Praise for Glenys Livingstone's original synthesis of seasonal ritual, female imagery for the Sacred and Western scientific story:

"… impressed with your work and with the vision, courage, and ardor with which you have followed through on a major aspect of the Great Work."
THOMAS BERRY, cultural historian, co-author of ***The Universe Story***, and author of ***The Dream of the Earth*** and ***The Great Work.***

"… marvelously impressive … It is a wonderful work you have done for women and the world."
ELISABET SAHTOURIS Ph.D., evolution biologist, futurist, author of ***Earthdance***, and co-author of ***Biology Re-visioned*** and ***A Walk Through Time***.

PaGaian Cosmology

PaGaian Cosmology

◆

Re-inventing
Earth-based Goddess Religion

Glenys Livingstone Ph.D.

iUniverse, Inc.
New York Lincoln Shanghai

PaGaian Cosmology
Re-inventing Earth-based Goddess Religion

iUniverse books may be ordered through booksellers or by contacting:

iUniverse
2021 Pine Lake Road, Suite 100
Lincoln, NE 68512
www.iuniverse.com
1-800-Authors (1-800-288-4677)

Because of the dynamic nature of the Internet, any Web addresses or links contained in this book may have changed since publication and may no longer be valid.

The views expressed in this work are solely those of the author and do not necessarily reflect the views of the publisher, and the publisher hereby disclaims any responsibility for them

ISBN: 978-0-595-34990-6 (pbk)
ISBN: 978-0-595-79701-1 (ebk)

Printed in the United States of America

For my son and my daughter
Joachim and Jesslyn,
who have engaged creatively and courageously
with their lives,
and for the Young One within all
- the Future,
for whom we refine the gold.

Contents

Preface

The term "PaGaian" requires some explanation: it expresses a reclaiming of the term "Pagan" as meaning a person who dwells in "country", yet with "Gaian" spliced in, it expresses a renewed and contemporary understanding of that "country". "Gaia" is a name for humanity's Habitat, an ancient yet new name, which I understand to include whole Earth and Cosmos—there is no seam separating Earth from Her context. And Pagan religious tradition offers a spiritual practice of celebrating Earth-Sun Creativity manifest in this Habitat. The cosmology described in this book makes a start on bringing all of this together. It is written from a Southern Hemisphere perspective which may enable a freeing of the Earth-Sun cycle and experience from the Gregorian calendar year: placing it more clearly for a moment in its Cosmic country.

Brian Swimme, a mathematical cosmologist, describes "cosmology" as "a wisdom tradition drawing upon not just science but religion and art and philosophy. Its principle aim is not the gathering of facts and theories but the transformation of the human."[1] PaGaian cosmology draws upon all of this and has the same principle aim. The cosmology described is based in the indigenous female-related religions of "Gaia", yet draws in contemporary knowledge/sense of Her from the sciences and humanity studies; it has many strands that are ancient, present and not-yet. This wisdom tradition is organic in nature, in the sense that its metaphor arose out of the human organism—which is this breathing body, this Earth, this Cosmos…human "country"—as an earliest and now contemporary expression of the Sacred. It is indigenous to each human as inhabitant of "Gaia"—this *materia*—whose primordial creative dynamics permeate all of existence as we know it; thus this cosmology's expression may be diverse and complex. Yet such conscious *place-ment* of ourselves in our Habitat with story from many disciplines and peoples, and with art and ceremony, may enable conscious human participation in Gaia's eternal transformation—both personally and collectively.

---

1.   Brian Swimme, *The Hidden Heart of the Cosmos*, p.31.

Throughout this book I will be capitalizing words such as Moon, Sun, Earth, Universe, Cosmos and sometimes Habitat (depending on the context) to re-invest these places with sentience, to name them as sacred places—not mere objects. It is central to the cosmology described herein that the world we live in is sacred space, and sentient. By sentient I mean an intelligent space, a capacity that is alive with potentialty.[2] For this reason also, I will at times omit the article "the", when speaking of these places. And just as it is common to capitalize "Western" when referring to Western culture for instance, so will I capitalize "Cosmic" when referring to the Cosmos' characteristics or patterns. I am thereby assigning "Cosmos" with at least as much credibility and diginity as "West", as a place, as a habitat. There are other instances where I capitalize words such as Dark, Light, Depths: I mean to invest these words with a numinosity—as names of actual aspects of the Sacred Universe. They are also aspects—Places—of our psyches. I capitalize "Seasonal Moments"[3]—traditionally known as the "Sab-bats"—as I mean to designate this term with the special "grace" of these transi-tions, as the holy day of any spiritual tradition is so designated. In the case of capitalizing "Female Metaphor" I mean it in the sense of female metaphor for the Divine, for the Sacred, for Ultimate Reality—I speak more of this in later chap-ters. I also capitalize "Creativity", as I mean it in the sense of the Absolute activ-ity—as another name for the Divine, the Absolute; I refer to the use of this name again in Chapter 1.

I also offer some explanation of my decidedly liberal use of slashes between words in the text (that is,"/"). Despite some initial dispute about it, I decided that the slashes needed to remain, as the words connected in this way support and enlarge each other's meaning. For example, in the case of "work/creativity", either word on its own would not convey my meaning to most minds, nor would "work *or* creativity": I don't mean "*or*" as in "either". I mean to integrate "work" and "cre-ativity"—to feel them as a whole, re-valuing each of them in the process. I was told that the slash-connected words stopped the flow of the words, made the reader stop a minute: I think that may be desirable in the case of such words, as

---

2.   The dictionary definition of "sentience" is "intelligence...the readiness to receive sensation, idea or image...unstructured available consciousness...feeling", *Webster's Third International Dictionary of the English Language*, p.2069.

3.   This is a term I sometimes use to speak of the "Sabbats", the eight Earth holy days of the Old European calendar. Thomas Berry has often referred to these Earth-Sun transitions as "moments of grace".

the very nature of the "re-inventing" described herein requires thought about what is meant.

This book is the presentation of a cosmology, and an art form—of ritual—that expresses and celebrates it. This cosmology represents for me a template of wholeness...which the Universe must be. I have been prepared to trust myself to this template—because it seemed to me to be so basic to Earth and Sun and Cosmos—our Place of being, our Habitat. I have come to represent this template in a three-layered arrangement—a mandala, a pattern which has inscribed itself within me through my conscious practice of its story and rhythm, in my place on the planet. At the edges of this particular mandala are the four elements in four directions—Water, Fire, Earth, Air.[4] These are things I can identify as held in common to all being on this planet, and "Their" sensate presence can be *felt* within any being. Within that boundary is a circle formed by eight objects, representing the eight seasonal points that I and many others have celebrated in recognition of the regional phases of our planet's relationship with our source of energy and life, the Sun. The centre of the arrangement is formed by three candles and associated objects which represent the Triple Spiral, the three faces of the Metaphor for the Creative Dynamic that I perceive continually unfolds it all. I came to perceive this ancient code—the Triple Spiral—as three dynamics of a mystery that was manifest everywhere, that I can touch, that I am, that I can become. The practice of the ritual celebration of the Seasonal Points may become a deepening into such a mandala—each being in a unique way; so that at a single glance something is known and felt.

The rituals of celebration of the Seasonal Moments as a whole year-long experience, when participated in fully as an art process and relationship with Gaia—our Habitat, become a sacred site. Caitlin Matthews, who has practiced the Wheel of the Year for decades, describes the "seasonal thresholds" thus:

> "The circuit of the earth about the sun is like the...revolving walk of a pilgrim about a sacred site: at each point of the circumambulation, there arises a different symbology in the changing weather and in the correspondences of the growing world."[5]

---

4. This is their order in the anti-clockwise direction in the Southern Hemisphere East Coast location—as many in this place choose to arrange them.
5. Matthews, Caitlin. *The Celtic Spirit*, p. 339.

One may enter into this sacred site through the particular Gaian seasons—Her particular modes of creativity. My practice of the ritual celebration of the Seasonal Moments—the great annual ritual of Earth and Sun—has enabled a shift in my *sense* of space and time, which is perhaps the most significant barrier to a return to an indigenous sense of being, to an archetypal relationship with the Universe.

This book shares some of the insights and transformational experiences gained from my doctoral research.[6] I was fortunate to be able to formally and academically document and study my experience and that of other participants in the ritual celebrations, some of whom had also participated in classes I taught. The thesis was in-formed by responses of women and men to these experiences, and to processes used that called forth imagination, presented in the form of teaching, meditations, dance, ritual, and storytelling, wherein female imagery was primary. The academic engagement of the ritual process which was already taking place was a form of "sacred science."[7] Many participants, in both the research and in general, have asked for the book. I envision it as a work that is never finished or complete. It hopefully says enough at this time to simply facilitate further re-storying and celebrating of Gaia-Goddess-Cosmos in much variation, by those readers who find it fires a passion of their own. I have retained a measure of the academic references in the form of footnotes to each chapter, so it might be used for academic purposes; also I am pre-disposed to remember the particular poetic expressions of my forebears, teachers and colleagues who have been part of the forming of this work. This work is a blend of both academic and personal text, that hopefully satisfies the minds and hearts of many who desire both capacities.

The structure of this book is layered—pieces that are at first introduced are later deepened. In the Introduction, I lay out some of the context, personal and cultural, and give an account of my method of approach. I introduce my perspective on ritual, which is in large part the central method of the re-invention being described. The place or region, which has been the site of the work, which is further context, is introduced. I describe the role of metaphor, and the need for a functional cosmology, and introduce the notion of the Female Metaphor ("Goddess") as a Cosmic Metaphor of Creativity. Chapter 1 introduces "Gaia" as a

---

6.   The full thesis is available at http://library.uws.edu.au/adt-NUWS/public/adt-NUWS20030731.103733/index.html

7.   As defined by John Heron, *Sacred Science: Person-Centred Inquiry into the Spiritual and the Subtle*, p.1-2.

name for our sacred context and develops further the term "Female Metaphor" as a way of speaking of "Goddess". I discuss language and introduce "Cosmogenesis"—the creative dynamic unfolding of the Universe.[8] The seasonal Wheel of the Year, an indigenous Western spiritual practice, is introduced. Chapter 2 discusses issues of embodiment and gender, and religion; and the significance of the Moon and Her three phases of waxing, peaking and waning. I describe more of my context—personal, cultural and cosmic. Chapter 3 develops the re-storying of the Female Metaphor—of Goddess in Her three aspects of Virgin, Mother and Crone—the necessity for such and how that may be possible. This "re-storying" that I present is based on evidence of past understandings combined with present experience and understandings. It is not a "proof", it is a "re-storying". In Chapter 4, pointing out the benefit of ritual and metaphorical connection with Gaia's Creative Dynamics, I deepen the piece of Cosmogenesis and its association with the Female Metaphor. Chapter 5 develops deeper layers to the piece of the seasonal points of the Wheel of the Year, telling the story of it in a new way: thus naming my telling of it as "PaGaian". I associate it with Gaia's story—the evolutionary story of the Universe, Her Creativity and the three faces of Goddess. Chapter 6 develops possible ritual format, processes and the poetic themes of each Sabbat—how they may enable the embodiment of the Creative Metaphor. Chapter 7 describes the actual ritual events as they have been done, and presents the full ritual scripts as they are at this time. Chapter 8 concludes with my experience of this shamanic process of re-creation, including how this created Con-text of cosmology and practice may meet what Thomas Berry calls the "meta-religious" challenge of our time.[9] This challenge he says, which goes beyond the human order to the entire geo-biological order of the planet, is the context in which "all human affairs need to establish their reality and their value—and their

---

8. Sometimes referred to as "evolution", which may be mistaken to imply "progress" of some kind. When I use the term "evolution" or "evolutionary" in this book, I do not mean to imply "progress" or any kind of "teleology" necessarily. It is simply meant in the sense of perceiving "a time-developmental process" (Swimme and Berry, *The Universe Story*, p.223). There is a story of the universe—that is, a sequence of events—that Western science has perceived as having taken place, and it is an "irreversible sequence of transformations", as Swimme and Berry describe. There does appear to be greater complexity, greater variety and intensity as can be observed on planet Earth, but this does not mean to imply an "ascent" as has been common to think in Western culture. I do not mean "evolution" to imply a heirarchy of development, simply perhaps a holarchy—which is an expansive nested reality that depends on what went before.

9. Thomas Berry, "The University: Its Response to the Ecological Crisis", p.8.

sense of the sacred."[10] The "sense of the sacred" in the practice of this PaGaian Cosmology is brought "Home"—a place where the domestic is cosmic, a Habitat that each being may know intimately.

---

10.   Thomas Berry, "The University: Its Response to the Ecological Crisis", p.8.

Introduction

I was perhaps one of Earth's most alienated of beings, and by that I mean that I did not sense belonging Here. My cultural context was such that I had no sense of relationship with my earthly and cosmic habitat. Cultural circumstance and story built over millennia converged to create a human who did not know her Place much at all—this included the place within my own skin, as much as the place in which I dwelt. Both were objects, *things*—inert matter of little cosmic significance. Apparently there are many humans in these times who are of such a tribe of alienated beings—albeit within many greatly different contexts. The religious stories, the cosmology of my cultural context did not include my place of being and dwelling in any particular way—did not include my "Place", this Earth, this Material, as significant.

I was born in the Southern Hemisphere—in the Great South Land of Australia—and as a white Western European girl child. Most of the texts and graphics explaining the Cosmos to an Australian and white child were (and still often are) drawn from the Northern Hemisphere perspective. The Moon's phases were "backwards"; Sun's daily movement from East to West was described as being "clockwise"; the seasons in the stories were always at odds with real experience. This was never regarded as important enough to mention, yet deep within me from the beginning there was scribed the cosmic essence of disregarding one's senses.

I was raised as a Protestant country girl in a land being colonized by the people of my blood-line. I was fortunate to spend my babyhood and some toddling years on a farm—eating lots of red dirt as I imagine it. I have later realised that this red dirt may have been part of the best cultural education I received in early years. The rest of my childhood and early adolescence was spent in a small country town. I never went into native bush although my brothers did; a girl would have been too vulnerable. In any case, the Earth/Nature itself was devoid of real consequence; it was human activity upon it that was of consequence. Humans made the best of it by growing gardens and crops, but even then they had to control its waywardness with sprays and fertilizers. It was a big dead ball of dirt upon which we played and travailed, and from which we would be saved by "God" eventually.

I had no understanding of the ancient land upon which I dwelt, or of the stories of its indigenous people. The new authorities to this ancient land had named the piece/"State" marked out as "Queensland", for their nominal divine representative. The white Europeans found themselves trying to make a living. My parents were the children and grandchildren of pioneers, but they themselves no longer had a vision, a reason, for being here in this "new" place—they just were. They were not even conscious of it being "new" any longer, as far as I could tell. My spiritual heritage was in contrast to, and at odds with, the rich red soil in which I played as a toddler. The spiritual heritage of both my parents, was largely unspoken—my mother was a "bush-Catholic" (that is, baptized a Catholic, but not instructed), and my father of Scottish descent was a nominal Presbyterian. It was the paternal lineage that held sway in the way things were understood. At the centre of the cosmology that I was handed, was a harsh father-god, who was no Poet; his creation of the cosmos in seven days was literal. He was a Mechanic, and the Universe was a machine, and he was definitely a male. He—this god, and indeed most of us white Europeans, were products of a long history of humanity in another part of the planet, and in more recent centuries, of events in Europe such as the Reformation and the witch-burnings; but now, these were no longer conscious. There was also now for these people in this new place, no visible memory of something that had been even earlier—some kind of ceremonially expressed relationship to the other-than-human world. These Europeans were Reformed Christianized people transplanted here from the Northern Hemisphere, with no sense of their historical roots, who knew no synchronicity of the religious festivals that they continued to pay homage to, with the seasons of Earth. Here in the South land, the supernatural Christian drama of God and Jesus was completely unrelated to place. It was a particularly cerebral religion, and in that sense barren—devoid of ritual recognition of the fertile Earthbody.[1] While at least in the Northern Hemisphere when my ancestors had lit candles and sang at the Winter Solstice, though they called it Christmas, there remained a resonance with the land, a memory of something earlier upon which this ritual was based. In the Southern Hemisphere, there was no such resonance of the religious practice of the Europeans with Earth; and the children here of this religious

---

1.   A term used by Charlene Spretnak, *States of Grace: The Recovery of Meaning in the Postmodern Age*.

practice inherited a poverty of spirit, a deep divorce from Earth that few other religions in the history of Gaia have ever known.

Being "Other"

The sense of being "Other"—out of the main play and text of things, and perhaps irrelevant—was exacerbated by being female. Perhaps this was actually central to the sense of alienation, since the religion—the main cosmology—paid her very little positive attention. It has been common for millennia that women have not been able to name themselves or their experience as sacred, because the metaphor of the Divine did not extend to their experience, their presence in the world. The historical, scientific and religious texts of my cultural context did not include the perspectives of a female-friendly cosmology. Woman as philosopher, shaman, priestess, spiritual authority, wise woman, healer, and also as mother in these roles, was barely identified, let alone her perspective taken seriously. Scholarly texts which purported to be whole and truthful objective accounts,[2] have used terms like "us" and "we"—presuming to speak for her, even as they burnt her, silenced her, kept her out of institutions, politics and texts. If the story had been told from within *her* perspective, that is, the perspective of a female-friendly cosmos…as wise woman, healer, priestess, mother, would she speak of herself for instance, as "just a mother"—if her mind was imbued with the integrity of Life happening in her? Would she allow a church to tell her she could not speak for the Divine?

The female body—and hence her presence—has not been included in most of humanity's thinking for some time. French philosopher Merleau-Ponty speaks about the body and its importance in human experience. For him,

> The body is first of all a way of viewing the world; it is at one and the same time the way a subjective attitude both comes to know itself and express itself. The lived phenomenal body must therefore not be thought of as an object in itself, but as a bodily presence in the world, a bodily awareness of the world.[3]

The denial of the body in general has certainly influenced Western thought;[4] so then it may be asked, how has the denial of the *female* body in particular affected

---

2.   I use the past tense here but I am aware that the situation is still very much current in most contexts around the globe.

3.   Madison, Gary Brent. *The Phenomenology of Merleau—Ponty*. p.23

thinking—by women themselves as well as by the men who wrote the texts? It is now a largely accepted fact that half the human race has rarely been allowed, or found access to the development of the mainly adhered-to texts of philosophies and sciences. Her body—for the last few millennia—was not supposed to do what it did; if her body was more like his, then it would have been better—and normal. St. Augustine for example, regarded it as an achievement when a nun's menstrual cycle ceased due to fasting—he regarded that she was getting holier. The body, at its best and peak of integrity, was not supposed to menstruate; what did this kind of thinking signify? What kind of worldview was being denied? Woman's fertility was thus frequently a source of shame, and certainly in the cultural context, it was at the base of her loss of power.[5] It is the worldview of the female body—this subjective presence in the world, that has been absent from our collective minds, even her own mind. She must now be written into the histories, the philosophies, the sciences, the cosmologies. This book participates in that movement along with many others at this time in the human story, wherein the female—as an embodied human—is moving out of being "Other" into the "norm", into the foreground of consciousness.

Method of Approach

My method of approach has been informed by my deep personal involvement in the topic, my need to "place" myself here—as feminist philosopher Luce Irigaray suggests that woman needs to do.[6]

Irigaray said that woman is not situated, "does not situate herself in her place", that she serves as a thing and is thus nude.[7] I have intuitively felt the need to "clothe" myself, to find the Place within me, to move from object to sentient subject. It has been a hunger which grew into a holy desire, a Passion. The early intuitive sense of this need was fanned by feminist philosophers, primarily Mary Daly,[8] who awakened me to the language that I and others spoke everyday—and

---

4.   See Lakoff, George and Johnson, Mark. *Philosophy in the Flesh: The Embodied Mind and its Challenge to Western Thought.*
5.   See Adrienne Rich, *Of Woman Born.*
6.   Luce Irigaray, *An Ethics of Sexual Difference.*
7.   Luce Irigaray, *An Ethics of Sexual Difference*, p.10-11.
8.   Other important early influences were poets and writers such as Adrienne Rich, Robin Morgan, Hélène Cixous and Charlene Spretnak who awakened me to the stories we lived everyday.

how the world was thus shaped: how my very own sacred Land, my bodily presence in the world was alienated from my consciousness by everyday expression and imagery. An ostensibly small but profoundly ubiquitous example is the use of the female pronoun *she* to designate only females, while the male pronoun *he* designates all humans as well as males: that is, the scope of maleness includes humanity, while femaleness is restricted to "the Other".[9]

> Any speaker internalizing such a language unconsciously internalizes the values underlying such a system, thus perpetuating the cultural and social assumptions...[10]

I have not been satisfied to accept this state of affairs, and as Daly indicated, "...the emerging creativity in women is by no means a merely cerebral process."[11] Thus my quest, and method of approach to this work has involved my whole being, my whole story. And the situation of the female pronoun turned out to become of central—essential—significance in the *Place-ment* of myself, as this whole cosmology describes.

I have been on a "quest for the Mother"—She within me and within Whom I am: this is how I have understood the complete transformation that I sought, such a complete coming home to an indigenous Self, a Place which was as surely within me as it was my actual Earthly and Cosmic Habitat—I could not separate these realms of myself. In approaching this search/research[12] then, I have been bold in my assumption of deep participation in the Matter of the world, the Matrix. I can identify this "Matter/Matrix" with Merleau-Ponty's "Flesh", which has been described as

> an elemental power that has had no name in the entire history of Western philosophy...(and) the mysterious tissue...that underlies and gives rise to both

---

9. Mary Daly, *Gyn/Ecology* p.18, citing Julia P. Stanley and Susan W. Robbins "Going Through the Changes:The Pronoun She in Middle English". The pronoun "he" is also used to designate all creatures unless it is known to be female or its femaleness specifically relevant; that is, even in reference to the other-than-human, "she" is still "Other".

10. Mary Daly, *Gyn/Ecology* p.18, citing Julia P. Stanley and Susan W. Robbins "Going Through the Changes:The Pronoun She in Middle English".

11. Mary Daly, *Beyond God the Father*, p.8.

12. Henceforth in the text I will often use the word "Search" to designate this process.

the perceiver and the perceived…(and) the reciprocal presence of the sentient in the sensible and of the sensible in the sentient.[13]

Such a subjective quest would once have found no carriage in formal academic process, but fortunately for me, by time I came to engaging with the academic and scientific "pursuit of the Mother" things had changed sufficiently at the edges, for me to proceed boldly with "laying claim to the power of Naming"[14] the sacred sites of my female land—my bodymind, and inhabiting my Place/Self, by means of acceptable academic methods as well.

Conventionally, scientifically acceptable discourse has disregarded all subjectivity—reality was in the domain of hard quantifiable matter only; while many spiritual discourses—both conventional and "new age"—have *only* valued subjectivity, that is, they have said that matter is not of consequence and is to be transcended. So both genres of discourse have perpetuated a notion of this "Flesh", this Matter, this Subject in Whom we are, as purely passive, without sentience, and available for exploitation. Neither of these viewpoints challenge the notion that our Habitat—our materia—is inert dead stuff…"just a big dead ball of dirt" as Brian Swimme describes the modern human's conception of Earth.[15] Neither viewpoint challenges the notion that it is possible to separate the one who is sensing from what is being sensed: as ecological philosopher David Abram says, "…contemporary discourse easily avoids the possibility that both the perceiving being and the perceived being are of *the same stuff*,…"[16] Neither the conventionally scientific nor the conventionally spiritual/religious viewpoint generally supports a sense of our context being essentially relational or a sacred whole—a mutual presence, that we are subjects within a Subject[17]—a sentient Universe. I therefore describe my engagement in my Search, my approach and the writing itself as a "con-course" instead of "dis-course".[18] I have been conscious of my relationship with my "topic"—Her intimate involvement and reciprocal presence. The method, the work, has been a process of en-trance-ment and

13.   David Abram, *The Spell of the Sensuous*, p.66 citing Merleau-Ponty 1968.

14.   Jane Caputi "On Psychic Activism: Feminist Mythmaking" in *The Feminist Companion to Mythology*. Carolyne Larrington (ed), p.438.

15.   Brian Swimme, *The Universe is a Green Dragon*, p. 133.

16.   David Abram, *The Spell of the Sensuous*, p.67.

17.   This is an expression used by Brian Swimme in *Canticle to the Cosmos*, video4.

18.   "Con-course" is a term used by Jürgen Kremer, in his paper *"Post-modern Shamanism and the Evolution of Consciousness"*.

inter-action. It has been a process of *changing* of mind, not just talking *about* it or *to* it.

My "method" has been organic and intuitive. I have allowed myself to be led by inner promptings, below my conscious rational understandings, which I then organised my conscious self around in various modalities; and the universe has come to meet me in these actions as well. Such methods of approach have been named in recent times as "transpersonal" research methods.[19] Such methods are defined as allowing identification with an expanded sense of self, a reciprocity, a participative relationship with the perceived. They

> incorporate intuition, direct knowing, creative expression, alternative states of consciousness, dreamwork, storytelling, meditation, imagery, emotional and bodily cues and other internal events *as possible strategies and procedures in all phases of research inquiry.*[20]

My methods may also be described as "sacred psychology" which is how Jean Houston has named the work of recovery and deepening of one's personal story.[21] Houston says that

> a deeper story sustains and shapes our emotional attitudes, provides us with life purposes, and energizes our everyday acts. It offers us both meaning and momentum. Everything coheres when a deeper story is present.[22]

Plants grow better with a depth of soil. So it is with humans: a perception of the organic depth of being, inclusive of Origins of the Universe, enables a being to flourish.

Layers of Action

There have been layers of action over a period of years, that nursed and created a context in which "She" could grow. They have been:

---

19. W. Braud and R. Anderson, *Transpersonal Research Methods for the Social Sciences*, *w*herein "Organic" and "Intuitive" are two methods that are named and described.
20. W. Braud and R. Anderson, *Transpersonal Research Methods for the Social Sciences*, p.xxx.
21. Jean Houston, *The Search for the Beloved.*
22. Jean Houston, *The Search for the Beloved*, p.91.

—the creation of seasonal ritual celebrations.

These started with one or two annually which grew over the years to include all eight of the pre-Celtic Old European calendar. At one very clear point I committed myself to the whole cycle, wrote the scripts and began practising and meditating upon them before each ritual. The participants in these events have been a varying group—of mixed gender though mostly women, some regular attendees, some only coming occasionally. In the early informal days, participants were mostly friends and later my Moon circle group.

For the period of the academic research, there was a core group of four women, who attended pre and post-ritual meetings, receiving teaching and background information on each Seasonal Moment and its celebration, and giving suggestions and feedback and assisting in the processes of the rituals. Their participation was always organic, that is, they always had the freedom to fit into it where it suited them, to mesh it with their lives as their lives were, rather than constructing an artificial situation. I felt that the participant's organic desire for the experience and knowledge must be present to make the research valid.

> If we want to know about people, we have to encourage them to be who they are, and to resist all attempts to make them—or ourselves—into something we are not.[23]

There was no requirement of attendance at any specific number of events, the organic needs of the individual were regarded as paramount to the validity of the research, acknowledging that participants may gain more from a hiatus than from an attendance, and that the nurturance that comes from the chthonic was essential to the real exploration of affects.

Since that focussed period, I sometimes currently have students in a year long class called "Celebrating Gaia—Goddess, Cosmos—in Seasonal Ritual", and they participate as co-celebrants in a similar way as this core group did: though all attendees at the ritual events participate actively and may take significant ritual roles.

My rewriting or refining of the seasonal ritual script and teaching usually takes place about two to three weeks into the particular seasonal process, by which time

23.   Peter Reason and John Rowan (eds), *Human Inquiry: A Sourcebook of New Paradigm Research*, p. xxiii

I am ready to seriously contemplate what will be articulated and dramatized in the seasonal ritual. The script for each Sabbat has remained fairly stable over the last few years, with changes—often quite subtle—made when my perceptions deepen or shift.

The changing and continuous seasonal decoration is a year long ritual art process of creation and erasure, kin to the construction of any other sacred art work—for example the Kalachakra Mandala—that is created and destroyed. Any house decorations, any garments to be worn, any headpiece, a wreath, the altar, preparation of ritual foods, all participate in the expression and learning of the Seasonal Moment/Sabbat; then the decorations are removed, changed, for re-creation. Engagement in the art process itself teaches—the art is ritual and the ritual is art. The *whole* ritual process—including the lengthy and detailed preparation, and the rituals themselves have been and are, central to the changing of bodymind—to the "con-course". They are a major Place of Conversation—Cosmic Conversation.[24]

My Search could not have evolved…the journey would not have happened, without there having been a responsive group of people who desired to participate, and share with me their experience. The people who have been and are, context for the ritual celebrations, are essential to their creation. I am doing my part of it—and I feel so privileged to have the role that I do—but it is their desire, their awareness, which allows it to be. I feel deeply graced and thankful for the receptivity and generous sharing of self of these participants.

—the presentation of a class series called
"Re-Storying and Celebrating Goddess in You".
This has involved the teaching of pre-patriarchal stories and perspective on Goddess cultures and metaphor, presentation and embodiment of images, meditations, sharing of stories, ritual and dance, focussing on the three faces/dynamics of Goddess—Virgin, Mother, Crone—and then Her embodiment and celebration in the seasonal Gaian cycle. These classes have been a place where women (and occasionally men) could tell their stories of how these three aspects of Goddess had manifest in their lives. And they could tell these stories in the context of a "Goddess" perspective—that is, within the context of nobler images of the

---

24. "Conversation" is a term used by Thomas Berry and Brian Swimme to describe human ritual as responsive participation in the Universe, *The Universe Story*, p.153.

female, from within the perspective of a cosmology that valued their experience—as distinct from the patriarchal context in which they had until now almost certainly, generally storied themselves. These classes built further a body of knowledge for each of us who participated: we in-formed each other.

—the presentation of a class series called
"En-Trancing Goddess: Entering into her More Fully".
This has involved the teaching of the triple Goddess metaphor as aspects of Cosmogenesis—the dynamic unfolding of the Cosmos, shared meditations, improvised dance and body movement, rituals of connecting with past and future—and thus the present web of life, a deepening into the personal story and practice of the seasonal Wheel of the Year, and a ritual developing one's sense of self as a "hera"/courageous individual.[25] These classes have been a place for enabling deeper immersion in awareness of the threefold Creative Dynamic present within, and to bring forth more of its power. This "entering more fully" into Her in ourselves and in All, may be an "entrancing" process—a word Swimme and Berry also use to describe the reality of the Universe, expressive as it is "of some ineffable mystery".[26] The creation of this series was my response to a request by one of the core research participants for "more", after the first series. I created the sessions using processes and meditations that had catalyzed my deepening into the Triple Metaphor, and that appeared to be successful in enabling me to make desired changes in my life. Together we entered into a process of transformation, each becoming "more". This series took us further into the informing of each other of our participation in the evolutionary Cosmic Dynamics.

—keeping a journal.
For the period of the academic research there was the disciplined recording of my own perceptions, imagination and intuitions of the Female Metaphor, and of my own experience of the yearlong seasonal process and rituals. Since I was passionately involved, and the whole inquiry relied heavily on my creativity, my thoughts were not "merely a reflection on reality, but also a movement of that reality itself".[27] I was aware of myself as a "mapmaker", the thinking and know-

---

25. Charlene Spretnak points out in *The Politics of Women's Spirituality*, p. 87, that the term "hera"—a pre-Hellenic name for Goddess, pre-dates "hero"—a term for the brave male Heracles, and thus it could be used as an expression for any courageous individual. The ritual that is done in the class series is one that is based on Jean Houston's exercise "A Friend in Court", *The Hero and the Goddess*, pp. 62-69.
26. Brian Swimme and Thomas Berry, *The Universe Story*, p. 224.

ing subject who was both a product and a performance of that which I sought to know and represent.[28] This is still the case as the work continues, for anyone who does this for themselves; so the noting is a good method of attention.

The journal process has been delineated into seasonal divisions, labelling them for example, as a "Summer Solstice 99 Process" and a "Lammas 2000 Process" and so on. There is no pre-determined beginning for the process of any season; I feel it intuitively—sometimes the beginning is felt soon after the previous ritual, sometimes not for a while. Sometimes during the academic process I would have two "processes" going at the same time. The important thing really was the noting of perceptions, events, ideas, thoughts and feelings. These things were noted whether or not I thought they had some imagined relevance to the seasonal Sabbat. I did not presume to know all that would emerge from this noting, but I had a record of my experience, which did serve academic purpose and when I do it now still serves my self-reflective purposes and awareness.

—a meditation practice.
Since what I have sought to know involves the subtle layers of my experience, the methods have included a personal daily meditational practice of various modalities, affirming the various aspects of self—sometimes a simple stillness, sometimes including dance and yoga, sometimes just being with the emotional self, sometimes being outside with Earth-Gaia. The meditation practice is an essential affirmation of my depths, and an opening to those depths. It is a practice of listening to my organism, knowing her as a nested reality of Her Larger Organism. I have also had many good teachers in this matter over the years—all of whom supported the premise of my own organic wisdom.

The Three Candles Ritual Meditation
One particular form that has been part of my meditation practice, is a reflective process that includes the lighting of three candles and the invocation of the triple metaphor in varied verbal valencies. I cannot remember when I first developed this, but I have a written record of it from the first year of the academic process. Over time, the invocation has complexified along with my understandings of the multivalent nature of each of the three faces. It continues to do so. There is a version of it in Chapter 8.

---

27.   Willis Harman and Elisabet Sahtouris, *Biology Re-Visioned*, p. 16.
28.   Willis Harman and Elisabet Sahtouris, *Biology Re-Visioned*, p. 16.

The Yoga Mudra as In-Corporation of Gaia's Breath
The daily meditation has also included this particular yoga pose, which I have understood as an in-corporation of the Triple Goddess Metaphor, and of the year long Seasonal Wheel. I have understood the seasonal Wheel as an embodiment of the triple-faced Creative Dynamic, like a year-long breath; that the seasonal Wheel manifests how Gaia breathes in my part of the world. The purpose of joining in that breath in ritual is in the hope of enhancing one's journey into the awesome Creativity that She manifests, to unfold this deepest identity, "to get with her Plot". So the Yoga Mudra has been a daily way of both invoking in my being the essence of my Search, and of remembering my actual immersion in it. The Yoga Mudra, as it was taught to me, integrates the multivalence of Gaia's Creative Dynamic very well. The first position at the beginning of the breath is a statement of love of Self (the Virgin aspect); the second position as the breath expands and the arms spread up and out, is a statement of love of Other (the Mother aspect); the third position as the breath releases and the torso folds over, is a statement of love of All-That-Is (the Crone aspect). So it may also speak the seasonal cycle—the play of light and dark, the waxing, peaking and waning of all being.

The Cosmos is a Ritual

Dawn and dusk, seasons, supernovas—it is an ongoing *Event* of coming into being and passing away. The Cosmos is always in flux, and we exist as participants in this great ritual, this "cosmic ceremony of seasonal and diurnal rhythms" which frame "epochal dramas of becoming", as Charlene Spretnak describes it.[29] Swimme and Berry describe the universe as a dramatic reality, a Great Conversation of announcement and response.[30] Ritual may be the human conscious response to the announcements of the Universe—an act of conscious participation. Ritual then is a microcosmos[31]—a human-size replication of the Drama, the Dynamic we find ourselves in. Swimme and Berry describe ritual as an ancient response humans have to the awesome experience of witnessing the coming to be and the passing away of things.[32] It is a way in which we may respond to this awesome experience of being and becoming—hold the beauty and the terror.

29.   Charlene Spretnak, *States of Grace*, p.145.
30.   Brian Swimme and Thomas Berry, *The Universe Story*, p.153.
31.   Charlene Spretnak, *States of Grace*, p.145.
32.   Brian Swimme and Thomas Berry, *The Universe Story*, p.152

Humans have exhibited this tendency to ritualize since the earliest times of our unfolding (evidence of burial sites dating back one hundred thousand years)—often going to huge effort, that is almost incomprehensible to the modern industrialised econocentric mind. The precise placing of huge stones in circles such as found at Stonehenge and the creation of complex sites such as Silbury Hill are expressions of some priority, indicating that econocentric thinking—such as tool making, finding shelter and food, was not enough or not separate from the participation in Cosmic events. Ritual seems to have expressed something essential to the human—a way of being integral with our Cosmic Place, which was not separate from material sustenance, the Source of existence: thus it was a way perhaps of *sensing* "meaning" as we might term it these days—or "relationship".

Swimme and Berry note that the order of the Universe has been experienced especially in the seasonal sequence of dissolution and renewal; this most basic pattern has been an ultimate referent for existence.[33] The seasonal pattern contains within it the most basic dynamics of the Cosmos—desire, fullfilment, loss, transformation, creation, growth, and more. The annual ritual celebration of the Seasonal Wheel—the Earth-Sun sacred site—can be a pathway to the Centre of these dynamics, a way of making sense of the pattern, a way of *sensing* it. One enters the Universe's story. The Sabbats when practiced in the art form of ceremony may be *sens-ible* "gateways" through the Flesh of the world to the Centre—which is omnipresent Creativity.

Humans do ritual everyday—we really can't help ourselves. It is simply a question of what rituals we do, what story we are telling ourselves, what we are "spelling"[34] ourselves with—individually and collectively.

Ritual as "Prayer" or Sacred Awareness

Ritual is often described as "sacred space". I understand that to mean "awareness of the space as sacred". All space is sacred, what shifts is our awareness—awareness of the depth of spacetime, all things and all beings. I understand "sacred

33.   Brian Swimme and Thomas Berry, *The Universe Story*, p.152
34.   This is a term Starhawk used on her email list in 2004 to describe the story-telling we might do to bring forth the changes we desire.

awareness" as an awareness of deep relationship and identity with the very cosmic dynamics that create and sustain the Universe; or an awareness of what is involved in the depth of each moment, each thing, each being. Ritual is a space and time given to expression, contemplation and nurturance of that depth...or at least something of it. Ritual may be both an expression of deep inner truths—perceived relationship to self, Earth and Cosmos, as well as being a mode of teaching and drawing forth deeper participation.

Essentially, ritual is a way of entering into the depth of the present moment...what is deeply present right here and now, a way of entering deep space and deep time, which is not somewhere else but is right here. Every-thing, and every moment, has Depth—more depth than we usually allow ourselves to contemplate, let alone comprehend. This book, this paper, this ink, the chair, the floor—each has a history and connections that go back, all the way back to Origins. This moment you experience now, in its particular configuration, place, people present, subtle feelings, thoughts, and propensity towards certain directions or outcomes, has a depth—many histories and choices that go back...ultimately all the way back to the beginning. Great Origin is present at every point of Space and Time—right here. In ritual we are plugging our awareness into something of that.

In this Holy Context then—in this mindframe of knowing connection, everything one does is a participation in the creation of the Cosmos: for the tribal indigenous woman, perhaps the weaving of a basket; for you, perhaps preparing a meal. It is possible to regain this sense, to come to feel that the way one breathes makes a difference—that with it, you co-create the present and the future, and you may even be a blessing on the past. In every moment we receive the co-creation, the work, of innumerable beings, of innumerable moments, and innumerable interactions of the elements, in everything we touch...and so are we touched by them. The local is our touchstone to the Cosmos—it is not separate. Ritual may be a way into this awareness, into strengthening it.

Starhawk says that "to do ritual, you must be willing to be transformed in some way",[35] because that is its very nature, that is, it is "trans-forming". Ritual can be as simple as having a cup of tea or reading a poem, or high drama like classical theatre or a rave concert; in either case it is "time out"—entering another realm,

---

35.   Starhawk. *Truth or Dare,* p.100.

to a greater or lesser degree. As with having a cup of tea, it is done with the expectation of rejuvenation/renewal. Humans actually do ritual all the time. Starhawk notes that "ritual is the way culture enacts and affirms its values."[36] But this enactment and affirmation is usually unconscious, and thus the participants remain unaware of what is actually being activated; for example, going to the pub or bar is a popular sanctioned ritual—time out, imbibing "spirit". And whereas once, the ancestors used to sit around the fireplace and tell the cosmic stories; now most often humans sit around the TV in the modern cave, and the story that is told is that the world is a collection of objects to be consumed.[37] As ritual is done consciously more often, we become aware of the symbols and myths that we live and can choose more consciously the tools with which we shape our lives. Ritual at its best is the art form of a living cosmology.

Ritual is actually "doing", not just theorizing. We can talk *about* our personal and cultural disconnection endlessly, but we need to *actually* change our minds. Ritual can be an enabling practice—a catalyst/practice for personal and cultural change. It is not just talking *about* eating the pear, it is *eating* the pear. It is not just talking *about* sitting on the cushion (meditating), it is *sitting* on the cushion. It is a cultural practice wherein we tell a story/stories about what we believe to be so most deeply, about who and what we are. Ritual can be a place for practicing a new language, a new way of speaking, or "spelling"—a place for practicing "matristic storytelling"[38] if you like, that is, for telling stories of the Mother, of Earth and Cosmos as if She were alive and sentient. We can "play like we know it", so that we may come to know it.[39] Ritual then is a form of social action.

I find it useful to describe ritual using and extending Ken Wilber's words to describe a "transpersonal practice" that is needed for real change: as one that discloses "a deeper self (I or Buddha) in a deeper community (We or Sangha) expressing a deeper truth (It or Dharma)".[40] It discloses a deeper beautiful self (the "I"/Virgin/Buddha), in a deeper relational community (the "We"/Mother/ Sangha), expressing a deeper transformative truth (the "It"/Old One/Dharma)". This is the "unitive body", the "microcosmos" that Spretnak refers to.

---

36. Starhawk. *Truth or Dare*, p.98.
37. Brian Swimme, *The Hidden Heart of the Cosmos*, p.8-20.
38. A term used by Gloria Feman Orenstein in *The Reflowering of the Goddess*.
39. As Dr. Susan Murphy described it to me in conversation.
40. Ken Wilber, *A Brief History of Everything*, p.306-307.

According to Swimme, the Universe is one huge celebration—expanding, exuberantly rushing away from a center with news of that center…an urgent unfolding of being.[41] Thus, he says, "Self-expression is the primary sacrament of the universe. Whatever you feel deeply demands to be given form and released."[42] He describes this innate dynamic of celebration as a "generosity of being" that "insists upon song and dance". Ritual must be a space where something deep in the self is free to be expressed—a space free of judgement and coercion—a space felt to be "safe" which allows and invites individual uniqueness, while affirming community.

Since ritual is an opportunity to give voice to deeper places in ourselves, forms of communication are used that the dreamer, the emotional, the body, can comprehend, such as music, drama, simulation, dance, chanting, singing.[43] These forms enable the entering of a level of consciousness that is there all the time, but that is not usually expressed or acknowledged. We enter a realm that is "out of time", which is commonly said to be not the "real" world, but it is more organic/indigenous, and at least as real as the tick-tock world. It is a place "between the worlds", wherein we may put our hands on the very core of our lives, touch whatever it is that we feel our existence is about, and thus touch the possibility of re-creating and renewing ourselves.

The Place/Habitat

The site of the seasonal ritual celebrations will always be significant. In my case, the place in which I have created them has been notably in the Southern Hemisphere of Earth. The fact of my context being thus—the Southern Hemisphere—has contributed in the past to my deep internalized sense of being "Other", yet hence in the present this context contributes to my deep awareness of Gaia's Northern Hemisphere and Her reciprocal Seasonal Moment—the whole Planet. My initial confusion about the *sensed* Cosmos—as a Place, has become a clarity about the *actual* Cosmos—which remains inclusive of my sensed Cosmos. PaGaian reality—the reality of our Gaian "country"—is that the whole Creative Dynamic happens all the time, all at once. The "Other", the opposite, is always present—underneath and within the Moment. This has affected my com-

---

41. Brian Swimme, *The Universe is a Green Dragon*, p.144-145.
42. Brian Swimme, *The Universe is a Green Dragon*, p.147.
43. Starhawk, *The Spiral Dance*, p.36.

prehension of each Sabbat/Seasonal Moment, its particular beauty but also a fullness of its transitory nature. Many in the Northern Hemisphere—even today—have no idea that the Southern Hemisphere has a "different" lunar, diurnal, seasonal perspective, and because of this there often is a rigidity of frame of reference for place, language, metaphor and hence cosmology.[44] Indeed over the years of industrialized culture it has appeared to matter less to many of both hemispheres, including then the "author-ities", the writers of culture and cosmos. Yet such "author-ity" and northern-hemispheric rigidity is also assumed by most more Earth-oriented writers as well. There is consistent failure to take into account a whole Earth perspective: for example the North Star does not need to be *the* point of sacred reference (there is great Poetry to be made of the void of the South Celestial Pole) nor the North rigidly associated with the Earth element and darkness, nor is there really an "up" and a "down" cosmologically speaking. A *sense* and account of the Southern Hemisphere perspective with all that that implies metaphorically as well as *sens-ibly*, seems vitally important to comprehending and sensing a whole perspective and globe—a flexibility of mind, and coming to inhabit the real Cosmos, hence enabling a PaGaian cosmological perspective.

It has also been significant that my Search in its particular perspective, has been birthed in this ancient continent of Australia. It is the age of the exposed rock in this land, present to her inhabitants in an untarnished, primal mode that is significant. The land herself has for millennia been largely untouched by human war, conquest and concentrated human agriculture and disturbance. The inhabitants of this land dwelt here in a manner that was largely peaceful and harmonious, for tens of thousands of years. Therefore the land Herself may speak more clearly; one may be the recipient of direct transmission of Earth in one of her most primordial modes. Her knowledge may be felt more clearly—one may be taught by Her. I think that the purity of this transmission, from my beginnings as a country girl—albeit below my conscious mind in the subtle realms of which I knew little, to the more conscious times of entering into the process of the Search, is a significant factor in the development of the formal research I undertook—in my chosen methodology and in what I perceived in the process, and documented. In this land that birthed me, "spirit" is not remote and abstract, it is felt in Her red earth.[45] Aboriginal elder David Mowaljarlai described, "This is a spirit coun-

---

44.   Caitlin and John Matthews are almost unique in their consideration of the Southern Hemisphere in their writing. See *The Western Way*, p.47.

try",[46] and all of Her inhabitants, including non-Aboriginal, are affected by the strength of Her organic communication.

It took me until the later stages of my research to realize the need to state the importance of this particular place—both the land of Australia, and the specific region of the Blue Mountains in which I was now dwelling—and the community of this region, for the advent of the research. The lateness of this perception on my part, has to do with the extent of my previous alienation; but the fact that it *did* occur, is perhaps at least in part attributable to the unfolding awakening to my habitat that was part of the project.

The specific region of the "Blue Mountains"—as Europeans have named them—is significant in that I don't think that this project could have happened as it did in just any region. David Abram says,

> "The singular magic of a place is evident from what happens there, from what befalls oneself or others when in its vicinity. To tell of such events is implicitly to tell of the particular power of that site, and indeed to participate in its expressive potency."[47]

The Blue Mountains are impressive ancient rock formations, an uplifted ancient seabed, whose "range of rock types and topographical situations has given rise to distinct plant communities";[48] and the presence of this great variation of plant communities, "especially the swamps, offer an abundance and variety of food sources, as well as habitats for varied fauna."[49] I feel that this is the case for this region's capacity to nurture this project—it received the particularities of my passion. Even though I have been bringing a Western European heritage to this site, singing songs and dancing dances that come from other sites and times, it has been done in accord with the Seasons of this place and increasingly in accord with the particular features of this place. The Search has been a journey of coming more deeply into relationship with my place, expressing and using the tools of my ancestral heritage—knowing this heritage in myself first so that I may come

---

45. as Australian writer David Tacey also articulates in all of his work, but referenced here particularly in "Spirit and Place", EarthSong journal, issue 1, p.7-9.
46. Quoted in David Tacey, "Spirit and Place", EarthSong journal, issue 1, p.7.
47. David Abram, *The Spell of the Sensuous*, p.182.
48. Eugene Stockton (ed), *Blue Mountains Dreaming*, p.43.
49. Eugene Stockton (ed), *Blue Mountains Dreaming*, p.43.

into relationship.[50] I have for some time felt "familiar" with this place, related/family with this place, and in the course of my Search, this place has received and enabled, and indeed invoked the seed within me. I am aware that the Poetry of this work has been enacted and enabled within the specific context, and it would not have been the same elsewhere and in a different community, which is itself a creation of the place.

The Role of Metaphor

Metaphor is not merely a matter of language, it is pervasive in everyday thought and action; "the way we think, what we experience, and what we do everyday is very much a matter of metaphor."[51] Lakoff and Johnson say that conventional ways of talking about anything "pre-suppose a metaphor that we are hardly ever conscious of".[52] They make the point that "the metaphor is not merely in the words we use", that it is in our very concept of the thing.[53] They say that "the essence of metaphor is understanding and experiencing one kind of thing in terms of another";[54] so (for my purpose here), "the Divine" or however one names what is Deepest in existence, is not female and is not male, though the metaphor used may suggest a likeness. The Webster's Dictionary defines "metaphor" as "a figure of speech in which a word or phrase denoting one kind of object or action is used in place of another to suggest a likeness or analogy between them",[55] and further that metaphor is an *implied* comparison, as opposed to an *explicit* comparison. As Starhawk notes, "an overt metaphor is a map, a description we may find useful or not, may accept or reject",[56] whereas if the metaphor is covert it is free "to restructure our reality by leading us to accept the map as the territory without questioning where we are going or whose interests are being served."[57] The fact that the Divine, the Essence of existence, is so

50. This Old European Pagan spiritual practice as I have re-created it here in Australia, is an imaginative response to the "challenge" of a "new cultural situation", as David Tacey calls for, though he has imagined that it would come mainly from old Christian traditions. See David Tacey, "Spirit and Place", EarthSong journal, issue 1, p.9-10.
51. George Lakoff and Mark Johnson, *Metaphors We Live By*, p.3.
52. George Lakoff and Mark Johnson, *Metaphors We Live By*, p.5.
53. George Lakoff and Mark Johnson, *Metaphors We Live By*, p.5.
54. George Lakoff and Mark Johnson, *Metaphors We Live By*, p.5.
55. *Webster's Third International Dictionary of the English Language*, p.1420.
56. Starhawk, *Truth or Dare*, p.21.

ubiquitously called upon as "God", systematically influences the shape "the Divine" takes, and the way it is talked about.[58] It suggests a likeness and it is usually a covert metaphor that restructures our reality without question.

"The Divine" may be metaphorised many other ways—"vibratory flux", "creativity", "relatedness".[59] Thus I frequently imply the Divine in many terms—"Deep", "Change", "Dark"—and capitalize the terms to signify this. I feel this is a necessary process for the changing and diversifying of minds. Mary Daly points out that "the word *metaphor* is derived from the Greek *meta* plus *pherein*, meaning to bear, carry" and that "*metapherein* means to transfer, change".[60] Metaphors may thus "transform/transfer our perceptions of reality, enabling us to 'break set' and thus to break out of linguistic prisons."[61]

Joseph Campbell describes a functioning mythology as "an organization of metaphorical figures connotative of states of mind that are not finally of this or that place and time…",[62] and such are made known in visual art and verbal narrative (written and oral). It is applied to communal life by way of a calendar of symbolic rites, festivals and ceremonies, that enable the community to participate "with its universe in eternity."[63] Campbell notes how, in the popular mind, "such metaphors of transcendence" get locked into chiefly functions of control and socializing, but that "the way of the mystic and of proper art (and we might add, religion) is of recognizing *through* the metaphors an epiphany beyond words."[64] Campbell was convinced of the necessity—"a social as well as spiritual necessity"[65]—of a new mythology that he felt was "already implicit among us as knowledge *a priori*, native to the mind."[66]

---

57. Starhawk, *Truth or Dare*, p.21.

58. George Lakoff and Mark Johnson, *Metaphors We Live By*, p.7. They are speaking of metaphor in general using the example of the word "argument". They are not adressing "the Divine" specifically here, though they do address metaphor and the "ineffable God" (sic) in *Philosophy in the Flesh* p.567-568), saying that "passionate spirituality" requires metaphor.

59. Charlene Spretnak, *States of Grace: the Recovery of Meaning in the Postmodern Age*, p.25.

60. Mary Daly, *Pure Lust*, p.26.

61. Mary Daly, *Pure Lust*, p.26.

62. Joseph Campbell, *The Inner Reaches of Outer Space*, p.21.

63. Joseph Campbell, *The Inner Reaches of Outer Space*, p.20.

64. Joseph Campbell, *The Inner Reaches of Outer Space*, p.21.

65. Joseph Campbell, *The Inner Reaches of Outer Space*, p.21.

At the heart of the metaphorical change that re-storying may enable, is a change of the felt need in the cultural psyche to "slay the dragon"—to be free of the matter, out of which we and all, arises. Re-storying may enable "embracing of the dragon". The Dragon—the serpent—represents a cosmology that assents to change, IS about change. Our culture and its metaphors has craved permanence, and is unable to deal with loss—which is essentially Change. The "Moon Goddess", the Female Metaphor in Her three aspects, passes through waning into the Darkness, from which there is renewal. Brian Swimme says that to enter into the terror of loss, offers the opportunity to accept what is real, and it is the way to unite with what is eternal.[67] I am not suggesting that human hunger for the eternal is aberrant; it may be met, in and through the Matter in which we are.

In my Search I have been seeking the essential nature of all things. This was also the aim of the early Greek philosophers and they called this essential nature "physis". As Capra notes, "The term 'physics' is derived from this Greek word and meant therefore, originally, the endeavour of seeing the essential nature of all things."[68] My quest is therefore very related to physics poetically—physics itself and my quest are both a kind of Poetry.[69] My understanding of Goddess is as a creative metaphor for the essential nature of all things. In Her three aspects, She is the "Triskele" of energy, the dynamics of Cosmogenesis, "the innate triplicity of the Cosmos…that runs through every part of the universe"[70] and is available to all. The "triskele" is a sacred symbol of the Celtic peoples, which consists of three legs radiating from a centre, understood to be in perpetual motion. To draw upon this triple-limbed wheel, was to "grace our lives with an ever-living energy that encompasses the beginning, middle and end of everything we undertake."[71] The term "triskele" itself, and its symbolic representation, could be said to be

---

66. Joseph Campbell, *The Inner Reaches of Outer Space*, p.19.
67. Brian Swimme, *Canticle to the Cosmos* video 5.
68. Fritjof Capra, *The Tao of Physics*, p.6.
69. I capitalize this term, as I use it in the sense of a language—a language of the Universe—much as one would capitalize "English" or "French". "English" or "French" are not generally thought of consciously as "sacred" media, although the terms are frequently treated as such. In this book, "Poetry" is definitely being used to refer to a sacred medium.
70. Caitlin Matthews, *The Celtic Spirit*, p.366.
71. Caitlin Matthews, *The Celtic Spirit*, p.366.

metaphor for the triple-action biospheric reality described by Russian scientist Vladimir Vernadsky:

> At each moment there are a hundred million million tons of living matter in the biosphere, always in a state of movement. The mass is decomposed, forms itself anew mainly by multiplication. Generations are thus born…unceasingly.[72]

A Functional Cosmology and Metaphor

Brian Swimme has said that

> to become fully mature as human persons, we must bring to life within ourselves the dynamics that fashioned the cosmos…That is our task: to create the human form of the central powers of the cosmos.[73]

To do this, many women, and men too, need the Female Metaphor…to become fully human, to embody these dynamics that created the galaxies, the stars. As Carol Christ noted, women "have not actively shaped their experiences of self and world nor named the great powers from their own perspectives."[74] Men too may find the Female Metaphor helpful in this matter of embodying the cosmic dynamics, since She is a participatory metaphor—relational—and She may restore him to the context, partnership, as opposed to centre-stage, dominance and alienation. Adam McLean makes a case for "the Triple Goddess figure" being "for men, a safe inner guide ",[75] free of the dangers of the "hero"/"saviour" identification.[76] John Heron has critiqued "gender-laden perennialism"[77] wherein the traditional, typically male, practitioner "claims to have become spirit as spirit",[78] whose spiritual practice involves sustained dissociation from the autonomous dynamic impulses of immanent spiritual life."[79] Heron describes this as "supremely alienated and inflated agency, a man wanting only to be the whole of reality, and in no sense whatsoever a part of it or participant in it."[80]

---

72. Vladimir Vernadsky, *The Biosphere*, p.34.
73. Brian Swimme, *The Universe is a Green Dragon*, p.87.
74. Carol Christ, *Diving Deep and Surfacing*, p.4.
75. Adam McLean, *The Triple Goddess*, p.120.
76. Adam McLean, *The Triple Goddess*, p.119.
77. John Heron, *Sacred Science*, p.3-4.
78. John Heron, *Sacred Science*, p.4.
79. John Heron, *Sacred Science*, p.4.

Part of the human memory that I have attempted to plumb in this Search is expressed by Swimme and Berry, in their telling of the Universe Story:

> Some 2.6 million years ago, at the close of the Pliocene period, the earliest expression of the human appears in its species identity, a form of human designated as Homo habilis....With Homo habilis an event of singular importance takes place: the beginning of the Stone Ages in the cultural development of the human....Exactly here in these transition years the more significant foundations for the human mode of being were established. The sense of time and space was developing; imagination was receiving the impress of its powerful images; the stock of primordial memories that would influence all future generations was being developed;...(and)...The ever-recurring sequence of seasonal decline and renewal was making its impress on the human psyche as one of the most basic patterns that would later find expression in ritual celebration.[81]

In these times, to re-invent ourselves as Thomas Berry suggests humans need to,[82] we would do well to remember as much wisdom as we can gather. The process of seasonal celebration that this project has re-created and reflected upon, has been and is, an intuitive archaeological dig into an early layer of human awareness, a meditation focussed on letting deep and ancient knowings arise, in the context of present understandings—the universe as our minds understand it today, and then to marry them. Georg Feuerstein, in describing the work of philosopher Jean Gebser speaks of an "archaeology of consciousness"—structures of consciousness—that "are not merely a matter of the past",[83] but do constitute our present whole field of cognition. These layers of modes of consciousness, each created at the various stages of human development over the millennia are all still present and essential to integral functioning of human capacity. The earlier layers/modes may help us understand "how our present responses and reactions are shaped by collective patterns of consciousness."[84] I am not suggesting that there is any one way of marrying an early layer of human awareness—Stone Age mind

---

80. John Heron, *Sacred Science*, p.4.
81. Brian Swimme and Thomas Berry, *The Universe Story*, pp.146-148.
82. Mark Matousek, "Re-Inventing the Human", Common Boundary Vol. 8 No.3, p.31.
83. Georg Feuerstein, "Towards a New Consciousness: A Review Essay on Jean Gebser". Noetic Sciences Review, No. 7, Summer 1988, p. 24.
84. Georg Feuerstein, "Towards a New Consciousness: A Review Essay on Jean Gebser". Noetic Sciences Review, No. 7, Summer 1988, p. 26.

as best one can intuit and imagine it—with present awareness of the Universe Story,[85] Gaia's story as we know it. I assume there are infinite ways to do this. The particular method and process as I have been part of, and is documented here in this work, is simply an illustration of a possibility.

Swimme and Berry say that: "Cosmology aims at articulating the story of the universe so that humans can enter fruitfully into the web of relationships within the universe."[86] The scope of their work is a synthesis of the questions common in traditional cosmology concerning the place of the human in the universe, with the factual investigations of scientific cosmology. Their articulation of the Universe Story is a new myth, a way of orienting the human anew in the universe, to enable a re-invention of the human. They say that to do this requires a reinvention of language to some degree:

> …for each extant language harbors its own attitudes, its own assumptions, its own cosmology. Thus to articulate anew the story of our relationships in the world means to use the words of one of the modern languages that implicitly, and to varying degrees obscures or even denies the reality of these emerging relationships. Any cosmology whose language can be completely understood by using one of the standard dictionaries belongs to a former era.[87]

Thus, they say, to understand the new cosmology in any significant way, "is a demanding task, requiring a creative response over a significant period of time."[88] This is kin to how Mary Daly speaks of "the very arduousness of the task of Naming and calling forth Elemental be-ing."[89] This project of re-storying and celebrating our Habitat/Place—this PaGaian process—as anyone undertakes it, is subject to such a requirement. New relationship with certain terms and names—the language we speak—needs to be established, and the Metaphor—the Female Metaphor/Goddess/Gaia—needs to be spoken, enacted, lived—until we who are the participants have begun to know this Language in our cells. Certainly the embodiment of this Creative Metaphor in the Seasonal ritual celebrations is a process that deepens my sensed knowing each time the year goes around—it

---

85. This term is capitalized to suggest that it may be understood to refer to sacred text, much as the "Koran" or "Bible" are capitalized.

86. Brian Swimme and Thomas Berry, *The Universe Story*, p.23.

87. Brian Swimme and Thomas Berry, *The Universe Story*, p.24.

88. Brian Swimme and Thomas Berry, *The Universe Story*, p.24.

89. Mary Daly, *Pure Lust*, p.25.

takes that kind of time, consistent practice over years. I realize that for myself, I am so far only scratching the surface; and other participants in this particular process have expressed feeling the same.

Some of the research participants commented in the interviews about how important the language used in the ritual celebrations was to them. They did this without the prompt of a specific question. One articulated how the old Western Christian cosmological language was no longer an adequate method of expressing his deep understandings of the cosmos. It has been my passion to find other language, other pathways to express those depths; and certainly for me it had to be a pathway that not only admits the Female/female, but celebrates Her/her, as an integral part of the Cosmos—in a way that patriarchal paradigms never have or could. It has been my passion to allow an experience of this for myself, and for others—WITH others…and that is where it really becomes meaningful, when communion is found. My self/Self re-creation became something that other people found resonance with, and I found resonance with them—and what has been *my* expression has been extended as I have felt for *their* expression. I have largely played the Poet, yet it is an inter-active process, that is growing over time—and into a plant we do not yet know.

The Female Metaphor

To clarify further what I mean when I speak of the "Female Metaphor": I am not referring to a "feminine" *part* of the Divine, nor to some complementary partner to the Great Mystery, nor to some "half" of the Creative Principle of the Universe. When I speak of Her, She is a name for the whole Creative Principle. In accord with this metaphorical understanding, Rainer Maria Rilke wrote:

> Some day there will be girls and women whose name will no longer signify merely an opposite of the masculine, but something in itself, something that makes one think not of any complement or limit, but only of life and existence.[90]

The re-storying articulated in the following chapters will be an illustration of how the Female Metaphor can be a name for the whole Creative Principle, of how this

---

90.   Edward C. Whitmont, *The Return of the Goddess*, p.214 quoting Rainer Maria Rilke, *Letters to a Young Poet*, p.59.

cosmology can be celebrated; and what difference it may make in the hearts and minds of women and men, and to the human response to Earth—our home.

A Cosmic Metaphor for Creativity

I propose that "She"—the Female Metaphor—in her three aspects, which I unfold in the chapters ahead, may be understood as a dynamic of Creativity—a dynamic innate to being, that may enable both women and men to participate more fully in the life of their own organism, and thus in the life of the Larger Organism of which we are part.

I propose that to participate in this year long process of ritual and celebration of Cosmic Metaphor for Creativity, with contemplation and consciousness, may enhance: (i) love of self, in a willingness to abide with the beauty and integrity of the particular differentiated self, and recognizing that this self is not separate from the Large Self which is Gaia (this is the work of the Virgin aspect). (ii) love of other, in a deep sense of relationship and communion with other people, the planet and the Cosmos—knowing both one's "support for" and how one is "supported by" (this is the work of the Mother aspect). (iii) love of All-That-Is, in the understanding of transformation as not only possible, but indeed, as intrinsic to the pattern—enabling one's more joyful participation in this intrinsic creativity (the work of the Crone aspect).

I propose that to participate in this Metaphor changes how one relates to loss; there is more willingness to let go. As one comes to identify with the Larger Self, and recognize one's place in the scheme of things, it turns around egoic hubris that would indulge in holding on, usually manifesting in behaviour destructive to self, other and planet. Apart from obvious personal and interpersonal conflict that such hubris may generate, there is wanton "therapeutic" consumerism on a large scale, which is symptomatic of disregard for Earth. I do not mean to imply that when egoic hubris is let go of then there is no conflict, I mean simply that the source of conflict may then more likely be the creative tension of being alive, rather than a desperate unwillingness to accept change.

I propose that participation in this Metaphor also changes how one relates to this life, especially if one has had uncertainties about the value of it. Spiritualities of the modern cultural context frequently stress the impermanence of this life, but in the cosmology presented in this book, life—manifest reality—is celebrated equally, *and* its perdurance becomes more obvious. When one is able to grasp something of the dynamic of Cosmogenesis from the earliest stages of the Cosmic Story as we currently understand it, Life's perdurance seems as insistent as the Void. It is true that one does not personally perdure, but one comes to know participation in a Process that does. For some people that is not sufficient, to be mere specks upon the road of a greater Journey, but that seems to be the situation; and the "specks" *do* create the Journey. The ritual celebration of the seasons may be an embodied reiteration of this truth, and enhance a willingness to participate creatively in this life.

1

Gaia, Goddess, Cosmogenesis and the Wheel of the Year

Gaia as a Name

I have long considered the practice of the spirituality described herein to be Gaian, perhaps encouraged by Charlene Spretnak's use of the term.[1] It is an Earth-based spirituality, which requires only birth, not baptism, for belonging. We are all native to Gaia; all humans are indigenous to Her. All humans can lay claim to relationship with Air, Fire, Water and Earth and to the Mystery at the Centre of it all. We do all issue forth from the same Origin—this is not just poetic flourish, this is biologically and cosmologically true. Gaia, as I understand Her, is not only Earth; She is Cosmos. Earth is that particular manifestation of Her with whom we are most intimate, and with whom all humans participate, whether conscious or not. The same Creative Dynamic[2] that flourishes in Earth is assumed to be the same Creative Dynamic present throughout the Universe. Earth-Gaia is Seed and Jewel of a larger living Organism. Earth-Gaia is our Mother, but She is Daughter too, of an essential Sentience that seethes through the Universe. Inasmuch as I am sentient, and I arise out of Her, out of Earth and Earth arises out of Universe, then Universe-Gaia is alive and sentient[3]. She is the eternal pulse, in which each one of us flows. Gaia is Earth, is Universe, is Ultimate Mystery, is you, is me—She is multivalent. The only faith required in this spirituality is in the Teeming Abundant Creativity that has been manifesting now for some thirteen point seven billion years, and which has survived on this planet

---

1. Charlene Spretnak, "Gaian Spirituality". Woman of Power Issue 20, Spring 1991
2. I capitilize this term here because I am implying or offering another name for the Divine.
3. This is not meant to be an axiom of logic. It is stated thus because its metaphoric base here is "family' or "nested realities".

in a particular way for millions of years. This is not a flimsy track record! Perhaps, as James Lovelock has said, this is "as near immortal as we ever need to know";[4] or as Susan Griffin said more poetically, "at no instant does She fail me in Her presence."[5]

Essential then, to this Gaian spirituality, is the development of relationship with Earth, entering into Her consciousness, expanding awareness beyond the human-centred perspective. It requires a remembering of the "real"—the situation of "all human thought, social or individual…in the processes of body, nature and place."[6] Or as Thomas Berry describes, it requires a return to our "native place", the recovery of a feeling of intimacy with "the earth community", which he describes as the recovery of

> a sense of presence, a realization that the earth community is a wilderness community that will not be bargained with; nor will it simply be studied or examined or made an object of any kind; nor will it be domesticated or trivialized as a setting for vacation indulgence…[7]

He says it requires remembering

> our sense of courtesy toward the earth and its inhabitants, our sense of gratitude, our willingness to recognize the sacred character of habitat, our capacity for the awesome, for the numinous quality of every earthly reality.[8]

This kind of presence is enabled by an identification of ourselves (the human) with the entire cosmic process—Gaia's story, which is also ours; and by an identification with the cosmic powers that sustain us—such as Air, Sun, Water and Earth. Gaian spirituality involves remembering the integrity of all elemental phenomena; that we are this, we depend on this, we come from this and we return to this.

---

4.   Cited in Connie Barlow (ed.), *From Gaia to Selfish Genes: Selected Writings in the Life Sciences*, p.42.
5.   Susan Griffin, *Woman and Nature*, p. 219.
6.   Charlene Sprenak, *The Re-Surgence of the Real*, p.4.
7.   Thomas Berry, *The Dream of the Earth*, p.2.
8.   Thomas Berry, *The Dream of the Earth*, p.2.

Gaia as Universe-Earth-Self: A Unity of Being

Earth-Gaia is not separate from Universe-Gaia. Earth is immersed in Universe. There is no seam that separates Earth-Gaia from Universe-Gaia…She is One. There is no "up" and "down". There is no "out there". Gaia is "in here", as much as anywhere, or She is nowhere. Gaia can be known, felt, in any single articulation of Herself—within any Self. We are IN it, Earth is IN it. Earth floats in the "heavens"—the "heavens" are where we are. This IS it. Gaia is a nested reality—many fold, but at least, Universe-Earth-Self; and inversely Self is Earth, is Gaia. Many spiritualities and most language imply that Earth is a world apart from the Heavens—and even that the Heavens are "higher' and thus "better". Yet we know that Earth is a Jewel in the Womb of Space—we have seen Her. We know that "Earth" is stardust—Her dirt is transfigured stuff of the stars. We know that we and all of it, are made from the same stuff—that we come out of the cores of stars, that a significant percentage of our "stuff" comes directly from the Origins, albeit recycled many times over. Spiritual language must catch up, if we are to stop killing ourselves and other beings with our words. "Higher" indicates "out there", in "loftier" realms beyond the earth, transcending lowly earthly nature. "Deeper" indicates "within", the depth of the earthly realm, enriched awareness of the multivalent numinous earthly nature/reality. The use of language such as "higher levels" by spiritual traditions in particular, and even by recently published ecological texts, and the worldview that accompanies it, has created and goes on creating a sense of alienation from what is here—the stuff we inhabit and where we dwell.[9]

In 1926—long before the human eye had actually seen Earth from space—Russian scientist Vladimir Vernadsky, was able to hold a vision of Her in her "cosmic surroundings."[10] He developed a hypothesis of the biosphere "as a unitary agent molding the earth's crust as a primary geological force"[11] that was in relationship with the cosmic energies of radiation, particularly solar radiation.[12] Throughout

---

9.   An example of recently published ecological work that calls for a change of metaphor, yet still falls into the use of "higher" meaning "better" in his text, is David W. Orr, *The Last Refuge: Patriotism, Politics and the Environment in an Age of Terror*; see Chapter 6.

10. Vladimir Vernadsky, *The Biosphere*, p.6. Elisabet Sahtouris questions whether Vernadsky really did perceive Earth as a whole live entity (*Earthdance* p.118), and refers to Scottish scientist James Hutton, as having such a view in 1785 (*Earthdance*, p.69).

11. Vladimir Vernadsky, *The Biosphere*, p.iv.

his work Vernadsky scientifically and poetically describes an wholistic vision of Cosmos and Earth, and at times refers to humankind as a "geological entity".[13] His concept of a biosphere is based on data from all Earth sciences, and because of this synthesis it is a comprehension of "the nature of the Earth on a planetary/ cosmic scale."[14] For Vernadsky, the biosphere is "a place of transformation" of cosmic energies.[15] He says

> The biosphere is as much, or even more, the creation of the Sun as it is a manifestation of Earth-processes. Ancient religious traditions which regarded terrestrial creatures, especially human beings, as 'children of the Sun' were much nearer the truth than those which looked upon them as a mere ephemeral creation...[16]

Vernadsky asserts that the phenomena in the biosphere cannot be understood "unless one takes into account the bond that unites it with the entire cosmic mechanism"[17]—the phenomena are "related to the structure of atoms, to their places in the cosmos and to their evolution in the history of the cosmos."[18]

Earth of course does not need to be named Gaia—Spretnak refers to "Earth-body"[19]—but it is a name that now has large appeal in the West, due to James Lovelock and Lynn Margulis' scientific theory named thus, first published in 1974. The name "Gaia" now not only invokes the ancient Greek myth of the Creator-Goddess, but also the present scientific inquiry. Lovelock points out that the Gaia theory is now

> spurring a great deal of scientific research into the geophysiology of our living planet (and) it is also spurring philosophic conceptions of what it means to our species to be part of a living planet. Some of these conceptions stay carefully within the accepted limits of science; others have a religious bent.[20]

12. Vladimir Vernadsky, *The Biosphere*, p.1.
13. Vladimir Vernadsky, *The Biosphere*, p.2.
14. Vladimir Vernadsky, *The Biosphere*, p.4.
15. Vladimir Vernadsky, *The Biosphere*, p.7.
16. Vladimir Vernadsky, *The Biosphere*, p.8.
17. Vladimir Vernadsky, *The Biosphere*, p.10.
18. Vladimir Vernadsky, *The Biosphere*, p.9.
19. Charlene Spretnak, *States of Grace*, p.144-145.
20. in James Lovelock's Foreword to Elisabet Sahtouris, *Earthdance*, p.xiii.

The religious bent is frequently problematic to the acceptance of the theory itself in the scientific community; but the scientific bent to this ancient religious story is most frequently beneficial to a prospective deepening of connection to the hearts and minds of a people seeking relationship with Earth. The naming of a spirituality as "Gaian" today, signifies the integration of scientific knowledge gained by humanity into the vision and metaphor of that spirituality. For Spretnak, knowing Gaia, is knowing that we are

> inextricably linked at the molecular level to every other manifestation of the great unfolding. We are descendents of the fireball…glimpsing the oneness of the sacred whole.[21]

The Gaia theory states "that our planet and its creatures constitute a single self-regulating system that is in fact a great living being, or organism."[22] Elisabet Sahtouris, evolutionary biologist, grounds her philosophy in this conception. She understands the scientific story of Gaian creation as a retelling of the ancient myth, and says that

> once we truly grasp the scientific reality of the Gaian organism and its physiology, our entire worldview and practice are bound to change profoundly, revealing the way to solving what now appear to be our greatest and most insoluble problems.[23]

As participants in Gaia, we may understand ourselves as Gaia, holons of the Large Self, as a drop of the ocean participates in (the whole of) the ocean. I regard the concepts of holons and holarchy[24] to be a crucial model for understanding a participatory universe. Harman and Sahtouris define a holarchy as "the embeddedness of living entities within each other (e.g., cell, organ, body, family, community, ecosystem, bioregion, planet, star system, galaxy, etc.)";[25] and they define a holon as "a living entity or system."[26] They describe the entire Universe

---

21. Charlene Spretnak, "Gaian Spirituality". Woman of Power Issue 20, Spring 1991, p.17.
22. Elisabet Sahtouris, *Earthdance*, p.xvii..
23. Elisabet Sahtouris, *Earthdance*, p.7.
24. Originally they are Arthur Koestler's terms. See Connie Barlow (ed.), *From Gaia to Selfish Genes: Selected Writings in the Life Sciences*, p. 89–100. Ken Wilber also describes the terms in *A Brief History of Everything*, p.20ff.
25. Willis Harman and Elisabet Sahtouris, *Biology Revisioned*, p.130.
26. Willis Harman and Elisabet Sahtouris, *Biology Revisioned*, p.130.

as a vast living entity or holon, and also as "a holarchy containing smaller holons in continual co-creation."[27] A most significant feature of a holarchy is that every layer/level has as much importance as any other, because they are embedded in each other—and actually the layers of simpler life forms are not dependent on the more complex, though the more complex are dependent on the simpler earlier layers. Within the context of holarchy, it may be possible to explain by physical principles how a quality of living systems "may apply all the way from the most simple single-cell life form to Gaia."[28]

Psychologist James Hillman recognizes that the cut between the self and the natural world is arbitrary, and wonders whether it can be made at all—"we can make it at the skin or we can take it as far out as you like—to the deep oceans and distant stars".[29] Lovelock refers to the human as Gaia[30]—"She has seen the reflection of her fair face through the eyes of astronauts...", and speaks of a "commonwealth of all creatures that constitutes Gaia."[31] In his early writings on Gaia, he did try to hold back from Her sentience:

> Occasionally it has been difficult to avoid talking of Gaia as if she were known to be sentient. This is meant no more seriously than the appellation 'she' when given to a ship by those who sail in her, as a recognition that even pieces of wood and metal may achieve a composite identity distinct from the mere sum of its parts.[32]

However, in 1988 Lovelock spoke of his relationship with Gaia as possibly kin to the relationship of some Christians to Mary. He says, "What if Mary is another name for Gaia?"[33] and later,

---

27. Willis Harman and Elisabet Sahtouris, *Biology Revisioned*, p.xxiii.
28. Willis Harman and Elisabet Sahtouris, *Biology Revisioned*, p.xxii. It is worth noting that a holon itself could be said to exhibit qualities that I identify with the three dynamics of the Female Metaphor and Cosmogenesis—agency, communion, and self-transcendence. See Sahtouris, *Earthdance*, p.51-53.
29. James Hillman, "A Psyche the Size of Earth" in *Ecopsychology: Restoring the Earth, Healing the Mind*. Roszak, Gomes and Kanner, (eds), p.xix.
30. Cited in Connie Barlow (ed.), *From Gaia to Selfish Genes*, p.19.
31. Cited in Connie Barlow (ed.), *From Gaia to Selfish Genes*, p.19
32. Cited in Connie Barlow (ed.), *From Gaia to Selfish Genes*, p.3.
33. Cited in Connie Barlow (ed.), *From Gaia to Selfish Genes*, p.41.

If their hearts and minds could be moved to see in her the embodiment of Gaia, then they might become aware that the victim of their destruction was indeed the Mother of humankind and the source of everlasting life.[34]

He had explained that

> Any living organism a quarter as old as the Universe itself and still full of vigor is as near immortal as we ever need to know. She is of this Universe and, conceivably, a part of (the Divine).[35]

Gaian researchers, scientists who study the global metabolism, generally tread more carefully, riding a fine edge in regard Gaia's sentience applying the principles of science yet "without postulating a global organism."[36] Nevertheless, there is evidence of ambivalence; Tyler Volk speaks of Earth (not "the" Earth) and of Gaian "physiology", implying a subject, while still using the pronoun "it". Volk speaks of all of us as "cells within the embracing physiology of...'Gaia'",[37] yet holds back from accepting Her as an organism. He says this because Gaia "does not evolve in a Darwinian sense",[38] but that leaves it open that She may evolve in some other sense. He, like other Gaian scientists, do participate in promoting an informed reverence for Gaia's body.

The restoration of the material reality, is a restoration of the maternal reality, is a restoration of the Mother.

> For so long we've considered the Earth as just a big dead ball of dirt. It shocks us nearly out of our minds when we discover we're involved with something that moves...(that) the whole process is alive.[39]

The entire Cosmos itself has been imagined as something dead and static—the heavens as a vacuous space "out there". Just as Aristotle storied the female body as passive matter, so the Womb of Space has been imagined. The cosmology of

---

34. Cited in Connie Barlow (ed.), *From Gaia to Selfish Genes*, p.42.
35. Cited in Connie Barlow (ed.), *From Gaia to Selfish Genes*, p.42. Lovelock actually uses the word "God", by which I assume he means "the Divine". I translate it in the text for the sake of continuity of my point.
36. Tyler Volk, *Gaia's Body*, p.ix.
37. Tyler Volk, *Gaia's Body*, p.viii.
38. Tyler Volk, *Gaia's Body*, p.ix.
39. Brian Swimme, *The Universe is a Green Dragon*, p.135.

Earth-based religious traditions, on the other hand, have always understood Earth as Mother, and the Mother as active Creator. Starhawk writes of Goddess as

> the living body of a living cosmos, the awareness that infuses matter and the energy that produces change. She is life eternally attempting to maintain itself, reproduce itself, diversify, evolve…[40]

Ecologist Stephan Harding, who teaches on Gaia and ecophilosophy at Schumacher College, says that "the whole reason for gathering scientific information is to provide a cognitive basis for developing wide identification with nature", that people love it when they "realize that the planet has life-like qualities of self-regulation"[41]—in my own words, people love to hear news of the Mother, that She is alive.

For many minds today Gaian research and knowledge of the evolutionary story, furthers our knowledge of the Mother, and at once, knowledge of ourselves. The definition of self-knowledge is extended to Self-knowledge—knowledge of Gaia: scientist Mae-Wan Ho says "It is in knowing her that we shall have intimate knowledge of ourselves."[42] Just as the prokaryotes, the first cells on Earth deeply effected the planet and its future, so our small organism and the many, many others effect the planet over long periods of time. This is Gaian spirituality—taking on the mind of the Universe, participating in the Dream of the Earth, beginning to "know" from within the perspective of Earth, Moon, Sun, Tree—and so on. And perhaps "PaGaian Cosmology", as I am coming to name this perspective, may more adequately express this totality, this integral sense of Gaia as Self-Earth-Universe, extending as it does the sense and vision of "country".

"Goddess"

"Goddess", as I understand the term, is the Female Metaphor for the Great Creative Principle of the Universe. As such, She is both the Matrix and an wholistic template of Being; that is, She is whole and complete within Herself, and is a complete illustration of the process of living and dying. Her three aspects are

---

40.   Starhawk, *The Spiral Dance*, p.228.
41.   Cited in Connie Barlow, *Green Space, Green Time*, p.216.
42.   Mae-Wan Ho, "Natural Being and Coherent Society" in *Gaia in Action*, Peter Bunyard (ed.), p.305.

based on chronological phases of a woman's life, but are not in any way limited to those phases. These three aspects are phases of the whole process of living and dying, that the ancients in many cultures noticed and celebrated. I contend that these three aspects were understood as a dynamic of Creativity—and witness to that is the Triple Spiral engraved in central position at New Grange in Ireland. The significance of the New Grange monument may yet to be fully understood, as our ethnocentric minds only now begin to remember the "Goddess" centred minds that built it, as well as other monuments in Old Europe, that have puzzled our patriarchal earth-alienated minds.[43] I propose that this Triple Spiral encoded at New Grange specifically celebrates the triple faced Female Metaphor as Cosmic Dynamic of Creativity, given that it is lit up at the moment of Winter Solstice, the Seasonal Moment that celebrates Origins and Earth-Sun creativity.

I understand "Creativity" as another name for the Mystery of Being, and it is what I understand as the essence of Being. As Loren Eiseley reflects,

> No utilitarian philosophy explains a snow crystal, no doctrine of use or disuse. Water has merely leapt out of vapor and thin nothingness in the night sky to array itself in form. There is no logical reason for the existence of a snowflake any more than there is for evolution.[44]

"Creativity" is also a term used by process philosopher Alfred North Whitehead for "the Category of the Ultimate"[45] and he refers to it as threefold.[46] Thus, as I understand "Goddess"—the dynamic, triple-faced Metaphor—She may enable the identification of Life itself, as we witness it, experience it, and inter-act with it, with the manifestation of the ultimate Mystery at the Heart and Origin. To further this identification I have associated the three Faces of the Female Metaphor—"Goddess"—with Thomas Berry's three characteristics of what is scientifically known as Cosmogenesis, the omnipresent creative dynamic essential to all structure and form in the Universe. Cosmogenesis is referred to by Brian Swimme and Thomas Berry in their story of the Universe as having three central

---

43. See Paul Devereaux *Earth Memory* p.34 and 120-124, Michael Dames *The Silbury Treasure*, Claire French *The Celtic Goddess*, p.22. See Appendix F, p.279-280 for more detail. See also the website http://gofree.indigo.ie/~thall/newgrange.htmltexts
44. Loren Eiseley, *The Immense Journey*, p.27.
45. Alfred North Whitehead, *Process and Reality*, p.28.
46. I describe more of this in Chapter 4: see "Whitehead's 'Threefold Creative Composition'".

tendencies which are "the cosmological orderings of the creative display of energy everywhere and at any time throughout the history of the universe."[47]

The three chronological phases of a woman's life in which these faces of Goddess are mirrored are:—pre-menarchal young one, menstrual mother, and post-menopausal elder; and thus they have been known as Virgin/Maiden, Mother/Creator, Old One/Crone. It will be necessary to "re-story" these terms, since women and men in our times, no longer understand them in their full integrity—diminished, trivialized and even demonized as they have been by millennia of patriarchal narrative. Whereas, in the earliest of times of consciousness, and even later, these phases seem to have been sensed as aspects of the Great Creative Process[48] whereby Life continued, they had in recent patriarchal times lost their sacred essence. Indeed the Great Creative Process itself, expressed in the female as sacred, had become background. The mother became mere vessel, and "useful" in this mode. The young virgin became a prize to be taken, the older virgin became a harsh deviant to be avoided. The old one became "used up" and troublesome. Adam McLean advises that:

> To find the Triple Goddess…we must go back to an early stratum of myth. Long before the ascendancy of the Christ myth, the primal myths of the Goddess had been overlaid with generations of masculine Gods usurping her place in the scheme of things, taking over her sacred centres and grasping for themselves some facet of her attributes. If we go back to the earliest myths of humankind we will find the goddess in her purest, usually triune, form.[49]

The re-storying of women—the Being of the female, is a preface to being able to speak sensibly of how Virgin-Mother-Crone could be a Metaphor for the Mystery of Being. It is then possible to relate these three aspects to the evolutionary cosmic dynamics—"Cosmogenesis"—as a way of deepening awareness of them in the present moment and as a way of entering into the Female Metaphor more fully, as a way of comprehending or *sensing* "Goddess". The seasonal celebrations then may become a way of accessing the Metaphor, embodying "Goddess" and developing personal and cultural relationship to the Cosmos, as one joins Earth in Her annual journey of descent and return.

---

47. Brian Swimme and Thomas Berry, *The Universe Story*, p.72.
48. I capitalize this term as I mean it as another name for the Absolute, for the Sacred.
49. Adam McLean, *The Triple Goddess*, p.12-13.

Language

It seems generally clearer for me to speak of the "Female Metaphor" rather than "Goddess" since I do not wish to imply a "God in drag". I will however, use the term "Goddess" sometimes, as I think humans do need to get acclimatized to Her expressed in this form—She has for too long been relegated to the fringes. According to the Webster's Dictionary, a metaphor is a word or phrase used "to suggest a likeness".[50] "Goddess" is a figure of speech suggesting a likeness of femaleness in the Divine, or the Divine in femaleness; few argue with that, though many do argue that "God" does not suggest a likeness of maleness in the Divine, or the Divine in maleness. The term "Goddess" does seem to evoke a different visceral impulse and visualization, which is worth noting. Some primal cultures seem to have never used an equivalent term, but neither was there any problem with a feeling for the Female as Sacred Entity: "Grandmother" spirits and ancestors were greatly revered.[51]

I will at times speak of many particular Goddesses with a capital 'g'—Demeter or Persephone for example, all of whom for me partake in the Female Metaphor; they are particular conflagrations of, are holons of, the Female Metaphor. I will use a capital "g" even for these particular Goddesses, partly for political reasons, that is, so Their Divinity is remembered; but also signifying that I am not simply speaking of an archetype of the Olympian pantheon. As evidence suggests, long before the Goddesses were colonized, married off, raped and caught in sordid plots against each other, they were faces of a Matrix and a Cosmic Power.

"Archetype" is a word frequently used to name/describe the Female Metaphor, though it is much less often used to describe other Deities. I prefer not to speak of Her as "archetype", as this tends to connote a "mindstruct"—something "merely" cultural—and what I wish to convey is the sense of Her as a "physic" of the Universe. Some who use the term "archetype" do appear to mean just that, that is, "archetype" as a "physic". Joseph Campbell's view is that "archetypes" arise not so much "from the mental sphere of rational ideation",[52] as from the single psychophysiological source common to all humans—the body.[53] In that

---

50. *Webster's Third International Dictionary of the English Language*, p.1420.
51. Hallie iglehart Austen refers to this in her discussion of "Language" in *The Heart of the Goddess*, p.xxi.
52. Joseph Campbell, *The Inner Reaches of Outer Space*, p.11.
53. Joseph Campbell, *The Inner Reaches of Outer Space*, p.12.

sense archetypes arise from "bioenergies that are the essence of life itself".[54] For Campbell, archetypes

> are biologically grounded and at once the motivating powers and connoted references of the historically conditioned metaphorical figures of mythologies around the world…(and)…are, like the laws of space, unchanged by changes of location.[55]

This would seem to be the sense in which I mean the Female Metaphor, and at home with the Cosmogenetic Principle which I will speak of later. However, in general I feel that the word "archetype" confuses the fundamental sense of the Triple Face Dynamic as I wish to convey it. The evolutionary cosmic dynamics—Cosmogenesis—are not culturally induced phenomena, nor is the cyclical dynamic of the Triple Goddess Metaphor. The Cosmogenesis in which we find ourselves is at once completely physical and manifest, as well as "intra"-physical and unmanifest—it is not "meta"-physical and separate, it is intrinsic with the physical. Physicist David Bohm speaks in terms of "implicate" and "explicate" orders, wherein the "explicate" (or "manifest", as I have termed it) is "a special and distinguished form contained within the general totality of all the implicate orders"[56] (or "unmanifest", as I have termed it). In this way Bohm develops a way of speaking about a "universe of unbroken wholeness"[57] which is how I understand the physics of the Female Metaphor.

Similarly, some common Pagan language that is used today does not communicate the actual physics of the Universe that it aspires to celebrate, or is at least unhelpful to the changing of our minds; for example, at times Light and Dark are spoken of as being in a battle,[58] where at Winter Solstice, the celebrations are languaged as marking Light's "victory over the darkness of winter."[59] Other Pagan sources say it is *Dark's* victory—Starhawk, for example, says that at Winter Solstice, "darkness triumphs".[60] Either way it is being storied as a battle, which in actual fact the Sun is not engaged in. I do not think that these expressions con-

---

54. Joseph Campbell, *The Inner Reaches of Outer Space*, p.13.
55. Joseph Campbell, *The Inner Reaches of Outer Space*, p.19.
56. David Bohm, *Wholeness and the Implicate Order*, p.xv.
57. David Bohm, *Wholeness and the Implicate Order*, p.xv.
58. Which is also the story told in many other religions, in various ways.
59. Vivianne Crowley, *Celtic Wisdom: Seasonal Rituals and Festivals*, p.40.
60. Starhawk, *The Spiral Dance*, p.182.

jure a desirable or insightful story about the Light and Dark phenomena caused by Sun's relationship with Earth. This kind of language does not do this ancient Earth-Wisdom tradition justice for our time, and perhaps it never did amongst those who observed, studied and reflected upon, and taught the Earth Wisdom. Our language needs to fit our understanding of the Universe, needs to fit us (humans and all beings) into—story us into—the Universe, as our minds know it.

Language is important to this work of re-inventing and re-storying. I have already noted some of my reasons for capitalizing words that would normally be in small case. I realize that there is argument for not capitalizing at all—any of it, the female metaphor herself: in which case, the base line is that it is all sacred, and nothing further needs to be said. However, the cultural reality is that all is not sacred, and that is a point that this work is speaking to. Thus I persist with the re-valuing of certain words by capitalizing as one method that goes in hand with the entire process of re-inventing, and opening those words up to the possibility of expressing a multivalent reality which is at once the Divine at all those valencies. The word "Divine" itself may also be problematic for some, as it may seem to imply anthropomorphic form: I think it need not be so, but agree that "Sacred" may be a better choice when possible.

In general, I like when possible to avoid "the", in front of "Source" or "Goddess" or "Mystery", since "That/She" is not an object. Just as those who do use "God" understand that "the" God, would seem to refer to a signifier of Divinity rather than referring to Divinity itself. I don't know that it is always possible to abandon "the"—this is an experiment, but the attempt may help us to change our minds.

Sometimes I may use the term "the Mother" to refer to the "Female Metaphor", as I mean "Mother" in the sense of Ultimate Creativity or Creator of All. One could also choose, as archaeologist Marija Gimbutas has done, to refer always to this Ultimate Creativity as "the Great Goddess",[61] however in our present cultural story I feel the meaning would not be clear. I will also try to be clear when I am referring to Ultimate Creativity, to the One, the "She-Who-Is-All" and when I am referring only to the aspect/face of Mother in the Triple Dynamic. I develop discussion of the complexity of the separation of the Three from the One, towards the end of Chapter 3.

---

61. Marija Gimbutas, *The Language of the Goddess*, p.316.

I frequently use terms like "we" and "ourselves", to speak of "humans", and sometimes to speak of "women". It will be clear as to which category I am referring, and I do understand that the experience of individuals and cultures within these categories are by no means monolithic. There are however some recurrent patterns that I refer to. In the case of using "we" for "women", I use it sparingly, and refer to the experience of those whom I have known both personally and via written word.

Feminist Theology—Thealogy—Poetry

This re-storying is not feminist theology. When at first I began I thought it may be a "thea-logy", which is a term thought to have been coined originally by Naomi Goldenberg in 1979.[62] Thea-logy is a study of Goddess. Some may prefer to call such a study, Sophialogy.[63] It is generally about relating with our Earth/Universe/Context; it is not simply "theology spelled with an *a*", as Barbara Walker points out.[64] Generally, thealogy speaks of our Place as sacred, and frequently, though not always, with an understanding that "Goddess" is immanent in this place, not an external Deity. However I find the term "thea-logy" to be cumbersome, and still seeming to indicate participation in "belief" in a Deity. I wish to be clear that what I am speaking of, is not a Deity: this is therefore not "theology" nor even "thealogy". It is a cosmology: what I am speaking of and with is Cosmos—a Place. Thomas Berry has preferred to be called a "geologian" or "cosmologist",[65] perhaps for a similar reason: he is speaking about a place, not a deity—as such has been understood by "theology". Earth-based religious traditions and Goddess traditions speak of this Place as sacred. "PaGaian" cosmology is a way of speaking about this Place: it implies a metaphor and a practice. It is a synthesis of "celebrating Gaia-Goddess-Cosmos"…a metaphor that one is IN. Thus I like to name the process of this synthesis as "Poetry". I feel that all "theology" and "thea-logy" was meant to be Poetry—what else could it be in its attempt to describe matters of an ultimate nature. Yet it seems to me that most of what has passed for theology has ended up actually a description of a dead butterfly pinned in a glass case, not one that is alive and flitting about the garden—a

---

62.   Cited in Carol Christ, *The Rebirth of the Goddess*, p.184 fn5.
63.   Coralie Ling, "Sophialogy and Croning Rituals", What's God Got to Do With It?" CONFERENCE PROCEEDINGS, Kathleen mcPhillps (ed.), p.83-90.
64.   Barbara Walker, *Restoring the Goddess*, p.27.
65.   Mark Matousek, "Reinventing the Human", Common Boundary Vol 8 No 3, p.31.

dynamic moving being. Cosmos is a Place, dynamic and moving, alive and changing, which is indistinguishable from participatory selves, which remains ultimately mysterious and indefinable; thus ultimately only able to be spoken of metaphorically. This then is Poetry.

Joseph Campbell has said that the best things can't be told since they transcend all thought; the second best things are misunderstood, since they are the thoughts that refer to what can't be thought about; and the third best things are what we talk about.[66] Campbell described life as a poem, and that we participate in a poem.[67] He recalled the Gnostic texts, saying that "one problem with Yahweh…is that he forgot he was a metaphor. He thought he was a fact".[68] I do not name Great Mystery—the "She" of whom I speak—as "God". In terms of human history, "God" is a recent name for the Mystery, or Source-of-All. A couple of millennia ago, the Greeks hesitated to use "God" as a name for Source-of-All lest the people became confused, as to whether the term was referring to Zeus[69]—their morphic god. Indeed in the minds of most, still today, I think "God" does precisely that; the image—the Body—invoked in the mind still looks the same even though it is not known as Zeus. The people tend to forget that "God" is a metaphor.

Even feminist theology can speak at great length about female metaphors for Divinity, and not once use or develop the term "Goddess", or sometimes not even use the female pronoun. Feminist theologians frequently do not perceive "God" as invoking Maleness, yet "Goddess" *is* perceived as invoking Femaleness, and this for some to whom feminist theology speaks, seems to be too dreadful a thought, and reveals an acceptance of "Goddess" as being an invocation of "Other". "God" can quite happily incorporate the maternal—"God" is frequently addressed as "Mother"—but there is nothing radically different about this incorporation; the Gods of recent human history have always done this, though they have left menstrual abilities alone.

On occasion feminist theology advises us to grow out of maternal metaphor altogether[70]—a move that I feel participates in a denial of the body. It falls into the

---

66. Joseph Campbell, *The Power of Myth*, p.49.
67. Joseph Campbell, *The Power of Myth*, p.55.
68. Joseph Campbell, *The Power of Myth*, p.62.
69. Dr. Joanmarie Smith CSJ, "Hen, Homemaker and Goddess" in PACE 14 issue D, p.2.

hands of the patriarchal mind that would have us deny Earthbody, along with female body, and the sensuous processes of Life—as Charlene Spretnak well describes in her book *States of Grace*.[71] Most feminist theology, as important as it is for women and men within the Christian paradigm, generally continues to be within that paradigm; and that is not what I am doing here. I am invoking an earlier human orientation to Mystery, something more primal to being, more organic, more dynamically essential to Life, more ubiquitous—that can be known in our bodyminds, in Earth, in the Cosmos. I feel that there is no longer the time to speak *to* the problem, as so many good minds still do; addressing issues with the "old guard". I suppose it still needs to be done—it does serve to identify and analyze the problem. I am glad that it is not my work. I feel that the hour is late, the urgent and sacred yearnings of the Earth call for real change, we must get on; we cannot be held up at the gate entertaining the old rules. I wish to be part of the re-creation—actually *"do"* something new, in the sense of actually changing the reality, situating us in a new Realm/Place.

Further to the case for naming what I am doing as "Poetry", is that the Earth tradition in which I have been nurtured, was in its origins, an oral tradition, which relied on its poets. It may be noted that the first among the attributes praised in the Great Goddess Brigid was Her function of poet—along with physician and smith-artisan. It would appear that Poetry was considered a critical discipline in which to engage—it was the way in which the culture was passed on, the transmission of the sacred stories, the cosmology of a people told, the bearing of a tradition. The poetic imagination may also allow for the ever-new that is innate to something that is alive. William Irwin Thompson speaks of the poetic imagination as a capacity to sense/intuit and to *be* more than one can *know*, a capacity that is important to scientific endeavour "because we are more than we know."[72] Poetry thus allows also for the bringing forth of a world, as well as the bearing of a tradition—using what is there yet allowing the sentience within it to reveal ever-new valencies. I am an inventor, a mythmaker, who has received/taken remnants of her indigenous religious heritage, and newly available parts, and spun and woven new threads, fabrics and stories.[73] When I became bold enough to assume such a task—out of a sensed necessity, I had long been encouraged by the words of Monique Wittig where she describes the attempt to remember an earlier

---

70.   Elizabeth Johnson, *She Who Is*, p.235.
71.   Charlene Spretnak *States of Grace: the Recovery of Meaning in the Postmodern Age*, p.122-127.
72.   William Irwin Thompson, *Gaia: A Way of Knowing*, p. 8-9.

mode of being, for which it is said "there are no words" and therefore perhaps "it does not exist." Wittig says, "Make an effort to remember. Or, failing that, invent."[74]

I do not regard this work as "feminist discourse", and I speak more of this later: rather I regard it as "PaGaian concourse"—perhaps that is another name for Poetry. This work may be regarded by some as feminist, and I have regarded myself as feminist, but I do think that this process ventures into new territory—that includes all the hard work done by feminism. The new territory is in the realm wherein we humans no longer primarily or simply engage in more talk and analysis, but we dare to attend sincerely and primarily to the complexity of actual relationship with, and comprehension of, our embodied engagement with our Earth-Universe-Gaian context.

Cosmogenesis—an Introduction

Central to this cosmology is Swimme and Berry's articulation of Cosmogenesis and its three "governing themes".[75] Brian Swimme is a scientist who tells the story of the evolutionary unfolding of the Universe with a feeling for its sacred nature. He and Thomas Berry offer an interpretation of the human in the Universe and Earth community, drawn from empirical scientific knowledge. Scientist E.O. Wilson has said that "the evolutionary epic is probably the best myth we will ever have"[76] and describes the story of the universe as a grand narrative that may utilize archetypes, use poetic form, charge people's souls to the critical task of participation and "inspirit" the material explanation of the world.[77] Swimme is a storyteller with that capacity. Thomas Berry, academically trained contemplative priest, co-author of *The Universe Story* and mentor of Brian Swimme forges "a partnership between the sciences and humanities" that humbly takes into account and includes the wisdom of indigenous peoples and the wisdom of women.[78] Swimme and Berry's cosmology is recognized as in keeping with the

---

73. As the process of invention and methods of qualitative research are described by Norman K.Denzin and Yvonna S. Lincoln (eds.), *Handbook of Qualitative Research*, p.584.

74. Monique Wittig, *Les Guerilleres*. NY: Avon Books, p.89.

75. Brian Swimme and Thomas Berry, *The Universe Story*, p.66-79.

76. Quoted in Connie Barlow, *Green Space, Green Time*, p.23, from Edward O.Wilson, *On Human Nature*, p.201.

77. Cited in Connie Barlow, *Green Space, Green Time*, p.24-28.

latest discoveries in astronomy, physics, complexity studies, and evolutionary theory. Connie Barlow describes in *Green Space, Green Time*, how Swimme and Berry's work catalyzes meaning-making that may actually make a social, political and cultural difference.

Amongst the broad range of influences upon Swimme and Berry's cosmological interpretations is Alfred North Whitehead's "process philosophy" which was an extrapolation from the quantum physics of the 1920's. Whitehead included in his philosophy a "Threefold Creative Composition" which I noted earlier, and later describe as resonant with the three faces of the Female Metaphor and hence with Swimme and Berry's three faces of Cosmogenesis. Swimme and Berry's articulation of the three is a development of Thomas Berry's fourth principle of a functional cosmology (See Appendix A). The three themes are offered as an interpretation of three fundamental principles of reality inductively drawn from empirical scientific knowledge. The three themes are not equations, nor are they laws like unto the laws of thermodynamics.[79] Swimme notes specifically some of the scientists whose work he and Berry draw on for the development and understanding of their three aspects of Cosmogenesis.[80]

Cosmogenesis, in brief, is the ongoing creative activity of the Universe, the unfolding of the Universe—referring to the form producing dynamics of the Cosmological Unfolding. Generally it refers to large-scale structures such as galaxies and stars, but a more inclusive understanding is justified:

> What we observe is that forms and structures in the universe arise, evolve in interactions, achieve stable if nonequlibrium processes, and then decay and disintegrate. The Cosmogenetic Principle simply states that the evolutionary dynamics involved in building the structures that appear in our own region of space-time permeate the universe as well.[81]

78. Connie Barlow, *Green Space, Green Time*, p.53-54. See Thomas Berry, *The Great Work*, p.176-195.
79. Larry Edwards helped me to clarify this.
80. In a personal communication (email 27/10/02) Swimme noted for example, G.G. Simpson *The Major Features* of Evolution p.243, and Karl Ernst von Baer as quoted in Stephen Jay Gould *Ontology and Philogeny* p.61, for differentiation; Jeffrey Wicken *Evolution, Thermodynamics and Information: Extending the Darwinian Program* p.8 for communion; and Ernst Mayr *The Growth of Biological Thought: Diversity, Evolution and Inheritance* p.533, and E.O. Wilson *The Diversity of Life* p.8, for autopoiesis.

Certainly in their discussion of the three dynamics, Swimme and Berry cover the full gamut of creative manifestation—from particles to biological life to stars. They later describe how the three biological shaping powers of mutation, natural selection and niche creation "are further illustrations of the root creativity of the universe" that they have identified with the Cosmogenetic Principle.[82] They consider their articulations of the meanings associated with these dynamics as a beginning, "a prologue for later treatments as our direct experience of the universe's development extends throughout space and time."[83]

In the background to this Cosmogenetic Principle, is a principle called the Cosmological Principle defined by Einstein, and it has been essential for the entire Western scientific research enterprise on the planet today. That principle states that every point in the Universe is the same as every other point[84]—basically that hydrogen in this part of the cosmos can be assumed to be the same as hydrogen in some other part of the cosmos. This is not something that can be proved but it is assumed as a reasonable principle. Swimme and Berry note that this foundational principle of cosmology came out of a context early last century, that believed we lived in a static cosmos—a context that was ignorant of the evolution of the Universe as a whole. Now that science recognizes that we live in a cosmogenesis, a developing evolutionary reality, which appears to have had a thirteen point seven billion year story, that principle of Einstein's is being extended to the Cosmogenetic Principle:

> Even though our knowledge of morphogenesis and cosmogenesis is in its infancy, we are assuming that the heightened scientific investigation of these dynamics will make the cosmogenetic perspective entirely ordinary in the next centuries.[85]

This Cosmogenetic Principle states not only that every point in the universe is the same as every other point, but in addition, that the *dynamics of evolution* are the same at every point in the Universe. What that means, amongst many other

---

81. Brian Swimme and Thomas Berry, *The Universe Story*, p.67.
82. Brian Swimme and Thomas Berry, *The Universe Story*, p.132. I provide a description of these three biological shaping powers and my association of them with the Female Metaphor in Chapter 4.
83. Brian Swimme and Thomas Berry, *The Universe Story*, p.71.
84. Brian Swimme and Thomas Berry, *The Universe Story*, p.66.
85. Brian Swimme and Thomas Berry, *The Universe Story*, p.129.

things, is that the same Creative principle that gives birth to the Universe, pervades every drop of it with the same creative potency—that the Centre of the Universe is everywhere. Thus it is here as much as anywhere.

Brian Swimme and Thomas Berry have stated that this omnipresent Creativity will be characterized by three features "throughout time and space and at every level of reality"—differentiation, communion and autopoiesis.[86] These three have been summarized as follows: differentiation—to be is to be unique; communion—to be is to be related; autopoiesis—to be is to be a centre of creativity.[87] Swimme and Berry call these three features, "cosmological orderings of the creative display of energy everywhere and at any time throughout the history of the universe."[88] They say these three refer to the "basal intentionality of all existence"[89] and importantly, they are "beyond any simple one-line univocal definition".[90] They are highly complex, interconnected and ongoing processes. The three features themselves are features of each other, for example:—a "multiform relatedness"—communion, is demanded by a differentiated universe, and that rests upon the fact of each individual thing's infinite creative depths—autopoiesis.[91] This book itself, as with any creative work, as it progresses, is ordered, structured and organized by these features. I refer to how this has characterized my process in this work, in the concluding chapter.

The Wheel of the Year—the Seasonal Ritual Celebrations

The ritual celebrations of Gaia as I have scripted them are based in the religious practice of the Old Western European Goddess tradition, wherein there are eight annual Earth holy days or "moments of grace" as Thomas Berry has often termed the seasonal transitions. These eight "holy days" are traditionally known as "Sabbats", and they were originally taught to me by Starhawk, both directly and in

86.   Brian Swimme and Thomas Berry, *The Universe Story*, p.71.
87.   This summary definition of the three aspects of Cosmogenesis is on the editorial page of issues of *Original Blessing*, a newsletter published by Friends of Creation Spirituality Inc., at 2141 Broadway, Oakland, CA., 1997. The Editor in Chief was Matthew Fox.
88.   Brian Swimme and Thomas Berry, *The Universe Story*, p.72.
89.   Brian Swimme and Thomas Berry, *The Universe Story*, p.71.
90.   Brian Swimme and Thomas Berry, *The Universe Story*, p.71.
91.   Brian Swimme and Thomas Berry, *The Universe Story*, p.74.

her book *The Spiral Dance*. Since I first began to celebrate them in the Southern Hemisphere, I have always done so at the correct dates for this location. I have adapted the celebrations significantly, re-languaging them for myself and for different groups of people, and as my understanding deepens and changes. It is my experience that the ongoing ritual celebration of these Seasonal Moments/Sabbats, couched in the participatory metaphor described in this book, enables women and men to actually experience participation in Gaia, identification and relationship with Her. The Wheel of the Year is a yearlong celebration of the Mystery—the light and the dark, which weave through our lives, and through all of existence. The annual Wheel is an expression of the dance of form and dissolution, that eternal dance in which we participate. It is an embodiment of the Creative Principle, the Triple Goddess, like a yearlong breath. The seasonal Wheel manifests how Gaia breathes in my part of the world, and the purpose of joining in that breath is in the hope of enhancing one's journey into the awesome Creativity that She manifests, to unfold this deepest identity.

The Western Way

Caitlin and John Matthews define two paths that form the "*prima materia*" of the Western Way—the body of teaching and knowledge dating from the "Foretime" in which the ancestors of Western Europe "first began to explore the inner realms of existence."[92] Those two paths are the "Native Tradition" and the "Hermetic Tradition". The "Native Tradition", also known as the "Old Religion"[93] because it is the earliest religion/spirituality in the West, is defined by Matthews as "more intuitive, earth conscious, Goddess-oriented", and they define the "Hermetic Tradition" as more focussed on "the pursuit of knowledge, oneness with the godhead, superconsciousness."[94] They say that Native Traditionalists see Deity "in terms of elemental forces", while Hermetic Schools shifts focus "from 'God out there' to God within the self."[95] I have learnt initially, about the Western Way from Starhawk's teaching of it. She is truly grounded in the Native Tradition, but there is no sense in which I have ever understood from her, that Deity in the elemental forces is separate from Deity in the self. It appears to me that Starhawk is

---

92. Caitlin and John Matthews, *The Western Way*, p.2.
93. Caitlin and John Matthews, *The Western Way*, p.22, and also Starhawk, *The Spiral Dance*, p.16.
94. Caitlin and John Matthews, *The Western Way*, p.3.
95. Caitlin and John Matthews, *The Western Way*, p.3-4.

part of the regeneration of the Western Mysteries that Caitlin and John Matthews also see their work as evoking. They encourage, as Starhawk does, a time

> for the symbols and systems to be regenerated by an influx of new yet ancient material, arising from within the group-soul and hereditary memory of ordinary people.[96]

Women particularly, and some men as well, of Goddess-centred spiritual tradition, have known deep stirrings and intuitions that are now forming the basis of a new era, a new branchpoint, as a new picture and sense of the Cosmos and the nature of humanity begins to be felt—in the crumbling of the old. A new story, grounded in ancient material yet with new "parts"/metaphors, and which is multivalent, is possible: enabling broader participation in human celebration of existence.

The Wheel of the Year in Stone

My ancestors built great circles of stones that represented their perception of Real Time and Space—cosmic calendars. They went to great lengths and detail to get it right. It was obviously very important to them to have the stones of a particular kind, in the right positions according to position of the Sun at different times of the year, and then to celebrate within it.

I have, for several years now, had a much smaller circle of stones assembled, representing the Wheel of the Year. I have regarded it as a "Medicine Wheel". I was assisted in the idea for this by Sedonia Cahill, when I participated in a guided meditation that she led, in which she had participants visualize our own circle of eight points.[97] I had already been celebrating some of the Sabbats, and felt a desire to construct my own circle of eight stones, in which I could sit in meditation. I did so, and I felt it as "medicine". My wheel of stones is a portable collection, that I can spread out in my living space, or let sit in a small circle on an altar, with a candle in the middle. Each stone/object (some are not stones as such)

---

96. Caitlin and John Matthews, *The Western Way*, p.15.
97. This was at a workshop at the Mind-Body-Spirit Festival in Sydney, 1995. In the meditation we each made our own imagined journeys around the circle. I learnt from her that there had perhaps been a lot of cultural exchange between the indigenous peoples of North America and the Celts.

represents a particular Sabbat, and is placed in the particular direction. I have found this assembled circle to have been an important presence. It makes the year tangible and visible as a circle, and has been a method of "changing my mind"—my feeling about space and time. My stone wheel has been a method of bringing me Home to my indigenous sense of Being, though I did not language it that way for some time. I simply knew I needed to do it. Abram writes that "medicine wheels" found on the high plateaus in the Rocky Mountains,

> enabled a person to orient herself within a dimension that was neither purely spatial nor purely temporal—the large stone that is precisely aligned with the place of the sun's northernmost emergence, marks a place that is as much in time (the summer solstice) as in space. [98]

The stone circles represent an understanding of, and the creation of, space-time unity, a Larger Picture of where we are, and who we are.

My understanding of sacred awareness is awareness of all that is involved in the present moment. The Wheel of Stones has offered to me a way of experiencing the present as "presence", as it recalls in an instant that

> That which has been and that which is to come are not elsewhere—they are not autonomous dimensions independent of the encompassing present in which we dwell. They are, rather, the very depths of this living place—the hidden depth of its distances and the concealed depth on which we stand. [99]

The Wheel of Stones, which may capture the Wheel of the Year in essence, locates the participant in the deep present, wherein the past and the future are also contained—always gestating in the dark, through the gateways. This is all continually enacted and expressed in the ceremonies of the Wheel of the Year. At Autumn Equinox, there is descent of the Beloved One to the underground for Wisdom, at Spring Equinox, She returns bringing with Her the presence of the underground. At Samhain/Deep Autumn, the future is conceived and gestates in the seething fertility of the Void. At Beltane/High Spring, the fertility of Life is accelerated, whipping into a "froth" of passion, that may be returned through the gateway of Summer Solstice, dissolving into the concealed gestating depths. At Winter Solstice, the concealed depths are birthed back into form.

---

98. David Abram, *The Spell of the Sensuous*, p.189.
99. David Abram, *The Spell of the Sensuous*, p.216.

Participation in the Wheel of the Year process may be a re-identification with the entire cosmic process—the time-developmental, as well as the seasonal-renewing processes—thus healing our estrangement from our place, returning us to presence to the Universe.

2

Embodiment, Gendered Language, and Personal/ Cultural/Cosmic Stories

The Body—Essential or Not?

All knowledge is an experience of body—what else can it be? Mind is body, body is mind. Humans know enough these days—including empirically—to end the dualistic notions of bodymind, to enter or perhaps re-enter in a new way, an integral comprehension of the bodymind we each are. In his recent book *The Spell of the Sensuous* David Abram affirms that

> Without this body…(could there be)…anything to speak about, or even to reflect on, or to think, since without any contact, any encounter, without any glimmer of sensory experience, there could be nothing to question or to know.[1]

I ask then: what difference if this body menstruates, lactates—if these body processes were considered and sensed as the norm? The "modern" woman—she of recent centuries—was held down by this difference, by the fact of her organic processes. The postmodern woman, convinced that the body can be "erased", that its substantive presence can be dismissed,[2] may be expected to deny that it matters, that it affects her experience in any way.

---

1. David Abram *The Spell of the Sensuous*, p.45.
2. Charlene Spretnak, *States of Grace: the Recovery of Meaning in the Postmodern Age*, p.122.

The organic processes of the female body, her "elemental capabilities",[3] are not cultural inventions, though I passionately agree that much cultural invention about woman's physicality has occurred (for example, the cultural idea that she was unsuited for education). And cultural invention continues to occur—across the full spectrum of thinking (for example, the persistent cultural notion that menstruation is a disability, or that physically strong women are "masculine"). And whilst it is true "that everything in human experience, including nature and human physicality,…(is already an)…entity shaped into cultural perceptions",[4] it is an error to deny any foundational experience. We are in deep relationship with our environment before we enter it—we are already shaped by environment as we form in the womb, as Swimme and Berry point out when discussing the Cosmo-genetic dynamic of communion.[5] We, like our primal forebears, breathe, drink water, excrete, feel. We do have a genetic code within each cell, that is a physical memory of origins…we are seeded with memory. This is especially true of the female body, whose ovum transmits the cytoplasm from one generation to the next. [6] The inability or unwillingness of a philosophical position to deal with a reciprocity between the being and environment—that the being itself has some innate foundational integrity, is a trait of the patriarchal mind in that it does not allow the *materia* any agency, sentience or autopoiesis. Scientific research is rampant with such minds, and as an example and typical of such a mind is that of Nobel award winning scientist Francis Crick[7] who claimed that human joys and sorrows, memories and ambitions, sense of personality and free will "are in fact no more than the behavior of a vast assembly of nerve cells and their associated molecules",[8] as if to assert that this "vast assembly of nerve cells and associated molecules" has no sentience.

---

3.   Charlene Spretnak, *States of Grace: the Recovery of Meaning in the Postmodern Age*, p.122.

4.   Charlene Spretnak, *States of Grace: the Recovery of Meaning in the Postmodern Age*, p.122 referring to Derrida.

5.   Brian Swimme and Thomas Berry, *The Universe Story*, p.77.

6.   See Irene Coates, *The Seed Bearers*, p.10.

7.   Francis Crick, was credited with the co-discovery of the double-helical structure of DNA along with James Watson. Rosalind Franklin whose work appears to have been crucial to the discovery remains uncredited and even discredited—see Ethlie Anne Vare & Greg Ptacek, *Mothers of Invention*, p.214.

8.   Referred to by Cameron Forbes in an article "Thirst for Thought", page 4 in *The Weekend Australian* February 3-4 2001.

I am suspicious of texts that would "erase" the body—deny physical sentience or difference, since in patriarchal cultures it is the female particularly that is associated with physical reality. Whose body is it then that is primarily being erased, that has been erased since the emergence of the patriarchal mind? (Yet artists have been obsessed with her body—as if trying to paint her back into the picture perhaps or at times to frame her there as object). The early Greeks denied her inclusion in the "kosmos" because of her messy body.[9] In other cultures where her body had been the lap upon which rulers sat and thus gained their right to rule,[10] her body was gradually stylized into furniture—a throne, and then forgotten: her body became "part of the furniture", utilitarian. Female sacrality—the sacrality of the female body—has been "unnamed non-data in secular culture; peripheral sub-data in the phenomenology of religions", and considered essentially "pagan" or unclean in Western religious culture.[11] All bodies exchange substances with the environment—the land—whether or not it is obvious to an etherealised and sanitised culture. Aboriginal cosmologies have never forgotten this exchange; as Heather McDonald describes in her book *Blood, Bones and Spirit*—a work on Aboriginal Christianity. The body of these cosmologies is

> an organic body which is consubstantial with, and permeable to, the living environment. It is composed of flesh and blood, bones and spirit, and is subject to the organic processes of fecundity, growth and decay.[12]

And the exchange of bodily fluids with land is valued and significant—a participation in the very flow of life, and relationship with "the ancestors".[13] Australian writer, David Tacey, points out that the spirituality that arises from the land in Australia, carried in the themes of its poets, and known by its indigenous inhabitants, is one that is profoundly continuous with the body.[14]

It is likely that when humans really remember the body, all bodies—this relational dynamic, this *materia*, in which we are—they will remember the female

9.   See W. K. C. Guthrie, *The Greek Philosphers*, p.34-40.
10. See Erich Neumann, *The Great Mother,* p.98-100.
11. Melissa Raphael, *Thealogy and Embodiment*, p.21.
12. Heather McDonald, *Blood Bones and Spirit: Aboriginal Christianity in an East Kimberley Town*, p. 20.
13. Heather McDonald, *Blood Bones and Spirit: Aboriginal Christianity in an East Kimberley Town*, p. 21.
14. David Tacey, "Spirit and Place", EarthSong journal, issue 1, p.9-10.

body, and once again will have to deal with a foundational cyclical experience of life—which includes birth and death.[15] How we story that experience is really very open, but it will be a recognition of the web of life into which we are woven, as well as being weavers.

Life—birth and death—does not seem like much of a "foundational cyclical experience" to most people. It seems more like a one way trip—linear, birth to death. But that depends on your perspective…if you take it from within our own small life, our own small perspective, then it appears that way. An analogy may be drawn to Euclid's parallel lines.[16] While his postulate that parallel straight lines will never meet, holds true within a limited space (or in a perfectly flat featureless space—limitless and three dimensional), it does not hold true in the actual world that we inhabit—a spherical Earth.[17] Within the context of Earth, the lines will meet. Over time, Euclid has been proved incorrect from within a larger perspective. So with our lifeline, viewed from a larger perspective, from the perspective of Gaia, there is rebirth (but it is not personal) because we participate in a larger picture. We are a small part of the parallel lines, which actually go around a much larger entity—Earthbody/Gaia.

I am aware that some of the text and premise of this book could be subject to critique by gender-skeptical feminist theory as essentialist, as a perceived collapse of "female" into "nature".[18] But I am actually identifying *all* being—not just female and male, or just human, but flora and fauna and stars and rocks as well, and even human culture—with nature. I then metaphorize the *dynamics* of all being as female, which again could be construed as essentialist. I think it does invoke "female sacrality" which for some indicates an essentializing of sacredness as female.[19]

I acknowledge that it *may* be so, but assert that it need not be. In the case of this book, there is a recognition or naming of "female-*referring* transformatory pow-

---

15. "Life" is not the opposite of "death"—"Life" contains both "birth" and "death". I feel it is good to correct this in our language on occasion.
16. David Abram, *The Spell of the Sensuous*, p.198, refers to Euclid's postulate in a slightly different context.
17. David Abram *The Spell of the Sensuous*, p.198.
18. See for example Val Plumwood 1993 and 1991.
19. See Melissa Raphael, *Thealogy and Embodiment: the Post-Patriarchal Reconstruction of Female Sexuality*, particularly p.8-10.

ers"[20] that are identified as cosmic dynamics essential to all being—not *exclusive* to the female. For example, "conception" is a female-referring transformatory power, that is, it happens in a female body;[21] yet it is a multivalent cosmic dynamic, that is, it happens in all being in a variety of forms. It is not bound to the female body, yet it occurs there in a particular and obvious way. In past ideologies, philosophies and theologies—many of which still make their presence felt (and hence are *presence*)—the occurrence of "conception" in *that place* (the female body) has been devalued; "conception" has only been valued in the *place* of the mind—usually the male mind—as "concept". Then in some circles of feminist spirituality particularly, there has been reversal of this so that the female body—and sometimes her bodymind—was the *only* place for significant "conception". This book is not saying that. It affirms "conception" as a female-referring transformatory power which manifests multivalently in all being, thus affirming female sacrality as part of *all* sacrality. It does thus affirm the female as *a* place; as well as a *place*.

My Search in its academic form—the doctoral research—was an inquiry into the affects of such recognition on the hearts and minds and actions of participants—female and male, and including myself.

The Terms "Feminine" and "Masculine"

It is popular for writers in the area of consciousness to describe different qualities of consciousness as "feminine" and "masculine", (for example, intuition as feminine and intellect as masculine), and to describe humanity's move out of an original participatory mind as "masculine". The image of St. George (masculine) slaying the dragon (feminine) is understood to speak of a necessary move in the evolution of consciousness, both of the collective and of the individual. It is popular to describe the active differentiating force of individuation as masculine. To quote one such writer: "The birth and development of the masculine principle in consciousness revolutionizes humanity's experience of itself and of the world."[22] It is implied that "maternal" consciousness is simply amorphous and chaotic, and

---

20. Melissa Raphael, *Thealogy and Embodiment: the Post-Patriarchal Reconstruction of Female Sexuality*, p.8 (emphasis mine).
21. Melissa Raphael, *Thealogy and Embodiment: the Post-Patriarchal Reconstruction of Female Sexuality*, p.8-9.
22. S. Colgrave, *The Spirit of the Valley: Androgeny and Chinese Thought*, p.71 cited in Peter Reason, *Participation in Human Inquiry*, p.21.

incapable of an evolutionary move. This is often seen as some justification for the patriarchal mind—that humanity needed to "get away from Mother". Yet the move out of original participation as a state of non-reflective consciousness[23] and the move into patriarchal mind appear to have been two different things. Peter Reason supports this in his citing of the work of Eisler, Swimme and Berry as opposed to the thinking of Colgrave and Wilber.[24] These former thinkers speak of evidence of sophisticated, complex, matristic Neolithic societies. Marija Gimbutas and Merlin Stone pioneered these insights into "Goddess" cultures, and many other scholars have developed it since. There appears to have been many pre-patriarchal cultures with highly developed reflective awareness, indigenous traditions knowing deep Wisdom. Reason says,

> It is difficult to believe that these complex societies were based on a pure form of original participation: that there must have been a high degree of purpose, planning and reflexiveness. Yet the social organization was articulated in terms of equality and partnership.[25]

Reason also cites Paula Gunn Allen[26] who describes complex and sophisticated gynocratic Native American tribal cultures. He says that these highly developed, self-reflective participative cultures are "not a description of original participation in the sense of being unconscious and unreflective."[27]

As Barbara Walker points out, reflecting on the historical and mythic view of motherhood,[28] it may well have been the female mind that instigated the radical changes in the way humans did things, that it was *her* desire for order, storage, abundance, tools, fire, medicine, art etc. that led to many of humanity's inventions, settlement in villages, writing, counting and social complexification. Walker asserts that it was precisely the female as mother who was the original "civilizing" force, which actually initiated the shift from spatial consciousness into time. The assumption that it must have been a "masculine" quality is perhaps part of the patriarchal mind set, which would rob maternity of its essential

---

23. Jürgen W. Kremer, "The Dark Night of the Scholar" in ReVision Vol. 14 No. 4, p.172-173, referring to Owen Barfield's definition.
24. Peter Reason, *Participation in Human Inquiry*, p.24-25.
25. Peter Reason, *Participation in Human Inquiry*, p.24-25.
26. Paula Gunn Allen, *The Sacred Hoop*, p..2.
27. Peter Reason, *Participation in Human Inquiry*, p.26.
28. Barbara Walker, *The Woman's Encyclopaedia of Myths and Secrets*, p.680-694.

active creativity. Judy Grahn develops this notion also with her insights into "menstrual mind", asserting the primal creativity of such a mind.[29]

I think that part of the reason for confusion on this issue, is that it is true biologically that the male did emerge "out of" the female cell—that is, meiotic sex was an evolutionary event.[30] This *is* a memory,[31] and it is celebrated in many ways. But it is a confusion to associate the advent of the male or masculinity with the advent of patriarchy, or consciousness, or enlightenment. The biological emergence of the male at about 1.5 billion years ago, is quite distinct from the so-called "emergence of consciousness", which is quite distinct from the development of Neolithic matristic cultures, which is again quite distinct from the development of patriarchy. It is perhaps even a mistake to speak of the "emergence of consciousness", since consciousness may now be assumed to have been primordial—according to some scientists, and in accord with many ancient Wisdom traditions, it is *matter* that emerged from consciousness.[32]

There is no need to masculinize this force/face that urges the move into individuation and complexification—it is an artificial construct to do so. I will, in the course of these chapters, describe how such a force/energy is an aspect of Cosmogenesis and contained within the Female Metaphor. Within the three faces of the One Creative Principle, is included the aspect of differentiation—the Urge to Be, to manifest; there is nothing innately or necessarily masculine about it. Nor ultimately would it have to be described as feminine/female, but it is a quality of the Female Metaphor, contained within Her. The point being made here is that the consciousness of the Mother is not an amorphous sludge, as the patriarchal mind has storied it. She—"maternal consciousness"—has full creative capacity, has always been quite capable of change; in fact, it is her very nature.

---

29. Judy Grahn, *Blood, Bread and Roses: How Menstruation Created the World.*
30. See Brian Swimme and Thomas Berry, *The Universe Story*, p.105-109 and Elisabet Sahtouris, *Earthdance*, p.126-131. And as Sahtouris writes: "All our mitochondria are descended from those of the egg cell with which we began, as they do not occur in sperm. Mitochondrial DNA is therefore referred to as maternal DNA." (in Sidney Liebes, Elisabet Sahtouris and Brian Swimme, *A Walk Through Time: From Stardust to Us*, p.78-79.)
31. Our human phylogenetic history lives within us. See Georg Feuerstein,"Towards a New Consciousness: A Review essay of Jean Gebser", Noetic Sciences Review No.7, p.23-26.
32. See Willis Harman and Elisabet Sahtouris, *Biology Revisioned.*

The incessant masculinization of things separative, rational, assertive, is harder than rocks in many imaginations and thinking of all genres—even amongst those who think they are New Age and ushering in some new kind of consciousness. "Wholeness" does not have to be understood in terms of a "feminine" plus "masculine" equation, and nor does it serve us. The Universe was not necessarily formed by "female" plus "male" energy, as is often loosely asserted even by those whose work could otherwise be considered helpful to gaining wholeness.[33] This dualism is not essential to the Creativity of the Universe. Creativity required such qualities as are stereotypically associated with "male" energy, long before the advent of the male, and even before the advent of the biosphere—the first cell. The so-called masculine attributes didn't suddenly appear in the Creativity of the Cosmos when the male appeared. Differentiation for instance is a quality innate to all being, and is primordial. The advent of gender and meiotic sex was an enormous leap for Cosmogenesis, enhancing the Cosmic project of Creativity, a major catalyst and immensely alluring one as far as I and many are concerned, but it is not required for "wholeness". I will illustrate the relativity of this mind-struct by developing the Female Metaphor, a complete and whole unity of Creativity.

Another dimension to the confusion on this issue is the lack of clarity about the primordial nature of the Power of Allurement—a Power that Brian Swimme lists among others as "coursing through the Universe and each of us".[34] Allurement may and does manifest between female and male, but it is a power that is not bound to female and male relationship. It has been present primordially, before the advent of maleness or gender. Allurement, or Holy Lust as it may be termed (as I do in Beltane ritual), unites the Cosmos, but it is not female and male united that unites the Cosmos: this is lovely poetry—a metaphor and an experience—the Power may take place here, but it is not bound to this relationship. All being knows it—within the self and in relationship.

Masculinity or maleness is a particular physical expression that can give rise to its own symbolism—but the interpretation of that symbolism is something else. For example, the phallus can be passive, vulnerable and flower-like if the mind-frame

---

33. Andrew Rothery, in *The Science of the Green Man*, makes one such statement in his Conclusion.

34. Brian Swimme, *The Powers of the Universe*.

is shifted. The Green Man metaphor may be developed as a deeply relational story of maleness—of "male-referring transformatory powers" as it may be termed: and there are some who are doing that well in recent times.[35] The story of maleness as innately "active, dominant, inflexible", by association with the phallus, is a patriarchal one that can be changed. "Masculinity" and "femininity" are largely cultural developments—developed over time by story, belief systems, even the foods each sex have been allowed to eat in some cultures, the activities they each have been allowed, so that certain styles, physical and psychic, have been bred into and out of maleness and femaleness to suit the mindframe. "Maleness" and "femaleness" on the other hand may be something quite different and more like a physical kaleidoscope: and it was a very creative move at a relatively recent point in the evolutionary story, that did enhance the Cosmogenetic enterprise of differentiation, communion and autopoiesis.[36] Both are embraced and immersed in the same Creative Principle/Dynamic of Being, up to that point of evolution and beyond. Both may be described as exhibiting these three characteristics of the Creative Dynamic of Being.

In the conclusion to his book on *The Triple Goddess*, Adam Mclean discusses how the triple facet may present itself within the male psyche, or as I would put it—in male "story form". McLean specifically identifies male versions of the Virgin, Mother and Crone.[37] These male story forms are Knight, Husband and Artist; and he does to some extent qualify these images, and restore them with a deep sense of Beauty, Integrity and Wisdom—as aspects of the Sacred. Generally I find that these images, as Mclean stories them, do mirror my own understanding of the triple qualities of the Female Metaphor. McLean still does use such concepts as "masculine side" and "feminine side", in a way that I think is completely unnecessary, especially when he is able to story the Triple Metaphor in male form and female form as he does.

Starhawk develops the qualities of these aspects in the male form in her chapter on "The God" in *The Spiral Dance*, though she does not specifically identify them with the three faces of the Goddess; she simply says that "Like the Goddess,

---

35. For examples: the work of William Anderson, *Green Man: the Archetype of Our Oneness with the Earth*, Andrew Rothery, *The Science of the Green Man*, and recent doctoral work of Phillip Costigan, "An Australian Man in Search of an Embodied Spirituality".
36. Brian Swimme and Thomas Berry, *The Universe Story*, p.108-109.
37. Adam McLean, *The Triple Goddess*, p.121-122.

the God unifies all opposites."[38] In Starhawk's tradition, the God moves through an equivalent three faces over the period of the Wheel of the Year along with the Goddess, and in the Creation story of Starhawk's Faerie tradition there are three evolving aspects identified as male—"the Blue God, the gentle, laughing God of love", then "the Green One, vine-covered, rooted in the earth, the spirit of all growing things", and "the Horned God, the Hunter whose face is the ruddy sun and yet as dark as Death."[39] These images may be identified as a male form of the triple faced Creative Dynamic, present within all. There is a dire need for the re-storying of these male forms; the patriarchal context has not generally provided stories of males that serve and nurture Life, as the Triple Faced Metaphor may do, and in our times the young particularly are starving for such. In recent decades, men have begun re-storying themselves, feeling for their own experience as "life-enhancing" beings. In recent doctoral work that is inclusive of personal art, poetry and imagination, Phillip Costigan does this re-storying. He describes it as a "re-positioning of men in a more life-enhancing engagement within the Sacred Network of All Beings", coining a new term to express this sense of male embodied sacredness—the male in "life-giving relationship with the Sacred within a cosmos imbued with this Sacred."[40] His term is "virism", which he derives from the Latin word for a specific man, 'vir' and the Latin word for green, 'viridis'. He also derives the term from 'viriditas' meaning greenness or ver-dure—a term coined by Hildegard of Bingen, the twelfth century German mystic, to name "the greening power of the universe".[41] Such work invokes a "male sacrality" as part of and within the Context of a Sacred Whole.

Feminist Discourse

This book then is not an exploration or statement of a difference between some concepts of "feminine" and "masculine", or "female" and "male". It is a development of a metaphor based in female bodily experience that is ubiquitous in natural phenomena such as all bodily cycles, the moon cycle, plant cycles, and the seasons. I do not spend time "dismantling a dualism based on difference" as feminist theorist Val Plumwood describes that task. [42] However, my work here does

---

38. Starhawk, *The Spiral Dance*, p.113.
39. Starhawk, *The Spiral Dance*, p. 31.
40. Phillip Costigan, "An Australian Man in Search of an Embodied Spirituality", p.38-39 of draft.
41. Phillip Costigan, "An Australian Man in Search of an Embodied Spirituality", p.36 of draft.

conform to features that Plumwood describes as required for "the reconstruction of relationship and identity in terms of a non-hierarchical concept of difference",[43] and I do believe this work, in its social action—its experiential concourse as already described—does conform to Plumwood's features of "appropriate relationship of non-hierarchical difference".[44]

Plumwood outlines two common problems that the female may be entrapped by, in the formation of identity as a "post-colonial" group, that is, as a group that has been "colonised", situated as "Other", or "backgrounded"—however one chooses to term it. Those two common problems are identified as (i) the denial of difference and (ii) the reversal syndrome (where the dualism and hierarchical arrangement are accepted, and value is reversed, that is, everything "female" is better than everything "male").[45] My work here does neither of these things. Difference is specifically addressed on various occasions, in theory and in regard to the visceral impact of language; and in the academic version it is further addressed in the experiences of participants in the rituals where there are people of both genders participating fully. In regard to the latter problem of "reversal syndrome" as defined by Plumwood, the Female Metaphor developed in this work does not fall into this entrapment as "the new identity", which is identification with the dynamics of all being, is not "specified in reaction to the coloniser…(or) in relation to him."[46] Also, (the new identity) has not accepted "the dualistic construction of identity."[47] Definition of the Female Metaphor is not "in relation to the master",[48] as Plumwood defines the possible problem: the nature of the Self in the Metaphor of this work always has agency and is centred in cosmic source, even while it remains deeply related, connected in the web of life.

42. Val Plumwood, *Feminism and the Mastery of Nature*, p. 60.
43. Val Plumwood, *Feminism and the Mastery of Nature*, p. 60.
44. Val Plumwood, *Feminism and the Mastery of Nature*, p. 60.
45. Val Plumwood, *Feminism and the Mastery of Nature*, p. 60-62.
46. Val Plumwood, *Feminism and the Mastery of Nature*, p. 61.
47. Val Plumwood, *Feminism and the Mastery of Nature*, p. 61. For a clear analysis of ways of dealing with "pairs"—in particular "masculine" and "feminine", see Rita Gross "The Feminine Principle in Tibetan Vajrayana Buddhism: Reflections of a Buddhist Feminist". She speaks of "dyadic unity", "hierarchical dualism" and "monolithic entity".
48. Val Plumwood, *Feminism and the Mastery of Nature*, p. 61.

Sometimes expressions used by some participants in their responses seem to indicate that some may still be caught in problems of "hierarchical difference", but I perceive and accept this as a remnant or an individual interpretation and difference of understanding, which is part of a dualistic cultural heritage. This cannot be abolished in one swift move. It is true as Plumwood asserts in earlier writing,[49] that Gaian symbolism is not an automatic guarantee of change, but I believe that when such metaphor is approached in a 'holarchical' manner rather than with a concept of hierarchy, that the Gaian symbolism and story *does* have the innate capacity for participants to change. A sensuous identification of the dynamic self with the dynamic Earth and Cosmos, through female metaphor, may serve as a gateway for some even beyond the female metaphor.

Others may explore the possibility of male metaphor as Cosmic Dynamic, but I am not doing that here or implying that it is not possible. As I have stated it seems like a highly desirable project, and feel that such projects are in process.

Goddess as Religion

This issue of the "status" of a "religion" needs to be addressed as the Female Metaphor is so often stated as—(given the status of)—"cult", as opposed to "religion"; that is, as opposed to having the status of any other "World Religion" as all the patriarchal, "historical" religions are known. Goddess "religion" has for the past few millennia been referred to as "fertility cult", and this has been understood to mean a more lowly status because matter itself had been reduced to insignificance. The reproduction of matter has been considered a trivial thing by most patriarchal religions themselves, and certainly by Western philosophy. It has been characteristic of the patriarchal mind to divorce itself from its embeddness in material reality. "Fertility" itself is a term that needs to be re-valued. There is no reason to assume that the ancients did not comprehend the multivalence—the depth dimensions, of "fertility". It is the Creativity of Earth, of the Cosmos, and it is concerned with the Life in which we are immersed. The modern mind frequently assumes that "primitive fertility rituals" came from an insecurity about survival. This may in fact be a massive projection. Frequently, our ancestors of earliest times partook in the abundance of nature, so perhaps the "fertility rituals" were as much a celebration of regenerative cosmic power. Heide Göttner-Abendroth, scholar of matriarchal cultures, now uses the term "faith of rebirth" rather

---

49.   Val Plumwood, "Gaia, Good for Women?" Refactory Girl.

than "fertility cult".[50] However I prefer to stick with a re-valuation of fertility. This eventuates further when I develop the three faces of the Female Metaphor, particularly in the re-storying of the Old One, that is, the post-menopausal elder. If the ancients were simply concerned with physical fertility (which only a dualistic mind can conceive), why celebrate this "useless" phase? The "fertility cults" seemed to have some understanding of the integrity of life—birth and death; certainly they seem to hold more than the "primitive", "unconscious" veneer they have been dealt by researchers of recent centuries, and by their conquerors of old.

The word "religion" itself is problematic, as it tends to imply a rigid system of belief. Its roots are in the word *religio* which may be interpreted as "binding" in a negative sense, or as a connectedness in a positive sense of relatedness and bonding. There is argument for the case that Goddess imagery and language is not another religion, since She underlies and is threaded through all of them; She is a Metaphor, but so is "God", as I have discussed. It would seem more accurate to speak of "Goddess spirituality", since that seems to indicate a fluidity and aliveness. Heide Göttner-Abendroth uses "matriarchal spirituality" for this reason.[51] Göttner-Abendroth re-defines "matriarchal" as meaning "in the beginning was the mothers", contending that 'arche' did not mean 'dominance' until later.[52] However, I am keen to have Her understood with the dignity of an in-depth spiritual practice, a coherent worldview; and the word "religion" does that. There are many different varieties of ritual and form within Goddess religiosity it is true, but so there are in God religions. She does deserve to be listed as a "World Religion", given that She was the main metaphor for Deity for so long and so pervasively, and still is revered in some form by millions of humans.

Most minds on the planet, at this time in the human story, are so used to reducing the Female Metaphor/Goddess to cult, archetype, consort, wife of, that it seems necessary to dwell for a while on this issue. Most minds are non-plussed as to who else She might be, if not in relationship to, or secondary to, or even a danger to, a male "major player". Was She ever anything else? In the following chapters I will address who else She might be, both from past evidence and from present experience of cosmological dynamics. These chapters will not directly address the "why" question—that is, if She was once something other than Her

---

50. Heide Göttner-Abendroth, *The Goddess and Her Heros*, p.xvi.
51. Heide Göttner-Abendroth, *The Goddess and Her Heros*, p.xiv.
52. Heide Göttner-Abendroth, *The Goddess and Her Heros*, p.xviii.

present reduced state, why did that change? I wish to focus on the present—who She is now, and, on what use that might be. What might be the consequences of changing our minds sufficiently, so that Medusa for instance, can be comprehended as metaphor for Divine Wisdom? Many scholars contend She once was understood this way. What might it mean for our minds to welcome Her back? Would that alter the way we relate to Earth, to Being?

A "Home-ly" Religion

My partner put forward the perception of Goddess religion being a "homely" religion, and he meant that with all the status that "homely" may have. It may be written as "Home-ly" to emphasize that it is connective to Home—as Earth, Self, Cosmos. Such a description as "Home-ly religion"—perhaps as a counter to "World religion"(!)—is based on evidence of the ancient practice of every house being a shrine, a sanctuary to Her; when there was no separation between the secular and the sacred, when "religion was life, and life was religion". This is described by Riane Eisler in *The Chalice and the Blade*,[53] referring to the archeological work of Marija Gimbutas. A "home-ly" religion then is a "domestic" religion—one that may be known in the familiarity of one's dwelling—bodymind, home, backyard, region, "country", Earth, Solar System, Universe.

The Moon Goddess

The triple-aspected Female Metaphor that has long captured my attention and imagination and lured me into the Search has in other times been known as "The Moon Goddess": that "aspect of Creativity of the Cosmos that manifests in the Moon" is the long modern title for Her perhaps.[54] The phases of the Moon have described for and since the first eyes, a pattern, that at some point was noticed to resonate with the human female cyclical pattern, and indeed, that of all human body cycles. Moreover, the Moon's cyclical pattern—of waxing and waning through lightness and darkness—was noticed to be reiterated in flora and fauna everywhere. The three phases have been known by the ancients of many cultures, and others since throughout the ages, as Virgin/Maiden, Mother/Creator, Old One/Crone, mirrored as they are in the three chronological menstrual phases of

---

53. Riane Eisler, *The Chalice and the Blade*, p.23.
54. Just as "Bear Goddess" is that "aspect of Creativity of the Cosmos that manifests as Bear" and so with other zoomorphic and descriptive Goddess titles. She—the Creative Principle—is as diverse as Being is.

the female:—pre-menarchal young one, menstrual mother, and post-menopausal elder. A Scots Gaelic prayer describes the Moon as "lovely leader of the way",[55] and so She has been for many humans, who have noticed Her cyclical pattern imbued in All, including in the seasons created by the annual Earth-Sun relational transitions or "movements". Moon was perceived as a teacher, *the* Teacher for many.

The Moon Herself is a Presence often taken as secondary, extraneous, romantic. Yet without Her gravitational pull on Earth, creating the tides—the ebb and flow—the biosphere may have never evolved.[56] The Moon's central role in our manifestation, in Earth's Creativity as we know it, largely goes without recognition. The same is true of the role that the female human cycle must have played in the early development of human consciousness: its role may well have been central yet it is never mentioned as a possible factor in mainstream texts. This *body* of conjecture is missing from much of what passes for real story of human beginnings. Rarely is it thought, as for example researcher Alexander Marshack thought, that the lunar notations found on bone, stone, antler and goddess figures may "have laid the foundations for the discovery of agriculture, the calendar, astronomy, mathematics and writing."[57]

As Judy Grahn points out, "human perception began, many creation stories say, when we could distinguish between light and dark"; that

> Disciplined separation is clearly a major factor of human culture, and the most complex and fundamental separation practice is that of the first menstruation, or…menarche.[58]

Yet a recently produced documentary about the earliest of humans[59] that put forth all kinds of detailed descriptions of their lifestyles and even projections about their emotions and why they did certain things, did not conjecture such a

---

55. Caitlin Matthews, *The Celtic Spirit*, p.302.

56. See Lynn Margulis' research into the beginnings of the biosphere, as referenced in Connie Barlow *Green Space, Green Time*, p.186-188, and Connie Barlow (ed.), *From Gaia to Selfish Genes:Selected Writings in the Life Sciences*, p.48-66.

57. Anne Baring and Jules Cashford, *The Myth of the Goddess*, p.20 referring to Alexander Marshack, *The Roots of Civilization*.

58. Judy Grahn, *Blood, Bread and Roses: How Menstruation created the World*, p.11.

59. *Neanderthal's World* shown on SBS in mid 2001.

thought. The text never flickered toward the possibility that the female cycle and its replication of the Moon cycle exactly in timing, may have impacted on the human psyche in a primordial, foundational way. Perhaps, as Grahn suggests, it was the "menstrual mind" that first connected to an external frame of reference—the Moon—and began to acquire external measurement and noninstinctual knowledge.[60] When humans first performed ritual burials, one hundred thousand years ago, what was their referent for thinking about death? What did they observe around them everyday about death and renewal? Could it have possibly been that "the Female Metaphor", in its lunar cycle and its human female cycle, may have played a central role in the earliest developments of the human mind—our sense of time, and existential wonderings and celebrations of life and death—just as its resonant Cosmic Moon Cycle played/plays a central role in the evolution of life on Earth? Could contemplation of the pattern that the Female Metaphor suggests, in its mandala-like rhythm have been the source of earliest human insight? Shuttle and Redgrove define a mandala as

> a pattern which is effective in connecting one part of experience with another, and the contemplation of which leads to insight. A mandala has a centre, a boundary or circumference, and cardinal points. It often depicts a rhythm, which one can see at a glance in a single image.[61]

They describe the Moon cycle as forming a mandala, and that the menstrual cycle can take a similar shape. Could the cosmic ubiquity of this metaphorical pattern have been the basis for knowledge/wisdom, that served humans and their growing conscious relationship to Cosmos? Could the primordial experience of witnessing this trustworthy rhythm have been the beginnings of "the inexhaustible creativity of humanity", as other Goddess researchers suggest?[62]

For a culture to have abstained from asking these questions, to have, for millennia been unable to form these questions in the mind, reveals an alienated mind—a mind that is out of touch with the Earth and Cosmic cycles, as well as that of the human female. An alienated mind is one that does not know participation, that "unconsciously participates" as Barfield describes[63]—a mind that has severed its

---

60. Judy Grahn, *Blood, Bread and Roses: How Menstruation created the World*, p.12-14.
61. Penelope Shuttle and Peter Redgrove, *The Wise Wound: Menstruation and Everywoman*, p.263.
62. Anne Baring and Jules Cashford, in *The Myth of the Goddess: Evolution of an Image*, p.19.

connections, wherein phenomena exist separately, a mind that has dissociated. Most humans today live in cultures that are alienated in this way, though it is expressed diversely. I speak mainly from within my own white Western Christianized culture, but it is by no means unique in regard to alienation from the Context/Earth/Universe—in which the human finds themselves.[64] If humans regard themselves as alive and sentient, then so is our Context/Matrix. We and our consciousness are "not some tiny bit of the world stuck onto the rest of it."[65] We are inside Her—our Matrix. Our Context appears to be alive and sentient, as Creativity spills up from within Her at local and universal levels; but it appears from the ecological crisis that we find ourselves in, that we humans have on a large scale shut ourselves off from this knowledge. Speaking for my own Western cultural context, we humans of this context today find ourselves living "on" a planet. For a long time, we have not participated "in" it. We have understood ourselves as apart from it, as an addendum or superior; and now, we often understand ourselves as inferior. Some humans who are still closely linked to their indigenous heritage have not lost the knowledge that She and they are alive in each other. These humans have remained intimate with our[66] Context, and the understanding of the local not being separate from the Cosmic, and that this Context is the Matrix of all humans and beings.

---

63. Jürgen W. Kremer, "The Dark Night of the Scholar" in ReVision Vol. 14 No. 4, p.172-173.
64. While "itself" may be "correct", I feel this useage further affirms human belief in self-alienation from Context—that we are "its". There are other problems associated with the use of "her" or "him" or both, so I'm choosing this "problem"—the one of "them".
65. Owen Barfield, *History, Guilt and Habit*, p.18 quoted by Jürgen W. Kremer, "The Dark Night of the Scholar" in ReVision Vol. 14 No. 4, p.169.
66. It is "our" Context, not "theirs" as some might describe it: all of us do live in Earth and in the Universe. Although it can be argued that in most cases, the indigenous person's mountain for instance, is not the mountain of the Westernized mind—"their world is not ours!" (Jürgen W. Kremer, "The Dark Night of the Scholar" in ReVision Vol. 14 No. 4, p.173), it can also be argued that at a deeper place, we may find " among the silent spaces, realities where cultures and their peoples touch in ways that are yet to be fully explored" (Kremer, p.174 referring to K.C. Forman, *The Problem of Pure Consciousness.)* Also I think it is time to move into the assumption that some previously Westernised minds have made steps towards their own indigenous mind; there is a growing "we" of "future participation"—a term Kremer uses (p.173) to speak of regained, intentional participation in our habitat.

I am re-linking with my own indigenous heritage, one that lives in my very body-mind. It has an actual tradition—of female-based metaphor—that has been nearly obliterated in relatively recent human history, that is, the last few millennia. It would be simplistic and short-sighted to single out the Inquisition of the last millennia of this Common Era as the only gynocidal event of the West, though it was certainly a horrific one. Though my indigenous heritage has its most recent roots in Old Western Europe—in the Earth-based tradition that goes back to pre-Celtic times—it also has roots in the bodyminds of other ancients of my line, who observed and knew a resonance of being with Earth and Cosmos. This heritage ran into difficulties long before the Inquisition, as Starhawk outlines in her overview of culture, politics and mythic cycles,[67] and as many others including Merlin Stone[68] and Gerda Lerner[69] document. Lerner says, "in the period when written History was being created, women already lived under conditions of patriarchy";[70] our roles, public behavior and sexual and reproductive lives were already so defined—our bodyminds had already been locked up, the Goddess temples had long been emptied, the integrity of the priestesses had long been trivialized. It had long been anathema to receive and speak Her Wisdom[71]—a Wisdom I call "Gaian", and of which in our time, we may come to know in a new way.

More Context—Personal/Cultural/Cosmic Stories

My personal context then, which cannot be separated from the cultural and cosmic context of my organism, and that fires my passion, is that I write as "a daughter born into the patriarchy". I know fairly well "my" story through these past few millennia. From my journal a few years ago:

> They said I destroyed the world with my sin—it was my fault. My wickedness was to blame—and Jesus, a man, had to suffer a terrible death to make it right. I, a woman, and all the other women like me, carried the burden for everything that was not right with the world.

---

67. Starhawk, *Truth or Dare*, p.37-40.
68. Merlin Stone, *When God Was a Woman*.
69. Gerda Lerner, *The Creation of Feminist Conciousness*.
70. Gerda Lerner, *The Creation of Feminist Conciousness*, p.249.
71. I mean "Wisdom" here to be understood as a name for a religious tradition—that has had no name—much as "Buddhism" or "Taoism" are understood to be names.

And I believed them. I did not disagree. At the trials, when they accused me, said what I did was evil—I could not remember, was I? I became confused. When I was a "qadishtu"[72] and the conquerors came, they said I was unclean, that their god regarded us as filth, that our kind had brought pain to the world. I was guilty. After a while, I couldn't remember—perhaps I was.
I now remember, my confusion clears, the veils are lifting. I remember my innocence. I lift the burden from my shoulders, and from other women's shoulders. I again walk proud and free.[73]

I write as a daughter hungry for the Mother, and I understand what Monique Wittig means when she says: "the language you speak is made up of words that are killing you."[74] Personally, I have been so hungry for the Female Metaphor, for the Mother—for words for Her, for knowledge of Her, that I could perform terrible and radical acts to find Her. I went away from my young children for a long period of time for this—to find the Mother for myself, and for them: I did not want to give my children the world I had grown up in—the world they needed had to be integral with Matter, or there would not be a world at all.

Queen Elizabeth I is known to have said, "I know I have the body of a weak and feeble woman, but I have the heart and stomach of a king."[75] Even a woman as great as this, of such astounding achievement and wisdom, felt driven to compare herself, to measure herself with male metaphor. Deep in the psyche even of great women, there has not been a female metaphor for greatness, for strength, for the wisdom which they themselves embodied. The female Deities had been so slandered, so stripped of essential integrity. Yahweh is after all God, Medusa is after all merely a goddess. We can forgive Yahweh his crimes…this is not myopia. The millennia of patriarchal narrative has left our minds locked up, unable to grasp the Female Metaphor…that she may stand sovereign, not as greater than, but in

---

72. Merlin Stone, *When God Was a Woman*, p.156-157, describes "qadishtu" as "the sacred women of the temples". They were holy women who were also sexual, but the word has often been translated as "prostitute".
73. With this story I am not telling women of races and ethnicities other than my own that they should be able to identify with my story. I am expressing my own resonance with this story, as one who has inherited elements from that culture via my religious heritage. I personally feel that I can identify with such stories of women; that is not to say that the reverse is true. See p.42 also for more on this issue.
74. Monique Wittig, *Les Guerilleres, p.114.*
75. It is quoted, though not exactly as written here, in the film *Elizabeth* (Universal 1998).

and of herself: so that, when a woman or a man desires to express greatness, nobility, strength they are able to easily reach for a female image.

I have been told that to look at history, theology, philosophy from the female perspective is myopic—one-eyed. It is commonly assumed that these disciplines have been regarded from the "human" perspective, that the male has incorporated both female and male perspectives, that he has been fair in all these matters, and indeed, capable. I have been expected to disregard it if the female is rarely mentioned as a factor in the first two million years of human existence, or if she is, that it is in a secondary placement or in a slanderous context. A casual perusal of most history, and "pre-history", from a "fair" perspective would leave one wondering how the human species reproduced itself, let alone that the female had any further creative input to the human enterprise. As an example, one such weighty tome called *The Last Two Million Years*,[76] has in all its four hundred and eighty-eight pages of text and plates, remarkably little evidence of female presence to the human enterprise. She rates a mention every now and then in relation to "problems of reproduction",[77] greater sexual receptivity than female apes,[78] and men insisting that "their sisters married outside the family".[79] The very occasional Goddess or woman of note is most often, a mistress, consort or wife. Queen Elizabeth I stands alone as a woman of power in the last two million years, and even then the caption under her portrait is couched in a negative, reading "Defeat of the Armada".[80]

Even a more recent text on the world's religions, which could be regarded as more "fair-minded", fails significantly in its balance. This text, *The World's Religions* by Ninian Smart, has five references to the women's movement, including note of Mary Daly, and to the fact that women are having an increasing role "in religions where in the past a patriarchal perspective has prevailed."[81] Smart is aware of the gender issues in the language and organization of religions. Yet in his own text, while he gives extensive treatment to the Holocaust, Marxism, various Chinese cults, and Malcolm X gets referenced twice, nowhere does he reference Mariology, nor is there any reference to the Inquisition. Witchcraft is mentioned

---

76. Reader's Digest
77. Reader's Digest, *The Last Two Million Years*, p.22.
78. Reader's Digest, *The Last Two Million Years*, p.17.
79. Reader's Digest, *The Last Two Million Years*, p.19.
80. Reader's Digest, *The Last Two Million Years*, p.235.
81. Ninian Smart, *The World's Religions*, p.586.

once in the context of Polynesian religions, as "using ritual means to bring about bad results for others".[82] The Great Isis is referred to as "Osiris' wife",[83] the main subject of the story being Osiris. Isis Herself is referred to twice in the context of a "cult". The Great Inanna is described as "associated with showers and thunder-storms", "goddess of war", "a harlot", and "supposed even to have become queen of heaven, as consort of An."[84] The "Enuma Elish", which is generally accepted as the Babylonian creation epic, but which is actually the creation of patriarchy in that culture describing as it does the murder of Goddess Tiamat, is here told by Smart completely unsympathetically to the indigenous tradition.[85] The epic is praised as "celebrating (the incoming god's) victory"; and the god, Marduk, is praised nonchalantly by Smart as "great". There is an apparent acceptance of the slaughter of the female at the base of creation. Philosopher Paul Ricoeur writes, in regard to this epic:

> Thus the creative act which distinguishes, separates, measures and puts in order, is inseparable from the criminal act that puts an end to the life of the oldest gods, inseparable from a deicide inherent in the divine.[86]

This "criminal act" then, this shedding of blood by the blade may be seen as a replacement of the "menstrual mind" that separated and distinguished, that Judy Grahn speaks of. Ricoeur goes on to describe creation as "a victory over an Enemy older than the creator"[87]—thus tracing the historical outcome of a "theology of war" and the enemy behind all enemies; but it is Catherine Keller who notes that Tiamat's sex is a salient fact.[88] To state Her sex, is to state/"status" Her—this "Goddess-Mother" as Her name means[89]—as the Enemy within all enemies. It is to understand war as the act of a Cosmically and Maternally alienated mind—not as inevitable essential beastly nature as most of us have been taught. Tiamat's slaughter, is described graphically in the epic, as it is by Smart in

82.   Ninian Smart, *The World's Religions*, p.169.
83.   Ninian Smart, *The World's Religions*, p.203.
84.   Ninian Smart, *The World's Religions*, p.200.
85.   Ninian Smart, *The World's Religions*, p.200-201.
86.   Paul Ricouer, *The Symbolism of Evil*, p.180 quoted in Catherine Keller, *From a Broken Web: Separation, Sexism and Self*, p.76.
87.   Paul Ricouer, *The Symbolism of Evil*, p.182 quoted in Catherine Keller, *From a Broken Web: Separation, Sexism and Self*, p.76.
88.   Catherine Keller, *From a Broken Web: Separation, Sexism and Self*, p.77.
89.   Barbara Walker, *The Woman's Encyclopedia of Myths and Secrets*, p.998.

his text: her corpse is used "to create the present universe, slitting her in two like a fish, one part being heaven and the other earth."[90] As Joseph Campbell points out, this

> great creative deed of Marduk was a supererogatory act. There was no need for him to cut her up and make the universe out of her, because she was already the universe.[91]

I suggest that this kind of unconsciousness, as exhibited by Smart, on the part of the writers of "humanity's" texts is analogous to the writing of Australian history wherein the Indigenous Australians are either ignored or labeled as "savages".

Most people naively assume that the history as told to them is the history of women as well—we are so used to our absence. Perhaps one only really notices it when reading a history that does include women in a conscious way, such as Margaret Wertheim's *Pythagoras' Trousers*. Such an inclusive history as she presents, in regard the education of women particularly, has informed me further of my context, my heritage, and what it has meant to be doing this work of unfolding the Female Metaphor and female-friendly cosmology.

Sex Object

A strong part of the cultural milieu in which I grew, was that I felt identified as sex object…with no subjectivity, no space to Be. Pornographic magazines of the day depicted women being constantly pursued by salivating men—either there was an assumption that she desired this, or they did not care to ask her. And Christian cosmology appeared to condone the imposition of a dominant will upon another—at the very heart of it is "the sacrifice of the lamb". Women have been especially vulnerable, with their submission openly advocated.[92]

"Marilyn", they sometimes called me, simply because of my babyhood waved platinum hair. I was not particularly cute as I grew up, on the contrary, I was

---

90. Ninian Smart, *The World's Religions*, p.201. The use of the metaphor of "fish" in the tale is perhaps a conscious reference to the Goddess' yoni (See Barbara Walker, *The Woman's Encyclopaedia of Myths and Secrets*, p.313)—this is where She was cut, and interestingly, women in cultures of this creation myth, continue to be genitally mutilated today.

91. Joseph Campbell, *The Power of Myth with Bill Moyers*, p.170.

92. See Rita Brock, "Can These Bones Live? Feminist Critiques of the Atonement".

skinny, had buck teeth, freckles and a bad haircut. But Marilyn was suggested to me by this naming, as someone I could model myself after. I didn't think about it a lot, but I don't remember any other significant famous women in the first decade of my life. As a child I was very conscious of being looked at, and perhaps on reflection, it was because I was female. I felt transparent and vacuous. I remember believing that others (particularly adults) could see my thoughts. The Great Male Metaphors of the day—God and Santa—knew everything about me. The male humans imitated the Deity with constant Gazing, in magazines, movies, wall calendars. I could only hope to be chosen to be worthy of his desire, yet at the same time it was known that he could be dangerous.

I felt acutely the identification of myself with the "inanimate" world, as it was understood to be—dead and inert. I had no words for it of course. Ursula Le Guin says,

> We are told in words, and not in words, we are told by their deafness,…(that)…the life experience of women, is not valuable…to humanity. (We have been valued by the patriarchal viewpoint only) as an element of their experience, as things experienced.[93]

The male in this worldview was also "inanimate", albeit the machine that was expected to perform.

I began to find words, and consciousness of my assigned cultural destiny as sex object. I wrote:

> What did it take to move from that, to develop a shell, a protective boundary, to pull the shades on the imposing mostly male Gaze, to allow a fertile darkness within my being, where "I" could begin? What did it take to create this kind of darkness, a safe place to Be, to shut out the world and scream "I"?…A sex object has to completely fall apart before she can rebuild herself in her own image. She has fall into the mud, begin again, perform her own acts of Creation, mold herself of this solid material. It is out of the mud that the lotus blossoms. It does not grow on some pedestal, under the light of the eternal Gaze.…How ironic that our paternal mythmakers made Medusa's gaze the deadly one!

---

93.   Ursula Le Guin, *Dancing at the Edge of the World*, p.155. Brackets my paraphrase.

I was fortunate, my life did fall apart, I was lost. The journey into Her story, means a participation in Her descent and return, it means a shattering of what went before. How does a woman stop being object, and become subject? How does she become the body in her own mind? It requires more than a headtrip, it requires the descent of Inanna, a falling apart. I was still a product of patriarchal narrative, and still seeking the Beloved (the Mother) outside myself. What did it take to move from that, to allow a fertile darkness within, from which the Self could begin? The regaining of integrity, and an understanding of why we lost it, or did not have it, can require a great darkness.

Thus my comfort with the Darkness of She, Her autopoietic aspect that I will re-story in the chapters ahead—I have found in my Search that this was also the experience of the Dark of other women who had known invasiveness/objectification of a sexual kind. My creativity comes out of my subjectivity, my inner depths; this is where my ability (able-ty) springs from. I have barely believed in this sentience myself—this Source of my ability. I am ambivalent about writing "Source" with a capital, as I also want to affirm that it is "source", with a small "s", to affirm that it is in *me*—and of course, it is the Ocean, it is Source; but my small part of it springs from the ground of my own small source. This Goddess Metaphor, this Wisdom tradition, is about recognizing the Power within each being, and making the Hera's journey, taking it for ourselves—female and male, all beings. This is empowerment—as opposed to a worldview that says some have this sentience and some don't. It is the difference between Kali, who is an agent of Creativity—Creator—who may rage and act, and Eve who is guilty and answers to a Creator outside of herself. In Goddess cosmology, I "participate directly in the cosmos-creating endeavour", as Swimme puts it when speaking of the autopoietic aspect of Cosmogenesis.[94] I am not a passive recipient or bystander.

Perhaps one of the earliest indications of a direction to take, came from my mother's hesitancy about the stories available, to read to her children. The stories had bits in them that she did not seem to want to tell. She would falter as she read, and then proceed as if making it up. It caused me to wonder, "what did the wolf *really* do to Little Red Riding Hood and grandma? What other horrible things were possible, that I had not yet imagined?" It seemed my mother would have spared us the whole tale if she could have. I felt my mother's wish for more

94. Brian Swimme and Thomas Berry, *The Universe Story*, p.75.

hopeful tales, tales of a better world. My mother had an ember in her heart that longed for a world that she could embrace, one that she could even just dream of…if something would help her imagine it. So I always listened for Something Else. Hints of Something Else did come through—in the revelation of the vast starred night sky; and in the revelation of the ancient relationship of sun and land, that I as a country girl had time to ponder. Something Else also came threaded through poetry that I loved at school, and music on the airwaves from far away places. The country girl knew she would have to travel a long way—into Other Times and Other Places, to find expression for the world that she and her mother wished for.

Another clue, not in a cognitive level but in a deep intuitive visceral level, came when I experienced the Creative Force of Life in my body—when I was pregnant for the first time. This was truly revelatory…it, the Cosmos, Ultimate Mystery, *was* in me! They had lied! It was a shock to realize that "something" could grow in me. There was nothing second rate about this. All previous stories had hidden its significance from me. But still I had no words to describe it—no possible expression for this. The knowledge sat in my heart like an uncut jewel, awaiting its time.

Re-Storying "Her"

It is not female biology that has betrayed the female, as Elizabeth Cady Stanton observed more than one hundred years ago, it is the myths and stories that have been told about her, what has come to be believed about her—even by the female herself.[95] In the Christian West, it is common for a woman to be described or to describe herself as "just a mother". It is common for "barefoot and pregnant" to connote powerlessness. Simone de Beauvoir suggested that it was as mother that woman was most fearsome, so it was as mother that she was enslaved.[96] Yet there

---

95. Elizabeth Cady Stanton actually said "Woman is made the author of sin, cursed in her maternity, subordinated in marriage, and a mere afterthought in creation…The first step in the elevation of women under all systems of religion is to convince them that the great spirit of the Universe is in no way responsible for any of these absurdities" February 29,1896 letter to the editor of *The Critic*. My particular paraphrase of what Stanton said could also be interpreted from resolutions passed at the Seneca Falls Women's Rights Convention in Irene M. Frank and David M. Brownstone, *Women's World: A Timeline of Women in History*, p.132-134.
96. Simone de Beauvoir, *The Second Sex*, p.171.

are cultures in the human community where a birthing mother is described as a "great warrior"—going to the gates of life and death, to heave and push a soul into the world.[97]

In regards to the understanding of virgin: where once it meant she who is "one-in-herself",[98] in patriarchal cultures it has been reduced to announcing the state of her hymen. Yet once virgins were just as likely, though not necessarily, sexually active, *and* holy women. The purity of the virgin was her freedom—it meant that all creativity was within her.[99] Artemis' devotees dressed in special tunics and celebrated an "uncompromising autonomy".[100] The virgin of the ancients embodied a holy Lust—a sacred ecstasy. She tended the flame—in many cultures[101]—kindling the spark at the Heart of existence—and it was not asexual.

The crone aspect of the Female Metaphor is not only about age, it is also about the acceptance and valuing of darkness as essential to the life process. Once this aspect was connected to regeneration and Wisdom, and some cultures understood darkness as the source of being. In a culture where the darkness is languaged as evil, where there is no place for the compost, this aspect is feared and loathed. Where only the Light is valued as positive, where the nurturance of the Dark has been forgotten, real wisdom and compassion will never be discovered.

Re-storying "Her" means re-storying "her"—the mere human (as well as our Habitat), and vice versa: Her stories are the stories of women (and therefore of men, who are co-Habitants) through the millennia, Her image is the image of women. The patriarchal re-writing of Persephone's voluntary descent to the underworld, as a rape of Her, expresses a change in the human psyche that was taking place.[102] She was no longer Sovereign, and no longer had the integrity and courage of a Hera/Redeemer who might go to the underworld voluntarily for the getting of Wisdom or the comfort of souls. She once had the same redemptive aura/power as Jesus later came to have,[103] and so She can again. When Perse-

---

97. Hallie Iglehart Austen, *The Heart of the Goddess*, p. 18.

98. Esther M Harding, *Woman's Mysteries: Ancient and Modern*, p.125.

99. Anne Baring and Jules Cashford, in *The Myth of the Goddess*, p.197.

100. Anne Baring and Jules Cashford, in *The Myth of the Goddess*, p.326.

101. Miriam Robbins Dexter, *Whence the Goddesses: A Source Book*, p.165.

102. Charlene Spretnak, *Lost Goddesses of Early Greece*, p.105-107.

103. Joseph Campbell notes that "Jesus took over what is really the Goddess' role in coming down in compassion", in Bill Moyers *The Power of Myth*, p.180.

phone's older story is re-constellated in the human psyche, She is allowed to move out of victim status.[104] Persephone had the Wisdom of Goddess, She had understanding of the fertility of the Dark terrain—the Mystery of life and death. When the integrity and grace of Her descent is restored, so is Her full participation in the Mystery and adventure of life. In the telling of Persephone's older story, the mere human female is also re-storied, re-visioned, re-imagined from within a framework that has her in mind and in heart; a story the way she or her mother would want to tell it, a story beyond victims and perpetrators where Divine Essence is expressed.

At this point in time the re-storying of Goddess has been happening for some decades amongst many on the planet, based upon the research of many over the past century or so, and particularly upon the research and reflection of many within the past fifty or sixty years. It is a complex creation—this is as it should be. How else could it be? The following chapter on Her re-storying is a gathering of the perspectives of many researchers, scholars, poets and storytellers. It is my particular blend, as I have collected it over decades. As I re-wrote it for this publication, it came to feel like the gathering of found shattered fragments of a vessel, that I have been piecing together: and now at last I begin to *sense* a Shape. Her Form and Her Shape have not been in any Atlas—it has taken many voyagers, seekers, mapmakers, diggers, stargazers, explorers: all willing to go beyond the bounds of the known world ("where there be dragons" as the Old Wisdom says!). The process of re-storying Goddess, as anyone undertakes it for themselves, for and with others, may be like a bird building a nest; and that indeed is what I feel I have been doing, and what all Her other hungry and lost daughters and sons have been doing.

---

104. See Charlene Spretnak, *Lost Goddesses of Early Greece*, p.109-118, and also Carolyn McVickar Edwards, *The Storyteller's Goddess*, p.178-183.

3

Re-Storying Goddess—Virgin, Mother, Crone

Almost every ancient culture's creation myth begins with Her.[1] In the beginning was the Matrix, and the Matrix was all there was. "Before creation a presence existed…(which)…pervaded itself with unending motherhood."[2] This Matrix was not "feminine", in any stereotypical way, which would limit Her to a certain mode of being. She was beyond all pairs of opposites. As the beginning and end of all things, She contained it all—she was yin and yang, right and left, light and dark, linear and cyclic, immanent and transcendent. There was not an either/or. She was not carved up into bits, apportioned a certain fragment of being—She was a totality. She bore within herself all of the polarities. Ancient Mesopotamian

---

1. There are many references for this statement, as there are for many of the statements I make in this chapter, so for the purposes of this publication I will dispense with the meticulous referencing which can be found in its entirety in Chapter 3 of the academic version as already referred to. The particular combined threads in this chapter are a complex weave, a complex wine, influenced and spoken by so many at this point in time; thus a specific reference is almost meaningless. Also the objectivity and subjectivity are hard to separate, which is really true for any text (though not usually admitted). Some of the story as I have come to tell it has arisen organically over the years of my own reflection and then later found affirmation from published academic researchers. There are however "objective" sources for all the storying I do here, and it has met academic requirements. "Objective sources" are those whose information is based in archaeological and mythological research and reflection, and is able to be checked. The prominent such influences and sources for this section are Marija Gimbutas, Erich Neumann, Hallie Iglehart Austen, Barbara Walker, Merlin Stone, Joseph Campbell, Anne Baring and Jules Cashford, Charlene Spretnak, Goeffrey Ashe, Marina Warner, Esther Harding, Lawrence Durdin-Robertson. These and others will be noted here in this text when specific and significant quotes are used, otherwise reference can be made to the academic version.
2. Lao Tzu, The Way of Life translated by Witter Bynner, p.40.

texts praise Ishtar of Babylon for her strong, exalted, perfect decrees as Lawgiver, and for her passionate, lifegiving sexuality, all in the one paragraph. As Vajravarahi, Goddess has been known as Mistress of all Knowledge, which included her physical being—quite a deal more expansive than more recent academic understandings of "Master of Arts". One of Ishtar's titles has been translated as "Great Whore", but this falls far short of the original understanding. As Merlin Stone has pointed out, the use of words like "prostitute" or "harlot" or "whore" as a translation for "qadishtu" negates the sanctity of this priestly role and reveals an ethnocentric subjectivity on the part of the writer.[3] The patriarchal bias in the minds of the writers disabled their comprehension of a holy woman who was sexual. The use of the word "Whore" to label One who embodied the Mystery of the Universe, has enabled patriarchal religions to denigrate the Female Metaphor—sometimes out of ignorance, sometimes with conscious intent.

As Isis of Egypt, the Great Goddess was "Mother of the Universe". This did not mean that there was a Father of whom she was partner, as most human minds of our time assume. This title meant that she was the One from whom all becoming arose. It meant that she was the Creator. Many minds get caught up here, with a need to affirm the now-known male role in reproduction; however, there has never been the same affirmation in the West, of the female role in reproduction when the God has been Creator. To comprehend Mother as Creator does not need to negate the integrity of the male, it simply re-instates the integrity of the female and her Creative capacity. As Mut of Egypt, She possibly preceded Isis. Mut is described as existing when there was nothing, the oldest deity, the original trinity. Her title meaning "Mother" was understood to hold within it the complete cycle that supported life—virgin, mother and crone—beginning, fullness, and ending; Mut's hieroglyphic sign was "a design of three cauldrons, representing the Triple Womb."[4] "Mother" was not a mere passive vessel, nor was she limited to the birthing and feeding aspects that later cultures allowed her; "Mother" was an wholistic title incorporating the beginning and the end. She was "Om", the letter of creation and "Omega", the letter of destruction.[5] Long before Jesus was said to have described himself as the "Alpha and the Omega", Goddess as Mother was comprehended in this complete form.

---

3.   Merlin Stone, *When God Was a Woman*, p.157. The term *Hierodule* is suggested as more accurate by Anne Baring and Jules Cashford, in *The Myth of the Goddess*, p.197.
4.   Barbara G. Walker, *The Woman's Encyclopaedia of Myths and Secrets*, p.702.
5.   Barbara G. Walker, *The Woman's Encyclopaedia of Myths and Secrets*, p.546.

As Neith, She was the Triple Goddess of ancient Egypt, the "World Body, the Primal Abyss from which the sun first rose…She was the Spirit Behind the Veil, whom no mortal could see face to face."[6] Throughout the ancient Mediterranean world this ancient One was known by various versions of Anatha, with Her triple aspects being Athena, Metis and Medusa. In later times, Neith was assigned a "father", as were many Great Goddesses around the globe—Brahma became the "father" of Sarasvati,[7] Chenrezig the "father" of Tara.

As Inanna of Sumeria, She was "primary one" for three thousand five hundred years. Her story of descent and return, death and resurrection, is the oldest story humans have of this heroic journey, and it influences the later stories of redeemer/wisdom figures such as Persephone, Orpheus, and Jesus. Inanna was known as Queen of Heaven. In one image, Her power was expressed with a crown of horns on Her head, Her foot on a lion, wings and thunderbolts sprouting from Her shoulders.[8] First known poet, Inanna's priestess Encheduanna of the second millennium B.C.E., and other such priestesses of her era celebrated and wrote erotically of the sacred marriage[9]—that of Inanna and her lover Dumuzi. It is one of the oldest surviving written records of the Sacred Marriage myth cycle;[10] and although Her sexuality is celebrated, Inanna's story never included pregnancy, as Starhawk notes.

In Greece, perhaps as early as the Paleolithic era, the Divine Female was known as Nyx, Black Mother Night, "the primordial foundation of all manifested forms", who laid the Egg of creation.[11] She was the full Emptiness, the empty Fullness. Aristophanes later sang of Her, "Black-winged Night…laid a wind-born egg, and as the seasons rolled, Forth sprang Love, the longed-for, shining with wings of gold."[12] Her Darkness was understood as "a depth of love", not a source of evil as later humans named Her.

---

6.   Barbara G. Walker, *The Woman's Encyclopaedia of Myths and Secrets*, p.721.

7.   Barbara G. Walker, *The Woman's Encyclopaedia of Myths and Secrets*, p.721.

8.   Hallie Iglehart Austen, *The Heart of the Goddess*, p.74.

9.   Judy Chicago, *The Dinner Party*, p.31.

10. Starhawk. *Truth or Dare*, p.40.

11. Demetra George, *Mysteries of the Dark Moon*, p.115–119.

12. Demetra George, *Mysteries of the Dark Moon*, p.115, quoting Aristophanes in *The Birds*.

As Aphrodite, She was said to be older than time. Aphrodite as humans once knew Her, was no mere sex goddess; She was once a Virgin-Mother-Crone trinity, and indistinguishable from the Fates and their power—perhaps more powerful. Aphrodite was "multivalent", had many names. This was characteristic of most Goddesses because the religion of the time was oral, and the stories of the diverse manifestations of the Ultimate Principle linked and were embellished upon as humans told them and travelled. Aphrodite was associated with the sea and dolphins, childbirth and the energy that opens seeds, sexuality and the longing that draws creatures together. The Love that She embodied as it was once understood was a Love deep down in things; it could be expressed as an "allurement" intrinsic to the nature of the Universe.[13] The Orphics sang of Her:

> For all things are from You
> Who unites the cosmos.
> You will the three-fold fates
> You bring forth all things
> Whatever is in the heavens
> And in the much fruitful earth
> And in the deep sea.[14]

Surely She who represented such a power, could be said to represent a fundamental cosmic dynamic. Scientists in the last few centuries have spoken of a basic dynamism of attraction in the universe that is primal, using the word "gravity" to point to it, but it remains fundamentally mysterious.[15] And what difference Hymns of this kind to the Psalms, which have been understood to praise the Divine—surely One who unites the cosmos and brings forth all things deserves the dignity of ultimate divine praise.

As Dana, She was Goddess of many peoples—the Danes, the biblical Danites, and the Celtic tribe "Tuatha De Danann", and in Russia she was called Dennitsa: the Daniel of the Bible was "Dan-El", his name really a title denoting his belonging to and knowledge of Goddess Dana.[16] Goddess was still very present to

---

13. A description of Aphrodite that is the coalition of the work of Brian Swimme and Charlene Spretnak, as described by Charlene Spretnak in *Lost Goddesses of Early Greece*, p.xvi.

14. This was referred to as "Orphic Hymn" in the 1994 calendar *Celebrating Women's Spirituality*, Crossing Press, Freedom California, week April 4–10. No further reference was given.

15. Brian Swimme, *The Universe is a Green Dragon*, p.43.

16. Barbara G. Walker, *The Woman's Encyclopaedia of Myths and Secrets*, p. 206-207.

human consciousness at the time of the writing of the Old Testament, a fact most often not taken into account, or at least not sympathetically explained, in exegetical accounts.

In China, the archaic Great Mother was named Shin-Mu, described as "Mother of Perfect Intelligence".[17] Also She was known as Guanyin, the Bodhisattva of Compassion—She who hears the cries of the world.

As Tara, She was known from India to Ireland as the primal Goddess Earth.[18] Praise and knowledge of Her has survived in Tibetan Buddhism into our times. In Tantric Buddhism She is understood to be at once both transcendent and immanent, at the centre of the cycle of birth and death, pressing "toward consciousness and knowledge, transformation and illumination."[19]

As Prajnaparamita in the Tibetan Buddhist tradition, the Female Metaphor is transcendent Wisdom and has been recognized as " 'Mother of all the Buddhas' because Buddha activity arises out of, results from, and is born from Wisdom."[20] Her space is not a passive place, it is fertile and vibrant.

As Vajravarahi, She has been offered praise in the following way:

> OM! Veneration to you, noble Vajravarahi!
> OM! Veneration to you, noble and unconquered!
> Mother of the three worlds! Mistress of Knowledge!…
> OM! Veneration to you, Vajravarahi! Great Yogini!
> Mistress of Love! She who moves through the air![21]

Vajravarahi is a face of the Fire of the Cosmos, the Dancer, the Unseen Shaper.[22] She represents the everchanging flow of energy.[23] She has been imagined as holding a sword of insight and discernment, and a cup of blood—the blood repre-

---

17. Barbara G. Walker, *The Woman's Encyclopaedia of Myths and Secrets*, p.933.
18. Barbara G. Walker, *The Woman's Encyclopaedia of Myths and Secrets*, p.976.
19. Erich Neumann, *The Great Mother*, p. 334.
20. Rita Gross, "The Feminine Principle in Tibetan Vajrayana Buddhism", The Journal of Transpersonal Psychology, p.186.
21. Hallie Iglehart Austen, *The Heart of the Goddess*, p.124, citing a poem to Vajravarahi from a Tibetan Art Calendar 1987, Wisdom Publications, Boston.
22. This is a title I have coined from Brian Swimme's name for Fire as unseen cosmic shaping power, in *The Universe is a Green Dragon*, p.127-139.
23. Hallie Iglehart Austen, *The Heart of the Goddess*, p.124, quoting Tsultrim Allione.

senting the life force and potential for renewal as any Goddess' blood does. Vajravarahi is a sharp, compassionate Intelligence, pervading all.

As Kali Ma, in the Hindu tradition, She is addressed as Supreme and Primordial, alone remaining as "One ineffable and inconceivable...without beginning, multiform by the power of Maya,...the Beginning of all, Creatrix, Protectress and Destructress."[24] The great mystic Ramakrishna of the 19th century, was overwhelmed by passion to realize Her and said he could not bear the separation any longer.[25] When She did reveal Herself to him, he experienced "a limitless, infinite shining ocean of consciousness or spirit"—he was "panting for breath".[26]

As Demeter of Greece, She is Mother of the grain, of wheat—"corn" as it was known, which was understood to reveal the Mystery of Being and was the core symbol of the Eleusinian Mysteries celebrated annually. The 'Vision into the Abyss of the Seed', was a vision of the Vulva—the Mother of all Life.[27] Demeter is always in relationship with Her Daughter Persephone—they are a union of the new reborn within and of the old. Demeter as Mother gives the sheaf of wheat to Persephone as Daughter, passing on the Knowledge, representing the continuity, the unbroken thread of life. Mother Goddess and Daughter, in this way reveal the Mystery of the seed in the fruit, the fruit in the seed, the eternal Creativity. The grain of wheat is both the beginning and the end of the cycle, and thereby may represent knowledge of life and death—Divine Wisdom; and it is also food, thus embodying all three aspects of Goddess. The bread that wheat becomes, sustains the human, who also eventually gives itself away becoming food for the Universe. Persephone, like Demeter herself—the Grain, "becomes the Goddess of the three worlds: the earth, the underworld, and the heavens."[28] They and their initiates are thus eternal.

In the Christian tradition, Mary of Nazareth came to embody Goddess, as many recount. This has been so mythologically and in the hearts and minds of the people regardless of the ambivalent official postures by the Church. Mary became

24.   Barbara G. Walker, *The Woman's Encyclopaedia of Myths and Secrets*, p.489, citing Sir John Woodroffe (trans), Mahanirvanatra, p.47-50
25.   Barbara G. Walker, *The Woman's Encyclopaedia of Myths and Secrets*, p.493.
26.   Barbara G. Walker, *The Woman's Encyclopaedia of Myths and Secrets*, p.493, citing Colin Wilson, The Outsider, p.254.
27.   Lawrence Durdin-Robertson, *The Year of the Goddess*, p.166-167.
28.   Erich Neumann, *The Great Mother*, p.319.

known as Moon Goddess, Star of the Sea, Our Lady and many other titles that recall more ancient Goddess roots. Mary has been the one to whom the people turned, certain of Her Love and mercy.

To the Sumerians the Divine was Queen Nana, to the Romans "Anna Perenna". She is Al-Uzza of Mecca, Artemis of Ephesus, Anatis of Egypt, Eurynome of Africa, Coatlique of the Aztecs. She is Rhea, Tellus, Ceres, Hera. The Female Metaphor has been known in innumerable ways and by innumerable names as humans tried to express their perception of the Great Mystery. She encompassed All. She has been present throughout the millennia in the myths, rituals, religions and poetry of humanity. She has been loved and revered.

And even before She appeared in human form, there were stones, trees, pools, fruits and animals that She either lived in or were identified with Her or parts of Her. For many peoples the stones and rocks were Her bones, the vegetation Her hair. Poppies and pomegranates and other such many-seeded flora identified Her fertility and abundance. The earth itself was understood as Her belly, the mountains as places of refuge, caves providing shelter for the unborn and the dead. Primal peoples everywhere at some time understood Earth Herself as Divine One—Mother. They languaged this in different ways. The pre-Celtic indigenous Europeans named Her—the Land—as Lady Sovereignty.[29] In Greece She was known as Gaia.

Central to understanding the Female Metaphor, is understanding the sacredness of vessels, pots, containers. These objects were understood as representations of Her. Pots, urns, pitchers "made possible the long term storage of oils and grains; the transforming of raw food into cooked;…also sometimes used to store the bones and ashes of the dead."[30] The vessel was felt as an extension of the female body that shaped life, carried the unborn, and provided nourishment. Kettle, oven, cauldron have to do with warmth and transformation; bowl, chalice and goblet are vessels of nourishment and their openness is suggestive of gift. The making and decorating of pottery was among the primordial functions of woman, often with taboos imposed on men to prevent them from going near. In later periods of human culture, in Eleusis, Rome and Peru and elsewhere the sacred vessels were supervised by the priestesses. The chalice was the holy Cup,

---

29. See Claire French, *The Celtic Goddess*.
30. Adrienne Rich, *Of Woman Born*, p.85.

felt as Her power to give life. Riane Eisler in *The Chalice and the Blade*, compares the chalice's power to give life with that of the blade, which is the power to take life, and develops how this was borne out culturally. In Christianity, woman was denied the right to handle the vessel as chalice—a ritual metaphor for the huge transition that had taken place in the human understanding; it was as if the female body no longer belonged to the female.

Water was a central Goddess abode, as it nourished and transformed, and also contained. She was identified with the water birds and ducks. As Bird Goddess She was the life giving force, nurturing the world with moisture, giving rain, the divine food—the very milk of Her breasts. So our ancestors frequently featured breasts set in rain torrents on the jars that they made.[31]

The tree as container and shelter, and also sometimes bearer of nourishment as in the fruit-bearing tree, was a central vegetative presence of Goddess. The figuring of such a tree in a negative context in later religious stories of humanity was not an arbitrary matter—this tree, particularly a fruit tree, was understood by the people of that time to be bearer of the Female Metaphor. The story was clearly a political statement, as many researchers now suggest.

Some animals were identified as particularly potent with Her; the deer with its fast growing antlers speaking of Her regenerative power, the toad with its pubic shape, the bull with its crescent shaped horns, the butterfly that emerged from its dark transformative space, the bear that so powerfully protected the young, the pig with its fast growing body and soft fats. The pig's identification with God-dess, with the Old Religion of the Land, had a lot to do with its later denigration, and taboos on its flesh.[32] Similarly, animals with which women have been "insulted"—cow, duck, hen—are animals once sacred to the Female. The snake was especially significant as symbolic of immortality, vitality and rejuvenation because of its shedding skin. The snake's intimacy with the earth, its knowledge of the darkness of the earth's womb as well as the light of the upper world, made it a symbol of power and wisdom. It was a Mother-power and wisdom that the later patriarchs rejected, as evidenced in their artwork and literature. The treat-ment of the snake's knowledge in the Genesis myth is a direct reference to the

---

31.   Marija Gimbutas, *The Goddesses and Gods of Old Europe*, p.116.
32.   Barbara G. Walker, *The Woman's Encyclopaedia of Myths and Secrets*, p.112.

Old Religion. In Christian art, Mary as Goddess is often depicted standing on the snake crushing it.

As the humans developed symbols, one of the earliest representations of Goddess was the downward pointing triangle, the pubic triangle. This was a recognition of the Source of life, the Gateway. Sometimes Goddess was depicted displaying her breasts, belly, genitalia, or entire naked body as a form of divine epiphany. Today, Western science has come to understand that the Universe is still rushing away from its birthplace, still expanding. The Mystery is still birthing. The Gateway still pours Itself forth. All of manifestation is divine epiphany—Her ecstatic irrepressible expression. This ancient Goddess symbol has been renewed empirically.

Central to the spirituality and understanding of Great Goddess is the recurrent cycle of birth and death, the immortal process of creation and destruction. It is a cycle seen most clearly in the moon, with its waxing, fullness and waning; which also corresponds to the body cycle of menstruation. The constant flux of things is manifest everywhere, in the seasons, in breathing, in eating. This is the nature of Goddess, Her manifestation, Her play. Anthropomorphized, this cycle is Virgin, Mother, and Crone. In Her most ancient and powerful depictions, Great Goddess embodies all three aspects—not just one; for example, Artemis is not only depicted as Virgin, in some images She clearly represents Mother and Crone too. These three aspects of the cycle, of Goddess, do belong together, and together they constitute a wholeness. Really they cannot be separated; one phase cannot "be" on its own, that is, a moon cannot always be full, the leaves cannot fall off the tree unless they grew there first, a new breath cannot be taken unless the old one is expired. The cycle has these aspects but it is One. And so Goddess of old was known, a union of three faces, complete and whole, yet ever in flux and dynamic. This triple aspect metaphor was later used to describe the triune nature of the patriarchal God, in both the East and the West, though in the Western teachings of the trinitarian Deity, its relationship to the cycle of Life was most often more abstract.[33]

---

33. a notable exception is where Jesus was characterised as the Green God, and this image portrayed on churches. See William Anderson, *Green Man: The Archetype of our Oneness with the Earth*.

Ultimately the Female Metaphor, Goddess, is about the celebration of Life, its eruption, its flux, its sustenance, with all that life demands and gives. She is an affirmation of the power symbolized by the chalice, the power to give life: initiate it, sustain it, pour it out. This is the power to Be, that all beings must have; not the power to Rule, that only a few might take. The popular Jungian understanding of the "Feminine" is not sufficient to contain Her, shuffled off as She usually is to a portion of reality. And frequently that portion in the popular mind consists of passive receptive qualities. These qualities are only part of the whole picture. As Virgin, Mother and Crone, She is eagle, bear, lioness, snake, as well as deer, gentle breeze, flower, rabbit.[34] She is not manifesting "masculinity" when she hunts for food, and neither is the human female when she operates in the world analytically or assertively.

The Virgin/Maiden Re-Storied[35]

The Virgin as she has been known in patriarchal times, is a distortion of the original understanding of Her. She is originally primarily in relationship with herself, and she is not asexual. She is decidedly self-determined, remains her own property, whether or not she has sexual relationships. The term *virginity* signified *autonomy*, and it was a power to be "at cause", instead of "at effect"; it was only in later patriarchal stories, that a Goddess' autonomy was "concomitant" with a loss of her sexuality, as in Athena's case.[36] The Goddess of old was always considered virginal; it was an ever-present quality of Hers. Even in some later stories, before the quality was completely diminished, She frequently "renewed" her virginity ritually[37]—sometimes to suit Herself, sometimes to suit the males with whom She mated.[38] Esther Harding expressed that,

---

34. See Marija Gimbutas, *The Language of the Goddess*, p.316-317 for a description of the wholeness by which "Goddess" was understood.

35. Other than the specific sources referred to in this section, I am indebted also to Marion Woodman, *The Pregnant Virgin*; Batya Podos, *The Triple Aspect of the Goddess*; Starhawk, *The Spiral Dance: A Rebirth of the Ancient Religion of the Great Goddess*; Hallie Iglehart Austen *The Heart of the Goddess*; and Robin Morgan, *Lady of the Beasts*; for the general understanding and tone of this re-storying of the Virgin.

36. Miriam Robbins Dexter, *Whence the Goddesses: A Source Book*, p.143.

37. Jane Ellen Harrison, *Prolegomena to the Study of Greek Religion*, p.311-312.

38. Miriam Robbins Dexter, *Whence the Goddesses: A Source Book*, p.167-170.

the woman who is virgin, one-in-herself, does what she does—not because of any desire to please, not to be liked, or to be approved, even by herself; not because of any desire to gain power over another…but because what she does is true.[39]

The Virgin's purity is this: Her unswerving commitment to Her truth, Her true Self. This Self-serving purity was a deep commitment to Being. Later patriarchal obsessions with unbroken hymens, turned the Virgin's essential "Yes" to Life into a "No".[40] She became reduced in Christian times to a "closed gate",[41] sometimes naive. In the Olympian pantheon the Virgin often came to be associated with harshness and indifference.

It was because of the Virgin's association with the beginning of things, the emergence of life, that She came to be understood as passionately protecting the flame of Being—"the 'hearth', which is also the original altar."[42] She loved all beings, desired their existence. She knew Creative Lust—Lust for Being. So Virgin Goddesses of many cultures have guarded perpetual flames, representing this purity of purpose and passion. Diana, Great Virgin of Rome, is depicted with a flame. The priestesses of Brigid, Goddess in Ireland, tended a flame; which was later, for a period of time, tended by nuns and Brigid was re-configured as a saint.

As Artemis in Greece, in Her Virgin aspect She was revered as midwife because of her single-minded drive to bring life into being.[43] The earliest stories of Artemis speak of a Goddess for whom "each creature—each plant, each wood, each river—is…a Thou, not an it."[44] Women called upon Her in childbirth, and the labour-easing herbs used by midwives in Old Europe were called *Artemisia*. Artemis came to be known as One that protected and nurtured the young and vulnerable, the will to life, the spirit.[45] She was as much concerned with physical being as with the making of soul—there was no separation. As Virgin, Artemis was associated with untamed nature, the pre-domesticated, the pre-informed, the

39. Esther M Harding, *Woman's Mysteries: Ancient and Modern*, p.125.
40. Audre Lorde, "Uses of the Erotic", in *Weaving the Visions: New Patterns in Feminist Spirituality*, p.208–213, influenced my understanding of the *yes* within ourselves, which I came to associate with the Virgin.
41. Marina Warner, *Alone of All her Sex*, p.73.
42. Erich Neumann, *The Great Mother*, p.284-285.
43. Charlene Spretnak, *Lost Goddeses of Early Greece*, p.77-79.
44. Christine Downing, *The Goddess: Mythological Images of the Feminine*, p.167.
45. Merlin Stone, *Ancient Mirrors of Womanhood*, p.381-386.

wild. She was the Possibility of the open mind, the new and untried. She had no need to be afraid, because She was certain of taking care of Herself. Artemis was known as a Mighty Huntress, and in earliest human cultures this was not contradictory to deep relationship with the animals that were hunted. She was also known as Lady of the Beasts; the deer was often Her animal—an animal associated with birth and renewal, and the bear associated with rebirth/hibernation and fierce mothering. Artemis is often depicted as an archer. Her arrow that flies true and on centre, is just as surely the arrow of Self. Christine Downing declares that "the spear of the goddess is a spear of passion", and notes Rene Malamud's perception that "all passion means fundamentally a search for self."[46]

Athena has, in Western secular culture, most commonly embodied the patriarchal version of Virgin—depicted as She has been in a suit of armour, with the head of Her sister Medusa on Her shield. In Athena's story as it evolved over time, can be seen a story of women throughout the ages.[47] Originally Athena was from North Africa where She was an aspect of the Triple Goddess Neith, along with Metis and Medusa.[48] While classic writers of later times insisted on Her asexual nature, "older traditions gave her several consorts" including Pan.[49] In Her oldest images and stories, Athena was associated with bird and snake, and was the inventor of all arts. She was one of the very early parthenogenetic Goddesses. Patriarchal myth accounts for Athena's existence by virtue of Zeus giving birth to Her from his head, after having swallowed her mother Metis when Metis was pregnant with Athena. Metis, Goddess of Wisdom Herself (and the old form of Athena), cannibalized by Zeus, was said to counsel Zeus from within his belly [50]—She was in effect, the first woman behind every great man. Athena became the archetype of the patriarchal dutiful daughter, Her father's mouthpiece, used to give authority to his edicts that included the denigration of Her own kind. In the Oresteia, one of the most frequently performed Greek dramas, standardly interpreted to be a lesson in the wisdom of state administered justice, Athena casts the deciding vote to acquit Apollo of the murder of his mother. The grounds for his acquittal is that the mother is not a parent, merely the nurse of the male seed, and Athena is proclaimed as primary witness to the glory of a child

---

46. Christine Downing, *The Goddess: Mythological Images of the Feminine*, p.180, quoting Malamud in James Hillman (ed), *Facing the Gods*, p.56.
47. MaryDaly, *Gyn/Ecology*, p.13-14.
48. Barbara G. Walker, *The Woman's Encyclopaedia of Myths and Secrets*, p.74.
49. Barbara G. Walker, *The Woman's Encyclopaedia of Myths and Secrets*, p.74.
50. MaryDaly, *Gyn/Ecology*, p.13.

brought forth from the father. Athena then persuades the Furies, the "last remaining representatives of woman's old powers" to submit to the new patriarchal order.[51] Whereas in the older stories, Athena was daughter of the Mother, indistinguishable from the Mother Herself. She was spiritual warrior—protecting the arts and wisdom, not a soldier.[52] Her holy quest had been in the service of Life, urging forward the creative spirit, that all may be fully what it is capable of being. It was Her vision, not armour, which was Her strength.

The Virgin aspect loves Herself, as She loves all, identified as She is with Life itself. To despise Self is to despise All. As Aphrodite, She "lifts Her robe to admire her own full buttocks";[53] Inanna too, Great Goddess of the Sumerian people rejoices in Her own sexual beauty very explicitly. Aphrodite, like her Sumerian Sister, is the Creative Force itself. In Aphrodite's case, She is identified with the oceans as Source of Life, and doves and waterbirds attend Her; the actual inseparability of the Mother and Virgin aspects is obvious here. It is interesting to contrast this perspective on Aphrodite with that of Jungian, Robert Johnson, who claims the patriarchal myths as the earliest sources on Her.[54] Johnson calls Aphrodite "primitive femininity", and after affirming that all women contain "the Aphrodite nature", proclaims "her chief characteristics…(as)…vanity, conniving, lust, fertility, and tyranny when she is crossed."[55] Charlene Spretnak wonders particularly about his inclusion of "fertility" in the "string of negative adjectives". Johnson goes on to label Aphrodite as "a thorough bitch".[56]

Persephone is a Virgin Goddess who has been to hell and back. In Persephone's story in its earliest version,[57] we see particularly the connection of the Crone and the Virgin, how these two aspects are really inseparable. Persephone chooses to go to the underworld and indeed becomes Queen of the Dead; she comes to know this realm and to guide others through it, but she is equally associated with re-emergence, re-generation. She is not a naive Virgin; she can go into the darkness

---

51.   Riane Eisler, *The Chalice and the Blade*, p. 81.
52.   Charlene Spretnak, *Lost Goddeses of Early Greece*, p.97.
53.   Hallie Iglehart Austen, *The Heart of the Goddess*, p.132.
54.   Robert Johnson, *She: Understanding Feminine Psychology*, p.1.
55.   Charlene Spretnak, *Lost Goddeses of Early Greece*, p.35 quoting Robert Johnson, *She*, p.6.
56.   Charlene Spretnak, *Lost Goddeses of Early Greece*, p.35 quoting Robert Johnson, *She*, p.7.
57.   as the pre-patriarchal version is referred to and described in Ch.2, p.78-79.

in trust, knowing its fertility, and trusting deeply her own impetus to sprout afresh, to begin again. She is a Virgin who has been around the block many times, and because of that (not in spite of it), she continues to believe in her capacity to take form again. This Knowledge of life and death, of the cycle, is the Mystery that was celebrated in the rites of Demeter and Persephone in Eleusis every Autumn. It was so, long before the Paschal Mysteries of Jesus crept in. Persephone's descent is a return to the depths for Wisdom, and Her emergence from the Earth, is an image of the power to Be, that surges through all Creation continuously and is manifest in individual life stories also. She is the Seed of Life that never fades away. Persephone tends the sorrows—as Spretnak tells in her version of the story. Persephone's pronouncement is:

> You have waxed into the fullness of life
> And waned into darkness;
> May you be renewed in tranquility and wisdom.[58]

Persephone goes into the heart of our sorrows to unfold the Mystery. She is an energy present in the seeds, in each person, creature, all of existence—at the heart of matter, of Life.

These Goddesses are the anthropomorphic forms of an energy, a dynamic that is Virgin. She has been named Artemis, Athena, Brigid, Aphrodite, and Mary…so that we may speak of Her. These forms that humans have given Her are only one of Her valencies, the way in which we may tell stories; there are other subtle valencies to be understood once it is clear that we speak of an aspect of Divine Essence (as opposed to a bit of patriarchally imagined female psyche). When I speak of Virgin, I understand Her as the *Urge to Be*—whatever it is in the dead looking branch that pushes forth the green shoot. She can be *felt* in you, as the Urge to take a new breath, as your hunger for food, as your hunger for anything. She is passionate. She can be felt in your longing—any longing. She is that in you which midwifes the soul, and any creative project. She is known when there is real self-love, one's beauty recognized, one's truth held firm and allowed Being. She is the hope, the Promise[59] of fulfillment—symbolized and expressed in the image of the new crescent moon, and felt, as that fine sliver of light enters your

---

58.   Charlene Spretnak, *Lost Goddeses of Early Greece*, p.116.
59.   I derived this name for the Virgin aspect from Starhawk's term "Child of Promise", which she uses to describe the new Young One, *The Spiral Dance*, p. 219.

eyes. She is all Possibility within you, within the seething quantum foam. She is essentially a big "Yes" to existence.

I associate the Virgin with the Buddha nature, that Shining One within all,[60] that calls us forward…She is the future that calls us to become all that we can become, for whom we "refine the gold". Virgin nature is *"She Who will Be"*, who can hold forth her song despite any forces of disintegration.[61] She is the courage, confidence and exuberance to say "yes" to each particular small self.

The Mother/Creator Re-Storied[62]

Where the Virgin is primarily in relationship with Self, the Mother is primarily in relationship with Other. She is the Network of relatedness, the Weaver of the Fabric. She is the peaking of Creative Power. As Mother, the Goddess is primal—the first concept of Divinity, the Creator. She is the beginning and end of all things, the Creative Force of the Universe, parthenogenetically giving birth to all life. The earliest human beings knew nothing of the male role in the process of reproduction—there was no reason or inclination to correlate copulation with childbirth. The women themselves must have eventually noted it, since they were the keepers of a lunar based calendar, which coincided with their menstrual cycles. The human community, the village, gathered around the primary dyad of mother and child. The woman as mother was perhaps the original civilizing force, though we have been led to believe, in the texts of our education that it was men who led the way in civilization, that motherhood distracted women from

---

60. I acknowledge Joan Halifax, *Being With Dying*, for a broadened understanding of the Buddha, the Sangha and the Dharma—which I now associate with the three faces of the Female Metaphor. Ken Wilber also associates I-Buddha, andWe-Sangha, It-Dharma, thus extending the valencies of what he names "the Spiritual Big Three" in *A Brief History of Everything*, p. 131-134.

61. This is similar to Wilber's understanding of the "agency" of a holon in *A Brief History of Everything*, p.21-22. Willis Harman & Elisabet Sahtouris in *Biology Revisioned*, p.17-18 describe agency as a holon's "capacity to maintain its wholeness in the face of environmental pressures which would otherwise obliterate it".

62. Other than the specific sources referred to in this section, I am indebted also to Robin Morgan, *Lady of the Beasts*; Batya Podos, *The Triple Aspect of the Goddess*; Starhawk, *The Spiral Dance: A Rebirth of the Ancient Religion of the Great Goddess*; and Marion Woodman, *The Pregnant Virgin*; for the general understanding and tone of this re-storying of the Mother.

this great enterprise. But there is evidence that in the earliest times, it was motherhood that gave the very impetus to grow, sustain, beautify, count, write.[63] It
was she

> who wielded the digging stick or the hoe: she who tended the garden crops
> and accomplished those masterpieces of selection and cross-fertilization which
> turned raw wild species into the prolific and richly nutritious domestic variet-
> ies.[64]

Indeed it is still she who comprises some eighty percent of the world's farmers. In
Egyptian hieroglyphics, "house" or "town" may stand as symbols for "mother".
Ancient civilizations traced their descent through the mother; the mother was the
basis for the clan, and it was named after her. Some ancient tomb inscriptions
disregarded fathers. Even the earliest patriarchies remained aware of and prepared
to admit the source of their power;[65] it was only later that the mother became
merely passive vessel, particularly in Greek philosophy. Pharaohs ruled by matri-
lineal succession. The throne itself is a stylization of the lap of the Mother; that's
where the power came from, being a child of the Mother. [66] The pharaoh's title
was originally Great Gate or Great House, symbolic of the cosmic Womb, by
whose power he ruled. Since women were the first measurers of time, the Sanskrit
word "matra" and the Greek "meter" both mean "mother" and "measurement".
In some civilizations the female skill in mathematics was thought to be associated
with their ability to give birth. In many cultures, ancient stories tell of the
Mother Goddess inventing the alphabet.[67]

Barbara Walker also notes how religions based on the Mother were free of what
she calls the "neurotic" quest for indefinable meaning in life, as such religions
"never assumed that life would be required to justify itself."[68] Such religions,
were generally free of guilt, fear and a sense of sin, since birth, not baptism was
the only pre-requisite for belonging. Even patriarchal religions have reached for

---

63. Barbara G. Walker, *The Woman's Encyclopaedia of Myths and Secrets*, p.684-685.
64. Barbara G. Walker, *The Woman's Encyclopaedia of Myths and Secrets*, p.681 quoting
     Lewis Mumford, The City in History, p.12.
65. Barbara G. Walker, *The Woman's Encyclopaedia of Myths and Secrets*, p.682.
66. Erich Neumann, *The Great Mother*, p.98-100.
67. Barbara G. Walker, *The Woman's Encyclopaedia of Myths and Secrets*, p.684-685.
68. Barbara G. Walker, *The Woman's Encyclopaedia of Myths and Secrets*, p.693.

maternal imagery to describe the love of the God. Buddha too described Universal Love in this way:

> As a mother...protects and loves her child...so let a person cultivate love without measure toward the whole world, above, below, and around, unstinted, unmixed with any feeling of differing or opposing interests...This state of mind is the best in the world.[69]

This maternal energy, seen here as the deep spiritual calling of all humans, has been for most women the zone where we frequently lost ourselves. Patriarchal religions have exhorted her to embody this unconditional love of the Other, with no balancing factor of love of Self. Where her capacity for this love of Other has been given its due, it has not at the same time, been recognized as a capacity for spiritual leadership. In the Catholic tradition, Mary is praised as a paradigm of virtue, and yet women and girls have sacramental roles withheld from them. If it is as perfect servant that she is praised, by their own theology that should make her perfect model for leadership. Mary is apparently the exceptional woman, yet Jesus is obviously the exceptional male—and that fact does not prevent male leadership. In the early days of Christianity, Mariology was a rival religion—there was grassroots allegiance to Mary as Divine—and that was evidently one of the factors in the decision to proclaim Mary Mother of God in 431 at Ephesus; the church thus took into itself this powerful image—rather like Zeus swallowing the Goddess Metis, thus incorporating her Wisdom and Creative power, and ensuring huge popular following. Simone de Beauvoir said that "it was as mother that woman was fearsome; it is in maternity that she must be transfigured and enslaved."[70] The fathers of the Christian church have been profoundly ambivalent about the details of Mary's motherhood, and her relationship to Divinity, Jesus and humanity; motherhood is a profoundly ambivalent role in many cultures. Many women remain very confused. It is clear that the maternal energy is indeed something that it would befit all humans to aspire to. It is a holy passion, but it has been unbalanced and short-circuited; frequently it is a woman locked into domesticity or a woman pouring her life's energy into mothering a man or an institution from whom she is getting no return. The potentially political and global significance of her consuming passion to sustain the world and make it better, has not been recognized within the cultural narrative,[71] and it has not

---

69. Barbara G. Walker, *The Woman's Encyclopaedia of Myths and Secrets*, p.694 referring to Nancy Wilson Ross, *Three Ways of Asian Wisdom*, p.123.
70. Simone de Beauvoir, *The Second Sex*, p.171.

been balanced with a consuming passion for her own being. The Mother's relationship to Other, Her Creative Power to give Life, in earliest mythologies, was not the prison that She was later contained in.

In patriarchal mythologies throughout the world, the Mother of All has frequently become "wife" of some god. Hera is such a One. Known in our times, as jealous, quarrelsome wife of Zeus, She pre-dated him by far as ancient face of the parthenogenetic Mother. The first "Olympic" races held every four years in ancient Greece, had been Hers, with runners—all girls—selected from three age groups representing the ancient Trinity.[72] Hera was the primordial Trinity, indigenous to this place, personifying all three aspects of Virgin, Mother and Crone. Hera and Zeus' constant mythological quarrels reflected real conflicts between the early matristic cultures and the rising patriarchate. She and the Amazon queens who represented Her did not go quietly, and they remained discontented with the new regimes. Hera's troublesome nature in the Olympic pantheon reflects One who had been "coerced but never really subdued by an alien conqueror."[73] Hera's first consort had been Heracles; the word "hero" referring to him and being the masculine form of "hera".[74] "Hera" predated "hero" and may serve as term for all courageous individuals as noted, and I do use it that way in the seasonal celebration of Eostar.

In some indigenous traditions around the globe, the birthing mother is understood as a model for courage—Iglehart Austen notes Native American, Samoan and Aztec cultures that honoured her as warrior.[75] There is evidence that many ancient cultures regarded birthing as a ritual act; in Catal Huyuk there is a ceremonial birthing shrine "with red-painted floors and images of the ubiquitous Open-legged Goddess in labor."[76] Vicki Noble describes the birthing woman as "quintessentially shamanic",[77] for in this act, she goes to the gates of life and

71. This is evident in derogatory references frequently made in political discussions, to "motherhood" statements and policies, as if "motherhood" describes the statement's/policy's small-mindedness and trivial nature. The word "trivial" itself has its roots in the sacredness of the "tri-via"—three way path.
72. Charlene Spretnak, *Lost Goddeses of Early Greece*, p.88.
73. Charlene Spretnak, *Lost Goddeses of Early Greece*, p.89 quoting Jane Ellen Harrison, *Prolegomena to the Study of Greek Religion*, p.491.
74. Charlene Spretnak, *The Politics of Women's Spirituality*, p.87.
75. Hallie Iglehart Austen, *The Heart of the Goddess*, p.18.
76. Hallie Iglehart Austen, *The Heart of the Goddess*, p.20.

death and with heaving and shoving and the most intense encounter with universal forces, experiencing trance states, she brings another being into the world. Perhaps the phenomena of "post-natal depression" in these times is a symptom of the lack of recognition of this.

Goddess as Mother is also the Weaver of the Fabric of the Universe, with many ancient Goddesses imaged this way. This power came to be feared, rather than revered—in Her "character as creator, sustainer and increaser of life" the Great Goddess came to be seen as "negative and evil", by a consciousness that desired "permanence and not change, eternity and not transformation, law and not creative spontaneity...(turning) her into a demon."[78] This consciousness, which Neumann calls an "antivital fanaticism", feared being "ensnared" in the "web of life, the veil of Maya".[79] Sometimes the weaving activity of women therefore became known as the cause of illness or a curse with some Christian traditions even forbidding knitting. The Fates of Greece have had nasty stories told about them—the classic texts of this culture telling how they had to be "submitted to the authority of Zeus who commanded them...".[80] Ixchel the Weaver, Mother, Queen, Grandmother to the peoples of Southern Mexico, the Yucatan Peninsula, and most of Central America,[81] came to be symbolized by an "overturned vessel of doom"[82]—yet "for centuries, women have made pilgrimages to Her holy places".[83] Iglehart Austen describes Ixchel as sitting "at Her loom with Her everpresent bird companion, the nest weaver, who is associated with Goddess throughout the world"—and how Ixchel "easily and with great presence...in the bliss of creativity" spins "from her deepest being" and breaths the "breath of eternity,...the life force into each being".[84]

This Mother energy, which sustains and nurtures the new life that the Virgin begins, participates in decisions that affect this life, and allows the Crone to cut the cord when it is necessary, has been named "ten thousand names", so that

---

77. Vicki Noble in "Female Blood Roots of Shamanism", quoted by Hallie Iglehart Austen, *The Heart of the Goddess*, p.18.
78. Erich Neumann, *The Great Mother,* p.233.
79. Erich Neumann, *The Great Mother,* p.233.
80. *Larousse Encyclopedia of Mythology*, p.163.
81. Hallie Iglehart Austen, *The Heart of the Goddess*, p.10.
82. Erich Neumann, *The Great Mother,* p.187.
83. Hallie Iglehart Austen, *The Heart of the Goddess*, p.10.
84. Hallie Iglehart Austen, *The Heart of the Goddess*, p.10.

humans may speak of Her. When I speak of Mother, I understand Her as Holy Context, *Place to Be*. She is the fullness that can be ***felt*** in the peaking of your breath, that dynamic interchange within you. She can be felt in the satisfaction of a well crafted project, the satisfaction of the successful tending of needs. Her power can be felt in the holding of another being, when life is given in some form to another. The Mother can be felt in the comfort offered by needed rain, seen and smelt in the full flower, tasted in the ripe fruit. She is so subtle, yet obvious, in the work of everyday, of strengthening networks, weaving and repairing, creating the world, raising children, teaching adults. She is the Promise fulfilled, Creativity in its fullness—symbolized and expressed in the image of the full moon, and felt, as that awesome disc of light enters your eyes. She is the Realization of Passion within you—most likely beyond your wildest dreams. She is the Bliss of Union.

I associate the Mother with the Sangha, that Community of support around the globe—it is complex and multifaceted, and specific facets may be focussed on, but at its broadest, it is the interdependent web without whom none of us would be sustained.[85] She is the present, the eternal now, the living of life as if it goes on forever—and indeed it does; if the thread were once broken, we would not be here. The form changes—every atom recycled infinite times, the shape shifts, but life does go on. She is the pure gift of every moment, filled as each moment is with the Creativity of the whole web since the beginning. She is *"She Who Is"*.

The Old One/Crone Re-Storied[86]

The Old One as a phase of Being is significant. The fact that life continues past reproductive fertility indicates an evolutionary interest in the creativity of this phase; Life has preserved it in the evolutionary story. The post-menopausal years

---

85. Similar to Wilber's understanding of the "communion" characteristic of each holon, *A Brief History of Everything*, p.21-22.

86. Other than the specific sources referred to in this section I am also indebted particularly to the following for much of my understanding and tone of this re-storying of the Crone: Pam Wright, "Living With Death as a Teacher"; Demetra George, "Mysteries of the Dark Moon"; Kathryn Theatana, "Priestesses of Hecate"; Patricia Reis, "The Dark Goddess" and "A Woman Artist's Journey"; Robin Morgan, *Lady of the Beasts*; Batya Podos, *The Triple Aspect of the Goddess*; and Sylvia Brinton Perera, *Descent to the Goddess: A Way of Initiation for Women*.

obviously have some impact on creativity as a whole, since it is an extensive part of the life-cycle before death.

The celebration of this threefold cycle of the Goddess is about the celebration of Life, about Creation and the sustaining of it. There is in it an acceptance of the waning of life, of death and the darkness as part of the life cycle. "The color black, now commonly associated with death or evil in Christian iconography, was in Old Europe the color of fertility and the soil."[87] Over the centuries, the Christian mind has imagined the religion of the Female/Goddess to be sordidly preoccupied with death, whereas in fact this may be considered a massive projection; the reverse being true. It is only in the denial of decline and death that we surround ourselves with it, because there is no place for new life to spring from. In the present cultural context where most people imagine or pretend that they are immortal, where death/darkness is seen as an aberration—not normal, we are surrounded by a fascination with it, and we struggle with a planet that is over-burdened by our waste. If the end part of the cycle was given a place, its reality accepted, we would always find ways of dealing with the garbage. It is in the compost, the de-composition, in the darkness, that new life is nurtured, fertility is found. It is in the acceptance of death that wisdom is gained, and life is lived more fully. Patricia Reis suggests that when the Female Metaphor was whole, death was not understood as separate. She points out that for 30,000 years (33,000 B.C.E.–3,000 B.C.E.) there were no images of a horrific Goddess, indicating perhaps that She only became terrifying when She lost her connection to the cycle.[88]

The Crone is primarily in relationship with All-That-Is (where Virgin is primarily with Self, and Mother is with Other). The Crone/Old One is that movement back into the Great Sentience out of which All arises, thus She sees into the elements behind form. She is often depicted with wide open eyes; often associated with the gaze of owl or snake—and knowledge of the Dark. In Her Egyptian form of Maat, She was known as the "All-Seeing Eye"[89] and Maat's plume/feather was the hieroglyph for "truth".[90] The Knowledge of this aspect of Goddess is beyond all knowledge; it is the Wisdom of the ages—of all Time and no

87. Marija Gimbutas, *The Language of the Goddess*, p.144.
88. Patricia Reis, "The Dark Goddess", Woman of Power, Issue 8, p.24. The research of Marija Gimbutas suggests this also: see *The Language of the Goddess*, p.316.
89. Barbara G. Walker, *The Woman's Encyclopaedia of Myths and Secrets*, p.294.
90. Barbara G. Walker, *The Woman's Encyclopaedia of Myths and Secrets*, p.561.

Time. The Crone aspect is the contraction that initiates destruction, when structure is no longer necessary or life-serving. Her contraction may also be understood as a systole, a contraction of the heart by which the blood is forced onward and the circulation enabled.[91] She is the systole that carries all away—She is about loss, but the contraction of the heart is obviously a creative one, it is the pulse of life. Is it only our short-sightedness that keeps us from seeing the contraction that way? Is it because we insist on taking it all so personally, when it is not, in fact?

As the end of the cycle, She is known in the breakdown of the endometrium, the shedding of the old, the flow of menstrual blood. She may be represented holding a bowl of blood, as Kali is, which signifies "birth fluid". The blood of Goddess is "'self-produced, primeval matter' the ocean of uterine blood before creation, holding future forms in the condition of formlessness or Chaos."[92] It is not blood that is shed by the blade, it is blood that naturally flows in the cycle of Life, to prepare for the new. Walker refers to it as "wise blood".[93] Menstruation has been such a source of shame and pain for women in our times,[94] and blood so associated with violence, that it is hard for us to re-imagine it as symbol of Wisdom and Regeneration. In the patriarchal narrative, blood shed by violence has been much preferred to that shed by the female. Seeing blood shed by violence even became a form of entertainment, and still is today, though the mythic advent of such acts (shedding blood by the blade), as a grasp for power, can be traced to the Epic of Gilgamesh in the second millennium B.C.E..[95] The power being grasped by shedding blood this way can be seen as a *synthetic* power—a substitute for the power to give life. The blood of the Female is very different; it is indeed awesome, indicating as it does, a dynamic of loss in the nature of things, but the larger arc of that dynamic is consistently creative. Our flesh, like all matter, is in constant flux. "Creation postulates change and any change destroys what went before."[96] The Crone is the one who "clears the decks", without which the new is not possi-

91. I owe the "systole" metaphor to Loren Eiseley, *The Immense Journey*, p.20. He uses it to speak of an eternal pulse that lifts Himalayas, and then carries them away.
92. Barbara G. Walker, *The Woman's Encyclopaedia of Myths and Secrets*, p.723.
93. Barbara G. Walker, *The Woman's Encyclopaedia of Myths and Secrets*, p.636.
94. See Penelope Shuttle and Peter Redgrove, *The Wise Wound: Menstruation and Everywoman* for a re-storying of menstruation. Also Taylor, *Red Flower: Rethinking Menstruation*.
95. Starhawk, *Truth or Dare*, p.47-60.
96. Starhawk, *The Spiral Dance*, p.95.

ble. She and the Virgin are always linked, the end and the beginning; One cannot exist without the Other. The snake that sheds its old skin, or eats its own tail, is Goddess' symbol of constant decomposition, constant renewal. It is in the burning that the fire creates warmth and light. The lioness must kill to feed her young. It is in the eating that our teeth and bodies break down what is needed for sustenance—the Crone is our constant companion.

Because of the snake's association with power, wisdom, transformation and renewal it came to be associated particularly with the Old One/Crone—the dark aspect of Goddess—although originally the snake/serpent *was* the Great Goddess herself. The snake has primordially been associated with the moon and the female, and in the Christian West all this became associated with evil, yet as Joseph Campbell affirms "the serpent represents immortal energy and consciousness engaged in the field of time, constantly throwing off death and being born again."[97] The Christian Goddess, Mary, has been imaged as standing on the serpent's head, crushing it; probably one of Mary's more powerful images, yet it is in opposition to Her ancient heritage. Campbell says that the portrayal of the serpent as a negative figure "amounts to a refusal to affirm life."[98]

Some of the Crone's names are Hecate, Kali, Caillech, Hel, Lillith and Medusa; the Aztecs have known her as Coatlique, the Egyptians as Selket. These Goddesses are associated with death, devouring, seduction, rebellion, anger, darkness and awesome power—not always seen wholistically or as agents of transformation as the Dark Goddesses may be seen, but at least they are still present. In the Christianized culture of the West She has almost completely disappeared in these forms. Her remnant is the wicked witch/hag of children's stories and cartoons, whose potency and intelligence is frequently fairly hollow. The term "old woman" is often used as a term of derogation in the Western cultural context; it is meant to reflect uselessness. Miriam Robbins Dexter points out that although patriarchal cultures could find a place for the use of the virgin and mother energies, they could find no such use for the old woman.[99] The young virgin could represent stored energy, and she maintained some numinosity for that reason. The mother transmitted energy, gave it to others. The old woman however, only had knowledge; this could be threatening, and was increasingly trivialized, as well

---

97.   Joseph Campbell, *The Power of Myth*, p.45.
98.   Joseph Campbell, *The Power of Myth*, p.47.
99.   Miriam Robbins Dexter, *Whence the Goddesses: A Source Book*, p.177.

as actually being truncated in its development by a discriminatory environment.[100]

Eve could be seen as a remnant of the Crone, since from the Judeo-Christian perspective, she is the cause of all death. In the fifth century C.E., a church council announced that it was heresy to say that death was natural rather than the result of Eve's disobedience.[101] As an Eve, every woman was "the devil's gateway" as announced by Tertullian. But Eve is really a very passive kind of Crone; even though she is to blame for death, she actually does not do the destroying, the God does; and Christian theologians noted that the devil tempted Eve because she was weaker willed than Adam. Eve is a far cry from a Kali or a Lillith or a Medusa. Most of what she carries around is guilt, not wrath. And many women have taken on Eve's burden.

Medusa is a good example of how Goddess in her dark aspect became demonized in the patriarchal context. Gimbutas points out that the earliest Greek gorgons were not terrifying symbols, but were portrayed with symbols of regeneration—bee wings and snakes as antennae.[102] Medusa with her serpent hair had been a widely recognized symbol of Divine Female Wisdom—the serpent representing Knowledge of Change, the very essence of Being, never-ending renewal, and thus immortality. Medusa was a face of Ultimate Mystery, of the One—She was "All that has been, that is, and that will be."[103] In our cultural mythology Perseus was celebrated as hero for being able to defeat her and cut off her head with its so called deadly gaze. It was said that her gaze was so fearsome it turned mortals to stone. There is no doubt that it is fearsome to look into the eye of the Divine; but patriarchal gods have carried the same characteristic, Yahweh for example, without threat of the same retribution. In the patriarchal context, is it really the gaze of the Female that is deadly? It is women who are the chronically gazed upon, whether as sex object or on a pedestal; perhaps this epitomizes Medusa's/Goddess' imprisonment—how She is "kept an eye on". The beheading of Medusa—one who is icon of Wisdom, may be understood as a story of dis-

---

100. Women were barred from education, yet at the same time denigrated as ignorant/ foolish. See Wertheim (1995) for some of the story of women and education through the recent millennia.

101. Barbara G. Walker, *The Woman's Encyclopaedia of Myths and Secrets*, p.290.

102. Marija Gimbutas, *The Language of the Goddess*, p.xxiii.

103. Barbara G. Walker, *The Woman's Encyclopaedia of Myths and Secrets*, p.629 quoting *Larousse Encyclopedia of Mythology*, p.37.

memberment of the Female Metaphor/Goddess.[104] The hera's journey today is to go against the patriarchal injunction and look Medusa straight on, as philosopher Hélène Cixous suggests.[105] She is at first fearsome, but the Dark Goddess' fierceness nurtures a strength in a woman, gives her back the "steel in her stomach" that she needs to live her life. This Old Wisdom tradition is about recognizing the Power within, and daring to take the journey into that Self-knowledge.

The Crone is known as the Dark One/Dark Goddess, since Her realm is that of the waxing Dark. She leads us into the Void. Hers is the Underworld, that Place at the foundations of Life, where things are broken-down, de-composed, dissolved; where the old ways are no longer known and the new can only be listened and felt for. It is necessary to come to a re-valuing of the Dark to understand Her. In the earliest of times the night was perceived as part of the day[106]—night was not the absence of light. The night was alive with its own kind of life. Even into more recent times (this past millennium), the day was reckoned from noon to noon; midnight was the centre position. A meridian then indicated the full moon overhead at midnight, not the high point of noon as it is now understood—the term "meridian" was coined from Mary-Diana, the Moon-Goddess.[107] The first calendars were lunar and menstrual. The light, or what we today call the "day", was understood to emerge out of the dark/night; as indeed all of manifest reality seems to. For some religious traditions the day still begins in the evening, and the Catholic Church still calculates many of its holy days on the lunar calendar. The seven day week is a calculation of the menstrual calendar.[108] The Darkness of Goddess is a rich fertile Place, seething with possibility and all that is necessary for Life to begin afresh. Her Darkness is where the new and undreamed of may be conceived. I think of it as the "quantum vacuum" that physicists speak about. Brian Swimme says,

---

104. Just as the rape of Persephone—one who is Seed of Life/Redeemer/Eternal Thread—may be understood as a story of the dis-integration of the Female Metaphor/Goddess. These stories may be understood as records of the loss of an integrity that went before, just as Campbell notes was true of the story of the dismembering of Tiamat by Marduk, *The Power of Myth*, p.170.
105. Hélène Cixous, "The Laugh of the Medusa", Signs 1 no. 22, p.885.
106. The day was "diurnal"—containing light and dark aspects. It is symptomatic of our present consciousness that "day" has come to mean only the light part.
107. Barbara G. Walker, *The Woman's Encyclopaedia of Myths and Secrets*, p.647.
108. Barbara G. Walker, *The Woman's Encyclopaedia of Myths and Secrets*, p.645.

> Modern science allows us to reapprehend…the superessential darkness of (the
> Divine) in what quantum physicists refer to as the quantum vacuum out of
> which elementary particles emerge and what I refer to as the all-nourishing
> abyss.[109]

The Crone's Dark Space is often symbolized in the Cauldron—a place of transformation, where the new is cooked up. She is the Wisdom, the "Organizing
Principle" that knows the recipe; She can be trusted to deliver from deep within.
Her cauldron is not for mixing poison as we've been told, but it is a Cauldron of
Creativity, frequently found at the bottom of deep fears, volcanic emotion, deep
sadness. Within Her dark Space is found the essence for re-membering. As Patricia Reis reflects,

> Whenever I have felt the Dark Goddess' consciousness filling me there is
> always an accompanying dread. I know my life will never be the same. I know
> that I am being initiated into a new aspect of myself, a new part of my jour-
> ney, which exists separate from my relationships to anyone else. And yet there
> is also a sureness, a firmness, a resoluteness, as in a re-solution.[110]

Often She is met unprepared: through an accident, an illness, an emotional
break—somehow we are broken down, torn apart. Sometimes change may have
been desired but the way unknown. Hers is an invitation to transformation.
When I speak of Crone, I understand Her as *"She Who Creates a Space to Be"*,
(where Virgin is *Urge to Be*, and Mother is *Place to Be*). She can be **felt** in the
need to exhale, to empty—in the release. She is felt in the ending of things, in the
shed skins of all your old shapes—who you have been, and are no longer. She
may be felt as pain, or as joy, or as both. Her symbol is sometimes the sword; She
cuts through illusion, and that vision is sometimes hard to bear. Hers is a fierce
love, which can be felt when you love but something needs to change. She is
known in the anger, in the "No more!",[111] in the chaos of dismantling a structure
no longer needed. The Crone can be seen in the seed pod, the peeling bark, the
pruned branches, the scissors cutting the thread. She is the Dissolver, the Trans-

---

109. Brian Swimme, in Dominic Flamiano, "A Conversation with Brian Swimme". Original Blessing Nov/Dec 1997, p.10—brackets my paraphrase: Brian Swimme had
  used the term "God", meaning "the Divine".
110. Patricia Reis, "The Dark Goddess", Woman of Power Issue 8, p.82.
111. An expression from *Song of Hecate* by Bridget McKern (1993), written in the last ses-
  sion of a series on Goddess that I was teaching. See Appendix B for the full text of
  her poem.

former—symbolized and expressed in the image of the waning crescent sliver of the moon, before she disappears. She is the Nurturant Darkness that fills your being, comforts the Sentience in you, allows new constellations to gestate in you.

I associate the Crone with the Dharma, the Truth-As-It-Is. She sees all Truth and can bear it, and Her Compassion is without end. She allows us to let go of our small self limitations,[112] and is *She Who Creatively Returns Us To All.*

The Triple Goddess

She has these faces, but She is One. These faces kaleidoscope into each other, they blur, they support each other, they are in each other—if they were not Life would not go on, for She is a continuous Thread, a multivalent Urge. The three are reflected in each other like a never-ending mirrored reflection, thus the numinosity associated with multiples of three since ancient times; all such multiples were considered to speak a Divine Harmony of some kind.

As Carolyn McVickar Edwards tells the Celtic version:

> ...the endlessly boiling Cauldron was stirred by Nine Sisters....The Nine Sisters represent the Holy Trinity of Maiden, Mother, and Crone, each able to manifest all three of Her selves.[113]

The Cauldron is "the Pot of the World", the Cosmos itself, and its magic "is that of endlessly shifting shapes", such as we are witness to in the evolutionary story of Gaia—this is Her everyday magic, displayed before us, and in which we are immersed. It is stirred by the Triple Goddess—the Female Metaphor in Her three aspects, the Evolutionary Cosmic Dynamics. As such, She is no simple linear Process, nor only two-dimensional, nor even just a few dimensions, but a web that radiates completely in all directions filling all space, like a Cosmic Sea of Superstrings.

As I deepened into each face, at the Sabbat that celebrated each one particularly, I came to insights into the particular face but also into the collective nature—the relationship—of the triad. There was sometimes a tendency and a temptation to

---

112. Similar to the capacities of self-transcendence and self-dissolution of holons, Willis Harman & Elisabet Sahtouris, *Biology Revisioned*, p.18.
113. Carolyn McVickar Edwards, *The Storyteller's Goddess*, p.152.

distinguish the Three from the One that they are, and to imagine a Background out of which the Triple One emerges; that is, to split this One into yet another aspect, to speculate about a fourth element.

In the third year of the academic research, as I worked on the Lammas teaching, and was reflecting on the face of the Crone as I was sensing Her, I was identifying this face almost completely with a perceived Background, the Great Void, the All-Nourishing Abyss[114]…as if the Old One/Crone was *the* One. And I have still done that here in these chapters at times; and yet I have felt there was/is something more. This is the text from my journal as I came to this dawning awareness:

> There is some distinction to be made between the formless Void/Great Sentience out of whom we all arise and the Old One who returns us to this. The distinction is always arbitrary. Is there any real distinction to be made between Manifestation/Form or the Light—the Virgin, and the Formless Void out of which it All arises? Perhaps it is that our distinctions are the mistake, the error. There is a fourth element then to this metaphor and it is the Background, the Deep Void, that is the Plenum upon which the three play out a movement, a motion. In fact none of them are distinct from the Formless Void, from Love, out of which All arises. All three are immersed in Love, are aspects of Love. Perhaps then my reason for identifying the Old One particularly with Love, in this Lammas celebration, is part of the re-storying of the Dark to Love. We so often associate Manifestation/Light with Love…that's easy, we've been doing that for quite a long time—Christmas, the Birth of the Holy Child, Winter Solstice. But to re-instate the Dark One as a manifestation of Love is what I need to do, to understand. Thus perhaps my particular association of this celebration with Her, with Love.

So while I was beginning to realize and sense that each face was a face of Love, of the Background, of the All-Nourishing Abyss, of All-That-Is, I still needed at this stage to express the Dark One particularly as this Totality. I understood that and allowed myself this counterbalancing indwelling and expression.

The point is that our minds will often want to separate the Three out from All-That-Is, and experientially They can't be. Further to this, sometime later, it was suggested that I add "Matrix" into the describing of the Mother aspect of Goddess. However, I did not really want to put it there, though it seemed correct to do so. I was aware that at that particular point I was making some arbitrary dis-

---

114. Brian Swimme's term for the void out of which all arises, *Hidden Heart of the Cosmos*, p.97.

tinction between the Mother aspect as "*a*" face of All/Matrix, and "*the*" All/Matrix. Really when we understand the faces, none of them are distinct from the All/Matrix. *Together* they *are* the All/Matrix—the "Background", the All-Nourishing Abyss, the Plenum. I hold out from naming the Mother aspect as Matrix, though She of course is, yet so are the aspects of Virgin and Crone—and that is the point. It seems to me that as we deepen into knowledge of the Virgin and Crone aspects, we will sense the "Matrix" in those facets too, that They-All-Three cannot be separated. They are indeed a Holy Trinity, a collaborative Cosmogenetic Dynamic that unfolds All, that "stirs the Pot". Most can sense or know a "Depth of Love"—the All—in the Mother aspect; I was just beginning through this process of re-storying and ritual to sense and know the Depth of Love—the All—in the Dark One, and to guess at the Depth of Love—the All—in the Virgin.

4

Cosmogenesis and the Female Metaphor

Charlene Spretnak has noted that:

> When a woman raised in patriarchal culture...immerses herself in sacred space where various manifestations of the Goddess bring forth the Earthbody from the spinning void...She will body the myth with her own totemic being. She is the cosmic form of waxing, fullness, waning: virgin, mature creator, wise crone. She cannot be negated ever again. Her roots are too deep—and they are everywhere.[1]

I propose that this may be true also for a man, who immerses himself in sacred space where various manifestations of Goddess bring forth Earthbody, where he may body the myth, the story, with his own totemic being, for She—the Female Metaphor—is the cosmic form of waxing, fullness and waning: a Dynamic that is everywhere, omnipresent. Brian Swimme has affirmed that "when he had reflected and meditated on the pre-Hellenic myths until he 'became filled with a myth'",[2] that his thinking about "natural phenomena and the entire universe were qualitatively different" from for instance, a "patriarchal, industrialized, competitive...frame of reference." His experience led him to conclude that the myths had a very deep biological basis, that could alter our relationship to the universe, and thus the universe itself, if we allowed ourselves to be filled with them.[3]

Swimme and Berry have noted often in their reflections on the story of the unfolding Universe, that Western industrialized peoples have become dissociated from, or autistic to, the Earth community and the Cosmos. Berry has suggested

---

1.   Charlene Spretnak, *States of Grace*, p.143.
2.   Charlene Spretnak, *Lost Goddesses of Early Greece*, p.xvii.
3.   Charlene Spretnak, *Lost Goddesses of Early Greece*, p.xvii.

that the only effective restoration of a viable mode of human presence on the planet is through a renewal of human intimacy "with the great cosmic liturgy of the natural world."[4] He suggests that the coordination of ritual celebrations with the transformation moments of the natural world—such as the "entrancing sequence" of the seasons—gives promise of a future "with the understanding, the power, the aesthetic grandeur, and the emotional fulfillment needed."[5] He suggests that such are the "entrancing qualities needed to endure the difficulties to be encountered and to evoke the creativity needed."[6] Berry believes that although we—the human and the entire planet—are in a moment of dangerous transition to a new era, a moment of significance far beyond our imagination, that we are "not lacking in the dynamic forces needed to create the future", that we need only invoke the abundant sea of energy in which we are immersed.[7]

If the Universe is understood to be "a single, multiform celebratory expression" as Thomas Berry and Brian Swimme affirm in their cosmic story, then we *are* the very Dynamics of Creativity, and only need to invoke these powers—these "originating powers" that permeate "every drop of existence".[8] As Charlene Spretnak affirms in *States of Grace*,

> we exist as participants in the greatest ritual: the cosmic ceremony of seasonal and diurnal rhythms framing epochal dramas of becoming…

and further,

> When people gather in a group to create ritual, they form a unitive body, a microcosmos of differentiation, subjectivity and deep communion.[9]

We may with practice—of a *religious* kind, as in a *connecting* kind—embody consciously, and grow into, our Earthly and Cosmic nature. This microcosmos—that we each are and that we may collectively express—of differentiation, subjectivity[10] and communion are three faces of Gaia's Cosmic method of Creativity, used everyday on planet Earth and throughout time and space in Her

4.   Thomas Berry, *The Great Work*, p.19.
5.   Thomas Berry, *The Great Work*, p.18-20.
6.   Thomas Berry, *The Great Work*, p.20.
7.   Thomas Berry, *The Great Work*, p.175.
8.   Brian Swimme and Thomas Berry, *The Universe Story*, p.78.
9.   Charlene Spretnak, *States of Grace*, p.145.

ever-transforming Cosmogenesis. In my Poetic Search, I have associated these three faces of Cosmogenesis with the three faces of the Female Metaphor—the three faces that the ancients noticed reiterated all around them. The dynamic was everywhere as I will describe, and the ancients—scientists in their observation of the world, of which they felt a part, noticed its dimensions.

Gaia's Creative Dynamics

The Moon was a sliver of light when She first appeared out of darkness, She waxed from there into fullness, and then waned to a sliver in the opposite direction, before disappearing into the darkness from whence She came. It was noticed by the women and perhaps some of the men, that the female body cycled with the Moon, waxing into desire and fertility, and waning into menstrual loss. All the body cycles repeated these faces: there was hunger, there was satiation, there was elimination. There was the urge to breathe, it waxed into fullness, there was the need to release—back into the emptiness from whence another could arise. The buds of flowers blossomed into fullness, then lost their petals, revealing seed pods from whence to begin again. The buds of leaves burgeoned out of dead looking branches, unfurled into greenery, then dropped away. Everywhere on the globe, on a daily basis, light emerged out of darkness—at dawn, waxed into the fullness of noon, then declined back into darkness. On an annual basis, the Sun's light emerged out of the darkness of Winter, waxed into fullness at Summer, then declined back into darkness.

The darkness itself each day, was understood as an equal part the "day"—a "day" was not only the light part. We have to speak of it today as the "diurnal" day, to recall the sense that the dark part was included. It may have even been the main part—the basis of measuring time. The darkness was a time for rest, perhaps relief from the heat, perhaps a time to seek comfort from the cold—but almost always felt keenly as a time of dreams, perception of subtleties not so noticeable in the world of light. And the darkness of the sky was sprinkled with pinpoints of light in which the ancients could imagine their own forms and those of creatures: the night sky told stories. When the ancients created their own pinpoints of light—made fire, they told their own stories as well. This darkness of the diurnal

---

10.   Swimme and Berry have at an earlier time, named the "autopoiesis" face of Cosmo-genesis as "subjectivity". By time they wrote *The Universe Story* they had changed the name to "autopoiesis".

day was fertile with life, a different kind of life. So too then, the death of the human must be a journey, like a long sleep, or an entry into a different kind of life. The plants grew above the Earth in the light, but the seeds sprouted in the dark, and emerged from there, and remained rooted in the dark to whence the plants would return. The darkness was understood to be the place of beginning—all things appeared to begin there—the womb, the Earth, the dead looking branch, the emptiness before a breath. Today Western science also suggests that the Universe itself seems to be mostly a sea of Dark Matter, out of which all emerges.

The triple dynamic as a whole, complexifies in the web of Life—the Universe itself is a display of these "primordial orderings" as Swimme and Berry describe them—and "the very existence of the universe rests on the power of these orderings", which govern the universe's arising "spontaneities".[11] Swimme and Berry state that "enshrined in the Cosmogenetic Principle, is that in this universe there are entirely natural powers of form production that, when given the proper conditions, will create galaxies."[12] Swimme and Berry name the three aspects/themes of Cosmogenesis as differentiation, communion and autopoiesis, yet with the understanding that each face/feature really defies pinning down to "any simple one-line univocal definition."[13] Swimme and Berry supply a list of perceived synonyms for each, that do indeed overlap in their definitions, though each remains a distinguishable dynamic of cosmic evolution. Those synonyms are: for differentiation—"diversity, complexity, variation, disparity, multiform nature, heterogeneity, articulation"; for communion—"interrelatedness, interdependence, kinship, mutuality, internal relatedness, reciprocity, complementarity, interconnectivity and affiliation"; and for autopoiesis—"subjectivity, self-manifestation, sentience, self-organization, dynamic centres of experience, presence, identity, inner principle of being, voice, interiority."[14] Swimme and Berry assume that "these three will undoubtedly be deepened and altered in the next era as future experience expands our present understanding."[15]

11. Brian Swimme and Thomas Berry, *The Universe Story*, p.72.
12. Brian Swimme and Thomas Berry, *The Universe Story*, p.70.
13. Brian Swimme and Thomas Berry, *The Universe Story*, p.71.
14. Brian Swimme and Thomas Berry, *The Universe Story*, p.71-72.
15. Brian Swimme and Thomas Berry, *The Universe Story*, p.72.

This complexity and "fuzziness" of the terms for the evolutionary cosmic dynamics is mirrored in the metaphor of the Triple Goddess. "Fuzziness" is a term used by scientist and philosopher Vladimir Dimitrov, who describes that:

> According to fuzzy set theory, the meaning of words cannot be precisely defined—each linguistic construct in use can be described by a set of 'degrees of freedom', i.e. ways of understanding (interpretation, transformation into actions) by individuals or groups.[16]

And so it is for these names of the faces of the Female Metaphor. Each face has a name and distinguishable qualities, and each face can be so suitably simplified, celebrated, mythologized and embodied—absorbed and understood in a Poetic way—enabling a creative alignment of the self and/or the collective, with this Gaian Power; yet each face is "impregnated with *virtual meaning* that provide space for extension, elaboration and negotiation…" as Dimitrov describes in reference to "fuzzy concepts".[17] Just so, is each embodied face of the Female Metaphor—a deep dynamic, a "primordial ordering" of being.

Adam McLean, a researcher who has spent much time studying and meditating upon the Triple Goddess, describes relationship/alignment with Her as releasing "such a powerful current of creative energy as few have ever experienced."[18] He contends that She "remains a key to unlocking the store of ancient energies and spiritual wisdom" bound up within.[19] He speaks of the complexity of her guises, how She challenges our usual thinking with seeming contradictions and inconsistencies, yet he senses that She holds within Her all polarities—an integration of being that seems necessary for the "spiritual energies of the future" as he describes.[20]

---

16. Vladimir Dimitrov, "Fuzzy Logic in Service to a Better World: the Social Dimensions of Fuzzy Sets", in *Complexity, Organisations, Fuzziness*, p.3. The website address of "Introduction to Fuzziology" is http://www.uws.edu.au/vip/dimitrov/fuzzysoc.htm

17. Vladimir Dimitrov, "Fuzzy Logic in Service to a Better World: the Social Dimensions of Fuzzy Sets", in *Complexity, Organisations, Fuzziness*, p.5.

18. Adam McLean, *The Triple Goddess*, p.12.

19. Adam McLean, *The Triple Goddess*, p.17.

20. Adam McLean, *The Triple Goddess*, p.12.

The Three Faces of Cosmogenesis Developed

Describing differentiation, which I associate with the Virgin aspect—the Urge to Be, passionate love of every individual self, Swimme and Berry say,

> From the articulated energy constellations we call the elementary particles and atomic beings, through the radiant structures of the animate world, to the complexities of the galaxy with its planetary systems, we find a universe of unending diversity…The more intimately we become acquainted with anything, the clearer our recognition of its differences from everything else…There has never been a time when the universe did not seek further differentiation. In the beginning all the particles interacted with each other with minimal distinction. But with the cosmic symmetry breaking, four branches of interactions differentiated from each other. From the thermal equilibrium of the fireball the universe sprouted into a universe differentiated by galaxies, with no two galaxies identical.[21]

Swimme and Berry note that although it is the endeavour of science to refer to the way in which structures are similar—stars, atoms, cells or society—the more deeply we come to know a thing—the Milky Way, the fall of Rome, the species on a particular tree in a rainforest—the more deeply we perceive its "ineffable uniqueness". They note then that not only is each thing new and different, but that the dynamics of relationship between the new structures are qualitatively and quantitatively different. They add that,

> This diversity of relatedness pertains to human knowing as well—knowledge represents a particular relationship we establish in the world…An integral relationship with the universe's differentiated energy constellations requires a multivalent understanding that includes a full spectrum of modes of knowing.[22]

They find that when the thirteen point seven billion year epic of the Universe's unfolding is viewed as a whole, with its extravagant creative outpouring, there is the revelation of the uniqueness of the creativity of each place and time, and the existence of each being.

---

21.   Brian Swimme and Thomas Berry, *The Universe Story*, p.73.
22.   Brian Swimme and Thomas Berry, *The Universe Story*, p.74.

My own Poetic translation of Swimme and Berry's expressions regarding Cosmogenesis proceeds in the following way. When they say that the universe "at each instant has re-created itself anew", and that this seemingly infinite power "speaks of an inexhaustible fecundity at the root of reality",[23] I imagine it in "Goddess-speak". That is, "the Virgin dynamic of unique beauty expressed and celebrated in early Spring, has layered within, the fertility that is expressed and celebrated in High Spring (Beltane), as She changes into the Mother dynamic of Summer, whose fertility rests in the Dark Interiority of the Old One expressed and celebrated particularly in Deep Autumn (Samhain)." This translation of mine is kin to William Irwin Thompson's translation of Lynn Margulis' description of her study of bacteria: he says that when he saw her film about bacteria, his thoughts "on the relationship between myth and science took a jump forward" as he began to understand what his Irish ancestors meant when they had spoken of "the little people" at work in the leaf mold at their feet.[24]

Even as Swimme and Berry define differentiation, the three aspects are constantly drawn into the equation, and again with this perception: "The multiform relatedness demanded by a differentiated universe rests upon the fact that each individual thing in the universe is ineffable."[25] The sentience or interiority or presence of each unique thing/being evokes relatedness in mind-boggling complexity. To help one understand the way in which the aspects support each other, Swimme and Berry imagine:

> Were there no differentiation, the universe would collapse into a homogenous smudge; were there no subjectivity, the universe would collapse into inert, dead extension; were there no communion, the universe would collapse into isolated singularities of being.[26]

Each aspect does not really exist without the others, yet each has its own integrity. In the case of the dynamic of differentiation, Swimme and Berry say that, to understand the Universe—the entire display—to get the full picture, we must understand the absolute freshness of each being and each moment.

---

23. Brian Swimme and Thomas Berry, *The Universe Story*, p.74.
24. William Irwin Thompson, *Gaia: A Way of Knowing*, p.7. He says that when Lynn Margulis spoke of bacteria laying down the iron ore deposits in the Gunflint formations of Ontario, he saw dwarves at work in the mines.
25. Brian Swimme and Thomas Berry, *The Universe Story*, p.74.
26. Brian Swimme and Thomas Berry, *The Universe Story*, p.73.

Describing communion, which I associate with the Mother aspect—the sustaining, relating Context, the reciprocal Place of Being, the passionate pouring forth for other, Swimme and Berry say,

> …relationship is the essence of existence. In the very first instant when the primitive particles rushed forth, every one of them was connected to every other one in the entire universe. At no time in the future existence of the universe would they ever arrive at a point of disconnection. Alienation for a particle is a theoretical impossibility. For galaxies too, relationships are the fact of existence. Each galaxy is directly connected to the hundred billion galaxies of the universe, and there will never come a time when a galaxy's destiny does not involve each of the galaxies in the universe.

> Nothing is itself without everything else. Our Sun emerged into being out of the creativity of so many millions of former beings. The elements of the floating presolar cloud had been created by former stars and by the primeval fireball…The patterns of nuclear resonances enabling stable nuclear burning was not the Sun's invention—and yet all that followed depended upon this pattern of interconnectivity in which the Sun arose.[27]

So it is with any entity, with any being—we arise within a pattern of interconnectivity, the beneficiaries of the creativity of former beings, supported by everything that has gone before.

Swimme and Berry point out that a sense of relatedness is at the base of being, present even before a first interaction—that this is true in the earliest eras of the Universe's unfolding at the quantum level of particles, present to each other in a direct and unmediated relationship; as well as in later eras as the biosphere of Earth unfolded. They give the example of an unborn grizzly bear, as being already related to the outside world in that she will not have to develop a taste for the foods bears eat, and she is already shaped for her environment and the survival tasks ahead of her; that is, we are already in relationship by the fact of our being—relationships then "are discovered, even more than they are forged."[28]

Once again, in the process of defining the one aspect—this time communion—all three aspects are drawn into the equation. They say, "…the universe

---

27.   Brian Swimme and Thomas Berry, *The Universe Story*, p.77.
28.   Brian Swimme and Thomas Berry, *The Universe Story*, p.77.

advances into community—into a differentiated web of relationships amongst sentient centers of creativity."[29] As I noted in the last chapter, quoting storyteller Carolyn McVikar Edwards, the Nine Sisters who stir the Cauldron "represent the Holy Trinity of Maiden, Mother, and Crone, each able to manifest all three of Her selves."[30] And so it is with the three faces of Cosmogenesis…as Swimme and Berry say: "These three features are themselves features of each other."[31]

The eating of food is a communion experience—it enters into the being. It is also a dissolution and a breaking down, in which the food becomes something new—it gets trans-formed into activity, thought, emotions and ideas. Swimme says that "we eat an orange, and it gets turned into poetry!"[32] All three dynamics are present and cannot be separated. Mating rituals—in the human world or in the world of other creatures—are communion experiences. Swimme and Berry note that the desire for relationships of true intimacy is obvious in the music and dance of the world, and in the energy given to attracting relationship—revealing something of the ultimate meaning of reciprocal presence.

Describing autopoiesis, which I associate with the Crone aspect—the Return to the Dark Sentience, the Wisdom of the Ages within, a passionate commitment to transformation, Swimme and Berry say:

> From autocatalyctic chemical processes to cells, from living bodies to galaxies, we find a universe filled with structures exhibiting self-organizing dynamics. The self that is referred to by autopoiesis is not visible to the eye. Only its effects can be discerned….the unifying principle of an organism as a mode of being of the organism is integral with but distinct from the entire range of physical components of the organism….Living beings and such ecosystems as the tropical forests or the coral reefs are the chief exemplars of self-organizing dynamics, but with the term autopoiesis we wish to point not just to living beings, but to self-organizing powers in general. Autopoiesis refers to the power each thing has to participate directly in the cosmos-creating endeavor. For instance, we have spoken of the autopoiesis of a star. The star organizes hydrogen and helium and produces elements and light. This ordering is the central activity of the star itself. That is, the star has a functioning self, a dynamic of organization centered within itself….With such an understanding of the term, we can see that an atom is a self-organizing system as well. Each

---

29. Brian Swimme and Thomas Berry, *The Universe Story*, p.77.
30. Carolyn McVikar Edwards, *The Storyteller's Goddess*, p.152.
31. Brian Swimme and Thomas Berry, *The Universe Story*, p.73.
32. Brian Swimme, *Canticle to the Cosmos*, video 4.

atom is a storm of ordered activity....A galaxy, too, is an autopoietic system, organizing its stars into a nonequilibrium process and drawing forth new stars from its interstellar materials.

Autopoiesis points to the interior dimension of things. Even the simplest atom cannot be understood by considering only its physical structure or the outer world of external relationships with other things. Things emerge with an inner capacity for self-manifestation.[33]

Swimme and Berry put forth the question then about the sentience of the elemental realm,

...for we now realize that where Earth was once molten rock, it now fills its air with the songs of birds. And if humans bask in an astounding feeling for the universe, and the human arose from the elements, what can be said of the inner world of the elements?[34]

They answer this partly, implying innate sentience, by affirming the need "to preserve the continuity holding together an integral universe" and the need to "avoid regarding consciousness as an addendum or as an intrusion into reality."[35] They do also allow for an apparent "discontinuity" which enables the universe to unfold through a sequence of transformations. Their interpretation is that the universe is "a place where qualities that will one day bloom are for the present hidden as dimensions of emptiness"[36]—qualities are not yet perceived or manifest. Swimme and Berry affirm that, the universe is a single "multiform energy event", that "everything comes forth out of the intrinsic creativity of the universe"—a "latent hidden nothingness of being", and they speak of the "potential sentience" in early elemental forms.[37] They say:

The rocks and water and air, just by being what they are, find themselves flowering forth with sentient beings. At the very least we can say that the future experience in a latent form is wrapped into the activity of rocks, for within the turbulence of molten magma, self-organizing powers are evoked that bring forth a new shape—animals capable of being racked with terror or stunned by awe of the very universe out of which they emerged.[38]

---

33. Brian Swimme and Thomas Berry, *The Universe Story*, p.75.
34. Brian Swimme and Thomas Berry, *The Universe Story*, p.76.
35. Brian Swimme and Thomas Berry, *The Universe Story*, p.76.
36. Brian Swimme and Thomas Berry, *The Universe Story*, p.76.
37. Brian Swimme and Thomas Berry, *The Universe Story*, p.76.

In a recent interview Brian Swimme gave a short version of the whole story of evolution: he said,

> You take hydrogen gas, and you leave it alone, and it turns into rosebushes, giraffes, and humans." He went on, "...The reason I like that version is that hydrogen gas is odorless and colorless, and in the prejudice of our Western civilization, we see it as just material stuff. There's not much there. You just take hydrogen, leave it alone, and it turns into a human—that's a pretty interesting bit of information. The point is that if humans are spiritual, then hydrogen's spiritual. It's an incredible opportunity to escape dualism—you know, spirit is up there; matter is down here. Actually, it's different. You have the matter all the way through, and so you have the spirit all the way through.[39]

By "autopoiesis", Swimme and Berry are pointing to an interior dimension of things. It seems to me that for them, this aspect/face seems sometimes overwhelmingly associated with the Great Mystery itself—much as I have at times overwhelmingly associated the Old/Dark One with Love itself (as mentioned in Chapter 3). Yet "autopoiesis" and the Old Dark One/Crone are both only meant to be an aspect of the whole Creative Dynamic, and so they are; perhaps in both cases, the emphasis on this aspect's centrality to Creativity is partly compensatory, given the cultural denial of it.[40] Certainly though, it taps the central Creativity of the All-Nourishing Abyss in a dramatic way—whether it be in the collapse of a star, or in the death of a loved one. Vision and perhaps trust are needed to comprehend such destruction as creative—creative of a larger picture than is ours to hold. When "autopoiesis" is described as "an inner capacity for self-manifestation",[41] the self that is being spoken of is the self that at once belongs and "knows"[42] it belongs, to the Larger Self—which is the Source of the Passion to manifest and to organize.

---

38. Brian Swimme and Thomas Berry, *The Universe Story*, p.76-77.

39. Susan Bridle, "Comprehensive Compassion: An Interview with Brian Swimme", What Is Enlightenment? No. 19, p.40.

40. The imaging by Swimme and Berry of autopoiesis as ***the*** place within, of direct contact with the cosmos—may suggest that the other two aspects are not. This would be an incomplete comprehension or expression of the other two aspects. Upon reflection, these other two aspects cannot be separated out from autopoiesis, and do also contact directly, simply in a different way; that is, the urge to differentiated manifest form and the weaving into relational being are as integral with the Larger Self as the creative centre.

41. Brian Swimme and Thomas Berry, *The Universe Story*, p.75.

Loren Eiseley refers to a mysterious organizing principle, without which life does not persist—

> yet this organization itself is not strictly the product of life, nor of selection. Like some dark and passing shadow within matter, it cups out the eyes' small windows or spaces the meadow lark's song in the interior of a mottled egg.[43]

He speaks of the manifest world as

> an apparition from that mysterious shadow world beyond nature, that contains—if anything contains—the explanation of men (sic) and catfish and green leaves.[44]

This organizing principle that he perceives, is the One I identify with Swimme and Berry's autopoiesis, and the ancient face of the Old Wise Dark One.

The Three Biological Shaping Powers and the Female Metaphor

Swimme and Berry note that biological life on planet Earth is shaped by "three fundamentally related, though distinct causes",[45] and they reflect that these powers further illustrate the "root creativity" of the Universe that finds expression in the three faces of Cosmogenesis.[46] These three shaping powers of the biosphere, of life's journey here on Earth, are genetic mutation, natural selection and conscious choice/niche creation. I in turn find in their descriptions of these three biological shaping powers, a further articulation of the nature of the three faces of the Female Metaphor.

Swimme and Berry find in genetic mutation a biological illustration of differentiation—it is this power of mutation that gives rise to genetic variation. They describe it as a "pressure toward the future within each moment (that includes) a

---

42. This "knowing" is meant in the broadest sense—not only referring to the human reflective knowing, but also to other ways of "knowing" by other beings and entities.
43. Loren Eiseley, *The Immense Journey*. p.26.
44. Loren Eiseley, *The Immense Journey*. p.27.
45. Brian Swimme and Thomas Berry, *The Universe Story*, p.125.
46. Brian Swimme and Thomas Berry, *The Universe Story*, p.132.

pressure for uniqueness",[47] and I have come to identify Virgin energy—*the Urge To Be*—this way. They describe this dynamic with various words such as "*chance, random, stochastic* and *error*", finally summarizing the quality as *wild*—"a great beauty that seethes with intelligence, that is ever surprising and refreshing."[48] I associate such a description with the Virgin, particularly as She is celebrated at Beltane—High Spring. I came to call this "the Poetry of genetic creation", which is an allusion to Thomas Berry's seventh principle of a functional cosmology, where he is stating the significance of the genetic coding process for life's expression and being.[49]

For Swimme and Berry, natural selection illustrates the dynamic of communion—it is this power that *sculpts* the diversity, *crafts* it. They describe natural selection as a

> dynamic of interrelatedness…that presses, always and everywhere, for a deep intimacy of togetherness…(deep into) the very structure of genes, body, mind.[50]

Swimme and Berry describe natural selection as a communal reality—a bonding process—wherein a species engages in finding its place in a biophysical community, and this seems similar to David Abram's understanding of it as a "reciprocal phenomenon"[51]—a dialogue or conversation between the organism and the environment. The conventional and popular notion of the environment being "fixed", and to which the organism must conform was challenged by biologist Lynn Margulis in her groundbreaking research.[52] These descriptions of the flux between organism and Earth, as a co-creation of place, have deepened my understanding of the nature of the Mother face of the Female Metaphor—as *the Place*

---

47. Brian Swimme and Thomas Berry, *The Universe Story*, p.133.
48. Brian Swimme and Thomas Berry, *The Universe Story*, p.126-127.
49. See Appendix A.
50. Brian Swimme and Thomas Berry, *The Universe Story*, p.134.
51. David Abram, "The Mechanical and the Organic" in *Gaia in Action*, p.247.
52. Margulis refers to the work of Russian scientist Vladimir Vernadsky and philosopher of science Karl Popper, saying that: "the activities of each organism lead to continuously changing environments. The oxygen we breathe, the humid atmosphere inside of which we live, and the mildly alkaline ocean waters in which the kelp and whales bathe are not determined by a physical universe run by mechanical laws; the surroundings are products of life interacting at the planet's surface." Cited in Connie Barlow (ed.), *From Gaia to Selfish Genes: Selected Writings in the Life Sciences*, p.237.

to Be; a Place that is a dynamic point of Interchange, a vibrant Reciprocity, that is celebrated particularly at the Winter and Summer Solstices. The Solstices are points of interchange between the light and the dark, the dark and the light, where one is seeded in the other. I came to call these Seasonal Moments, "Gateways"—places of Birth, either into form or into dissolution; they are points that celebrate life's transitions of birth and death, the holy Moments of the annual cycle that celebrate the interchange between the biological self (a singularity, be it species or individual) and existence (All-That-Is).

Swimme and Berry describe the third biological shaping power of niche creation or conscious choice as a biological illustration of the Cosmogenetic dynamic of autopoiesis.[53] Ordinarily, scientific accounts do not give niche creation/conscious choice as much importance as the other two biological shaping powers, but Swimme and Berry argue for its equal inclusion saying that at points of major evolutionary change, conscious choice becomes the primary explanation for the change. They call for more recognition of the self-organizing dynamics within all life forms—"behavior that can be interpreted as manifestations of memory, of discernment concerning questions of temperature and nutrient concentration, of a basic irreducible intelligence."[54] They express that even minimal powers of this kind have resulted in primal decisions on the part of organisms which have sent the biosphere into pathways forever characterized by those decisions. As a premise to their perception Swimme and Berry argue against the conventional notion of a "fixed environment" pointing out its limitations, stating rhetorically that a species always creates its own niche. They present the example of the horse and the bison who come from a common ancestor but are now very different forms of life—the different choices made by their primordial ancestors created two different worlds, with different selection pressures constellated for each, and these shaping the genetic diversity accordingly.[55] They describe this dynamic of niche creation as a felt "vision" or simple thrill wherein the creature responds to this inner attraction to pursue a particular path—much like the power of imagination draws the human. I associate this energy with the Crone, particularly as She is celebrated at Samhain—Deep Autumn, drawing forth the future, conceiving the new, from Her Dark Sentient Depths. In the human this imaginative power is sometimes simply felt, sometimes "seen", always an act of will. I came to

---

53. Brian Swimme and Thomas Berry, *The Universe Story*, p.132.
54. Brian Swimme and Thomas Berry, *The Universe Story*, p.132.
55. Brian Swimme and Thomas Berry, *The Universe Story*, p.136-138.

call this "the Poetry of trans-genetic creation" which is an allusion to Thomas Berry's ninth principle of a functional cosmology, where he is stating the significance of human language—"cultural coding".

Whitehead's "Threefold Creative Composition"

Process philosopher, Alfred North Whitehead also perceived the Universe as including a composition of a "threefold creative act". He describes these three as

> (i) the one infinite conceptual realization, (ii) the multiple solidarity of free physical realizations in the temporal world, (iii) the ultimate unity of the multiplicity of actual fact with the primordial conceptual fact.[56]

I note some congruencies of this threefold composition with the Female Metaphor, as well as some points of departure. Whitehead conceives his first and the third aspects as having a unity, which is also true of the Virgin and Crone aspects of the Female Metaphor—the beginning and the end are barely distinguishable in their felt proximity to Source; the continuity of the "Urge to Return" and the "Urge to Be" may be more obvious than their continuity with the "Place of Being". We are always returning to the Unity—it is integral with Life; and we are always being regenerated—reconceived: our bodyminds in a constant state of renewal, and both the Virgin and Crone energies inseparably allow this. We are part of some Great Cycle of Returning and Renewal, and the Manifest Reality—the Mother, the "physical realization" as Whitehead describes his second aspect—is the place of Communion. However Whitehead puts the first and third aspects "over against" the second aspect. He admits the power of the second aspect, as he describes that the "sheer force of things lies in the intermediate physical process: this is the energy of physical production",[57] but his "God" is merely "patient" with it. Whitehead says that "God's role…lies in the patient operation of the overpowering rationality of his conceptual harmonization."[58] Whitehead's point was that "God" did not create the world, that "he" was the poet of the world—leading it with "tender patience", but the language that he uses invokes

---

56. Alfred North Whitehead, "God and the World", in Ewert H. Cousins (ed), Process Theology, p.91.

57. Alfred North Whitehead, "God and the World", in Ewert H. Cousins (ed), Process Theology, p.91.

58. Alfred North Whitehead, "God and the World", in Ewert H. Cousins (ed), Process Theology, p.91.

and indicates a remnant of dualistic thinking, as does his splitting of the "three-fold creative act" into this oppositional situation. The cosmology of the Female Metaphor has resonances with Whitehead's philosophy, however he still speaks of a God as an entity as if external to creation, albeit at times also Creature and of "consequent nature"—that is, partly created by the world.[59]

Theologian Nancy Howell notes that Whitehead's "philosophy of organism", as she describes it, does provide a cosmology that radically differs from "dominant mechanistic and patriarchal worldviews", thus providing support for the constructing of a promising feminist theory of relations, a feminist ecological cosmology.[60] She describes how Whitehead's process philosophy has provided a "helpful conceptual framework" for the interpretation of women's experiences based as it is in relational, organic thinking that is systemically inclusive of an infinite range of experience, and promotes a continuity of the human with the cosmos/nature. Howell notes that Whitehead's philosophy promotes and reflects change, and enables the reinterpretation of many dualisms—subject/object, body/mind, reason/emotion, God/world.[61] Feminist theologians, for whom in general "God" remains an indelible metaphor, find the reinterpretation of the last mentioned dualism particularly hopeful. Howell describes that "the genius of Whitehead's metaphysics" is that "God and the world" truly affect each other, create each other, receive from each other—are "truly in relation":[62] Howell is thus confident that this metaphysics feeds "a feminist vision of mutuality".

This helps clarify then that the cosmology I am describing in this book goes further than a "feminist vision of mutuality". Howell still speaks of this "God" as a separate entity: to my mind this is still a "meta"-physics, not the "intra"-physics of the cosmogenetic dynamics of which I speak. Howell comes closest in her language to this "intra"-physics where she notes Rita Nakashima Brock's metaphor of "God/dess as Heart, the present divine erotic power".[63] Brock appears to have made the connection, the transition to an integral cosmology, where Whitehead's

---

59. Charles Hartshorne, "The Development of Process Philosophy", in Ewert H. Cousins (ed), Process Theology, p.53.

60. Nancy R. Howell, *A Feminist Cosmology: Ecology, Solidarity, and Metaphysics*, p. 13-14.

61. Nancy R. Howell, *A Feminist Cosmology: Ecology, Solidarity, and Metaphysics*, p. 22.

62. Nancy R. Howell, *A Feminist Cosmology: Ecology, Solidarity, and Metaphysics*, p. 31.

63. Nancy R. Howell, *A Feminist Cosmology: Ecology, Solidarity, and Metaphysics*, p. 32, quoting Rita Brock, *Journeys by Heart: A Christology of Erotic Power*, p.46.

metaphysics comes up short. As mythologist Joseph Campbell points out, " 'God' is an ambiguous word in our language because it appears to refer to something that is known"; elaborating that "in religions where the god or creator is the mother, the whole world is her body. There is nowhere else."[64]

The Spirochete as an Example of the Female Metaphor

The spirochete is a bacterium—one of the earliest forms of life on the planet. It is a prokaryote, a cell without a nucleus—of the kind that has been swimming around on Earth for four billion years, and with which Life proceeded to build further. The work of biologist Lynn Margulis on the earliest of life forms—bacteria—has been ground breaking and has changed the way Life may be perceived.[65] In her general theory of evolution, the spirochete—an ancient single rod bacterium that has neither head nor tail—is seen as the fundamental building block of life's unfolding. Many other later developments of Life—such as axons attached to neurons, spermatozoa attached to ova—Margulis saw as "a variant of the biological architecture of the attachment of the spirochete to the larger cell of the protist."[66] The spirochete, fundamental to the biosphere, moves randomly in a wave-like motion in its viscous aqueous medium seeking nutrition. William Irwin Thompson uses the spirochete to begin his story of the evolution of consciousness, and points out three factors associated with the spirochete dynamic—"the meat" or the rod of the spirochete, "the motion" or wavelike pattern, and "the waves it makes in its liquid medium by writhing in space."[67] These three factors associate very well in themselves and in their developing complexity, with the evolutionary cosmic dynamics of Cosmogenesis and the Female Metaphor; at the simplest layer of perception, the materia/meat is the Mother, the wavelike motion of the materia is the Urge/Virgin, the waves created in the liquid that ripple out in search of nutrients are the Crone/the Transformer.

Further, Thompson notes that even at this level of biological development, we encounter the factor of "distinction"—between one end of the rod that may have found food and thus becomes still and "listens" and "sucks", and the other end of the rod that may not have yet encountered a strong presence of food and contin-

---

64. Joseph Campbell, *The Power of Myth*, p.48-49.
65. See Connie Barlow (ed), *From Gaia to Selfish Genes: Selected Writings in the Life Sciences*, p.47-66, and also Elisabet Sahtouris, *Earthdance*, Ch.6 particularly p.100-103.
66. referred to in William Irwin Thompson, *Coming into Being*, p.18.
67. William Irwin Thompson, *Coming into Being*, p.21.

ues to writhe.[68] I find this factor of distinction kin to the primary distinction of light and dark—manifest and unmanifest—which is a major distinction in the Female Metaphor, and celebrated in the Wheel of the Year. In the case of the spirochete, the emergent property of the distinction between one end's activity and the other end's stillness, is "directional motion"; in the case of the light and dark parts of the Metaphor, the emergent property is ongoing creativity.

All this fires my poetic imagination, as it did Thompson's when he saw Lynn Margulis' film of the bacteria,[69] although mine specifically sees the ancient Triple Metaphor and the triple-fold cosmic dynamics at play. A further development to the first simple layer of perception of the three distinct factors of the spirochete is this: within the materia/meat of the rod—the Mother—is another whole depth…which is Sentience/Crone, and with its own differentiated entities—Virgin. And the wave in the liquid—associated with the sentience/interiority of autopoiesis—is also a communion, and also establishes a new relationship. The motion itself—the Urge—can only exist in the materia, or at least can only be seen/manifest there. At this time in scientific research, its manifestation remains a mystery. The Urge to writhe responds to feedback or presence in the liquid medium, either in the form of nutrition or of other spirochetes—its flagellating movement comes into synchrony with others after a period.

There is the question of explaining the stilling and "listening" of one end. Contemporary science favours a chemical explanation, while Thompson's "poetic imagination" entertains the theory that the stilling occurs when the spirochete receives back an echo/sonar wave from the "Other", though he suggests it may be "an interesting interaction of the two on the membrane of the bacterium."[70] My poetic imagination sees the Reciprocity between the unmanifest and the manifest—Dark and Light—as celebrated in the Wheel of the Year.

Beneath or within the form of the spirochete is another whole world, wherein the "microtubule" is the primary form, and the distinction is no longer the two states of writhing and stillness, and the emergent property is no longer directional motion, "but the single quantum state", as Thompson describes. By shifting one's threshold of perception, one may comprehend a different reality, "an emer-

---

68.   William Irwin Thompson, *Coming into Being*, p.22.
69.   William Irwin Thompson, *Gaia: A Way of Knowing*, p.7.
70.   William Irwin Thompson, *Coming into Being*, p.23.

gent property of coherence".[71] So it is with the Metaphor, and Her embodiment in the seasonal cycle of light and dark, when one shifts one's threshold of perception.

---

71. William Irwin Thompson, *Coming into Being*, p.26.

5

The Seasonal Moments—a PaGaian Wheel of the Year

The eight Sabbats/holy days in the traditional pre-Celtic Wheel of the Year are as follows: two Solstices—Winter and Summer, two Equinoxes—Autumn and Spring, and four cross-quarter days, that is, meridian points of each quarter of the year. There is a simple division into a light half during which the light is waxing—Winter through Spring to Summer, and a dark half during which the dark is waxing—Summer through Autumn to Winter. There is another division of the year into one half when the hours of light in a day are longer than the hours of dark—Spring Equinox through the Summer to Autumn Equinox, and the other half being when the hours of dark in a day are longer than the hours of light—Autumn Equinox through Winter to Spring Equinox. (See Figure 1[1]). On its simplest level, the light that is "born" at the Winter Solstice waxes through the Spring—at first being young and tender, before coming into balance with the dark at Equinox, then waxing into the strength and passion of High Spring (Beltane) and Summer. At the Summer Solstice, the dark that is "born" waxes through the Autumn—at first being a remembering of letting go or "harvest", before coming into balance with the light at Equinox, then waxing on into the dark transformation of Deep Autumn (Samhain) and Winter.

---

1.   The actual date of the Seasonal Moment varies from year to year. A good site to check for the details of global time and place is: http://archaeoastronomy.com/seasons.html The dates on my diagram are traditional and for the Southern Hemisphere. Annabelle Solomon notes that the South should really be at the top of the page for the Southern Hemisphere perspective. She does this in her diagram of the Wheel of the Year, *The Wheel of the Year: Seasons of the Soul in Quilts*, p.105—see APPENDIX E.

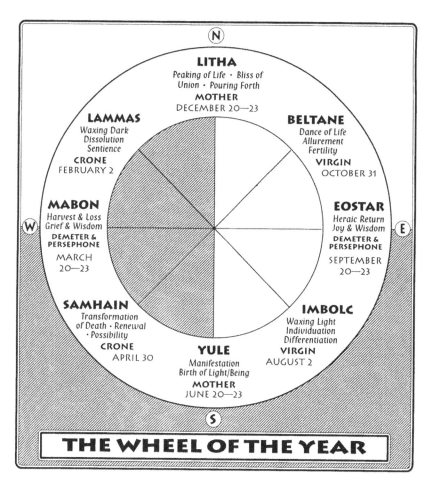

Figure 1: The dates are for the Southern Hemisphere. See footnote 1.

I commonly think of the light part of the cycle as acknowledging and celebrating the "manifest" reality, and the dark part of the cycle as acknowledging and celebrating the "unmanifest" or "manifesting" reality. I take these terms from David Abram's explanation of Benjamin Lee Whorf's work in analyzing the Hopi language:

> While Whorf did not find separable notions of space and time among the Hopi, he did discern, in the Hopi language, a distinction between two basic modalities of existence, which he terms the 'manifested' and the 'manifesting'.[2]

Abram summarizes the meaning of these terms with:

> The 'manifested',…is that aspect of phenomena already evident to our senses, while the 'manifesting' is that which is not yet explicit, not yet present to the senses, but which is assumed to be psychologically gathering itself toward manifestation within the depths of all sensible phenomena.[3]

It is easy enough for the average modern Western mind to associate light with manifestation; the birth of light at the point of Winter Solstice and its waxing through to the fullness of Summer Solstice, is fairly easily taken on as cause for celebration. However, the celebration of the dark is quite another thing; the average modern Western mind finds it very hard to comprehend, having metaphorized the dark as a dead-end, bad, even sordid. Within a linear time frame, where it is disconnected from the cycle, the dark is no longer a space for transformation, for "manifesting". Participation in the Wheel of the Year process, re-enables the "sense" of the dark. With experience of the Wheel's cycle, one comes to always be aware of the polar opposite Sabbat, in the midst of a seasonal celebration; that is, to be aware of the presence of the "manifested" in the "manifesting"/"unmanifest", and vice versa.[4] For example, at Lammas (Early Autumn), where individual self is given over to the dark, there is a memory of Imbolc (Early Spring), when the differentiation of individual self was celebrated; at Lammas, one may become aware that "I" am simply *returning* the "manifested" to the Source or the "*heart*…behind and within all the forms and appearances of nature".[5] I have adopted the terms because it seems from Abram's interpretation of Whorf's work that the Hopi had a sense of space and time that was similar to that invoked by practice of the Seasonal Wheel of the Year, wherein

---

2. David Abram, *The Spell of the Sensuous*, p. 191. I came to using the terms "manifest" and "unmanifest", which does alter the sense slightly, but it has seemed clearer to me given my cultural context of lack of familiarity with the unseen. I now prefer to use the terms "manifested" and "manifesting" if the meaning to others is clear, but it usually requires qualifying.
3. David Abram, *The Spell of the Sensuous*, p.192.
4. This awareness/memory of the polar opposite Sabbat being within the one being celebrated is also enhanced by awareness of the other Hemisphere's polar opposite inclination/Moment; that is, by a global/PaGaian perspective.
5. David Abram, *The Spell of the Sensuous*, p.192, quoting Whorf in Dennis Tedlock, and Barbara Tedlock, (eds). *Teachings from the American Earth*, p.122.

one's own feeling, thinking, desiring are a part of, and hence participant with, this collective desiring and preparing implicit in all things—from the emergence and fruition of corn, to the formation of clouds and the bestowal of rain. Indeed, human intention, especially when concentrated by communal ceremony and prayer, contributes directly to the becoming manifested of such phenomena.[6]

Participation in the Wheel process, particularly when practised as a whole year-long experience and over the period of years, re-identifies one's small self with the Larger Gaia-Self. It is the experience of many indigenous cultures that their communal ceremony and prayer, along with their daily activities, participate "in acts that evoke the ongoing creation of the cosmos."[7] Increasingly, as I practice this Wheel of the Year process, I come to understand how we create the Cosmos, whether conscious or not. I did not know this when I began; this awareness has grown in the practice of identifying with the Creativity of Gaia Herself, through the cycle of the "manifest" and the "manifesting", the light and the dark, the differentiation and the transformation. Gradually I come to understand how these seasonal ceremonies are a response to awakened relationship with Cosmos—thus in some sense, the celebrations become a

> *responsibility* to the cosmos…to know grace, to know as intimately as possible the mysterious interrelatedness and spiritual powers that infuse being and to live our lives accordingly.[8]

Perhaps the central/essential significance of the Sabbats is that they are points of expression of relationship with Gaia, who is a Phenomena of storied events. These "events" are not accomplished and "located in some finished past", but are "the very depth of the experiential present", as Abram describes this sense when describing his understanding of the Aboriginal Australian notion of Dreamtime.[9] Abram understands the "Dreamtime"—as the indigenous term has been commonly translated[10]—to refer to the "implicit life" of a place, the storied events

---

6.   David Abram, *The Spell of the Sensuous*, p.192.
7.   Charlene Spretnak, *States of Grace: The Recovery of Meaning in the Postmodern Age*, p.95.
8.   Charlene Spretnak, *States of Grace: The Recovery of Meaning in the Postmodern Age*, p.100.
9.   *The Spell of the Sensuous*, p.193.
10. Some Aboriginal groups are dissatisfied with this translation insofar as it may imply something "not real".

that "crouch within" a place, that the human may rejuvenate with "en-*chant-ment*" and action.[11] The human is thus enchanted and rejuvenated simultaneously—human and Habitat know relationship, intimacy. This seems resonant with what I have called the "sacred awareness" of the Universe we live in, that may be conjured by the ceremonies of the Wheel of the Year. After celebrating the seasonal ceremonies for a period of time, I came to have a clear sense, at each Sabbat, as I/we prepared to celebrate the ritual, of the uniqueness and depth of this space-time moment in the history of the Universe; I understand this as "sacred awareness". It is a sense of the deep time and space of the moment, and that it is significant Cosmically.[12] The moment becomes a Moment, as actually all moments are; this sense then was often carried over into my life at other moments.

Each Sabbat has its roots in relationship of Earth with Sun primarily, then in how this has affected Earth's response, and our response—in the growing of our food and in the tending of animals (both pre and post-domestication); then in how it has affected human understanding of the Mystery at the Heart of existence—how we have storied it, metaphorized it, how we have come to understand Life and Death through "observing" it, in a participatory sense. This then expresses how humans have come to understand personal stories—the search for the Harmony within our stories' pain and ecstasy. All these layers of story over time, and even varying within a place, and a culture, are intermingled, making a web that is complex, and ever more so; but each Sabbat does retain a particular moment of relationship, a particular "slice" of the Whole Creative cycle of Light and Dark essentially—of "manifest" and "manifesting"—that invites celebration. And gradually, the place in which one celebrates this Great Story...the place which is local-particular and cosmic at the same time, becomes the sacred site that author Caitlin Matthews, speaks of when she describes the experience of consciously joining Earth in Her circumambulation of Sun.[13] The ritual celebration of each Sabbat—the moment in time, the particular "slice" of the Whole Creative cycle of Light and Dark, may embed one in a growing *sense*—felt knowledge—of being at the Centre and Origins of All.

---

11. *The Spell of the Sensuous*, p.193.
12. Even though the actual Cosmic significance does lie well beyond anyone's comprehension.
13. Caitlin Matthews, *The Celtic Spirit*, p.339.

Some of the words/poetry in the rituals as I have celebrated them are taken directly from the traditional expressions/stories that Starhawk articulates. I have also added much of my own understanding, and storied in the particular emphasis of the Triple Goddess/Triple Spiral/Cosmogenesis. Starhawk has always invited adaptation of the rituals as need, place and circumstance predicated. Her version includes a much stronger presence of the God, which is a later (Celtic) adaptation of a story originally based in the phases of the Triple Goddess.[14] There is no right and wrong way to tell this story of the Wheel of the Year; there seems to be as many interpretations as there are groups of people. These Sabbats/festivals have taken different names in different ethnic groups over the centuries, and their significance altered slightly according to the culture. As one example, Emma Restall Orr gives various names of the festivals and some of the different emphases;[15] and from a reading of Shirley Toulson's explanation of the Celtic Year[16] it seems that the ancestors moved dates around to suit their perceptions of the light and dark, and the stories they wanted to tell. Starhawk points out that the story will be different for specific places and climates, and that "the way we celebrate the seasonal festivals also changes over time."[17] She explains the celebrations as described in *The Spiral Dance*:

> Some of these rituals—or some aspects of them—we still do very much as is described here. For some festivals, new traditions have evolved that are repeated year after year. For others, each year's ritual is different. Some festivals have specific children's rituals involved; others don't as yet. The opening invocations reflect the old imagery based on heterosexual polarity. Please feel free to change or adapt them. I may rewrite them someday, after a few more turns around the wheel.[18]

Caitlin and John Matthews, scholars and practitioners of the Western Way, point out that the seasonal festivals have much deeper significance than the exoteric celebration of them makes apparent.[19] They note how the forms and names of the

---

14. Susan Gray, *The Woman's Book of Runes*, p. 17-18. Adam McLean, *The Four Fire Festivals*, and Lawrence Durdin-Robertson, *The Year of the Goddess*, also note this earlier (pre-Celtic) Goddess version of the Wheel of the Year, and detail its celebration to some extent.
15. Emma Restall Orr, *Spirits of the Sacred Grove*, p.234-235.
16. Shirley Toulson, *The Celtic Year*.
17. Starhawk, *The Spiral Dance*, p.245.
18. Starhawk, *The Spiral Dance*, p.245.
19. Caitlin and John Matthews, *The Western Way*, p. 47.

festivals have changed, but declare that "the inner protective energy remains the same", and that "they are the times when the way to the Otherworld stands open."[20] The festivals, they say, can become "hidden doorways in your life" for vital inner energy and "fostering sensitivity to the important psychic tides which energize the world."[21] It has been so, in my experience, and also in the experience of the participants who spoke of it.

I have adapted the Wheel as a way of celebrating the Female Metaphor—Cosmogenesis, the Creativity that is present really/actually in every moment, but for which the Sabbats provide a pattern/Poetry over the period of a year—in time and place. The pattern that I unfold is a way in which the three different phases/characteristics interplay. In fact, the way in which they interplay seems infinite, the way they inter-relate is deeply complex. I think it is possible to find many ways to celebrate them. There is nothing concrete about the chosen story/Poetry, nor about each of the scripts presented here, just as there is nothing concrete about the Place of Being—it (She) is always relational, a Dynamic Interchange. Whilst being grounded in the "Real", the Poetry chosen for expression is therefore at the same time, a potentially infinite expression, according to the heart and mind of the storyteller.

Swimme and Berry call for "a more symbolic language…to enter into the subjective depth of things, to understand both the qualitative differences and the multivalent aspects of every reality."[22] The Wheel of the Year is such a multivalent language, I believe. It can speak any number and layers of experiences in the dynamic of the waxing into fullness and the waning into emptiness—in our individual lives, in the life of a group, in the life of Earth, in the evolution of the Universe. It happens in time, it is an objective event, but its interpretation is multivalent. I use the Wheel of the Year, and its traditional base, to spell out a cosmology as I perceive it. In the following description of the Wheel, as one Sabbat kaleidoscopes into the next, I will place a relevant moment of the Universe's Story as perceived by Swimme and Berry, and quoted from their book.[23] This is for the purpose of poetically aligning Cosmogenesis with the Wheel of the Year. This alignment is drawn into the Poetry of the rituals, as later described in chapter 6. The diagram—Figure 1 in this chapter—has a summary of each Sabbat's

---

20.   Caitlin and John Matthews, *The Western Way*, p. 47-48.
21.   Caitlin and John Matthews, *The Western Way*, p. 48.
22.   Brian Swimme and Thomas Berry, *The Universe Story*, p.258.
23.   Brian Swimme and Thomas Berry, *The Universe Story*.

associations. The dates given below are for the Southern Hemisphere (designated "S.H."), and as noted earlier the actual dates anywhere on the globe do vary from year to year.[24]

Samhain/Halloween—April 30th (S.H.):

Samhain marks the New Year in this tradition because it is the meridian point of the darkest phase of the year, wherein the new is understood to be conceived. Much like any New Year, when "re-solutions" are made, there is particular magic felt in this moment; all is possible, one could decide anything and will it to be—so, it is. This is of course true of every moment, and this celebration can remind one of that, if its significance is not rigidified.

Traditionally, as Starhawk tells it,

> This is the night when the veil is thin that divides the worlds. It is the New Year in the time of the year's death, when the harvest is gathered and the fields lie fallow. For tonight the King of the Waning Year has sailed over the sunless sea that is the Womb of the Mother, and steps ashore on the luminous world egg, becoming the seed of his own rebirth. The gates of life and death are opened; the Sun Child is conceived; the dead walk, and to the living is revealed the Mystery: that every ending is a new beginning. We meet in time out of time, everywhere and nowhere, here and there, to greet the Lord of Death who is Lord of Life and the Triple Goddess who is the circle of rebirth.[25]

I have adapted it in the following way:

> This is the time when we recognize that the veil is thin that divides the worlds. It is the New Year in the time of the year's death—the passing of old growth. The leaves are turning and falling, the dark continues to grow, the days are getting shorter and colder. Earth's tilt continues to move us away from the Sun.

---

24. See footnote 1, this chapter. Also of note, Vivianne Crowley (*Celtic Wisdom: Seasonal Rituals and Festivals*, p.104) points out that prior to reliance on calendar and clock time, some seasonal festival dates were not fixed, but were timed according to harvest and weather and locality. Caitlin and John Matthews, *The Western Way*, p.47, say that: "In inner terms, the right time is more important than the right date. Those living in the Southern Hemisphere are already well aware of this."
25. Starhawk, *The Spiral Dance*, p.193-194.

The story of old tells us that on this night, between the dead and the born, between the old and the new, all is possible; that we travel in the Womb of the Mother, the Dark Shining One within, from which all pours forth, and that we are the seed of our own rebirth. The gates of life and death are opened: the dead are remembered, the Not-Yet[26] is conceived. We meet in time out of time, everywhere and nowhere, here and there…to transform the old into the new in our own bodyminds.

Samhain is a profound celebration of the Void—the Void before time, the Space between one exhalation and the next inhalation, the All-Nourishing Abyss, the Sea of Generosity[27] from which all pours forth, the quantum vacuum. It is regarded as the time for remembering the ancestors—those who have gone before us. From the point of view of Gaia/All-That-Is, death is a transformation; Samhain is a time for remembering this, and being done with the old and conceiving the new. It is a time for recalling the many changes each participant has come through in their particular lives. It can recall the many cultural changes of our human story, the many evolutionary changes—Gaia's transformations, which are also ours—anywhere in the spectrum of thirteen point seven billion years. We can remember how old we really are, and we can remember that we are yet "much More", as is stated in the ritual—personally and collectively. We may articulate some of these conceptions. This is the autopoiesis of the Cosmos.

Samhain is a celebration of the Crone's process of the transformation of Death. She is the Old One who remembers, and from whose Sentient Depths the new is drawn forth. The imagined conceptions will continue to gestate in the Fertility of the Old One's growing Dark. At Samhain, Her face has begun to move into Mother—the Womb of Winter Solstice.

> *A billion years after the birth of the universe, when the galaxies have just emerged, great regions of hydrogen and helium drift about the centre of the Milky Way. In the collapse of our galactic cloud, the spinning of the matter flattens out, disclike, as the angular rotation carries the clouds into the gentle movement of the twirling spiral galaxy. After another hundred million years the invisible density arm sweeps through the cloud and shocks it into collapsing upon itself. No further energy from the galaxy is now required. The cloud that has drifted undisturbed for eons sud-*

---

26. A term used by Brian Swimme, *The Earth's Imagination*, video 8.
27. William C. Chittick and Peter Lamborn Wilson (trans), *Fakhruddin 'Iraqi: Divine Flashes*, p.76. Brian Swimme also speaks of how "all being has gushed forth because Ultimate Generosity retains no thing", *The Universe is a Green Dragon*, p.146.

denly undergoes a profound transformation that destroys its basic form but gives birth to a cluster of ten thousand diamond lights in a sea of dark night.[28]

Winter Solstice/Yule—June 20–23 (S.H.):

This is one of the easiest of Earth's holy days for people of our time in general to relate to, particularly in Christianized cultures, where it has been celebrated as "Christmas" since the Middle Ages. The Winter Solstice marks the stillpoint in the depths of Winter, when Earth's tilt and orbit cause the Sun to begin its return. It may have been the first Earth-Sun event that the ancients noticed, it is the most obvious and dramatic, and it has been especially marked cross-culturally. It is this Sabbat for which the ancients in Ireland built New Grange, thought until recently to be a burial mound or "temple-tomb",[29] but which may in fact be specifically a celebration of Earth-Sun creativity. The inner chamber wall is carved with the Triple Spiral, which at this Seasonal Moment is briefly illuminated by the rising sun; thus expressing the significance of the Winter Solstice.

In this tradition since Celtic times, and in many other cultural traditions, this Moment has been celebrated as the birth of the God (of the Sun). Yet for most of humanity's history, the Sun was understood as Mother, not as a male principle,[30] so the story may vary accordingly. I vary the story as Starhawk tells it, only slightly, to emphasize that what is born, is within each one—the "Divine" is not "out there", we are each Created and Creator:

> This is the time of Winter Solstice in our Southern Hemisphere. Earth's tilt leans us away from the Sun to the furthest point at this time in our annual orbit. This is for us, the time when the dark part of the day is longest—darkness reaches Her fullness, She spreads her cloak, and yet gives way, and moves back into light. The breath of nature in our part of the world is suspended. She rests. We wait…within the Cauldron, the Dark Space, for the transformation.
>
> The stories of Old tell of the Great Mother giving birth to the Divine Child on this night. This Divine Child is the new being in you, in me…is the bringer of hope, the light in the darkness, the evergreen tree, the centre which is also the circumference—All of Manifestation. The Divine Child being born is the Miracle of Being, and the Unimaginable More that we are becoming.[31]

---

28. Brian Swimme and Thomas Berry, *The Universe Story*, p.47.
29. Anne Baring and Jules Cashford, *The Myth of the Goddess*, p.98.
30. See Patricia Monaghan, *O Mother Sun! A New View of the Cosmic Feminine.*

Winter Solstice is the time for rejoicing in the awesome miracle of Manifestation—at the beginning of time, and in every moment. It is a celebration of the Primeval Fireball—the Original Big Birth, as well as the actual birth of our Sun from the "Grandmother" supernova, and the birth of the first cell, and our own personal manifestation, and it is the time for the lighting of candles, and expressing what we will birth in ourselves in the coming year. It can be a moment for recalling the Great Turning of these times, as Joanna Macy calls it[32]—the hope we might hold for the future.

Winter Solstice is a celebration of the Mother aspect of Creativity, the ripening of Her Darkness into the awesome act of creation of form, the Web of Life, the Field of Being. It is a celebration of Communion, a point of interchange from the "manifesting" into the "manifest"; it is a time for feasting, and experiencing this essence of existence. At this point in the Wheel She is the Alpha, and at the Summer Solstice She will be the Omega—both Gateways, points of interchange, when dark and light turn. At this Winter Gateway, the Crone's face passes through the Mother to the Virgin. The process of the three Sabbats of Samhain, Winter Solstice and Imbolc, as a group, may be felt as the three faces of Cosmogenesis in the movement towards form.

> ...the first living cell.... emerged from the cybernetic storms of the primeval oceans.... Life here was born in a lightning flash....(the first cells—prokaryotes) were the most fragile autopoietic structures yet to appear...and yet they were essential for the next advance.... For four billion years the prokaryotic organisms have been remembering the composition from the beginning....Though fragile, though liable to destruction and change in an infinity of ways, they could nevertheless perform an aboriginal magic that would enable them to pervade the world: they could swallow a drop of seawater and spit out a living version of themselves....Besides these new powers of autopoiesis, cells exhibited a new depth of differentiation as well. Once every million births, a cell was created that was new.[33]

Imbolc/Early Spring—August 2nd (S.H.):

Imbolc, the meridian point of the new quarter, is quintessentially the celebration of the new. It is the first celebration proper, of the light part of the cycle, and as

---

31. Starhawk The Spiral Dance, p.182, blended with my words from Winter Solstice 2004.
32. Joanna Macy and Molly Young Brown, *Coming Back to Life*, p.17.
33. Brian Swimme and Thomas Berry, *The Universe Story*, p.86-88.

such, it recognizes the vulnerability, the fragility of that new light or being, of those first tendrils of green, that new self.[34] It is especially dedicated to the Virgin, inviolable in Her commitment to Being; She is traditionally invoked as Brigid, who is the tender of the Flame of Life.

Using Starhawk's words,[35] in combination with my own emphasis, I state the seasonal purpose thus:

> This is the season of the waxing light. Earth's tilt is taking us back towards the Sun. The seed of light born at the Winter Solstice begins to manifest, and we who were midwives to this Flame now see the Light grow strong as the light part of the day grows visibly longer. This is the time when we celebrate individuation: how we each light our own light, and become uniquely ourselves. It is the time of beginning, when the tendrils of green emerge tentatively from the seed. We meet to share the light of inspiration and creative intentions, which will grow with the growing year.
>
> This is the Feast of the Virgin—Brigid, She who tends the Flame of Being; Artemis, She who midwifes body and soul. She is deeply committed to the Creative Urge, to manifestation, deeply committed to Self. She is uncompromised, unswerving, noble, true, a warrior of spirit. She will protect the stirrings of Life.

For women particularly, the Imbolc process/ritual can be an important integrating expression and movement, used as many women frequently are, to fragmentation in relationship—giving themselves away too easily. This seasonal celebration of movement into form, individuation/differentiation, yet with integrity/wholeness, especially invoking She-who-is-unto-Herself, can be a significant dedication. It is a "Bridal" commitment to Being, in the original Brigid-ine sense.[36] Yet men too may find this celebration of Brigid within themselves to be an integrating invocation—at last an opportunity to identify with "Her". For any being—female or male—it may be a statement of taking up courage to be and a celebration of the individual quest.

---

34. The Light has just been "born" at the Winter Solstice, and the cold has usually been increasing since then, so the inhabitant has the experience of wanting to "rug up" and seek the warmth and nourishment of the Light.
35. Starhawk, *The Spiral Dance*, p.186.
36. "Bride" is another name for Brigid—Great Celtic Goddess—from pre-Christian times. See Vivianne Crowley, *Celtic Wisdom: Seasonal Rituals and Festivals*, p.57.

The lighting of candles and a central flame is again a big part of this Sabbat as it was at Winter Solstice, this time recognizing that each self is a Promise of Life. Each individual Promise is identified with Gaia Herself, with "the beauty of the green earth and the white moon among the stars and the mystery of the waters".[37] It is a time for purification, that is, for recognizing what it is in you that inhibits the Spark, the growth, the Power to Be, and what enhances it; then for making a commitment to the tending of this Self. This Earth holy day celebrates differentiation, diversity, the multiform beauty of Gaia, all of which is indeed brought to us through the many challenges that Gaia Herself has encountered as She has developed—our individual lives are no different. The challenges we have encountered and midwifed ourselves through, may add to our complexity, strength and beauty. The Virgin is that aspect that finds the "yes" to being—beyond the complete awesomeness of it both personally and collectively. This aspect finds the "yes" to loving the self/Self beyond all failings, and is able to step into the Power of Life—so She moves into the balance of Eostar/Spring Equinox.

> *A cloud of elements hovered, floated…far from the centre of the Milky Way galaxy.…In our universe, the originating powers permeating every drop of existence drew forth ten thousand stars from this quiescent cloud. To varying degrees, these stellar beings manifested the universe's urge toward differentiation, autopoiesis, and communion. And at least one of these, the Sun, managed to enter the deeper reaches of the universe creativity, a realm where the complexity, self-manifestation, and reciprocity at the very heart of the universe revealed themselves in a way transcending anything that had occurred for ten billion years—as an extravagant, magical, and living Earth burst into a new epoch of the universe story.[38]*

Eostar/Spring Equinox—September 20–23 (S.H.):

As the light continues to grow, it comes into balance with the dark. Eostar, or Spring Equinox, is one of two points in the year when the Sun is equidistant between North and South, creating this light and dark balance. Yet the trend at this Equinox is toward increasing light—longer hours of light. Earth in this region is still tilting further toward the Sun. Traditionally it is the joyful celebration of Persephone's return from the underworld; this is when the balance tips—the certainty of the return of light is assured, the darkness has been navi-

---

37. Starhawk, *The Spiral Dance*, p.90-91, quoting Doreen Valiente's "The Charge of the Goddess".

38. Brian Swimme and Thomas Berry, *The Universe Story*, p.78-79.

gated successfully. As is said in the seasonal celebrational statement, rewording Starhawk slightly:

> Life bursts forth with new strength. The story of Old tells us that Persephone, beloved Daughter, returns from Her journey to the Underworld—Demeter stretches out Her arms—to receive and rejoice. The Beloved One, the Lost One, returns with new Wisdom from the depths.
>
> We may step into a new harmony. Where we step, wild flowers may appear; where we dance, despair may turn to hope, sorrow to joy, want to abundance. May our hearts open with the Spring.[39]

The patriarchal version of Persephone's story is that She is abducted and raped by Hades. I think it is particularly important that this myth be re-storied. As it has been known in patriarchal times, it is an account of what did happen historically; that is, in the human story. However, in the oldest tale, Persephone *voluntarily* descends to the underworld—she is not forced.[40] She has the Wisdom of Goddess, who understands the fertility of the Dark terrain, who understands the Mystery of life and death. In this old account, Persephone journeys seeking Self-knowledge and Compassion, retaining Her integrity and sovereignty:[41] She is thus restored to Her former grace, and to the gaining of a sense of Her full participation in the mystery and adventure of Life.

Persephone's return is the certain return of manifest Creativity. She brings with Her, knowledge of the Depths (autopoiesis), from whence springs all Creativity. Persephone's journey is about becoming familiar with the inner realms in herself, falling in Love with these depths. In the Creation story of the Faery tradition, all manifestation springs forth from Goddess falling in Love with Her reflection in the curved mirror of black space.[42] The ancients understood that the essence of Creative Power springs from Self-Love, known and seen only completely in the Dark.

---

39. Starhawk, *The Spiral Dance*, p.187.
40. Charlene Spretnak, *Lost Goddesses of Early Greece*, p.105-118.
41. As explained also in Ch.2, p.78-79. This retention of Her integrity does not mean that She does not really lose Herself as the Hera/Hero must in the Descent to the Underworld. It simply means that She remains a Wisdom figure—the Hera, just as for instance, Inanna of Sumeria retains Her identity as Queen (sovereign) in Her Journey to the Great Below where She becomes a rotten piece of meat.
42. Starhawk, *The Spiral Dance*, p.31.

I story this celebration as a "Stepping into Power", identifying ourselves as Heras, rejoicing in how we have made it through, having faced our fears, the chthonic, and our demise (in its various forms). It is a time to welcome back that which was lost, and step forward into the light, to fly. Eostar is the time for enjoying the fruits of the descent, of the journey taken into the darkness. It is a point of balance of the three faces of Goddess—Persephone representing both the Wise One from the depths and the newly Emerged, being embraced by the Mother, rejoicing and affirming the harmony of All. It is the three aspects of Cosmogenesis in "a fecund balance of tensions".[43]

Earth is perfectly poised in this balance for a moment, before She tips into the increasing fertility of Spring. The freedom of empowerment, the exhilaration of the full flight of Being, brings with it increasing passion for Life. Allurement awakens, desire reaches for "More" (promised at Samhain), for fullness; it is the wild, untamed nature of the Virgin who would give Herself to the ecstatic Dance of Life. This is the energy of Beltane.

> *Love begins as allurement—as attraction. Think of the entire cosmos, all one hundred billion galaxies rushing through space: At this cosmic scale the basic dynamism of the universe is the attraction each galaxy has for every other galaxy....Gravity is the word used by scientists and the rest of us in the modern era to point to this primary attraction....(but) the mystery remains no matter how intelligently we theorize....The attracting activity is a stupendous and mysterious fact of existence. Primal....this alluring activity permeates the cosmos on all levels of being....By pursuing your allurements, you help bind the universe together. The unity of the world rests on the pursuit of passion.[44]*

Beltane/High Spring—October 31st (S.H.):

Earth's holy day of Beltane marks the meridian point of the lightest phase in the cycle—some name it High Spring; the time when the light part of the day is longer and continuing to grow longer than the dark part of the day. Beltane is polar opposite Samhain on the Wheel of the Year, when the dark was still climaxing.

---

43. Brian Swimme and Thomas Berry, *The Universe Story*, p.54.
44. Brian Swimme and Thomas Berry, *The Universe Story*, p.43-48.

Based on Starhawk's telling of it,[45] but mostly in my own composition, I express the seasonal celebrational purpose thus:

> This is the time of Beltane, when the light part of the day is longer and continues to grow longer than the dark part of the day. In our region of the world, Earth continues to tilt us further toward the Sun—the Source of Her pleasure, life and ecstasy. This is the time when sweet Desire for Life weds wild delight—it is met; when the Promise of Spring—which you are, weds the Passion of Summer—fulfillment is nigh. The fruiting begins. It is the celebration of allurement...Holy Lust...that which holds all things in form and allows the dance of life.
>
> The ancients called this Holy Lust, this primordial essence 'Aphrodite'...they sang of Her:
>
> > 'For all things are from you.
> > Who unites the cosmos.
> > You will the three-fold fates.
> > You bring forth all things.
> > Whatever is in the Heavens.
> > And in the much fruitful earth
> > And in the deep sea.'
> > Let us celebrate our erotic nature, that brings forth all things.

Beltane is an opportunity to recognize and ritualize our desire for Life, which we feel in so many ways; and to recognize that it is a Holy Desire. On an elemental level, there is our desire for Air, Water, the warmth of Fire, and to be of use to Earth. There is an essential longing, sometimes nameless, sometimes constellated, experienced physically, that may be recognized as the Desire of the Universe Herself—desiring in us.[46] We may remember that we are united in this desire with each other, with all who have gone before us, and with all who come after us—all who dance the Dance of Life. Beltane is a time for dancing and weaving into our lives, our heart's desires; traditionally the dance is done with participants holding ribbons attached to a pole.[47] There is also the exhilarating tradition of leaping the flames, exclaiming what one wills to leave behind—it may be understood as letting the Flame of Love burn away the perceived blocks to one's desires. Beltane is a time for assenting to the frenzy of the Dance of Life, with only Passion as the guide for where to place one's feet; much like the dancing Goddesses and Gods of

---

45. Starhawk, *The Spiral Dance*, p.188.
46. Brian Swimme, *Canticle to the Cosmos*, (Video series), video 2 and 10.
47. I have named this a "Novapole", for our Southern Hemisphere, whereas in the Northern Hemisphere it is known as a "Maypole".

many spiritual traditions. It is being with Life and its intense fertility, in the moment.

One of the shaping powers of life is a wild energy, that Swimme and Berry associate with the causal factor of genetic mutation; and "Genetic mutation refers to spontaneous differentiations taking place at life's root."[48] Wild energy is also associated with Artemis in Her Virgin aspect;[49] She and many other Goddesses were named as "Lady of the Beasts". Swimme and Berry describe wildness as "a face ultimacy wears", "a primal act within the life process".[50] They say:

> A wild animal,…alert and free, moves with a beauty…far beyond the lock-step process of a rationally derived conclusion. The wild is a great beauty that seethes with intelligence, that is ever surprising and refreshing…The discovery of mutations is the discovery of an untamed and untameable energy at the organic centre of life.…For without this wild energy, life's journey would have ended long ago.[51]

At Beltane the Virgin's Passion moves Her more deeply into engagement with the Other—Her face is noticeably changing into the Mother. Her desire for complete fullness continues to wax. Her movement, Her Lust, is to open completely into the Omega of Summer Solstice.

> *In the primeval fireball, which quickly billowed in every direction, we see a metaphor for the infinite striving of the sentient being. An unbridled playing out of this cosmic tendency would lead to ultimate dispersion. But the fireball discovered a basic obstacle to its movements, the gravitational attraction. Only because expansion met the obstacle of gravitation did the galaxies come forth. In a similar way the wings of birds and the musculature of the elephants arose out of the careful embrace of the negative or obstructing aspects of the gravitational attraction. Any life forms that might awake in a world without gravity's hindrances to motion would be incapable of inventing the anatomy of the cheetah.*[52]

48.   Brian Swimme and Thomas Berry, *The Universe Story*, p.125.
49.   Charlene Spretnak, *Lost Goddesses of Early Greece*, p.75.
50.   Brian Swimme and Thomas Berry, *The Universe Story*, p.125.
51.   Brian Swimme and Thomas Berry, *The Universe Story*, p.127.
52.   Brian Swimme and Thomas Berry, *The Universe Story*, p.55.

Summer Solstice/Litha—December 20-23 (S.H.):

The "moment of grace" that is Summer Solstice, marks the stillpoint in the height of Summer, when Earth's tilt and orbit cause the Sun to begin its decline—its movement back to the North. This Sabbat is polar opposite Winter Solstice when it is light that is "born". At the peak of Summer, in the bliss of expansion, it is the dark that is "born".[53] It is a celebration of profound mystical significance, that in a culture where the dark is not valued for its creative telios, may be confronting. This is the Sabbat for which Stonehenge was apparently built.[54]

The purpose for the seasonal gathering is stated thus, in my own adaptation of Starhawk's version:[55]

> This is the time of Summer Solstice—the time when the light part of the day is longest. In our part of the world, light is in Her fullness. She spreads Her radiance, Her fruits ripen, Her greenery is everywhere, the cicadas sing. Yet as Light reaches Her peak, our closest contact with the Sun, She opens completely, and the seed of darkness is born.
>
> As it says in the tradition, this is the time of the rose, blossom and thorn, fragrance and blood. The story of Old tells that on this day Goddess and God embrace, in a love so complete, that all dissolves, into the single Song of ecstasy that moves the worlds. Our bliss, fully matured, given over, feeds the Universe and turns the wheel. We join the Beloved and Lover in the Great Give-Away of our Creativity, our Fullness of Being.

Summer is a time for celebrating our realized Creativity, whose birth we celebrated at Winter, whose tenderness we dedicated ourselves to at Imbolc, whose certain presence and power we rejoiced in at Eostar, whose fertile passion we danced with at Beltane. Now, at this seasonal point, as we celebrate Light's fullness, we celebrate our own ripening—like that of the wheat, and the fruit. And like the wheat and the fruit, it is the Sun that is in us, that has ripened—the Sun is the Source of our every thought and action. The analogy is complete in that

---

53. And in Australia the heat usually increases after Summer Solstice, so the inhabitant frequently has the experience of wanting to close out the heat and light and enter the relief of the Dark.
54. Ken Osborne (ed), *Stonehenge and Neighbouring Monuments*. p.2.
55. Starhawk *The Spiral Dance*, p.189, with additions from p.219 where she describes Summer Solstice as "the Give-Away time of the Sun."

our everyday Creativity and we ourselves are ultimately also Food for the Universe.[56] Like the Sun and the wheat and the fruit, we find the purpose of our Creativity in the releasing of it; just as our breath must be released for its purpose of Life. The symbolism used to express this is the giving of a full rose or flower of choice to the flames.[57] We, and our everyday Creativity are given over. In this way we each are the Bread of Life; just as many other indigenous traditions recognize everyday acts as evoking "the ongoing creation of the cosmos",[58] so in this tradition, Summer is the time for particularly celebrating that. Our everyday lives, moment to moment, are built on the fabric of the work/creativity of the ancestors and ancient creatures that went before us. So the future is built on ours. We celebrate the blossoming of Creativity then, and the bliss of it, at a time when Earth is pouring forth Her abundance, giving it away. We aspire to follow Her example. In this cosmology, what is given is the self fully realized and celebrated, not a self that is abnegated—just as the fruit gives its full self: as Starhawk says, "Oneness is attained not through losing the self, but through realizing it fully."[59]

Summer Solstice is a celebration of the Fullness of the Mother—in ourselves, in Earth, in the Cosmos. It is the ripening of Her Manifestation, which fulfills itself in the awesome act of dissolution. It is a celebration of Communion, the Feast of Life—which is for the enjoying, not for the holding onto. I represent this Sabbat on my Wheel of the Year with a horseshoe, because its yonic shape is symbolic of Goddess' "Great Gate": "Greeks assigned the yonic shape to the last letter of their sacred alphabet, Omega, literally, 'Great Om', the Word of Creation, beginning the next cycle of becoming."[60] Summer Solstice is such a Gateway. At this interchange, the Virgin's face has passed through the Mother into the Crone. The process of the three Sabbats of Beltane, Summer Solstice and Lammas, as a group, may be felt as the three faces of Cosmogenesis in the movement towards entropy.

> *Eventually, in a million years or in several billion years, a star's resources against the collapse are all used up. If the mass of a star at this point is large enough, its*

---

56. This is a metaphor I learnt from Brian Swimme, *Canticle to the Cosmos*, video 5.
57. This also resonates with Summer being the season of fires, and something can be made of that in the ritual.
58. Charlene Spretnak, *States of Grace: The Recovery of Meaning in the Postmodern Age*, p.95.
59. Starhawk, *The Spiral Dance*, p. 27
60. Barbara Walker, *The Woman's Encyclopaedia of Myths and Secrets*, p.414.

gravitational pressures will destroy the star. The remaining materials will rush toward each other. Nothing in the universe can now stop them.…This stellar being that burned brightly for billions of years, that may have showered sentient creatures with radiant energy that they transformed into their living bodies and into cathedrals that rose in wheat fields, has gone, only a black cinder left.[61]

Lammas/Early Autumn—February 2nd (S.H.):

Lammas is the meridian point of the first dark quarter of the year, after the light phase is complete, and as such, it is a special celebration of the Crone. Within the Celtic tradition, it is the wake of Lugh, the Sun King, and it is the Crone that reaps him. But within earlier Goddess traditions, all the transformations were Hers;[62] and

> the community reflected on the reality that the Mother aspect of the Goddess, having come to fruition, from Lammas on would enter the Earth and slowly become transformed into the Old Woman-Hecate-Cailleach aspect…[63]

I dedicate Lammas to the face of the Old One, just as Imbolc, its polar opposite on the Wheel, is dedicated to the Virgin face. The Old One, the Dark and Shining One, has been much maligned, so to celebrate Her can be more of a challenge in our present cultural context. Lammas may be an opportunity to re-aquaint ourselves with the Crone in her purity, to fall in love with Her again.

I state the purpose of the seasonal gathering thus:

> This is the season of the waxing dark. The seed of darkness born at the Summer Solstice now grows…the dark part of the days grows visibly longer. Earth's tilt is taking us back away from the Sun. This is the time when we cel-

---

61. Brian Swimme and Thomas Berry, *The Universe Story*, p.48.
62. Susan Gray, *The Woman's Book of Runes*, p. 18. This is also to say that the transformations are within each being, not elsewhere, that is the "sacrifice" is not carried out by another external to the self, as could be and have been interpreted from stories of Lugh or Jesus.
63. Lawrence Durdin-Robertson, *The Year of the Goddess*, p.143, quoting Adam McLean, *Fire Festivals*, p.20-22. Another indication of the earlier tradition beneath "Lughnasad" is the other name for it in Ireland of "Tailltean Games". Taillte was said to be Lugh's foster-mother, and it was her death that was being commemmorated (Mike Nichols, "The First Harvest", Pagan Alliance Newsletter NSW Australia).

ebrate dissolution; each unique self lets go, to the Darkness. It is the time of ending, when the grain, the fruit, is harvested. We meet to remember the Dark Sentience, the All-Nourishing Abyss, She from whom we arise, in whom we are immersed, and to whom we return.

This is the time of the Crone, the Wise Dark One, who accepts and receives our harvest, who grinds the grain, who dismantles what has gone before. She is Hecate, Lillith, Medusa, Kali, Erishkagel—Divine Compassionate One. We meet to accept Her transformative embrace, trusting Her knowing, which is beyond all knowledge.

Lammas is the seasonal moment for recognizing that we dissolve into the "night" of the Larger Organism that we are part of—Gaia. It is She who is immortal, from whom we arise, and into whom we dissolve. This celebration is a development of what was born in the transition of Summer Solstice; the Dark Sentient Source of Creativity is honoured. The autopoietic space in us recognizes Her, is comforted by Her, desires Her self-transcendence and self-dissolution; Lammas is an opportunity to be with our organism's love of Larger Self—this Native Place. We have been taught to fear Her, but at this Sabbat, we may remember that She is the Compassionate One, deeply committed to Transformation, which is actually innate to us.

Whereas at Imbolc, we shone forth as individual, multiforms of Her; at Lammas, we small individual selves remember that we are She and dissolve back into Her. We are the Promise of Life as we affirmed at Imbolc, but we are the Promise of *Her*—it is not ours to hold. We become the Harvest at Lammas; our individual harvest *is* Her Harvest. We are the process itself—we are Gaia's Process. *We* do not breathe (though of course we do), we borrow the breath, for a while. It is like a relay: we pick the breath up, create what we do during our time with it, and pass it on. The harvest we reap in our individual lives is important, *and* it is for us only short term; it belongs to the Cosmos in the long term. Lammas is a time for "making sacred"—as "sacrifice" may be understood; we may "make sacred" ourselves. As Imbolc was a time for dedication, so is Lammas. This is the Wisdom of the phase of the Old One. She is the aspect that finds the "yes" to letting go, to loving the Larger Self, beyond all knowledge, and steps into the Power of the Abyss, encouraged and nourished by the harvest—so She moves into the balance of Mabon/Autumn Equinox.

If the atoms in the prestellar cloud had been given language and the power to reflect upon inner experience, so that they could ponder the significance of the density waves sweeping through them and the rush of atoms ramming up against them, they would even then not have been able to speak in clear terms about the star they were destined to become....The beauty of the star gripped the atoms in some primordial manner; the beauty of the new flowering of Earth's realities likewise grips us and is in many ways the central significance of all our experiences of obstacle, disappointment, dismay, and despair....We cannot know with certainty...what is required of us now. We will find our way only with a deep and prolonged process of groping—considering with care a great variety of interpretations, weighing evidence from a spectrum of perspectives, attending with great patience to the inchoate, barely discernable glimmers that visit us in our more contemplative moments.[64]

Mabon/Autumn Equinox—March 20-23 (S.H.):

Mabon is a time of thanksgiving for the harvest—for its empowerment and nourishment, and it is also a time of leavetaking and sorrow, as Life declines.[65] As the dark continues to grow, it comes into balance with the light; Mabon/Autumn Equinox is that point of balance. Sun is equidistant between North and South, as it was at Spring Equinox, but in this phase of the cycle, the trend is toward increasing dark. For millennia, in Greece, this Sabbat has been the holy celebration of Persephone's descent to the Underworld, and as mentioned earlier, in the earliest Goddess tradition, Her descent is voluntary—She simply understands the necessity of the Journey.

As I say in the statement of purpose for the seasonal ritual,

> Feel the balance in this moment—Earth as She is poised in relationship with the Sun. Feel for your own balance of light and dark within. Breathe into it. Breathe in the light, swell with it, let your breath go into the dark, stay with it. Feel for your centre, shift on your feet, from left to right, right to left.
>
> In our part of Earth, the balance is about to tip into the dark. Feel the shift within you, see in your mind's eye the descent ahead, the darkness growing, remember the coolness of it. This is the time when we give thanks for our harvests—the abundance we have reaped. Yet we remember too the losses. The story of Old tells us that Persephone is given the wheat—the Mystery, knowledge of life and death—for this she gives thanks. But she sets forth into the darkness—both Mother and Daughter grieve that it is so.

---

64. Brian Swimme and Thomas Berry, *The Universe Story*, p.58.
65. Starhawk, *The Spiral Dance*, p.192.

Like its Spring counterpoint, Autumn Equinox is also a "stepping into power", but it is not necessarily perceived as such; it is usually felt as loss. Autumn Equinox is a time for grieving our many losses, as individuals, as a culture, as Earth-Gaia, as Universe-Gaia. At this time we may join Demeter—and any other Mother Goddess from around the globe—in Her weeping for all that has been lost. The Mother weeps and rages, the Daughter leaves courageously, the Old One beckons with Her Wisdom and Promise of Transformation; yet all three know Each Other deeply, and share the unfathomable Grief. But Persephone as Seed represents the thread of Life that never fades away. The revelation of the Seed, central to this seasonal celebration, is that:

> Everything lost is found again,
> In a new form, In a new way.
> She changes everything She touches, and
> everything She touches changes.[66]

And so it will be. In this way Persephone as Seed, tends the sorrows, "wholes" the heart.

All at once, the three faces of Cosmogenesis are present. As Seed, She is Queen of the Underworld—Old Wise One, and the irrepressible Urge to Be; and She is the Mother, Source of Life. This is a blessed Moment of Harmony/Balance that streams through the grief and the ecstasy of Life.

This point of balance tips further into the dark, as Earth's tilt and Sun continue their relational dynamic. The dark of night keeps growing, the seed is in the Earth, the grub is in the chrysalis, the Abyss is accepted—the metamorphosis of the dark Sentience is awaited, the fertile Emptiness of the Crone is the moment of Samhain.

> *...after billions of years of striving...Tiamat found herself pressed to the wall, exhausted by the effort, helpless to do anything more to balance the titanic powers in which she had found her way. When her core had been transformed into iron, she sighed a last time as collapse became inevitable. In a cosmological twinkling, her gravitational potential energy was transformed into a searing explosion,...But when the brilliance was over, when Tiamat's journey was finished, the deeper meaning of her existence was just beginning to show through.*[67]

---

66. Starhawk, *The Spiral Dance*, p.103.
67. Brian Swimme and Thomas Berry, *The Universe Story*, p.60-61.

With Samhain, the annual cycle—the Wheel of the Year—is complete. It is the time of Death, and the beginning of the New Year.

In Summary—Contemplating How Creativity Proceeds

There are two celebrations of the Virgin/Young One/Differentiation—they are the meridian points of the waxing light phase. At Imbolc, the first in the light phase, we *identify* with She, who is Shining and New—as we take her form; at Beltane, we participate in Her *process* of the Dance of Life. This light part of the cycle is about coming into Being—nurturing it (the midwifing of Imbolc), stepping into the power of it (the return of Eostar), the fertility (of Beltane), the peaking of it (at Summer).

There are two celebrations of the Old One/Crone/Autopoiesis—they are the meridian points of the waxing dark phase. At Lammas, the first in the dark phase, we *identify* with the Dark and Ancient Wise One—dissolve into Her; at Samhain, we participate in Her *process* of the Transformation of Death. This dark part of the cycle is about dissolving/dying/letting go—nurturing it (the midwifing of Lammas), stepping into the power of it (the departure of Mabon), the fertility (of Samhain), the peaking of it (at Winter).

There are two celebrations of the Mother/Communion—the Solstices. If one images the light part of the cycle as a celebration of the Productions of Time, and the dark part of the cycle as a celebration of Eternity, the Solstices then are meeting points, and are celebrations of the communion/relational field of Eternity with the Productions of Time. This is a relationship which *does* happen in this Place, in this Web. This Place, this Web, is a Communion—it *is* the Mother; the Solstices mark Her Birthings.

There are two celebrations wherein the balance of all three Faces are particularly present—the Equinoxes, that are also special celebrations of Demeter and Persephone—the Mystery and Awesomeness of the continuity of life, its Creative Tension/Balance. Both are celebrations and contemplations of empowerment through deep Wisdom—one contemplation during the dark phase and one during the light phase. The Autumn Equinox is a descent to it, the Spring Equinox is an emergence with it. I like to think of the Equinoxes, and of the ancient icons of Demeter and Persephone, as celebrations of the delicate "curvature of space-time", the fertile balance of tensions which enables it all.

The Mother aspect then may be understood to be particularly present at four of the Sabbats, which are also regarded traditionally as the Solar festivals. I recognize them as points of interchange. At the Autumn Equinox, Mother is present as Giver—She is letting Persephone go. At Spring Equinox, She is present as Receiver—welcoming the Daughter back. At Winter Solstice the Mother gives birth, creates form. At Summer Solstice, She opens again/further, dissolves form. The Mother is Agent/Actor at the Solstices. She is Participant/Witness at the Equinoxes, where it is then really Persephone who is Agent/Actor, embodying an inseparable Young One and Old One.

Another possible way to visual it, or to tell the story, is this:
The Mother—Demeter—is always there, at the Centre if you like. Persephone cycles around. She is the Daughter who returns in the Spring as flower, who will become fruit/grain of the Summer, who at Lammas assents to the dissolution—the consumption. At Autumn Equinox She returns to the underworld as seed—Her harvest is rejoiced in, Her loss is grieved, as She becomes Queen of the Underworld—the Dark One, Crone. In the light part of the cycle She is Virgin. Persephone is that part of Demeter that can be all three aspects—can move through the complete cycle. The Mother and Daughter are really One, and embody the immortal process of creation and destruction. Demeter hands Persephone the wheat, the Mystery, and the thread of life is unbroken—it goes on forever. It is immortal, it is eternal. Even though it is true that all will be lost, and all is lost—Being always arises again. This is what is revealed in the ubiquitous three faces. The Seed of Life—She never fades away, She is always present; even though it may not be apparent. As Swimme and Berry note, galactic clouds may drift for eons before undergoing transformation,[68] but the fertility/potency seethes there.

As one participates in this year long process of ritual and celebration the complexity of the three aspects does become more apparent. Indeed all three aspects/faces/energies do occur simultaneously—sometimes obviously so, as mentioned, sometimes perceived only at deeper levels; and at deeper levels, one can perceive how the three are features of each other. Usually it is fairly clear that the Virgin and Crone aspects are inseparable, and this is true also of the cosmogenetic characteristics of differentiation and autopoiesis. For example, differentiation/diversity/uniqueness has been enhanced by the advent of death in the biological

---

68.   Brian Swimme and Thomas Berry, *The Universe Story*, p.47.

story;[69] and the autopoietic dynamic is ambivalently self and not-self, it is Self who is larger Self at the same time. This inseparability is congruent also with the ancient perception that the day begins with the evening. The severance comes first—is it birth or is it death? It is not always clear where something ends and where it begins.

There is a symmetry or reciprocity between the polar opposites on the Wheel, some of which I have already noted. One begins to feel these, as one's familiarity with the Metaphor and the celebrations grows. I have noticed the connection of Samhain-Winter Solstice-Imbolc as the movement through the three faces towards form, from Dark One to Birth to Light; and the connection of Beltane-Summer Solstice-Lammas as the movement through the three faces towards entropy, from Light/Passion of Being to Birth to Dark One. This is a useful contemplation as it teaches how Creativity proceeds. When it is practised as a whole, it becomes a Gestalt, one may begin to Know.

There is also a pattern of the Star of Aphrodite that emerged as I contemplated the Wheel Diagram when I first mapped it out[70]—the Crone of Samhain with the Virgin of Imbolc and the Mother of Summer as the upward pointing triangle; and the Virgin of Beltane with the Crone of Lammas with the Mother of Winter as the downward pointing triangle. I like this emergent pattern because it speaks of the essential Desire which is at the centre of the Wheel, which turns the Wheel; something I came to understand ever more deeply as I practised the rituals. I speak more of this in the concluding chapter. The connection of these particular Sabbats, and their creative impetus, is worth further contemplation: they may be contemplated also in connection with the balance points of Spring and Autumn Equinoxes where all three are celebrated.

---

69. See Elisabet Sahtouris, *Earthdance*, p.134-135 and Ursula Goodenough, *The Sacred Depths of Nature*, p.143-149.
70. See Appendix D. This is the six-pointed star that is commonly thought of as the Star of David but which was only adopted by Jewish mysticism in the 12th century due to its association with sex and Eastern Goddess religious practice. See Barbara Walker, *The Woman's Encyclopaedia of Myths and Secrets*, p.400-403. I have named it the Star of Aphrodite, as 666 was Her number, though it could equally be known as the Star of Ishtar for similar reasons.

There may be many other patterns and relationships between the Sabbats that individuals and groups may notice and learn from, and draw into the Story and their ritual celebrations.

6

Ritual Celebration of the Creative Dynamic

This chapter and the one following are somewhat practical guides as to how I have been doing the ritual celebrations of the Sabbats, as a means to embody this Wholly Creative Dynamic—to get with Gaia's "plot" as I see it. There is nothing necessarily pre-scriptive or "correct" about the way I have been doing the rituals, but I will tell it and offer it as a possible way to proceed, as an illustration of how one can and might put such ritual celebration together. One does not need to be a hierophant, a trained ordained person to begin: it may even be an advantage not to be,[1] although care is essential.

Overall it has been very important to me to make the ritual space one of "ease", that is, accessible and comprehensible to people, to allow it to be relevant to people's experience. Yet without compromising its sacred depths and solemnity, nor compromising the story that I wanted to spell out—which was also the story the participating people *wanted* to have spelled out. As much as possible, in any group preparation for the rituals, I have de-constructed the language often used in traditional Pagan circles to describe the ritual processes. My sense of freedom to do this is partly drawn from Starhawk's encouragement and style when I was taught by her. It is also partly drawn from an early background in de-constructing Catholic rituals (known as "Mass") almost a decade before that, when the people in that context began to take spiritual expression into their own hands.

---

1. This is not to denigrate or deny the wealth that comes from training and years of experience, it is simply to recognize that many ordained persons or qualified witches/ priestesses may not necessarily facilitate as nurturant a sacred space as they are "authored" to do. A person who has less "hocus-pocus" (that is, "correct" terminology, holy robes and tools) but more care, real commitment to the Cosmos and simple psychological skill, may facilitate a more deeply affective ritual space.

And so it is now: the people in the larger community are increasingly desiring to take spiritual expression into their own hands. My priorities in ritual are also affected by my training in liturgy at the Jesuit School of Theology in Berkeley, where we were taught carefully to enable the real Presence in the people.[2] These days I interpret that to mean enabling participants to bring their personal and collective stories to the story of the Sabbat ritual and therein to find deep communion with self, other and all-that-is.

Ritual Format

The format/structure that I have used for the rituals is based on Starhawk's format for the traditional seasonal rituals that she outlines in *The Spiral Dance*.[3] Everyone or every group will have their own preferred emphases, additions, and somewhat varied understandings of the processes. Briefly, the ritual processes as I have done them, flow like this:

"Warming the Energy"—This is partly done in the preparation of the space before the event—with decoration appropriate to the Sabbat, with a sense of presence conjured by aroma and music and meditations I have done there during the weeks or days before. It is also "warmed" in the greetings and conversation that goes on as the gathering of participants happens, and as they select their positions in the prepared circle and place their ritual "accessories" (masks, stones, photos, flowers or whatever depending on the Sabbat) in designated areas. There is eating and drinking of a light kind that goes on at this time also—in the kitchen, as part of the welcoming and settling in. The "warming" is also done in the group preparation for the ritual, which is when I regard the circle as formally beginning, and the point at which I close the doors to any latecomers. This group preparation will be detailed more later, but it is essentially the time for going over the "order of service", and learning the dances and/or songs, followed by ten minutes of individual reflection/meditation before we re-gather for the actual ritual.

Gathering—This is the formal gathering moment of the ritual. Just prior to this, participants have been in individual meditation, possibly wandering or sitting in the garden or some other room, and/or taking care of physical needs, in preparation for the "sacred space".

---

2.   This was the instruction and practice of James Empereur S.J. specifically.

3.   Starhawk, *The Spiral Dance*, p. 181-196.

Centering or Breath Meditation—A breath meditation is the usual method of "Centering/Grounding" at the beginning of the rituals. It is a process of establishing connection with ourselves as "breath-taking" beings, becoming present to the moment, moving into a deeper reflective space. The way I have languaged them follows the flow of Gaia's breath over the year—connecting the individual breath cycle to the Larger Creative cycle. I focus on the part of the breath pattern that matches the particular Sabbat, sometimes adding quite extensive poetic flourish that introduces the theme of the ritual celebration.

Statement of Purpose—stating the reason for the gathering, which in this case is the celebration of a Seasonal Moment. All the statements that I have written into the scripts are based in theme and expression on Starhawk's, as noted previously, with my own additions and changes that include emphasis on Cosmogenetic and female metaphor. I am always careful to express what is actually happening with the light part and the dark part of the day, and to express it in this way; that is, with language that acknowledges the "day" as diurnal—having a "light part" and a "dark part" that is in dynamic movement through the year. Such expression participates in spelling the dark back into the "day".

Creating Sacred Space—Traditionally this is known as "the calling of the directions" and their associated elemental powers, and "casting the circle". The four elements of Water, Fire, Earth and Air are represented in the centre—posted in associated directions that may vary according to the Place of celebration.[4] The recognition of the directions signifies the presence of the Whole Cosmos here and within each one: we are each indeed recycled bits from everywhere and everytime. We don't have to go anywhere, it is all "right-here" within each participant: we simply have to recall it. The essence of this ritual process then, as I see it, is the remembering of our common origins, remembering who and what we are, and

---

4.   This variation of direction for the associated elements is one of those realities particular to the mind of Southern Hemisphere people who have been transplanted within the last couple of hundred years from the Northern Hemisphere. Traditionally the elements correspond to particular definite directions, but practitioners of the tradition in the Southern Hemisphere have learnt to be flexible about the corresponding directions, since the sensed experience is actually different—most obvious is that North is definitely the direction of "hot". Anyone anywhere may vary the elemental-directional association according to sense—this flexibility and relativity acknowledges the Great Big Universe we live in.

from whence we come, thus creating awareness of a deeper space and time in which we all participate. It de-constructs our usual personas and social complexities, taking participants into a deeper more basic reality of being—which we share in common, and in which it is safe to speak deep truths and be heard and known. This can be done with lots of poetry and drama, or with a simple group chant. As I have done them, there is almost always a direct involvement and identification of each participant with each element. Generally individuals are invited to add in their own words to the addressing of the elements, in addition to the formal script which is following a Seasonal theme in its pattern.

Always I conclude this process of "casting the circle" with a statement like: "This is the Centre of Creativity", drawing attention to the fact that the Centre of the Universe is here,[5] that the Ultimate Sentience of the Universe is present. This is true of every place, being and time, and yet the ritual is a space wherein this is made conscious, and that for me, is what "casting the circle" means—awareness of being at Centre, in that Awesome Creative Space.

"Invocation"—After setting up the safe space in which deeper truths may be spoken, it is traditional to "invoke the divine" in whatever way that is understood. I re-language that to mean, a recalling that we are each expressions of something Awesome, that in fact the truth of each person is that "here is the Source of everything, here is the Ultimate Mystery of the Universe."[6] This can be done in any number of ways…poetry, anointing, a simple gesture shared in pairs or with the group. Quite often as celebrant I will speak it to each person, though just as often participants will pass it to each other. Generally people can memorize any words that are used adequately, with some improvisation and prompting. Ideally, if whatever is said, is said with conviction, a deep knowing—it is an invocation of Presence. As I see it, that is what "transmission" is: that is, if a person can tell another with a deep knowing that "Here is the Source of everything, here is the Ultimate mystery of the Universe", the receiver will most likely get it on some level. That is what blessing is supposed to be, what invocation is. It is a deep knowing that the Power of the Universe is present. That, to my mind, is what it means to be "between the worlds", as traditional Pagan language describes the ritual space. This deep knowing is nurtured by meditation and practice over time,

---

5.   We live in an omnicentric Universe, noted by Brian Swimme, *Canticle to the Cosmos*, videos 1 and 9.

6.   Brian Swimme, *Canticle to the Cosmos*, video 1.

as well as by good teaching, and will usually be felt more deeply within a ritual context of experienced participants.

The Invocation as I have always done it, includes either a response from each participant that is central to the process—an affirmation that they accept this as a truth, or sometimes the Invocation is scripted as a space for each to announce themselves—in some way identifying themselves as a Larger Self, in accord with the Seasonal theme. Participants are encouraged to write or speak their own words, or at least to add their own words to any formal pre-scripted ones offered. I have found that it is also important in the preparation of the group for this process, to verbally offer participants the freedom not to speak, but to simply gesture in some way so that they may be welcomed as a Presence. Some may be far too shy, others may simply not have words—there may be any number of reasons for choosing a silent but conscious gesture.

Seasonal Rite or Body of the Ritual—This is the particular dramatic processes that give expression to the Seasonal Moment. These can be of great variation, according to personal, communal and regional aesthetics and factors. It includes what is traditionally known as "raising of energy" and the "working of magic"; that is, the transformational processes that are possible in ritual space. These, as I and participants currently do them, are in the ritual scripts in Chapter 7.

Sharing of Food or Communion—This is a formal recognition of how we are sustained, what gives us life, and of the fundamental communion experience of the Universe. It is a time within the ritual for thanksgiving, some relaxation and enjoyment. The food that is shared varies, and it is given to each participant formally with a blessing—sometimes from the celebrant or celebrants, sometimes from each other as it is passed around the circle. The food and the process connect with the theme of the Season.

Storytelling—a listening circle, wherein participants may speak to the group without having a discussion or being argued with. Any response from the group is formal and brief, such as "May it be so" or "thank you" or some other appropriate empathetic affirmation of having heard the speaker. It takes some discipline and sensitivity for participants to restrict themselves to hearing and only responding formally; usually the nature of the process has to be mentioned during the ritual preparation and re-iterated when introduced during the ritual. Often the celebrant will need to keep drawing the group consciousness back to the formal agenda with further invitation to others who may wish to speak. Sometimes patience and tolerance are required as some participants seem to go on, and not all may find the story being told pertinent. Yet this space is always an exercise in respect, sensitivity, true receptivity, and group trust. Each seasonal ritual script in Chapter 7 has a suggested agenda for this process that relates to the seasonal theme, but it is really an open space for whatever individuals need to speak of.

Opening of the Circle—a retracing of the "calling of the directions" and associated elements, and a summarized recapitulation of the seasonal ritual process that we have just participated in, with a peace blessing. Then the final words that I use are my version of the traditional ones[7]—sometimes sung, sometimes spoken:
The circle is open but unbroken. May the peace of Goddess go in our hearts. It has been a merry meeting. It is a merry parting. May we merry meet again. Blessed Be.

Usually a kiss is passed in both directions simultaneously, but this would depend on the nature of the group.

Celebrant and/or Co-celebrants as Evocators of Presence

In presiding as Mistress of Ceremonies/Priestess in the rituals, I have been conscious of the importance of my voice, my invocation of the reality of which I speak, when I speak. Spoken words—everyday ones—are actually always an invocation, a spelling of reality, but in ritual this may become more conscious. The celebrant and/or co-celebrants are participating in the calling forth of Presence within the consciousness of those present—the sacred depths. They will be enabled in that process by prior meditations upon, and awareness of, the truth of the Poetry they speak. They will also be enabled by the confident use of their breath and voice, which may involve some singing or voice lessons, and expressive therapies. Then in their voice:

> ...the meaning is inseparable from the sound, the shape, and the rhythm of the words...it remains rooted in the sensual dimension of experience, born of the body's native capacity to resonate with other bodies and with the landscape as a whole.[8]

---

7.   See Starhawk, *The Spiral Dance*, p.171.

All others present participate in the calling forth of this Presence, in themselves and in others, and may take roles in this regard in some of the processes. It is my understanding that the Poetry itself has its own integrity, as does the speaker, and as do the recipients; the Poetry is not a monolithic inert slab of information, It speaks to our depths in a relational particularity—each person "selecting" Its valency for them. As Charlene Spretnak tells it in *States of Grace*, in the ritual creation of sacred space, the narrator and listener become "engaged witnesses, weavers of a web of being" where articulations of mythic dramas are "acts of relation that place all participants in deep accord with the life processes of the unfolding universe."[9] The role of Priestess or celebrant is a deeply relational role; it is not just putting out questions, statements. She is evoking, drawing forth, and is already in response to the particular person's being—how they "select"/elicit a particular approach from her. The celebrant or co-celebrant listens deeply to the response, so the person is received. Sometimes, a particular invocation/blessing may be passed around the entire group, allowing individuals the opportunity to bless another, and to speak it. This kind of participation may also be structured into the creation of the sacred space—the remembering of the elements of Water, Fire, Earth and Air—whenever possible, enabling individuals to practice speaking with or "*to* the world", instead of *about* it;[10] that is, to practice PaGaian relationship.

HOW SPECIFIC RITUAL PROCESSES MAY DEVELOP THE THEME OF THE SEASONAL MOMENT

The actual Poetry of the Wheel as I have written it and understand it currently has evolved over time through a process that in itself reflects the threefold Cosmogenetic Shaping Powers—in the form of (i) my personal genetic "whisperings" or story, (ii) relational "natural selection" or how the Poetry feels when played out with others in ritual, and (iii) cosmic intuitive creativity…inspirations/images/words that simply arrive. Whilst this creative process is ongoing and opens the processes to change, there has been a consistency for the past several years that participants have been able to look forward to and deepen into each time.

---

8.   David Abram, *The Spell of the Sensuous*,p.74-75.
9.   Charlene Spretnak, *States of Grace*, p.141.
10. David Abram, *The Spell of the Sensuous*,p.71.

CALL TO GATHER:

Imbolc[11]—a single small bell rung three or more times, with each ring being separate. It is the beginning of the light part of the cycle, the flicker of Life, of Being, in its solitary tenuous Beauty allowed to resonate for a period of time. When the gathering is assembled, the celebrant suggests listening to the bell as if listening to the sound of each one's unique ringing. It is rung once more, and accentuated with the djorge for a few minutes.

Eostar—drums. It is a seasonal moment of stepping into Power, heralding dramatic Emergence and Return from the Underworld.

Beltane—when possible, a conch shell made into a horn, meant to be representative of Aphrodite who is especially invoked at this Seasonal Moment celebrating Desire/Allurement. Otherwise, vigorous drumming reflecting the fertile alluring beat of Life.

Summer Solstice—drums, with participants coming into the circle moving to the rhythm, and continuing to circle several times. This Season is about fullness of expression—being an "open channel for the moving energies of Life".

Lammas—a bell rung at a slow paced tempo. It is the counter reflection of the bell used at Imbolc; this time it is used to recall funeral rites. It is the beginning of the dark part of the cycle, the flicker of Death, of Return to Source. When the gathering is assembled, the ringing stops and the celebrant continues with "The Hour is come. For whom does the bell toll?" She asks the question three times, then finishes with "It tolls for thee."

Mabon—drums. It is another seasonal moment of stepping into Power, reflecting that of Eostar, but at this time heralding dramatic Descent.

Samhain—vigorous drumming. It is a dramatic Season, when all is possible.

Winter Solstice—a chant, with participants coming into the circle moving around the centre to the rhythm and joining in the chant. There are movements

---

11. Traditionally, in Pagan practice the year begins at Samhain, but "the beginning" may be felt throughout the three Sabbats of Samhain-Winter Solstice-Imbolc, so I am "fuzzy" about it.

that may go with the chant; all meant to encourage a recalling of our galactic location in the Milky Way. This Seasonal Moment is traditionally a time for singing together, in the depths of the Dark and the cold, affirming Being and keeping each other warm.

CENTERING—THE BREATH MEDITATIONS:

Winter Solstice—over the years this has developed into a relatively lengthy meditation, beginning with a focus on the "Void" at the bottom of the emptying of breath and feeling the Urge to breathe as it arises. This is drawn into a recalling of the many birthings of all kinds in personal lives—remembering how one has been Creator and Created. That is then extended to recalling Gaia-Earth's many birthings in this moment, everyday and throughout the eons, and then Gaia-Universe's many birthings in this moment, everyday and throughout the eons. Attention then is again drawn back to the breath, associating it with the birthing—of all—in every moment, the seamless Gaian self.

Imbolc—once again it begins with a focus on the Space between the breaths, the emptiness, and imagining it as the "Sea of Generosity" from which all springs forth. The experience of the breath then is imagined as a "ripple stirring upon the Sea", extending to imagining the self as being that ripple. The breath is then used to speak "the Mother's word of Creation—'Om'",[12] contemplating how we "spell" the world personally and collectively.

At the Equinoxes—the focus is on the experience of balance of light and dark, as Earth is so balanced in these Moments; imagining the breathing in as a swelling with Light, and the letting go of the breath as a letting go into Dark. It is spoken as "a fertile balance of tensions" that at the Spring Equinox is visualised as about to tip into increased light, and at the Autumn Equinox is visualised as about to tip into deeper dark.

Beltane—the focus begins with feeling the breath as it waxes towards fullness, and feeling one's desire for this breath. There is recall of how in each breath we share in the life of all who have danced and will dance, the Dance of Life—how each breath is actually filled with the Presence of all creatures who have known/

---

12. Barbara Walker describes "Om" as "mantramatrika, Mother of all Mantras" spoken by Kali, "an invocation of her own 'pregnant belly'. This was the primordial Logos...", *The Woman's Encyclopaedia of Myths and Secrets*, p.546.

will know breath.[13] This is extended to a physical gesture of embrace of the Present, as Beltane is a "Meeting of Desire"—an embrace, a "wedding". The recognition at this Sabbat of all who have come before—"and danced the Dance"—both in this ritual process of the breath meditation and also in the process of creating the sacred space, is a recognition of the resonance with the polar opposite Sabbat of Samhain.

Summer Solstice—the focus is on the experience of the peaking of the breath, beginning with a visualisation of deep connection to the core of Earth as sinking into full relationship with Her. The focus is on the filling of the bodymind to capacity, to feeling the fullness, and the felt need to release, and then "giving it away". I have also added into the format of Summer Solstice, after the statement of purpose, a "banishing" process. This would be traditionally understood as "cleansing the space". I have languaged it as making conscious those inner voices that impede one's full expression.

Lammas—the focus is on the passing of one's individual breath, the breath "that is yours, and not yours", how we pick the breath up at birth, let it go at death. We breathe a collective breath, that belongs to All.

Samhain—the focus is on following the breath down as it empties, and noticing the Space between the breaths "into which all who have gone before us have travelled, from which to enter again the dance of Life". This Space is again felt after the calling of the elements/directions and identified with the "Womb of All, fertile with possibility".

CREATING THE SACRED SPACE—REMEMBERING THE ELEMENTS—CALLING THE DIRECTIONS—"CASTING THE CIRCLE":

Winter Solstice—the elements are remembered as Cosmic Dynamics, dynamics that translate into particular capacities within the human—sensitivity, shaping power, memory and wisdom, exuberance and expression: this is drawn from Brian Swimme's understandings of the elements.[14] Remembering them in this way at Winter Solstice extends the theme of this Moment's breath meditation as connecting the layers of the seamless Gaian self—our presence to Origins.

---

13.   Brian Swimme, *Canticle to the Cosmos*, video 1.
14.   Brian Swimme, *The Universe is a Green Dragon*, p.87-109 and p.127-151.

Imbolc—since this is a celebration of physical manifestation, of differentiated being, the particular self, the language in the calling of the elements focuses on the individual internal physical experience of each element—each one's sensed feeling of each element. At Imbolc then, the external actual elements around the altar are not actually handled as usual, but attention is simply paid to the personal internal sensation of each.

Spring Equinox—since the celebration focuses on "Stepping into Power"—the Power of Being, the Heraic Return from the Depths, the focus is on the elements as Powers and feelings that we do know. It continues and deepens the Imbolc focus on feeling the elements, but now with an ability to act with them, an empowerment. The associations with each of the elements at this Sabbat are based on psychologist Sarah A. Conn's four aspects of global responsibility—direct experience, understanding, action and awareness.[15]

Beltane—since this is a celebration of Desire/Allurement, the focus is on our experience of desire for each of the elements—our thirst, desire for warmth and gathering around, our desire for fulfilment of purpose, and for breath and inspiration. Each participant engages in a tactile sensuous way with each element. There is an identification of that desire with all Desire, the Desire of all who have come before us, and the Desire of all who will come after us, and with the Desire of the Universe.

Summer Solstice—the focus repeats that of Winter Solstice, recalling the elements as Cosmic Dynamics present in human capacities, and thus reflecting a seamless Gaian self. However at this Summer Moment there is specific invitation for each one to speak of or be conscious of their relationship with each element as it is brought to them. This is an emphasis on the fullness of expression, as well as the celebration of the Mother aspect and its quality of relatedness and deep communion.

---

15. I have not arranged them in the order Conn has put them in, as my arrangement reflects the order of the elements in my particular location in the Southern Hemisphere. Conn describes growth in the process of global responsibility as non-linear, so I think my varied arrangement may be OK. Sarah A. Conn, "The Self-World Connection" Woman of Power Issue 20, Spring 1991, pp. 71-77.

Lammas—since the celebration is primarily about Dissolution, the Return to the Cosmic "soup", the focus is on identifying with the elements as part of the Old One's "Recipe". Each participant affirms their elemental presence in "Her Cauldron of Creativity"[16]—the Soup of the Universe. The drum beats for a few moments echoing the tempo of the bell that called to gather—a solemn paced beat, while participants wait.

Autumn Equinox—the directions are referred to as Places that we all come from. This is a way of recalling the ancient ritual of the Eleusinian Mysteries upon which this ritual is based; that is, it is said that people came to this annual event from every corner of the Earth to be initiated. These Mysteries were thus thought to hold the entire human race together.[17] Referring to the directions in this manner also alludes to our elemental presence in many forms throughout Gaia's entire transformational story—our ancient and multifold initiations in Her. We are from everywhere. Included in this process there is also an affirmation that "She is alive in me, and I in Her." This echoes part of the Seasonal rite of Spring Equinox. And in particular, it recalls the Seasonal theme of the continuity of Life, as the Mother Demeter passes all knowledge to the Daughter-Self Persephone, who thus becomes Mother—the Seed in the Fruit becomes the Fruit in the Seed,[18] they are in each other: so the elements of Water, Fire, Earth and Air are associated with this continuity of Life within us. The rhythm of the calling of the elements is quicker than usual, to create a cacophony effect and a sense of this continuity.

Samhain—since the celebration is about the Transformation of Death, the focus is on how ancient each element within us is, how we are its recycled presence, thus how old we each really are. This is a remembering that there is nothing we have not been—we are fertile with possibility. The elements are not handled by each participant as usual; instead they are ceremonially processed around the circle for viewing and contemplation. This is also a reverse reflection of the Imbolc element/directions process.

---

16. My understanding of Her "Cauldron of Creativity" is the all pervading constant flux of all matter in which we are immersed, and which has been described scientifically by Vernadsky in *The Biosphere*. See p.22 *PaGaian Cosmology*.
17. Lawrence Durdin-Robertson, *The Year of the Goddess*, p. 158.
18. a metaphor used by Starhawk, *The Spiral Dance*, p.196.

Overall, throughout the Light part of the cycle, there is a continuation of focus on the sensual experience of the elements, a focus on the individual sensate knowing of the elements, and in this way knowing participation in All. Whereas in the Dark part of the cycle, the elements are acknowledged primarily in their collective aspect, how we are each a drop of, and inseparable from that collective, how we are elementally immersed in something much Larger—not individual at all, how we elementally belong to that "Soup".

INVOCATIONS:

At Winter Solstice, which is a birthing, and a particular remembering of Origins, participants anoint each other with oil, and pronounce with authority the Divinity[19]—Creator and Created—in each other: "Thou art Goddess, thou art the Divine Child, thou art All of That." These words are offered, and participants are encouraged to take this opportunity to "try them on", but also to maybe add something that they find expressive of the reality, like perhaps, "You are a whole Universe." This Invocation is extended then into the "Cosmogenesis Dance"[20] which expresses in movement the three aspects of the Sacred Dynamic Cosmological Unfolding that we participate in. The dance begins with an inner and an outer circle, that move into relationship in a middle space, before passing into the opposite places—becoming outer and inner respectively.

Imbolc—where the flame/light is tender and new, and the One who is the "Urge to Be" is celebrated and nurtured, participants each light a candle from the centre candle and gaze into the flame, contemplating how the Flame of Being is within them. In their own time each one places the candle on the altar affirming in their own words the Presence of this Virgin quality in their being. The midwifing and

---

19. This word does not need to be used—some may find it problematic, others may need it. "Sacred" can usually be substituted.

20. This dance is originally named as "Adoramus Te Domine" and the instructions for it come with the music by the same name, on an audio tape called "Sacred Dances" produced for Dr Jean Houston's work. New music for this dance is being composed by Tanna Kjaer-Dona (www.tannakjaer.com) of the Goddess Association in Australia. It was only in the second year of doing the dance at Winter Solstice, that I realised its three layers were resonant with the Female Metaphor and the three faces of Cosmogenesis. I thereafter re-named and storied the dance that way in the ritual preparation and teaching—see the Winter Solstice teaching in Appendix F, p.280-281. For the dance instructions, see Appendix I.

"true" qualities of Artemis are then invoked with the tasting of Artemisia herbs and the holding of Her arrow.

Spring Equinox—we are invoking the Hera, the Courageous One who has returned from Journeying in the Darkness. Each participant holds up a special stone or rock representing the precious gem of Wisdom gained from the Darkness, and announces themselves as Hera or Hero or Courageous One. Placing the stone on the altar they affirm their Return and Presence and gained Wisdom.

At Beltane—we are invoking Beauty and Desire. The Charge of the Goddess is read or spoken,[21] and participants are invited to name themselves as "the Beauty whom She desires".[22] To facilitate this identification of self with Beauty, each one brings an object or a photo, or recalls some thing, being, or place that they experience as beautiful, recognising it within themselves. This may be extended, as each one wishes, to expressing themselves as the Beloved, wholly desirable, and their desiring being as holy.[23]

At the Summer Solstice—we are recognizing and invoking Fullness of Being and Full Expression of Creativity. Participants are invited to greet each other with a bow of reverence and "Thou art the Sacred Fullness of the Mother—She is fully present in you. Thou art Queen of Summer/Summer King". In this spiritual tradition, all the seasons have a significance that has been lost to most minds today, but to the ancients "Summer" had a special numinosity: it was understood as a Place of abundance, ripeness and eternal fulfillment (similar to the Christian "heaven" except that there was nothing ethereal about it). So, to be recognised as "Summer Sovereign" is to be blessed with eternal Creativity and Union. The

---

21. Actually only the last paragraph of it is used on this occasion. See p.219-220. The full text is quoted in Starhawk, *The Spiral Dance*, p.90-91.

22. This is an expression that Brian Swimme has used to describe what he perceives as the required aspiration of the male in sexual relationship to the female; that is, to be "the beauty that she desires". I like to use it here meaning it as something which all Being actually is and may consciously aspire to; that is, to be the Beauty and delicious morsel that the Universe desires.

23. At a subtle level this celebrated Desire is a desire for mergence—union. With practice of the Wheel of seasonal ritual one begins to get a SENSE of growing light associated with this dissolution—we are actually moving towards entropy with the waxing and alluring Light. This gets "written" into the bodymind with this ritual practice—though it may be unconscious scribing for some.

invocation is continued with a "Conversation of Union" or "Dyad Poem" as I call it,[24] wherein at this Solstice Gateway from the Light into the Dark, an inner and an outer circle express the Union—the reciprocity—of form and formlessness. This dialogue poem may express the flux and interchange of the "manifest" and the "manifesting" of the Cosmos. This formation of an inner and an outer circle in conversation also recalls the formation at the Winter Solstice invocation for the Cosmogenesis Dance—which is done in silence. The Summer Solstice dyadic conversation/poem culminates in a unified "prayer" and then a toning—a harmonising of voices that may be felt as an exercise in relationship with self, other and all-that-is…the three layers of Cosmogenesis.[25]

At Lammas—where we remember the Dark One to whom we return, that we are the Harvest, we are recognizing and invoking the Presence of this Dark and Ancient Sentience within—the One who "creates Space to Be", who is the Transformation of the Ages. Participants receive grains of barley in their hands, and ash on their foreheads, and affirm that they are: "She, Dark and Ancient Wise One", adding or expressing their own words to this theme. There is then a meditative space for contemplating Her within.

Autumn Equinox—this is a rite of initiation into the Dark Mysteries, the Heraic Descent of the Courageous One, the Beloved Daughter-Self, who must know the processes of the Depths. Demeter is invoked with a chant, and She hands to each participant three stalks of wheat tied with red ribbon, signifying the passing on of the sacred knowledge[26] of Life. The Mother is acknowledging their readiness for the Journey, wherein they will receive and *per*ceive the Wisdom necessary for Life

---

24. It is an adaptation of a poem in Starhawk, *The Spiral Dance*, p. 119.
25. The way I teach it in the ritual preparation is that each participant is feeling for their own true expressive voice (Virgin/differentiation), as well as listening for the other voices (Mother/communion), and it is all coming out of and going into a Larger Self (Old One/autopoiesis); the toning that arises is co-created and yet coming from the Well of Creativity itself. See Appendix F, p.297.
26. This "knowledge" that the wheat signifies is as much genetic, body memory, as much as it is mind, trans-genetic cultural memory. This passing on of knowledge was originally understood as particularly expressed in the mother-daughter relationship: this turns out to have some basis genetically. See Irene Coates, *The Seed-Bearers*. It may be understood to represent all that each being is given by the Universe in every moment.

to continue: in fact, with the gift of the wheat, She hands each one All that is needed. We are the Bearers of Life as much as we are Borne by Life.

Figure 2: The Mother Demeter hands the wheat to Her Daughter-Self Perse-phone, expressing the passing on of all knowledge—the continuity of Life.[27]

---

27. This image is adapted from Hallie Iglehart Austen, *The Heart of the Goddess*, p.73, where credit is given to Alinari/Art Resource, New York. Eleusis Museum, Greece.

Samhain—we are invoking All Possibility in this Moment of deep formlessness, our capacity as Co-creators. Each participant is invited to name themselves as they will, wherein they may identify imaginatively with the mythic, the fanciful, and other subtle dimensions of themselves that they may wish to be more conscious of.[28]

COMMUNION—THE SHARING OF FOOD:

At Winter Solstice, as we celebrate the Birthing of All from the full Darkness of the Mother, each participant is offered dark fruit cake and red wine, and poetically identified as *Her* Cake and Wine—made by and for Her, integral with the Cosmic processes. We are Her Communion, we are the Place/Space where it happens: in that sense we are Her—the Mother. Communion at this Sabbat, affirms that we, as Cosmic/Earth participants, are "wine poured out for the Mystery"—that is our Origin and our purpose. This resonates with the Communion words of Summer Solstice where participants affirm that they are Food—Bread and Wine—that has ripened, ready for consumption.

At Imbolc, the first celebration of the Light part of the cycle, the fruit bread and the wine/juice are white or light in colour and we also share white gourmet chocolates. As each participant is given the food, they are blessed with a version of the Annunciation to Mary from the Christian tradition, as a way of reclaiming that metaphor of Annunciation for all; that is, as a recognition of the Holy One, as the Young One, present in the Self.

At Eostar, where confirmed emergence from the depths is being celebrated, with the main story being that of Demeter and Persephone, the words of Pindar, the Greek philosopher and poet, are used in part, for the blessing: "Blessed are you—you have seen these things…"[29] Added to this is a re-worded version of an admonition commonly used in the Christian communion rite, which some participants would be aware of: "Do this in remembrance of She who gives Life"—it is a conscious reclaiming, as Persephone in this Goddess tradition is a Redeemer/

---

28. At a subtle level this celebration of deep formlessness is a desire for creation, for emergence of form—polar opposite Beltane. With practice of the whole Wheel of seasonal ritual one begins to get a SENSE of growing dark associated with becoming—this gets "written" into the bodymind—though it may be unconscious scribing for some.

29. Jean Houston uses these words as participants in her exercise "The Realm of the Ancestors" emerge from the "Underworld". See Jean Houston, *The Hero and the Goddess*, p.197.

Wisdom figure. The food given is poppy seed cake: the poppy is associated with Persephone because of its many seeds, representing the abundance and fertility of the Dark. Each participant is also offered a "Golden Egg" (a gourmet chocolate wrapped in golden foil), partly because of participants' familiarity with the tradition of eggs at "Easter", the Christian festival—which is held during Autumn in Australia (!)—and I wish to call to their sensed experience, chocolate eggs in the right Season—Spring. They are told of the Goddess roots of this tradition in the teaching before the ritual, and they are blessed as they take the egg, with: "Remember the Ancient One who lays the Golden Egg—take it, it is yours—laid out for you everyday."

At Beltane, it is the sweetness of Life that is emphasized, with honey cake and sweet white wine being offered, with the admonitions to "consume your Desire" and to "enjoy it". Sweet sugary doughnuts are also offered, partly because these sweet cakes can be hung in trees and bushes around the circle if practical, but the "hole" shape is also a good metaphor for this Seasonal Moment of "Holy Desirability" and fertility. Since Aphrodite is especially invoked, and the rose is Her flower, rose water is used in the honey, and rose petals are sprinkled on the cake which is coloured pink. The light use of roses in this way also previews the central role of roses in the seasonal rite at the next Sabbat, Summer Solstice.

At Summer Solstice, which is quintessentially a celebration of Communion—the ripening of the Promise of the light part of the cycle, whose purpose is to be given to Other and All-That-Is and consumed, each participant affirms, "I am the grain, I am the Bread of Life", as they take the bread in their own hands and break off a piece. Each one similarly affirms, "I am the grape, I am the Wine", as they take the decanter and glass from the celebrant and pour wine for themselves. The response to this, from other participants, affirms that it is the Sun in each of us that has ripened: "It is the Sun that is in you, see how you shine."[30]

At Lammas, the first celebration of the Dark, dark bread and red wine/juice are offered to participants, with blessings for being nourished by Her Harvest, and letting "Her Rich Creative Darkness soak through you." The latter blessing is, in my mind, a reference to the Womb of the Mother wherein Her Blood is for gestating, is for Life. It also may recall the dis-solution theme of this Season.

---

30. A variation of words from Starhawk, *The Spiral Dance*, p.190-191.

At Autumn Equinox, which is the main thanksgiving harvest festival, the food that is shared is all brought by the participants, as a representation of their abundance gained, their "Harvest". The presentation of the food is part of the Seasonal rite, as they state the "harvests" for which they give thanks.

At Samhain, apples and apple juice are the chosen communion food, as the apple in this Goddess tradition represents never-ending renewal.[31] In the tradition as Starhawk does it, an apple is frequently ritually cut at this Season's celebration.[32] Using the apple as a holy food is an opportunity to re-story and re-experience it, given that most participants will have been imbued with the Judeo-Christian story, wherein the apple is a fruit of temptation representing knowledge that is ruinous. The patriarchal religion storied it this way *because* it represented the Mother Knowledge. At the Samhain communion then, as each participant is offered the apple and juice, they are admonished and blessed with, "Stand tall, daughters and sons of the Mother. Daughters and sons of Eve, stand tall—enjoy the fruit and drink of never-ending renewal."

HOW GAIA'S STORY—THE UNIVERSE STORY—MAY BE CELEBRATED IN THE SEASONAL MOMENTS

Woven throughout the Seasonal ritual celebrations, may be the conscious celebration of Cosmogenesis, the Creative Unfolding of Gaia-Universe&Earth. These ritual celebrations begin with Earth-Sun relationship—that is the reason for their existence since the earliest of human times. The resulting Creativity of the play of Light and Dark in this Earth-Sun relationship has translated into food, and into human psyches. The creative telling of our personal and collective stories, and how we wish them to unfold, may be folded into the seasonal moment because that is where we may each interface intimately with Gaia. Then also, as participants in the Larger Story of Gaia—*knowing* this is our full story—there is always this Deeper layer to be expressed, and it may be drawn specifically into the Seasonal Moments.

---

31. See Barbara Walker, *The Woman's Encyclopaedia of Myths and Secrets*, p.48-50.
32. Starhawk, *The Spiral Dance*, p.195-196.

On the surface of it, the dark Crone phase particularly celebrates Autopoiesis—sentience, subjectivity, interiority, the creative centre; the light Virgin phase particularly celebrates Differentiation—diversity, complexity, multiform nature, articulation. Communion—the Mother phase, reciprocity, deep relatedness, interconnectivity, mutuality—is celebrated throughout, though particularly at the Solstices, and in balance with other two at the Equinoxes.

There may be many ways of folding in aspects of Gaia's story, of languaging in moments of her Story that one wants to celebrate, but I have been conscious of some as follows, and written them in to the ritual scripts and the pre-ritual teachings.

At Winter Solstice, it is the Original Flaring Forth, the Primaeval Fireball, the Great Origin, that is echoed in the Sun's "return" and the movement out of darkness. Also echoed is the birth of our Solar System, from the Grandmother Supernova Tiamat[33]—this is our particular Cosmic lineage whom we may remember at this time. It is the time to recall and proclaim any birth, and the births in our psyches, imaginations, and minds.

At Imbolc, it is the continued birthing—the rushing away of the Fireball, the continued rippling forth of Creation, the early Universe. It is understanding the difficulties, the resistances that even Gaia-Universe has encountered, and how this has served the Unfolding of the Story as we know it. Imbolc celebrates Gaia's rush to diversity, differentiation; we commit ourselves to this, beginning with ourselves. The ritual process of "purification and strengthening" may be understood as a feeling for where it is in us that the Universe is acting now—where each one feels the excitement of Creativity calling to them in their lives. [34]

At Eostar, when the Light reaches a new level of power, and "Persephone" returns with Wisdom gained, Her emergence may be understood as a collective experience of emergence into a new era—the Ecozoic Era that Berry and Swimme speak of.[35] As I say in the teaching that prefaces the ritual:

---

33. Tiamat" is Swimme and Berry's name for the Supernova that was the Mother of our Solar System, *The Universe Story*, p.49.
34. Brian Swimme speaks of such feeling in "The Timing of Creativity", *Canticle to the Cosmos*, video 10.
35. Brian Swimme and Thomas Berry, *The Universe Story*, p.253-254.

we may contemplate not only our own individual 'lost' wanderings, but also that of the human species. We are part of a much Bigger ReTurn that is happening. The Beloved One is ReTurning[36] on a collective level as well. We affirm that tonight—we are part of making it happen.

At Beltane, the essential primordial power of Allurement is celebrated. It is this power of attraction, in particular as gravitational bonding, that holds the universe together, as Brian Swimme describes it.[37] "This primal dynamism awakens the communities of atoms, galaxies, stars, families, nations, persons, ecosystems, oceans, and stellar systems."[38] In the experience of the ritual, individuals may sense and express their participation in this Allurement, in its many valencies—feel and affirm how this Desire is at the core of their Being, and all that they do. Beltane is also a good time to celebrate the advent of meiotic sex, a step in Gaia's Story some one billion years ago, that was an evolutionary leap for all three aspects of Cosmogenesis.[39] This evolutionary move may be understood as the advent of gender, as a particular manifestation of Creativity. This moment in the Story of the Universe is also connected to the advent of death,[40] which is poetically resonant with the polar symmetry of Beltane and Samhain.

At Summer Solstice, it is Gaia's Teeming Abundant Creativity that is celebrated—how "She gives it away, She pours it forth" as we say in the ritual. We recall that this is what Mother Sun does, this is what Earth does, and this is what we may do with the abundant Creativity that ripens in us. This cosmology assents to, and nurtures a concentration of Being that innately demands to be poured forth—it creates a generosity within since abundance is its very nature. We celebrate the innate Generosity of the Universe, for which Sun may be our model. As Swimme reminds, "There is not a single solitary thought or action in the history of humanity that is not a Solar event."[41] It is a time for remembering

---

36. This way of writing "ReTurning" is inspired by Jennifer Berezan's CD ReTURN-ING referred to p.213. fn.43. Joanna Macy also speaks of the "Great Turning" of our times, Coming Back to Life, p.17.
37. Brian Swimme, *The Powers of the Universe*, lecture 2.
38. Brian Swimme, *The Universe is a Green Dragon*, p.49.
39. Brian Swimme and Thomas Berry, *The Universe Story*, p.107-109. See also Elisabet Sahtouris, *Earthdance*, p.126-131.
40. See Elisabet Sahtouris, *Earthdance*, p.134-135, and Ursula Goodenough, *The Sacred Depths of Nature*, p.143-149.
41. Brian Swimme, *Canticle of the Cosmos*, video 2.

our Source, and the ongoing Event that we are part of, that even the Sun is part of.

Lammas celebrates the beginning of dismantling, de-structuring, cutting the harvest, after the peaking and ripening of Summer Solstice. There are many such moments in the evolutionary story which could be specifically remembered, including our present ending of the Cenozoic Era, as Swimme and Berry describe the present extinctions and planetary destruction.[42] Gaia has done a lot of this de-structuring, it is in Her nature to Return all to the Sentient "Soup". In the Lammas celebration, as I have languaged it, we recall the Dark Sentience at the base of Being, to which each is returned. I also use Swimme's term, the "All-Nourishing Abyss", expressing as it does, that this Mystery at the base of being, is both generative and infinitely absorbing—a Power out of which particles simply emerge and into which they are absorbed.[43] We image this "Power" as the Great Receiver, the Old Compassionate One, complete forgiveness, the Transformer, a Depth of Love—She is all of That.

At Mabon when Dark reaches a new level of power, and it is storied as the departure of "Persephone", the Beloved One, there is opportunity to recall and express all the grief of the losses involved in Gaia's penchant for Change and "dis-mantling". In the long evolutionary story, there have been many told and untold losses—species of flora and fauna that will never arise again, cultural losses, genocides, individual tragedies. Mabon is a time for remembering both the rich harvest gained and apparent, and also this deep loss and pain. Another layer to this recognition of Loss at Mabon, is the Loss of every moment of Existence—the fact that every moment dissolves, and is never repeated: the Story of Gaia-Universe is irreversible and nonrepeatable.[44] It is also then true that every moment is totally new. We may grieve the Loss, *and* celebrate the Moment. Mabon is also then the time to celebrate the Delicate Balance, the Creative Curvature of Space-Time, that Creative Edge upon which all Life proceeds. The red thread with which the wheat is tied for this ritual has come to represent that to me.[45] Also the seed, the

---

42. Brian Swimme and Thomas Berry, *The Universe Story*, p. 241-250.

43. Brian Swimme, *The Hidden Heart of the Cosmos*, p.100.

44. Brian Swimme, *Canticle to the Cosmos*, video 10. See also Appendix A, Thomas Berry's principle 10.

45. It was traditional for Eleusinian initiates to wear threads. In our current times the thread may also represent the superstrings conjectured by Western science to form the basis of matter: see Brian Greene, *The Elegant Universe*.

"Persephone" that is planted ritually represents that very perdurable balance and fecundity that has enabled the entire evolutionary story. Six months later, at Eostar, the flowered seed is held up, as evidence of Her never-ending Presence and Generativity.

At Samhain, the theme is one of journeying yet further into darkness—the Transformation of Death, and therein the conception of the new. It is a time for celebrating the Becomings, the unimaginable More that Gaia has become, and will still yet become. It is a time for remembering the ancestors—creatures, plant and human—out of whom we and the present have arisen, that we are the ancestors of the future, and that we are completely free to imagine/conceive Much More.

7

The Ritual Events and the Scripts

Following is a description of various aspects of the ritual events, how they actually unfold generally—including inviting the people there, the place, how we spend the time, how the group is prepared for the ritual, who helps facilitate, and then the ritual scripts/dramas themselves as they are currently. I understand any particular ritual event as an invitation to participate in a Poem, an invitation into a Poetic experience, much like going to theatre except that it is participatory theatre. It is ritual theatre, wherein there is a script known in part by at least one facilitator/celebrant, but it is not completely known, as the "actors" are not yet all assembled with their full parts spliced in. There is an expressed intention in the gathering, but the actual unfolding is unpredictable. The Poetic experience is co-created though there is a guiding story—there is hearing and speaking, learning and expression, receiving and giving, that is ever reciprocal. The sum of the whole cycle of the year of ritual events then is an invitation to participate in a Poem over time—over the period of the year or years; and that has another whole dimension to it.

Invitations

I produce an "invitation" or flyer for each Sabbat, which is meant to orient the prospective participants to the Seasonal Moment. These invitations spell out the reason for the season, give a summary of the Seasonal Moment and a sense of the celebration, along with some details of what to bring. It is usual each year, for me to re-consider the wording and make some changes as my understandings develop and change, and especially if any changes have been made to some of the ritual processes. These invitations are sent out to an interested list of persons that has grown over time. Even people who choose to come to only very few of the ritual celebrations, express their enjoyment of receiving these invitations, as reminders of the Season. It may encourage them to make the transition to Gaian time-space, and to create their own manner of celebration.

Place

Although over the years almost all of the seasonal rituals that I have facilitated have taken place within the Blue Mountains—my region, each ritual has not taken place in the same location. I would have preferred that it did, but it was not possible. I had to move for a time from my home, a ritual place with which I was "familiar"—"family". This dislocation was a source of some disruption to me, but one that was expressive of the whole situation of this work at the time: that is, there was not really a space for it, a place, a situation, a site. One of the outcomes of the academic research, which enabled the deepened practice of the rituals (and also the meeting of my supportive and participatory partner) was the development of a place, a site. This place for the rituals turned out to be a return to my home where they have been held ever since. I now consider it important that I am present in my ceremonial place—my home—at the time of the Seasonal Moment, participating with my community in the ritual. I do not go away during these times: I feel committed to the ceremony on this site and its multivalent significance.

When I had left my home just prior to beginning the research, I realized then that I felt that the trees and plants there knew me—many seasonal rituals had already been celebrated there. After that, quite often the rituals were held in places with which I was un-familiar, that is, I was very aware that I was not "family" with the place; or within structures that had probably never witnessed such ceremony before. It was important to me that I visited, familiarized myself, and meditated in the space, at least a week before the ritual. On the day of the ritual, I was always keen to get into the space as soon as I could, to set up and settle in. It was always a relief when the ritual was able to be celebrated at my place of dwelling, where I had plenty of time in the space, and also where I did not have to vacate as soon as it was concluded. I did notice that when a particular place was repeatedly the location for sequential Seasonal rituals, that the memory of the previous Seasonal motifs and rites would present themselves spontaneously, as the present one was being prepared and carried out. This was a great pleasure and added to my real understanding of this religious practice.

I relate all of this so as to say that compromises may sometimes need to be made for a time, but in my experience, the determination to proceed as best one can, with a generosity of spirit, and continued vision and feeling for what one is essentially celebrating, will eventuate in fulfillment or deeper practice.

Ritual Preparation of the Group

Between the stated time for arrival of the participants and the formal beginning of the event, there is time allowed for the participants to settle in—place their ritual objects and "bits" and themselves, and to meet and greet others, and to nibble. The formal beginning of the event takes place when we all come to sitting in a circle in the ritual space—which may be inside or outside depending on the Seasonal Moment, the nature of the ritual processes and the weather. We begin with a teaching about the Seasonal Moment. At this time the door is closed to any latecomers, as the teaching is important to participant comprehension of the occasion and their ability to creatively and sincerely engage in the processes of the ritual. Thus closing the door to latecomers is felt to be part of creating the "sacred space"—a space safe and known, for the unfolding of each participant's particular dearly held understandings, interpretations and expressions.

The teachings themselves have evolved over time, and continue to, according to my understanding. I always ask for comment, additional input and questions. Some participants who have been coming for years don't seem to mind hearing some of the same information over again each year, and neither do I, as we all seem to grow in our comprehension each time. I have included the teachings—as they are currently—in this book as Appendix F. They repeat much of the information already within the main text of this book, but in a collected, synthesised and somewhat augmented form, directly related to the particular ritual scripts. They are included here, not because I think they are definitive in any way—I regard myself as a novice yet—but because they provide a summary of the Earth-Sun Moment and its layers of significance, and may be of use to some to get started in their own Seasonal practice, meditations and further research.

After the preparatory teaching I go over the ritual format with the group, teaching any dances and songs that need to be known, and explaining and evoking participants' particular possible actions and expressions. I have found that it is important to each person's comfort that I specifically state that individual speaking is not required, that what is paramount is each one's own consciousness of their intentions. They need only participate by means of gesture or minimal words according to their desire, for their own sense of presence, and also that others may respond to their presence. On the other hand, each one is encouraged to express themselves as dramatically as they like, to seize the opportunity. There is always a great range of chosen modes of presence to the processes and rites, and care needs to be taken to encourage this. For some processes, words will be offered on pieces of paper—as some participants have requested this, but it is made clear that they are meant only as guides. Some people will choose to use these words, most will write their own and a few will speak spontaneously.

The next stage of the preparation as it has been done, is ten minutes for individual meditation or contemplation of personal intentions and contributions. Participants wander into different spaces—the garden, the kitchen, the meditation room, some stay in the ritual space. Some participants will write during this time, some simply sit quietly. This time is also used for the taking care of physical needs, switching off mobile phones, taking care of details of all kinds—lights, candles, kitchen appliances, and personal—so that the ritual circle can proceed as smoothly as possible and without interruption.

Artful Expression—Headpiece, Decoration and Wreath

I have always worn a special headpiece for the rituals: I feel that any participant may do so, not just the celebrant. My ritual headpiece with its changing and continuous Seasonal decoration took on increasing significance over the years; it became a personal central representation of the year long ritual art process of creating, destroying and re-creating. For the research period particularly, it came to represent for me the essence of "She"—as Changing One, yet ever as Presence—as I was coming to know Her. In my journal for the Mabon process notes one year I wrote:

> As I pace the circle with the Mabon headpiece in the centre, I see "Her" as She has been through the Seasons…the black and gold of Samhain, the deep red, white and evergreen of Winter, the white and blue of Imbolc, the flowers of Eostar, the rainbow ribbons of Beltane, the roses of Summer, the seed pods and wheat of Lammas, and now the Autumn leaves. I see in my mind's eye, and feel, Her changes. I am learning…The Mother knowledge grows within me.

The headpiece, the wreath, the altar, the house decorations, all participate in the ritual: they are part of the learning, the method, the relationship—similar to how one might bring flowers and gifts of significance to a loved one at special moments. Then further, the removal and re-creation of the decorations are part of the learning—an active witness to transformation through time.

Co-Celebrants

These rituals—this art form of ceremony—always required others who could take on roles of helping facilitate processes, ensuring an active participation of those assembled—not passive watching. In the earliest of days when I first began to create a few of these celebrations, there were friends—female or male—who took these roles. Later when I was part of a Moon Circle of women, we all took on co-celebration, though I took the role of initiating the events and scripting the dramas. Within the context of another group—Women-Church—there was frequently co-celebration of various types of ritual celebrations, with one or a few scripting the process. These rituals were usually not of seasonal theme specifically. At that stage I had not committed myself to the full cycle of the Seasonal celebrations nor did I have any idea of the significance and power of the story of the Wheel as I have come to understand it and articulate it. This awareness has only dawned on me over time, as the particular synthesis grew within me and as others responded. I was drawn into scripting the full annual cycle of the rituals, and it all very quickly blossomed, attracting participation and co-celebration, as well as opening the pathway of academic research and documentation.

Central to the real development, deepening and articulation of this art form of ritual during the research period was the participation of four core women, as mentioned in the Introduction, and the organic nature of their participation was described. I considered them to be co-celebrants. They began as drummers initially, and their roles expanded quickly. Throughout the research period, these four women were given copies of the script weeks before each Sabbat. They were free to give their opinion and participate in the altering of details, though the story remained fairly much intact. They were conscious, as I was, that we were experimenting to some extent, with a particular expression/story of the Creative Wheel of the Year. They were happy to go with it.

These women, and one other who also sometimes drummed, always handled the elements in the rituals—volunteering themselves for different elements as they felt each time. They frequently served the Communion and spoke the blessings, they often played key roles in the Invocations, and sometimes other special roles that were part of particular rituals, for example, at Lammas offering the bread figures, and at Winter, lighting the cauldron fire. Their participation and understanding was an important part of the whole experience. These particular women still sometimes play any of these roles, but there are also others now, or sometimes students in current seasonal classes, who may volunteer at the time during preparation when the ritual format is being previewed. Some roles, such as the handling of the elements and lighting of the Winter Solstice candle, or carrying communion trays of glasses or food, lend themselves to an opportunity for children, who love to serve in this way. Frequently now there are long periods when there is no team preparing for the rituals, though I would like it if that happened again. My partner now co-hosts the events with maintaining and preparation of the ritual place, and the clean-up, and by serving various roles within the ritual such as drumming, carrying communion glasses around, and some very practical roles such as lighting the ritual fires or torches and overseeing safety matters.

Another role for co-celebrants for which I sometimes spontaneously choose an experienced participant, or for which one volunteers spontaneously, is to play the Priestess role when for example, at Mabon, it is my turn to receive the wheat, or at Eostar when it is my turn to be welcomed back, or at Samhain when it is my turn to be given a gingerbread snake.

At the time of each ritual, whenever there has been a prepared team of co-celebrants, we gather in a small circle before the formal Call to Gather, joining hands, to centre ourselves as a group.

Participation of Children

Some Seasonal celebrations may seem to lend themselves better to the participation of children, but children themselves are usually eager to attend any of them. Any hesitance to include children usually has more to do with adult discomfort with the nature of the Seasonal Moment, or a perceived compromise of the parent's need for the process of the ritual space. All of the Sabbats have been at one time or another attended by at least one child. In each case, the child participated in the whole ritual process, at their own level of understanding, and it was always with a guiding parent. The children have always seemed to have a good experience—often expressing thanks. Children who were too young to participate have never attended.

The Ritual Scripts

As I have mentioned, I consider most of the specific phrases and language important, it is not a casual thing—I consider it Poetry; yet there is also some variation in the moment, as the particularity of the people, the person, the flow is sensed—and there is a lot of variation in the responses. The scripts, as I have written them, have evolved over time.[1] The scripts continue to evolve, according to my understanding of the Seasonal event and the creative dynamic face of Mystery that it seems to me to express. I am conscious of these scripts as being a "scribing" process, an "authoring"; primarily as a Creative process that is being "authored" largely by me, yet wherein each participant may choose to articulate and "scribe" their personal experience of this particular story. Generally only minor changes have been made to the scripts in the last several years, and the community of regular participants enjoy that consistency, finding that it allows a deepening into the Poetry.

Participants are encouraged to add their own words to responses even in places where there is particular wording significant to the Sabbat and a relationship/theme that I feel is important to be expressed.[2] This freedom to add or articulate their own felt response avoids any feeling of "parroting", and invites a felt resonance for participants with what they are saying. That may mean at times that the group response to say, the calling of the elements is of varied individual statements—then it becomes simply a chorus of felt response. Most often the participants use the response that is offered in the script—they seem to desire to try out this particular expression, to participate in this particular Poetry, and then some add to it. Sometimes there has been a request for the responses to be printed out

---

1. The process of the evolution of some of the ritual scripts is described in detail in Chapter 7 of the academic version of this book, which is accessible at: http://library.uws.edu.au/adt-NUWS/public/adt-NUWS20030731.103733/index.html

2. This was not always done so freely during the research period, when I sought to create a specific context, wherein "She" was definitely spoken, and responses to that context were being sought. I am now more confident of the Poetic context having been created, wherein participants understand and desire the particular metaphor and story, so they are free within that to express their own relationship.

on slips of paper, so they could express it just so, and/or onto which they could write additional expressions during the meditation time before the ritual.

Starhawk says it is best to memorise or improvise. It took me some courage in the early days, to let go of having the script in hand during the ritual, but it was important to do so, for both personal and dramatic/aesthetic reasons. I then had to learn the Poetry, which is what I really wanted to do: I have been learning a new language, a new reality that required new language, a language not readily accessible to me—so I memorised the scripts. This has filled me with the Poetry; it has become readily accessible to my mind and my lips. Increasingly then improvisation and sensing of the moment become possible—one first needs the "tools", the skills of the craft, before the art is possible. I have been a novice, starting from "scratch", so I had to take care to include all the steps in my learning, to be meticulous in my preparation.

The process of preparation for me as celebrant has involved rehearsing the ritual—the words and actions—in the space when possible. I begin this some weeks before the Sabbat. Again, this is much like the rehearsal necessary for any dramatic event: this enables a sense of the details, and I make notes as I become aware of these and any changes that I desire to make. In the weeks before the ritual, my daily meditation includes going through the script, deepening into its dimensions—feeling it for myself and for the imagined group. Sometimes I also rehearse the script as I walk or travel somewhere, sometimes over a cup of tea in bed, anywhere really.

Below are the scripts, in their most recent form. Acknowledgement of the work and inspiration of others are noted. I have already noted the use of Starhawk's work in particular. All words in quotation are spoken by me as the celebrant, unless otherwise noted. A dotted space—(......)—indicates that a co-celebrant is taking the action and/or speaking. In indented print at the beginning of each Sabbat's script is some detail about the props and setting required for the ritual drama. At the end of each script I include a list of the particular themes for the contemplation of participants in their preparation for the ritual.

SAMHAIN

Participants may come dressed in costume. Each bring photos/objects that represent "old selves"—to have with them at circle. Covered basket of gingerbread snakes. Scissors. Sliced apples—rubbed with lemon, apple juice poured. Ball of golden thread. Photos of ancestors for side altar. Dark centre altar cloth with gold stars/webs in it, or a dark golden cloth.[3] Cauldron or large clay pot full of soil, overlaid with wreath of dried leaves (both left over from Mabon), as centrepiece with the centre candle. "Mists"/veils of varied colours as decorations. Music ready.

Call to Gather—vigorous drumming

Centering/Presence

"Welcome to all you creatures and beings, who have slipped in from your dreams and wild places—the possibilities between the worlds. Breathe, go within for a moment.

Breathe deep....as you let go of your breath, follow it down, and notice the Space before you inhale. Don't hold it, just notice it. And again, breathing deep and following the breath down to this Space—that is always with you, feeling it. Breath deep—and as you let go, noticing this Space...into which all who have gone before us have travelled...from which to enter again the dance of life in some form. Feel this Space between your breaths."

Statement of Purpose

"We are gathered to celebrate Samhain. This is the time when we recognize that the veil is thin that divides the worlds. It is the New Year in the time of the year's death—the passing of old growth. The leaves are turning and falling, the dark continues to grow, the light part of the day is getting shorter and colder. Earth's tilt continues to move us away from the Sun.

The story of old tells us that on this night, between the dead and the born, between the old and the new, all is possible; that we travel in the Womb of the Mother, the Dark Shining One within, from which all pours forth, and that we are the seed of our own rebirth. The gates of life and death are opened: the dead are remembered, the Not-Yet is conceived. We meet in time out of time, every-

---

3.   I have come to associate gold fabric—preferably weblike—with Samhain, because the Gaian reality is that death is a transformation, and that is what I have been coming to learn.

where and nowhere, here and there…to transform the old into the new in our own bodyminds.

Let us enter this realm, the vast sunless sea within us—the Womb of All. We can proceed by remembering our elemental origins."

Calling the Directions/Casting the Circle

All turning to the East—
"Hail the East, Powers of Water. We remember that we are Water."
All: We remember that we are Water.
"Water, that has nursed our beginnings in the primordial soup, that walks around in our flesh. We are old, so old."[4]
……slowly walk the circle spooning water with shell. DRUM.
All: I remember that I am Water and there is nothing I have not been.[5]

All turning to the North—
"Hail the North, Powers of Fire. We remember that we are Fire."
All: We remember that we are Fire.
"Fire, that has surged through every thought, and action, that dances at the root of all life. We are old, so old."
……light pot of fire[6] and slowly walk the circle with it. DRUM
All: I remember that I am Fire and there is nothing I have not been.

All turning to the West—
"Hail the West, Powers of Earth. We remember that we are Earth."
All: We remember that we are Earth.
"Earth, whose intelligence has conceived us and all creatures, and to whom we all return. We are old, so old."
……slowly walk the circle with the rock/earth. DRUM.
All: I remember that I am Earth and there is nothing I have not been.

---

4.   This a line from "Song of Hecate" by Bridget Mckern. See Appendix B.
5.   The last part of this sentence is from Robin Morgan, "The Network of the Imaginary Mother", *Lady of the Beasts*, p. 88.
6.   A pot of sand onto which methylated spirits is poured and lit, creates a gentle flame that may be used indoors.

All turning to the South—
"Hail the South, Powers of Air. We remember that we are Air."
All: We remember that we are Air.
"Air, that passed through the lungs of ancestors, dinosaurs, and every breathing creature. We are old, so old."
……light smudge, slowly walk the circle w/smudge and feather. DRUM.
All: I remember that I am Air and there is nothing I have not been.

All turning to the Centre—
"We are this Mystery—Water, Fire, Earth and Air (PACING THE CIR-CLE)—we are from all time and no Time, everywhere and no Where. Feel the space within you…the Womb of All, fertile with possibility. Breathe…this is the Centre—the Centre of the Cosmos.
The circle is cast, we are between the worlds, beyond the bounds of time and space,where light and dark, birth and death, joy and sorrow, meet as One."
(Light centre candle)

Invocation

"We are Co-creators—we are divine. We call the Divine by a thousand names, uttering ourselves.[7] Name yourself as you will."
Each one: I am……
Group response: (Deep bow) "Welcome (full name as announced), spark of Goddess, the Divine One."

Transformation Journey

"Let us now remember some the old selves we have been. Let us all take the journey now, remembering some of our transformations." (the circle joins hands, with the exception of one person who will "journey" first[8])

The circle raises joined hands, the journeyer goes in and out the gaps of the circle, as the circle chants:
In and out the windows

---

7. Robin Morgan says in her poem "The Network of the Imaginary Mother", *Lady of the Beasts*, p. 88: "You call me by a thousand names, uttering yourselves".
8. Usually the order of "journeyers" has already been worked out in the preparation—it is simplest in this case if it is around the circle in turn.

In and out the windows
In and out the windows
As we have done before.[9]
The circle brings their hands down at the end of each round of chant allowing the person to be "in". The chant stops.

Celebrant: "Who have you been?"
The person shows a photo/object—around the circle (walking around if they like), saying "this is someone I have been" (and whatever further description).
OR the person describes some "old self" they have been—as long as they have a clear picture of this "old self" in their own minds.

Group response: Hail to you and your becomings.
(Each receives the response with a bow and continues "in and out" for another round, repeating the process a few times.)

(After all have woven in and out.)

Presentation of Snakes

Celebrant takes basket of snakes and walks the circle saying:
"O Great Ones, you have come through so many changes,…(elaborate—with DRAMA)…as Gaia Herself has done. Gaia, like you, has come through so many changes…and yet—and YET: She and you…are More,[10] much more.
Accept these snakes, symbol of life renewed—as you, like Gaia, have done so many times." (uncover snakes)

Servers/celebrant distribute snakes, repeating to each: "You are More, much more."

---

9.   This is from a children's game called "In and Out the Windows" where a person caught outside the "windows" at the end of each round of the chant was out of the game. The group would try to keep the person "out"—close the "windows" on them. In this ritual game there is no attempt to keep the person out, and in fact they are helped to be "in" to speak of each "old self".

10. I think I may have got the idea for this expression from Jean Houston. She says, "You are more than you think you are and something in you knows it", *A Mythic Life*, p.329. I capitalize the term as I mean it as a name for the sacred potential gestating in the plenum which is within and without all.

Response: It is so.

ALL SIT

Consuming Old Selves

"Drawn from the first by what you might become,
You did not know how simple this secret could be
The carapace is split
the shed skins lie upon the ground,
(hold up snake)
Devour now all your old shapes, wasting no part."[11]
(Celebrant breaks off a part of her snake.)

All: I devour now all my old shapes. (or some affirmation of what they are doing)
All eat some of their snakes. MUSIC[12] ON.

Remembering the Ancestors

"Let us remember our ancestors, those who have gone before, bring them into our presence."

Each may name any who have passed on, that they wish to remember.

After all have spoken:
"We welcome all these, who have been food for the Universe, and we remember that we also will become the ancestors. We will be consumed. May we be interesting food."[13]

Celebrant hold up her snake and break off a part.

---

11.   Most of these lines are directly from Robin Morgan, "The Network of the Imaginary Mother", *Lady of the Beasts*, p.84.
12.   I have used "The Shores of the High Priestess" on an audio tape *Dreams* by Sky, 1988 Ronny R. Bunke, Magic Music PO Box 1111, Mill Valley CA 94942. It seems to be no longer available. I currently use "Shamanic Healing", Cave of Bones, Oliver Baldwin and Richard Bottom, 2001 GOOD MOVE MUSIC LTD LC 01027.
13.   Brian Swimme uses this metaphor, *Canticle to the Cosmos*, video 5.

All: We also will become the ancestors. We will be consumed. (or some affirmation of what they are doing)

All eat the more of their snakes. MUSIC ON.

Remembering the Old Shapes of the Culture

"Let us remember some of the old shapes of our human culture and story that we would leave behind."

Each name the memories and "shapes" they choose.

After all have spoken:
"We devour these old shapes of our culture, of our world, transform them in our beings."

Celebrant hold up her snake and break some more.
All: We devour these old shapes, transform them in our beings. (or some affirmation of what they are doing)
All eat more of their snakes. MUSIC ON.

Silence or Music Down

"Let us sit for a while with these endings in the vast sunless sea."

MUSIC OFF

Building the Web—Conceiving the Future

Celebrant takes golden ball of thread and holds it up.

"Having devoured your old shapes, wasting no part
you are free…free
to radiate whatever you conceive,
to exclaim the strongest natural fibre known
—your spirit, your creative self,
into such art, such architecture
as can house a world made sacred by your building."[14]

ALL STAND. Put snakes down to finish eating later.

"Take the golden thread now, that emerges from your creative centre, and spin what you will." (start chant)
All chant: Free to radiate whatever we conceive.

Celebrant passes the golden ball, having wrapped it around herself.
Each takes it and wraps it around themselves a few times.
When each has the ball, each chants: "Free to radiate whatever *I* conceive", then back to *we*.

Let the chant build.
When thread gets back to celebrant, she holds it up.
"What would you conceive/spin from your bodymind? What do you want to create in your life?"

Pass ball of thread for each in turn to hold—wrap one more time.
Each: " I want...create/conceive/spin into my life..."
Group response: So be it!
Each cuts both threads for the person next to them saying: "You are free."
Pass scissors.

When ball of thread has gone full circle:
"May all these conceptions, desires, imaginings—spoken & unspoken—house a world made sacred by our building."[15]

All: May it be so.

Communion

Celebrant put thread down, put tray of glasses with juice in centre, hold up cut apples & juice.

---

14. Most of these lines are from Robin Morgan, "The Network of the Imaginary Mother", *Lady of the Beasts*, p.84, with some re-phrasing.
15. A paraphrase of words from Robin Morgan, "The Network of the Imaginary Mother", *Lady of the Beasts*, p.84.

"Stand tall, daughters and sons of the Mother. Daughters and sons of Eve, stand tall—enjoy the fruit and drink of never-ending renewal."

Servers, repeating the blessing: "Stand tall daughter/son of the Mother—enjoy the fruit and drink of never-ending renewal."

Offer more apple, cider and juice. More gingerbread snakes and lolly (candy) snakes.

Story Space—stories of transformation, or anything else.

Open the Circle

All turning to the South—
"We have remembered that we are Air, as old as She, and present in the lungs of all who have ever breathed. May there be peace within us."
All: May there be peace within us.

All turning to the West—
"We have remembered that we are Earth, as old as She and constantly changing. May there be peace within us."
All: May there be peace within us.

All turning to the North—
"We have remembered that we are Fire, as old as She, and surging with Her dance. May there be peace within us."
All: May there be peace within us.

All turning to the East—
"We have remembered that we are Water, as old as She, and nursing all possibility. May there be peace within us."
All: May there be peace within us.

All turning to the centre—
"We have remembered that we are Co-creator, we are Divine. We have remembered some of our transformations, and those who have gone before us, and we have conceived our futures. We have remembered that we are More, much More. May there be peace within us and between us." (all join hands)

All: May there be peace within us and between us.

Pass the kiss both ways.

"May the peace of the One go in our hearts.
The circle is open, but unbroken…"
All: It has been a merry meeting
It is a merry parting
May we merry meet again
Blessed Be!

Music:[16]

Points for individual contemplation prior to the ritual:

—Naming yourself (at Invocation)
—Old selves you have been
—Ancestors or those who have gone before whom you would like to name
—Old cultural shapes, stories, events you see yourself as helping transform
—What you would like to create in your life…conceive, imagine

WINTER SOLSTICE

Cauldron ready for fire.[17] Evergreen wreath around centre candle. Deep maroon altar cloth with white ribbon. Darkened room, or outside, lit with candles. Basket of candles and holders. Trays of sand on altar for placing candles. Tree or trees with fairy lights. Bowls of oil. Cake and wine and juice. "Solstice" music[18] playing during arrival time. Music ready. Songsheets handed out during preparation.

---

16. I use "1492" by Vangelis, Warner Music UK 1992.
17. I use a large clay disclike pot full of dry sand, onto which methylated spirits is poured and lit. If it is outside it may need to be covered so the sand does not get damp, and the methylated spirits will need to be kept warm. Sometimes we are able to make a real bonfire.
18. I use *Gregorian Waves* by Pascal Languirand. Canada:Imagine Records 1991. IMD 2015. It says on the cover, this music "pays joyous homage to the Earth Goddess Gaia: the haunting magic of Gregorian music is rediscovered and transformed…".

Call to Gather—celebrant starts chant, moving around the circle in an anti-clockwise direction (in the Southern H.—opposite in the Northern H.). All join in:
"A circle around, a circle around, the boundaries of the Earth.
A circle around, a circle around, the boundless Universe.
Spreading my long tail feathers as I fly,
spreading my long tail feathers as I fly,
Higher, higher, higher and higher. Deeper, deeper, deeper and deeper."[19]
All join in movement and chant for some time.
All move back to places.

Centering

"Let us focus on our breath for a while. Take a deep breath and let it go. Notice the Void at the bottom of emptying your breath…feeling it, and feeling the Urge to breathe as it arises. And again…feeling it over and over. Trusting it.

—Recall some of the birthings in your life, your actual birth—see it there in your mind's eye…coming into being. Recall projects you have brought into being, new selves, perhaps children, new selves in others, how you have been Creator and Created. Staying for a while with the many, many birthings in your life.

—imagine yourself as Gaia-Earth and all her birthings out of the Dark—everyday…the dawn is constant as She turns. See Her in your mind's eye—imagining the constant dawning around the globe, the constant birthing—feeling this. Recall Earth's many births right now of all beings—as day breaks around the globe—the physical, emotional, spiritual births. The many, many birthings everyday, and throughout the eons.

—Imagine yourself Gaia-Universe and all Her birthings—everyday…supernovas right now, stars and planets being born right now. The many, many birthings everday and throughout the eons.

---

19.   There are arm movements and spinning that may go with the chant. I also instruct during the preparation to "imagine ourselves as the arms of our Milky Way galaxy—remembering where we are." I don't remember where this chant comes from; I apologize for lack of acknowledgment.

Come back to your breath—this wonder—none of it separate…birthing you in every moment—in real time and space."

Statement of Purpose

"This is the time of Winter Solstice in our Southern Hemisphere. Earth's tilt leans us away from the Sun to the furthest point at this time in our annual orbit. This is for us, the time when the dark part of the day is longest—darkness reaches Her fullness, She spreads her cloak, and yet gives way, and moves back into light. The breath of Gaia in our part of the world pauses. She rests. We wait…within the Cauldron, the Dark Space, for the transformation.

The stories of Old tell us of the Great Mother giving birth to the Divine Child on this night. This Divine Child is the new being in you, in me…is the bringer of hope, the light in the darkness, the evergreen tree, the centre which is also the circumference—All of Manifestation. The Divine Child being born is the Miracle of Being, and the Unimaginable More that we are becoming.

Let us join the breath of Gaia in her suspension, the Great Mother in Her birth-giving. Let us recall this Dark Space, this Holy Cauldron within. Let us begin by remembering who and what we are and from whence we come."

Call the Directions, Create the Sacred Space—

All turning to the East—
"Hail the East, Powers of Water, Water that we are, we remember you."
All: Water that we are, we remember you.
"Cosmic Dynamic of Sensitivity,[20] that absorbs, becomes, whatever you touch; may we *feel* what we are, and respond compassionately."
All: May we feel what we are and respond compassionately.
DRUMS as……sprinkles water w/pine branch.

All turning to the North—
"Hail the North, Powers of Fire, Fire that we are, we remember you."
All: Fire that we are, we remember you.

---

20. This understanding of Water comes from Brian Swimme, *The Universe is a Green Dragon*, p.87-95.

"Unseen Shaping Power of the Cosmos,[21] that gives us form—flames that we are; may we dance with you and act with Creative Lust for all of life."
All: May we dance with you and act with Creative Lust for all of life
DRUMS as......lights fire in the pot, takes it around.

All turning to the West—
"Hail the West, Powers of Earth, Earth that we are, we remember you."
All: Earth that we are, we remember you.
"Always present to us, you hold all the stories of life in your Body, we can learn it all from you; may we remember who we really are, may we hold the Wisdom of all time and no Time."[22]
All: May we hold the Wisdom of all time and no Time.
DRUMS as......holds up rock & carries it around.

All turning to the South—
"Hail the South, Powers of Air, Air that we are, we remember you."
All: Air that we are, we remember you.
"Cosmic Dynamic of Exuberance and Expression,[23] Wind that moves the trees, the clouds, and allows us voice; move us and inspire us to unfurl our being."
All: Move us and inspire us to unfurl our being.
DRUMS as......lights smudge stick, carries it around.

All turning to the centre—
"This is what we are—Water, Fire, Earth, Air (PACING THE CIR-CLE)—Divine Mystery manifest in this Place and Time. The Centre is Here. The circle is cast, we are between the worlds, beyond the bounds of time and space, where light and dark, birth & death, joy & sorrow meet, as One.

Invocation. (Celebrant taking bowl of oil and holding it up)
"As the oil comes to you, turn to the person next to you and pronounce with the authority in you: 'Thou art Goddess, Thou art the Divine Child, Thou art all of

---

21. This understanding of Fire comes from Brian Swimme *The Universe is a Green Dragon*, p.127-139.
22. This understanding of Earth is inspired by Brian Swimme, *The Universe is a Green Dragon*, p.99-109.
23. This understanding of Air comes from Brian Swimme, *The Universe is a Green Dragon*, p.143-151.

That. You are a whole Universe', annoint with oil on the forehead and bow deeply, as you recognize the Sacred."

"Cosmogenesis" Dance[24]—"Let us celebrate this Sacred within, Her eternal Cosmogenesis, in the dance."

MUSIC

Sit in the Dark

"Sit in the stillness now, wrap the Dark Space of the Mother around, and await the transformation."

LIGHTS OFF. CANDLES OUT.

Lighting of the Fire

After some time of sitting in the dark:
"Out of Her fertile Dark Matter, the Light is born—all Manifestation is born."

......and a young person, both wearing special garland and clothing, feel their way (in the dark) to the centre......pours methylated spirits on the sand in the cauldron/large clay pot and lights the fire.

She says: "We recall our Beginnings—the Primeaval Fireball—the Great Flaring Forth, and Grandmother Supernova Tiamat, and our Star the Sun. We are Gift of Tiamat, out of her stardust we are born. Carbon, hydrogen, oxygen, nitrogen, sulphur, phosphorus and trace elements. We are Gift of Tiamat—out of her stardust we are born."[25]
The young person lights the centre candle.

---

24.   See Chapter 6 fn 20, and Appendix I for dance instructions.
25.   This is largely the composition of "The Tiamat Song" by Connie Barlow, *Green Space, Green Time*, p.83.

Lighting the Candles

Celebrant: "The *Universe* wants to speak you, the Universe wants to speak *you*. Take a candle, light it, hold it up ceremoniously and recall, and speak if you like, of the light—the new being—in you, being born this year."
Each in turn moves to the centre, takes a candle, puts a holder on it, lights the candle and speaks if they wish, then holds the lit candle up ceremoni-ously—which is the cue for all to respond with:

"So be it. Let your new being and light be born."

Song

When all have lit candles in hand:
"Let us sing together in praise of these new beings and Her Creativity—which is also our own."
All sing "PaGaian Joy to the World"[26] standing in a single circle.

The Spiral Dance

"And let us dance the Spiral."
Collect songsheets and move cushions. All join hands each holding their candle in linked right hand. Celebrant leads into a spiral, all singing the first verse and chorus of "PaGaian Joy to the World" over and over, making sure to look in the eyes and faces of the passing people, then re-forming the circle.

Re-Lighting the World

"Let us take our lights—these new beings—and re-light the world, as the Sun re-lights it. What do you wish for the world, what is the flame in your heart? Join it with all the others."

Each one in turn steps into the centre and speaks if they wish, takes the holder off the candle, and puts their lit candle down firmly in the sand—which is the cue for all to respond with:

---

26.   See APPENDIX G.

"May we be like the Sun and re-light the world."
Assistants to switch on lights and re-light candles while this is in process.

Communion

"All glory and praise be to Her who daily gives us more than we can ask or imagine. We will now enjoy some of Her delights (hold up cake and wine), and remember that we also *are* Her delights.
You are Cake—Divine Cake—to enjoy and be enjoyed.
You are Wine poured out for the Mystery."

Servers and celebrant serve cake with the blessing:
"You are cake for the Queen of Heaven and Earth. May you enjoy and be enjoyed."

Assistants hold trays of glasses and wine/juice, while servers ceremoniously pour wine/juice in front of each with the blessing:
"You are wine poured out for the Mystery. May your flavour be full."

Toasts—short

Dance

"May we choose a joyful response to the awesome fact of our being in the Universe, and express that response through the art and dance of our lives.[27] You are the choreographer of your dance of life, we are the choreographers of the dance...so enjoy!"

MUSIC[28]

Co-celebrants lead off in improvised free dance, others may join in.

---

27.   This is a slightly altered quote from Matthew Fox. I can't remember where he said it.
28.   I currently use "Santiago" by Loreena McKennitt on the CD *the mask and mirror* 1994, Quinlan Road Limited.

Open the Circle

All turning to the South—
"We have remembered that we are Air—cosmic dynamics of exuberance—unfurling our being. May there be peace within us."
All: May there be peace within us.

All turning to the West—
"We have remembered that we are Earth—deep memory and presence. May there be peace within us."
All: May there be peace within us.

All turning to the North—
"We have remembered that we are Fire—vessels of the unseen shaping power of the cosmos—dancing. May there be peace within us."
All: May there be peace within us.

All turning to the East—
"We have remembered that we are Water—cosmic dynamics of sensitivity—feeling what we are. May there be peace within us."
All: May there be peace within us

All turning to the centre—
"We have remembered that we are Goddess, the Divine Child, all of this Sacred Mystery. We are That. We have remembered our Origins and the light—the new form—birthing in us. We have remembered the flame in our hearts.
May there be peace within us and between us." (all join hands)
All: May there be peace within us and between us.

"May the Peace of the One grow in our hearts."

All: The circle is open, but unbroken
It has been a merry meeting,
It is a merry parting,
May we merry meet again.
Blessed Be.

MUSIC[29]

Points for individual contemplation prior to the ritual:

—how you are Water, Fire, Earth and Air
—how you and other are Goddess, Divine Child, all That—a whole Universe.
—What new being is birthing in you this year—what is growing.
—What do you wish for the world? What it is that you would like to make a difference to.

IMBOLC

Large "well" of salt water under a clay bowl of sand for flame. Smaller bowl of salt water, and hand towel. Each wear "bridal" gear, and a "crown"/veil. Bow and arrow. Fruit bread, Tray of glasses with light colour fruit juice or white wine. White chocolate treats, white foods such as ricotta, fetta cheese. Greenery, buds. Artemis herbs. Candles & trays of sand. Red cloth/carpet laid down—facing in towards edge of circle. Music ready. Double-sided copies of "Bridal" commitment and processional praise. Bundle of sprigs of wattle.[30] Bell and djorge.

Gathering—Ring the bell three or more times—with space between each ring. All come to sitting in the circle.

Centering

"Listen to the bell as if listening to your ringing, your Being—the Beauty of your differentiated unique being, ringing."
Ring the bell again, and accentuate with the djorge.

"Take a deep breath, and as you let the breath go, follow it down to the space before your next breath. Imagine this space, this emptiness, as *the* Sea of Generosity…from which All springs forth. Feel the Urge of Creation springing forth—as the Urge to breathe arises. Imagine it as a Ripple upon the Sea of Generosity.

---

29. Some appropriate Gaian Solstice music. Once again I often use I use *Gregorian Waves* by Pascal Languirand, as noted in this chapter footnote18.
30. This is the seasonal flower of my region.

Imagine it rippling out of this Sea as your breath expands. Imagine your-Self as this Ripple. We are ripples stirring upon the Original Sea of Generosity now."

Speaking the Word of Creation

"Next time you take a deep breath, we will do it together, and as we let the breath go, let us speak the Mother's word of Creation "Om"—let it come from your belly. You may contemplate how you spell the world, create it with your self-expression, and how this weaves with others. Let us Spell it three times together:"

Statement of Purpose

"This is the season of the waxing light. Earth's tilt is taking us back towards the Sun. The seed of light born at the Winter Solstice begins to manifest, and we who were midwives to this Flame now see the Light grow strong as the light part of the days grows visibly longer. This is the time when we celebrate individuation: how we each light our own light, and become uniquely ourselves. It is the time of beginning, when the tendrils of green emerge tentatively from the seed. We meet to share the light of inspiration and creative intentions, which will grow with the growing year.

This is the Feast of the Virgin—Brigid, She who tends the Flame of Being; Artemis, She who midwifes body and soul. She is deeply committed to the Creative Urge, to manifestation, deeply committed to Self. She is uncompromised, unswerving, noble, true, a warrior of spirit. She will protect the stirrings of Life."

Let us begin our celebration of Her, by remembering our beginnings, from whence we come—our *true* nature.

Creating the Sacred Space

"We are from the East, and we are Water—filled with the ocean tides, feel the moistness in you, taste it. We are juicy with it, soft with it. Feel how you are Water…we are Water, we are this."
Response: We are Water, we are this.

"We are from the North, and we are Fire—sparks of ancient heat, feel the warmth of your body. Your metabolism an echo of the Great Fire at the Beginning, and of the Sun. Feel how you are Fire…we are Fire, we are this."

Response: We are Fire, we are this.

"We are from the West, and we are Earth—geological, Gaian formations, feel your weight, your memories. She is alive in us and we in Her. Feel how you are Earth…we are Earth, we are this."
Response: We are Earth, we are this.

"We come from the South, and we are Air—drawn from and drawing from this ancient river that all have breathed, feel it in you, expand with it. Feel how you are Air…we are Air, we are this."
Response: We are Air, we are this.

We have always been from the very beginning, and so we always shall be. We are at the Centre of Creativity—a multiplicity of centres. The circle is cast, we are between the worlds, beyond the bounds of time and space, where light and dark, birth and death, joy and sorrow, meet as One."
Light the candle.

Invocation

Pass basket of candles, each take one.
"Let us each light our own lights. When you have done so, sit for a few moments gazing into the flame. Contemplate how the Flame of Being is in you, how it is given to you, and how it is yet ever-new."
SITTING QUIETLY FOR A FEW MOMENTS.
"When you are ready, one at a time, place your candle on the altar, affirming that you are She—this ever-new Flame of Being, this Young One, the Virgin-Self, a unique beautiful being of the Universe…however you'd like to express it."
Each put candle down in the sand when ready to.
Each one: "I am She—shining and new" (or "I am this ever-new Flame of Being, Virgin-Self", or some variation as is meaningful).

Celebrant holds up the herbs and pronounces:
"Taste the herbs of Artemis—and contemplate the One within you who mid-wifes you, who is always birthing you."

Pass the herbs around and each rub and taste the bitterness on their fingers.

Celebrant holds the arrow to her heart and pronounces:
"…hold Her arrow. She is the One in you who is true."

Pass the arrow around for each to hold to their heart.

Purification and Strengthening[31]

"Take the bowl of salt water, breathe into it and say where in your life does your Urge to Be wilt? What are your vulnerabilities? Where can the delicate new being be torn? What holds you back from the Beauty and strength of Being?"

Pass bowl of salt water, clockwise.[32]
Each one may speak…and breath into the water.
Drum beat as each washes—drums stop when person stops.
Group response for each one's washing: May you be cleansed.

Let us raise some power, some of our energy.
All stand. Drum…and improvised voice, raising energy—moving.

All return to sitting.

Celebrant holds up the bowl of salt water, and asks:
"Where in your life do you feel power, strength of Being? What encourages your "nwyfre"[33]—life force? Your Passion? Where do feel the excitement of Creativity?"
Each one may speak…and breathe into the water.
Drum beat as each washes again—drums stop when person stops.
Response for each one's washing: "We bless your power."

Pass the bowl of salt water, counterclockwise.[34]

---

31. This process with the salt water is adapted from Starhawk, *Truth or Dare*, p.304-305.
32. This is the chosen direction for the Southern Hemisphere. Starhawk does it opposite for the Northern Hemisphere.
33. This is a Welsh word (pronounced NWIVE'ry) meaning a sense of vigour and energy. See Caitlin Matthews, *The Celtic Spirit*, p. 207 and 208.
34. This is the chosen direction for the Southern Hemisphere. Starhawk does it opposite for the Northern Hemisphere.

After the bowl has gone full circle, celebrant pours water into the centre bowl. "We commend our power to and from its Source—the Well[35] within."

Celebrant lights the centre flame. "We are tenders of the flame."
All: "It is so. We are tenders of the Flame."

"Take up your flame now and let us sing to the ancient One Brigid, She within who tends the flame of Being. Let us invoke Her."
All stand and take up their candles, putting a holder on.
All sing: "Ave Brigid"[36] a few times.

Celebrant takes up the bundle of wattle (or other seasonal flower), walks the circle—as "Brigid", and stands near the red carpet.

The "Bridal"/Brigid-ine Dedication

"Now is the time for your commitment to Being, your dedication to Self."

Each steps forward to the red carpet in turn, and may speak:
(each may use these words or add or write/speak their own words)
"I commit myself to Self—my particular small self, understanding that I am She—Gaia—She who is All. I am connected to Her as the tree bud is to the branch. 'I am the beauty of the green earth and the white moon among the stars and the mystery of the waters'. I will protect Her and honour Her in myself—this ever-new beautiful Self. I am a Promise of Life. Whatever She needs I will give Her. I will tend Her in myself."

Celebrant (as "Brigid"): "Rejoice O highly favoured. Gaia Herself rejoices in your commitment and freedom to Be, for you are a Promise—of Life."
She gives each a sprig of wattle (or early Spring flower).

Each processes slowly up and down the red carpet a couple of times, holding up their candle, with arms raised like Eurynome (the Bird-headed Snake Goddess),[37] if they like. Then stands, until group finishes its response and praise.

---

35. This "Well" has traditionally been associated with Brigid, and may be extended to include the Well of Creativity that the whole Universe itself is. Swimme uses this "Well" metaphor in "The Timing of Creativity", *Canticle to the Cosmos*, video 10.

36. We sing this to the tune of "Ave Maria".

Group response—"processional praise": (Written on paper)
"Brigid of the holy well and the sacred flame!
Artemis of the arrow, flying true and on Centre!
Ancient One, Eurynome, whose passion is Life!
Aphrodite,who sings love songs to her own beauty.
We celebrate you in (person's name)."
All sing: "Ave Artemis!"[38] twice.
All state: Ave (person's name)!

Dance[39]

Re-light centre flame.
"Let us celebrate our commitment to Being in the dance. Let us dance it into Being."
All put candles down—in the sand trays on the altar.
MUSIC ON.

Communion

Celebrant holding up fruit bread and wine/fruit juice:
"Let us enjoy our manifested state with food of the Mother, brought to us by Her and by the creativity of our ancestors."

Assistant holds tray of poured wine/juice. Server and/or celebrant offer a glass and fruit bread to each, saying:
"Rejoice O highly favoured.
Blessed are you amongst women & men & children
And blessed is the fruit of your Creativity."

Pass around white chocolate treats, ricotta, fetta cheese.

---

37. See image in Hallie Iglehart Austen, *The Heart of the Goddess*, p.9. It is good to have this image visible, as well as images of any other Goddess named.
38. Sung to the tune of "Ave Maria".
39. The dance that we do at this Seasonal festival of the Virgin is one that I learnt as the "Miserlou" from Jean Houston, at her workshop in Sydney in 1990. The music for this dance is listed by that name in a selection of "Sacred Dances", available from Dog Ear Productions, 32 Cat Swamp Road, Woodberry CT 06798-3018.

Story Space

Let us share stories of creative projects and intentions.

Open Circle

"We have remembered that we are Air, we feel Her in us—this ancient river, expanding. May there be peace within us."
All: May there be peace within us.

"We have remembered that we are Earth, we feel Her in us—our weight, a geological formation. May there be peace within us."
All: May there be peace within us.

"We have remembered that we are Fire, we feel Her in us—our warmth an echo of the Great Fire. May there be peace within us."
All: May there be peace within us.

"We have remembered that we are Water, we feel her in us—our moistness, the primordial ocean.May there be peace within us."
All: May there be peace within us.

"We have remembered that we are creative Ripples stirring upon the Sea of Generosity, the Divine One, Flames of Being ever-new, spelling the world with ourselves. We have dedicated ourselves to tending the Flame of Being. May there be peace within us & between us." (all join hands)
All: May there be peace within us & between us.

Song

"The circle is open but unbroken. May the peace of the Goddess be ever in our hearts. Merry meet and merry part, and merry meet again."

All: Blessed be!

Pass the kiss in both directions.

Points for individual contemplation prior to the ritual:

—how the Flame of Being is within you—affirming that you are this beautiful, unique being, ever-new…this Virgin-self.

—What causes your Urge to Be to wilt? What holds you back? What are your vulnerabilities?

—What encourages your strength of Being, your power?

—Your commitment/dedication to self—how you might express that.

EOSTAR

Each one bring a stone/rock, a Spring mask, a large bouquet, "laurel" head garland. Potted flower from Mabon on altar. Centre cauldron or large clay pot of soil, overlaid with wreath of greenery and flowers, with centre candle. Green altar cloth. A "gateway" from the circle to the "Underworld"/house[40] marked with stones and a flame torch. Lit lantern, bulb seeds, 3 stalks of wheat tied with red ribbon, poppies, near gateway. Masks around altar, stones in basket, bouquets near gateway. Poppyseed ring cake—sliced, but left whole. Chocolate eggs wrapped in gold paper/foil. Copies of "Stepping into Power" words. Music ready. Boiled coloured eggs for decorations.

Each one to take special stone/rock and head garland to pre-ritual contemplation with them. Place rock/stone in basket on altar upon gathering to the circle, and wearing garland.

Call to Gather—drums—STRONG BEAT

Centering/Breath Meditation

"This is the time of Eostar, the Spring Equinox, the moment of balance of light and dark in the light part of the cycle. The light and the dark in the South and in the North of our planet, are of equal length at this time.

Feel the balance in this moment—Earth as She is poised in relationship with the Sun. Feel for your own balance of light and dark within—this fertile balance of

---

40. The "Underworld" may be inside a house or outside in a garden. It is worth considering that "inside" a house/building may be more "outside" of Gaia, and thus perhaps better represents a place of getting lost.

tensions. Breathe into it. Breathe in the light, swell with it, let your breath go into the dark, stay with it. Breathe in the light, swell with it. Shift on your feet, from left to right, feel your centre….breathe it in.

In our part of Earth, the balance is about to tip into the light. Feel the shift within you, see in your mind's eye the energy ahead, the light expanding. Feel the warmth of it. Breathe it in."

Statement of Purpose

"This is the time of Spring's return. Warmth and growth may be sensed in the land. The young light that we celebrated at Imbolc, has grown strong and come to balance with the dark. Life bursts forth with new strength. The story of Old tells us that Persephone beloved Daughter, returns from Her journey to the Underworld. Demeter stretches out Her arms—to receive and rejoice. The beloved One, the Lost One, returns with new Wisdom from the depths.
We may step into a new harmony. Where we step, wild flowers may appear; where we dance, despair may turn to hope, sorrow to joy, want to abundance. May our hearts open with the Spring.

Let us begin our celebration by remembering our true power of Life, let us enter the eternal Space and Time in which we are immersed and embraced."

Creating the Sacred Space

All facing the East
DRUMS
"Hail the East and Powers of Water—powers of sensitivity, emotion and response: I am wet with you, I taste you, I know you."
……take the water, for each to wet their hands and wipe it on themselves.
Response: I am wet with you, I taste you, I know you.

All facing the North
DRUMS
"Hail the North and Powers of Fire—powers of shaping, passion and understanding: I am spark of you, I feel your warmth, I know you."
……light the fire, take it around, each passes their hand over it.
Response: I am spark of you, I feel your warmth, I know you.

All facing the West
DRUMS
"Hail the West and Powers of Earth—powers of memory, presence and action: I hold the story of you in my body, I feel your weight, I know you."
......take the basket of rocks around, each takes their own.
Response: I hold the story of you in my body, I hear you, I know you.

All facing the South
DRUMS
"Hail the South and Powers of Air—powers of perception, awareness and inspiration: I breathe you in, I expand with you, I know you."
......light the smudge stick and take around to each.
Response: I breathe you in, I expand with you, I know you.

All facing the Centre
"This is the truth and Power of who we are—Water, Fire, Earth and Air (PACING THE CIRCLE). We are beyond the bounds of time and space, we are at Centre—the Centre is here, where light and dark, birth and death, joy and sorrow meet as One."
(Light candle)

Invocation

"Let us invoke and recognize the Divine Heraic self in each other—emerging and present. Announce yourself."
Each person, holding up their rock/stone: "I am a Hera, Courageous One, Beloved One...returned and Wise."
(option to say more—in terms of your own experience, perhaps what and how you feel you have made it through.)
Each place the rock/stone on the centre altar.

Response: Beloved One, (repeat however they named themselves), we welcome you.

Story

"Let us sit and listen to the traditional story of this season."

ALL SIT DOWN

......reads:

"Persephone had gathered three poppies and three sheaves of wheat. Then Demeter had led Her to a long, deep chasm and produced a torch for her to carry. She had stood and watched Her Daughter go down further and further into the cleft of the Earth....

For months Persephone received and renewed the dead without ever resting or growing weary. All the while Her Mother remained disconsolate... In Her sorrow She withdrew Her power from the crops, the trees, the plants. She forbade any new growth to blanket the Earth. The mortals planted their seed, but the fields remained barren. Demeter was consumed with loneliness and finally settled on a bare hillside to gaze out at nothing from sunken eyes. For days and nights, weeks and months She sat waiting.

One morning a ring of purple crocus quietly pushed their way through the soil and surrounded Demeter. She looked with surprise at the new arrivals from below and thought what a shame it was that She was too weakened to feel rage at Her injunction being broken. Then She leaned forward and heard them whisper in the warm breeze: "Persephone returns! Persephone returns!"[41]

Celebrant holding up a potted flower:

"Persephone returns! The Seed of life never fades away. She is always present. She is returning. Let us put on our masks, we are the Persephones."

Each put on their Spring mask.

Chant and Dance

All: "Persephone Returns! Persephone Returns! Rejoice, rejoice! Persephone Returns!"—with arms raised, and free individual movement.

Link hands and grapevine steps counterclockwise: "We are the Persephones" X 4. Repeat as desired.

---

41.   An excerpt from Charlene Spretnak, *Lost Goddesses of Early Greece*, p.114-118.

Raising Energy

"In the tradition of our ancestors, and the people of this land too, let us wake up Mother Earth and ourselves!"[42] Foot stomping on the Earth in time to: "She who is alive, is alive in us, and we who are alive, are alive in Her."

Return to the "Persephone" chant and dance in the circle for a while.

Stepping into Power/New Wisdom/New Strength of Being

"Now is the time for us to step into the Power of growth, to emerge, to soar, to feel the Power of Being, to welcome back that which was lost, and to welcome the New Wisdom."

……go to the gateway and light the lantern, and the torch.
Celebrant stand near the gateway.

(If there is enough people, 2 may form an archway for re-entry.)

MUSIC[43] on

Each one in turn, goes to the gateway, takes off their head garland and picks up the lantern, and also wheat, poppies and seed as they wish, and walks into the "Underworld"/house for their Journey.

Group waits and watches—like Demeter.

---

42. This footstomping done at Spring Equinox is traditional to this Earth-based Goddess religious practice, yet it also finds resonance with Australian Aboriginal religious practice. In Aboriginal dance and celebration the movements of the feet are significant, as David Tacey describes in "Spirit and Place", EarthSong journal, issue 1, p.8. It is traditional "for the feet of the dancer…(to)…strike the earth with much energy and vigour."

43. I have used *ReTURNING* by Jennifer Berezan, with Linda Tillery and Sharon Burch. Edge of Wonder Records, 2000. EW 13. Recorded in the Oracle Chamber in the Hypogeum at Hal Saflieni, Malta. Make sure it is set to repeat if is thought necessary, so it doesn't need attending during the process.

The Journeyer returns to the "gateway" and puts the lantern down, and whatever else they have taken with them, and stands waiting. Music pauses.

Each: (Optional words—some choices…each write their own)
"I have gained new Wisdom. My bodymind feels new knowings. I have ReTurned from…. I am gaining in strength and real Power—Gaia's Power. I leave behind the binds of the past—they are for me…

I welcome back my beloved Daughter/Child within. I welcome back the Beloved Lost One. She/This One is for me…

I step with Her/Him into the light & strength of Spring and Being."

Each steps through the threshold of the gateway, takes off their mask, is embraced by the celebrant, given a bouquet and their laurel garland placed back on their head. Others may embrace the returned One too.
Celebrant may greet with words like: "You are a champion, a hera, welcome", according to how the journeyer has expressed themselves and the intuitive sense of the celebrant.

Group response: "Yay, yippee!" (cheer, clap) "What a hera! We bless your empowerment. You made it!"
(Switch music back on, and await next person to take the Journey)

Sitting

"Let us sit quietly for a while-rest on our laurels!"
(harp music for a few minutes)

Communion

"Blessed are you—you have seen these things. You know the end of life and you know the divine—given beginnings. May you enjoy the wisdom of your journey."

Celebrant hold up the cake:
"Take and eat this holy cake—with its many seeds, remembering Her fertility and abundance. Do this in remembrance of She who gives Life."

Celebrant puts pieces on two plates and passes a plate in each direction. Each repeats blessing as they hand to next person:
"Take and eat—do this in remembrance of She who gives Life."

Servers take glasses to all. Celebrant holds up the wine:
"Blessed are you—you have seen these things. Take and drink—do this in remembrance of She who gives Life."
Pass a decanter of wine in each direction. Each repeat the blessing as they pour for the next:
"Take and drink—do this in remembrance of She who gives Life."
Offer juice for those who wish.

Offer Eostar eggs, around the circle:
"Remember the Ancient One who laid the Golden Egg, who **lays** the Golden Egg—take it, it is yours—laid out for you everyday."

Stories

Let us tell each other stories of empowerment.

Open Circle

All turning to the South
"We have remembered that we are Air, we are the breeze, She expands in us. May there be peace within us."
All: May there be peace within us.

All turning to the West
"We have remembered that we are Earth, we are the story, She speaks in us. May there be peace within us."
All: May there be peace within us.

All turning to the North
"We have remembered that we are Fire, we are the dance, She is our form. May there be peace within us."
All: May there be peace within us.

All turning to the East
"We have remembered that we are Water, we are the juice, She feels with us. May there be peace within us."
All: May there be peace within us.

All turning to the Centre
"We have remembered that we are Divine Ones—Heras, Persephones, Courageous Ones—Beloved Ones. We have remembered something of our Journeys, our Lost Places and welcomed and embraced New Strength of Being, New Wisdom. We have welcomed our Lost Beloved Ones. May there be peace within us and between us." (all join hands)
All: May there be peace within us and between us.

"The circle is open but unbroken, may the peace and courage of Goddess go in our hearts."

All: It has been a merry meeting,
It is a merry parting,
May we merry meet again.
Blessed Be!

Song

"Shine"[44] (hand out words for all to sing along.)

Points for individual contemplation prior to the ritual:

—the balance of this Moment, the light and dark in balance on the planet and within you…this fertile balance of tensions.
—yourself as a Hera/Hero/Courageous One…some of what you have made it through, how you have returned from the depths with Wisdom—represented with the rock/stone (take it with you for contemplation).
—stepping into Power/New Strength—your Journey, what/whom you are welcoming, how you might like to express this (spontaneous or written).

---

44. From *Deity* by Wendy Rule. Shock Records, 1998. WENDY007. See APPENDIX H.

BELTANE

Outside altar. A firepit/large clay pot with sand, pole hung with rainbow streamers. Red altar cloth with streamers of rainbow colours. Doughnuts hung in bushes. Pink ring cake, with rose honey and petals-cut up but whole. Sweet wine and champagne. Rose water in East. Earth paint in West, card paper, water & towel. Each bring object or photo representing Beauty for them. Wear head garlands of flowers. Copies of invocation words. Rose petals scattered about.

Each one to take object or photo of Beauty to pre-ritual contemplation with them.

Call to Gather—Conch horn if possible, or drums

Centering/Breath Meditation

"Breathe deep. Feel your breath as it waxes towards fullness—as it rushes in. Breathe deep and feel your breath as it waxes towards filling completely. Feel your desire for this breath. This is how Gaia breathes in our part of the world at this time. The light is waxing towards fullness. Feel your breath as it rushes in. Feel your desire for this breath.

Breathe deep…in that breath we share in the life of all who have come before us, and danced the dance of life: and we are present to all who will come after us and dance the dance of life. Breathe deep…and feel the Presence of all these…and the Present that always is. You may if you like make a simple gesture that embraces this Present Moment and this Presence—reaching back and down, bringing your hands and arms up and forward…reaching, and folding over in reverence if you like as you embrace it all."

Statement of Purpose

"This is the time of Beltane, when the light part of the day is longer and continues to grow longer than the dark part of the day. Light is waxing towards fullness. In our region, Earth continues to tilt us further toward the Sun—the Source of Her pleasure, life and ecstasy. This is the time when sweet Desire for Life weds wild delight—it is met; when the Promise of Spring—which you are, weds the Passion of Summer—fulfillment is nigh. The fruiting begins. It is the celebration of Allurement…Holy Lust…that which holds all things in form and allows the dance of life.

The ancients called this Holy Lust, this primordial essence 'Aphrodite'…they sang of Her:

> 'For all things are from you.
>   Who unites the cosmos.
> You will the three-fold fates.
>   You bring forth all things.
> Whatever is in the Heavens.
>   And in the much fruitful earth
>   And in the deep sea.'

Let us celebrate our erotic nature, that brings forth all things.

Let us begin by remembering the Sacred Space present, and our deep Desire for it."

Creating the Sacred Space

All turning to the East
"All hail the East, presence of Water!"
All: All hail the East, presence of Water!
"We desire you, thirst for you, as all have done before us."
All: We desire you, thirst for you, as all have done before us.
Soft but constant drums, as……takes water jug around, pours a little into each one's hands, for them to drink.
Each one affirms: I desire you, thirst for you, as all have done before me.

All turning to the North
"All hail the North, presence of Fire!"
All: All hail the North, presence of Fire!
"We desire you, gather around you, as all have done before us."
All: We desire you, gather around you, as all have done before us.
Soft but constant drums, as……lights the fire, and each one in turn comes to the flame and passes their hands over it.
Each one affirms: I desire you, gather around you, as all have done before me.

All turning to the West
"All hail the West, presence of Earth!"
All: All hail the West, presence of Earth!
"We desire you, are held by you, desire to make our mark with you, as all have done before us."
All: We desire you, are held by you, desire to make our mark with you, as all have done before us.
Soft but constant drums, as........ attends the wet earth, bowl of water and towel for washing, and each one in turn comes to the wet earth, puts in their hand and impresses their print on a piece of card paper.
(Each rinses and dries their hands)
Each one affirms: I desire you, desire to make my mark with you, as all have done before me.

All turning to the South
"All hail the South, presence of Air!"
All: All hail the South, presence of Air!
"We desire you, reach for you, as all have done before us."
All: We desire you, reach for you, as all have done before us.
Soft but constant drums, as......takes perfumed flowers around to each.
Each one affirms: I desire you, reach for you, as all have done before me.

All turning to the Centre
"We are united in our Desire—for Water, Fire, Earth and Air (PACING THE CIRCLE), in our longing, with each other, and with all who have come before us and all who will come after us, in their Desire and their longing. Our desire, our longing, *is* the Beloved, is the Universe, desiring in us.[45] Feel it. This is the Centre of Creativity—beyond the bounds of time and space, where light and dark, joy and sorrow, birth and death meet as One."
(light candle)

Invocation

......: "Hear the words of the Star Goddess, the dust of whose feet are the hosts of heaven,.....

---

45. This is inspired by Brian Swimme, *Canticle to the Cosmos*, video 5, and various other teachings of his.

I who am the beauty of the green earth and the white moon among the stars and the mysteries of the waters, I call upon your soul to arise and come unto me. For I am the soul of nature that gives rise to the Universe. From me all things proceed and unto Me they must return. Let My worship be in the heart that rejoices, for behold—all acts of love and pleasure are My rituals. Let there be beauty and strength, power and compassion, honour and humility, mirth and reverence within you. And you who seek to know Me, know that your seeking and yearning will avail you not, unless you know the Mystery: for if that which you seek, you find not within yourself, you will never find it without. For I have been with you from the beginning, and I am that which is attained at the end of Desire."[46]

Celebrant: "Name yourself as the Beauty, the Beloved—whom She desires."

Each one: (wording as you want…this is a suggestive collage of phrases. Add, change or leave out what you want. Hold object or photo of Beauty, if you like, as you speak).
"I am the Beauty of the Rose (or whatever…). Aphrodite (this Allurement, this primordial essence, Holy Lust, She Who holds all in form)—is within me. I am Desirable. The Cosmos (Universe, Aphrodite, She…) desires me. The Promise of Spring that I am, has become (becomes) the Rose (Passion) of High Spring. I am waxing towards fullness. I celebrate my Beauty and my (Holy) Desire (my Body—who is the Universe, and my Desire). The Beloved is within me. I am the Beloved."

Response: Welcome, we recognize your Beauty and your Desire.

The Dance[47]

"With all this Holy Desirable Beauty, let us dance the dance of life."
(All move to the pole)

Celebrant: "Take a ribbon of your choosing and weave in to your life what you will."
Each person: "I choose red, for......or "I choose blue, for....." etc.

---

46. Excerpt from *The Charge of the Goddess* by Doreen Valiente, in Starhawk, *The Spiral Dance*, p.90-91.
47. Dance Instructions: number off as 1's and 2's. All 1's face right, all 2's face left. All 1's go in and under first, all 2's go out and over first.

Response: May it be so.

All chant as the group dances:
"We are the Dance of the Earth, Moon and Sun
We are the Life that's in everyone
We are the Life that loves to live
We are the Love that lives to love."[48]

After it is woven, the chant continues, with improvised dancing and clapping, eventually over to the firepit/altar. Drums start up, dancing continues.

Leaping the Bonfire

Drums abate.

"Let the flame of Love burn away your petty disharmonies and habitual negativities. Leap the Flame, and leave behind what you will."

Light the fire.

Each takes a turn leaping the fire, saying what they leave behind to the flames. Each make take several turns.

Drum roll for each leap.
Response: claps and cheers. "May it be so."

Sitting

When the excitement quietens down, and all are done.
"Let us sit with this healing, and name others for whom we desire this."
After the naming:
"Feel this desire in you now. This is the primordial essence, that brings forth all things. May all these desires spoken and unspoken, be so."

---

48. Written and taught to me by thea Gaia, with some added changes.

Communion

Celebrant holding up the plates of cake:
"Take and eat this Holy Cake, consume your desire."
Put pieces of cake on two plates and pass in each direction. Each one repeat blessing to next.

Server take glasses to all. Celebrant holds up the wine.
"Take and drink. Taste and enjoy the sweetness of life."
Pass a decanter of wine in each direction. Each repeat the blessing as they pour just a little (it is sweet) for the next. Offer juice for those who wish.

Open champagne: "Life, the Universe is a happening, a party and we are the champagne.[49] May you enjoy a lightness of Being."
Invite all to find and eat the doughnuts hanging about.

Storytelling

Space for speaking, and telling stories of Passion.

Open the Circle

All turning to the South
"We have remembered the presence of Air, how we desire Her, reach for Her. May we know peace within us."
All: May we know peace within us.

All turning to the West
"We have remembered the presence of Earth, how we are held by Her, how we desire to make our mark with Her. May we know peace within us."
All: May we know peace within us.

All turning to the North
"We have remembered the presence of Fire, how we desire Her, gather around Her. May we know peace within us."
All: May we know peace within us.

---

49.   This is inspired by Brian Swimme, *The Universe is a Green Dragon*, p.123.

All turning to the East
"We have remembered the presence of Water, how we desire Her, thirst for Her. May we know peace within us."
All: May we know peace within us.

All turning to the Centre
"We have remembered that we are the Beauty whom She Desires—that the Beauty and Holy Desire of the Universe is within us, uniting us with all and with the cosmos. May we know peace within us and between us." (all join hands)
All: May we know peace within us and between us.

"May the Delight and Ecstasy of the Divine—Goddess and God, Beloved and Lover—go in our hearts."

Song

"The circle is open but unbroken. May the peace of the Goddess be ever in our hearts. Merry meet and merry part, and merry meet again."

All: Blessed be!

Pass the kiss in both directions.

Dance Music[50]

Points for individual contemplation prior to the ritual:

—your desires as the Universe desiring in you
—how you are the Beauty of the Rose, the Tree, or whatever you choose…"the Beauty whom She desires."
—what you would weave into your life
—what you would leave behind to the flames—let the Flame of Love burn away.

---

50. I have used "Huron 'Beltane' Fire Dance" by Loreena McKennitt, from *Parallel Dreams*, 1994, QUINLAN ROAD LIMITED.

SUMMER SOLSTICE

Fire ready off to side. Each brings a full rose or flower. Wrapped lollies (candy), small fruits, flowers in baskets. Golden yellow altar cloth with black ribbon. Wreath of roses, wildflowers, black ribbon near fireplace. Loaves of bread near fireplace and on altar. White wine and white grape juice. Queenly/"regal"/"best clothes" attire, and a small shoulder bag/pocket for "small edibles". Dyad poem copies. Olive oil. Rattles, tambourines, drums.

Each one take their rose/flower to pre-ritual contemplation with them—place in basket on altar upon gathering to the circle.

Call to Gather—drum beat, people come in moving in a circle to the rhythm—several circles, feeling the rhythm.

Centering/Breath Meditation

"Breathe deep, feel the weight of your body—sink into it. This is how Earth holds you. Visualise roots coming from your feet going deep into earth through the mantle and crust all the way down into her core. Breathe deep, and sink into your relationship with Her.

Breathe deep now and be aware of filling your bodymind to capacity, until you can draw it no longer, feel the fullness…let it go. Again, breathe deep, fill your bodymind to capacity. Hold it a moment, feel the need to let go. Giving it away. This is how Gaia breathes in our part of the world at this time. She is filling to capacity, and giving it away, letting go."

Statement of Purpose

"This is the time of the Summer Solstice—when the light part of the day is longest. In our part of the world, light is in Her fullness, She spreads Her radiance, Her fruits ripen, Her greenery is everywhere, the cicadas sing. Yet as Light reaches Her peak, our closest contact with the Sun, She opens completely, and the seed of darkness is born.

As it says in the tradition, this is the time of the rose, blossom and thorn, fragrance and blood. The story of Old tells that on this day Goddess and God, Beloved and Lover,[51] embrace, in a love so complete, that all dissolves, into the single Song of ecstasy that moves the worlds. Our bliss, fully matured, given over, feeds the Universe and turns the wheel. We join the Beloved and Lover in the Great Give-Away of our Creativity, our Fullness of Being."

Banishing

"Let us begin by remembering that we are each open channels for the moving energies of Life—Goddess and God, Beloved and Lover. Let us recall those voices that hold us back from being these open channels, fully who we might be—that block the flow.

Turn to a partner or group of three—expressing some of this if you like…dramatic if you like. If you would rather not speak, your consciousness is all that matters; but do listen to your partner—without comment."

ALLOW A FEW MINUTES

"Let us banish those voices—move some of that energy, raise some energy—open up the channels."

DRUMS AND RATTLES AND VOICE.

"Having made a start on banishing those states of being which throw us off balance, let us call upon those with which we may be in harmony."

Creating the Sacred Space

All turning to the East
"Hail the East, Powers of Water—Cosmic Dynamic of Sensitivity."
All: Hail the East, Powers of Water—Cosmic Dynamic of Sensitivity.
Celebrant: "…that absorbs, becomes, whatever you touch; may we *feel* what we are, and respond compassionately."
DRUMS as……sprinkles water with oak branch.(each speak as they wish as water goes by—or conscious of their own relationship with water)

---

51. I use this ungendered form of metaphor for lovers when possible, for the sake of inclusiveness—not just of same-gender sexual relationships, but also of all inner metaphor for the Beloved of the soul.

When water is placed back on altar:
All: May we *feel* what we are, and respond compassionately."

All turning to the North
"Hail the North, Powers of Fire—Unseen Shaping Power of the Cosmos."
All: Hail the North, Powers of Fire—Unseen Shaping Power of the Cosmos.
Celebrant: "...that gives us form—flames that we are; may we dance with you and act with Creative Lust for all of life."
DRUMS as......lights the fire in the pot, carries it around. (each speak as they wish as fire goes by—or conscious of their own relationship with fire)
When fire is placed back on the altar:
All: May we dance with you and act with Creative Lust for all of life.

All turning to the West
"Hail the West, Powers of Earth, deep Sentient Presence and Memory."
All: Hail the West, Powers of Earth, deep Sentient Presence and Memory.
Celebrant: "You hold all the stories of life in your Body—as each of our bodies do also; may we remember who we really are, may we hold the Wisdom of all time and no Time."
DRUMS as........ holds up rock and carries it around. (each speak as they wish as earth goes by—or conscious of their own relationship with earth)
When rock is placed back on the altar:
All: May we remember who we really are, may we hold the Wisdom of all time and no Time.

All turning to the South
"Hail the South, Powers of Air, Cosmic Dynamic of Exuberance and Expression."
All: Hail the South, Powers of Air, Cosmic Dynamic of Exuberance and Expression.
Celebrant: "Wind that moves the trees, the clouds, and allows us our voice; move us and inspire us to unfurl our being."
DRUMS as......... lights smudge stick, carries it around.(each speak as they wish as smudge goes by—or conscious of own relationship with air)
When smudge is placed back on the altar:
All: Move us and inspire us to unfurl our being.

All turning to the Centre
"This is what we are—mysterious Flashes of Water, Fire, Earth and Air (PAC-ING THE CIRCLE)—in this dynamic Place of Being, and we are at Centre. The circle is cast, we are between the worlds, beyond the bounds of time and space, where light and dark, birth and death, joy and sorrow meet, as One." (light the centre candle)

Invocation

Celebrant: "Let us recognize and invoke the Sacred Fullness of the Mother, the Wholeness of the Universe, the Summerland—in each other."
Celebrant start in two places—one immediately to her left and one opposite in the circle. Then each person pass the invocation to the next, around the circle:
"Hail ...... thou art the Sacred Fullness of the Mother: the Wholeness of the Universe—the Summerland is within you. (Thou art Sovereign of Summer)".
(bow of reverence, take their hand-optional)
Response: It is so.

"Let us continue the invocation of the Sacred Fullness present in us with the poem—a Conversation of Union."

Dyad Poem[52]

(inner and outer circles—facing each other)

Inner:	**Outer:**
Nameless One	of many names
Eternal	and ever changing One
Who is found nowhere	but appears everywhere
Beyond	and within all
Timeless	circle of the seasons
Unknowable Mystery	Known by all
Mother of all Life	Young One of the Dance
Engulf us with your love	Be radiant within us

52.　See Chapter 6 fn24.

Inner circle step back into outer circle:
All (with actions): See with our eyes. Hear with our ears. Breathe with our nostrils. Touch with our hands. Kiss with our lips. Open our hearts…that we may live free, joyful in the Song of all that is.

Song/Toning

Begin with "O—Ah—Ay—Ee", building on this, each flowing into their own sound and listening for the others—harmonising voices. Let it flow for a while, building and ebbing, until it comes to its own conclusion.

SILENCE FOR A MOMENT

The Give-Away[53]

Celebrant and a few others pick up baskets of blossoms first, then baskets of lollies (candy), throwing handfuls of contents into the air—repeating the blessing;
"She gives it away, She pours it forth.
They—Beloved and Lover, give it away, They pour it forth."

Celebrant and a few others do the same with baskets of small fruits, or hand larger fruits to people, with the same blessing.
(Everyone pick up lollies, fruit—puts them in pocket/bag.)

Spiral Dance and Chant

"Each pick up the rose or full flower you have contemplated, which represents your Fullness of Being, your radiance, and let us dance the Mystery of the Spiral."
All pick up rose/flower and join hands, each holding their flower in linked right hand.
Celebrant leads into a spiral, as all chant, making sure to look into the eyes and faces of the passing people.

All chant:
"She is shining, crowned with light.

---

53. My first experience of this "Give-Away" process was with Moonskins ritual group in Woolongong NSW, Summer Solstice 1995, Margi Curtis and Graham Wykes.

We are radiant, we are bright.
We dissolve into the night."[54]

The Fire

As the circle opens back out, lead to the fire at the side…light it.
"Let us join in the Great Give-Away, each give it away, give your Creative Fullness away…to the Universe—however you'd like to express it. Take your time."

Each one comes forward in turn, and speaks if they wish, and throws their rose on the fire.
Response: "We bless you, and the Gift that you are".

Silence and the Wreath[55]

All stand watching the flowers burn.
Celebrant holds the wreath to each person's face, so they can see the flames through it and says: "See with clear sight."

She holds the wreath aloft, where person can see it, and says:
"And know the mystery of the unbroken circle."

Communion

(Bread near fireplace)
Celebrant holds up the bread: "We are each the Bread of Life—feeding the world with our everyday acts and being. It is the Sun that ripens in us—bringing us to this creative fullness, this Radiance. We are the Sun. We are the grain, we are the Bread of Life."

Each comes forward in turn, takes the bread from the celebrant and breaks off a piece, holds it up and affirms: "I am the grain, I am the Bread of Life." (add more if they like)
Response: "It is the Sun that is in you. So may you shine!"

---

54. My own variation of a chant in Starhawk, *The Spiral Dance*, p.190.
55. A process from Starhawk, *The Spiral Dance*, p.190.

Celebrant holds up the wine: "We are each the Wine, poured out for the Mystery. It is the Sun that ripens in us—bringing us to this creative fullness. We are the Sun. We are the grape, we are the Wine."

Each comes forward in turn, takes the decanter of wine from the celebrant and a glass, pours their wine/juice, holds it up and affirms:
"I am the grape, I am the Wine." ("I am the grape, I am the juice.")
Response: "It is the Sun that is in you. So may you shine!"

Stories

"Let us sit and enjoy some of our fruits and lollies and tell each other stories of the fullness of Creativity, what you are creating—perhaps every day, what is peaking in you, flowering in you, perhaps what you want to give or have given—or whatever you would like to say.

Response: "May you be fruitful" or "We bless your creativity" or other appropriate formal response.

Open the Circle

All turning to the South
"We have remembered that we are Air,
Cosmic Dynamics of Exuberance and Expression
unfurling our being.
May there be peace within us."
All: May there be peace within us.

All turning to the West
"We have remembered that we are Earth,
deep Sentient Presence and Memory
holding all the stories of life in our bodies.
May there be peace within us."
All: May there be peace within us.

All turning to the North
"We have remembered that we are Fire,

vessels of unseen shaping power—
dancing flames.
May there be peace within us."
All: May there be peace within us.

All turning to the East
"We have remembered that we are Water,
Cosmic Dynamics of Sensitivity
absorbing, becoming all that we touch.
May there be peace within us."
All: May there be peace within us.

All turning to the Centre
"We have remembered that we are open channels for the moving energies of
life—the Sacred Fullness of the Mother, of the Universe—that the Creativity that
pours forth from us is Divine—is what the Cosmos is made of. We have remembered that we are the Bread of Life—that our Passion released, may feed the
world.
May there be peace within us and between us." (all join hands)
All: May there be peace within us and between us.

"The circle is open but unbroken,
May the Peace of the One go in our hearts."

All: It has been a merry meeting,
it is a merry parting,
may we merry meet again.
Blessed Be.

Pass the kiss in both directions.

Points for individual contemplation prior to the ritual:

—the voices or what holds you back from being fully who you might be—what
blocks the flow.
—how you and others are the "Fullness of the Mother, of the Universe". Contemplate the Dyad Poem as a conversation of the interchange of form and formlessness.

—the rose/flower—what you give away to the Universe, how you feed the Universe with your daily creativity, your Passion, your actions.

—how you are the Bread of Life (connected to the third contemplation)—how it is the Sun in you that ripens, as much as Earth.

LAMMAS

Each bring a bread figure that they made with contemplation on what they fear. Wear black preferably, bring dark veil or dried garland. Black felt altar cloth. Dark rye bread on two plates & dark beer, red wine and dark grape juice. Dark foods such as licorice, prunes, black olives. Fire ready. Star carrots/cookies near fireplace. Small bowl of ash. Small basket of grain. Cauldron-like clay pots for all the elements. Centre candle on large cauldron-like claypot of earth with wreath of dried roses from Summer with wheat/grain heads, rosehips, flower pods. Music ready.

Each take bread figures to to pre-ritual contemplation with them—place in basket on altar upon gathering to the circle.

Put on veils or garlands before contemplation.

Call to Gather...a bell, ringing several times continuously.

Centering

"The Hour is come. 'For whom does the bell toll?' (three times—different emphasis on toll, bell and whom each time.) 'It tolls for thee.'

Breathe this breath that is yours, as if it were your first...do you remember that it was so? Breathe this breath that is yours, as if it were your last...do you remember that it will be so? Breathe it now, this breath that is yours...but not yours. We breathe this breath together (take hands)...we are the breath of the Cosmos in this time and in this place—Her breath-taking manifestation, in this Moment."

After a few moments let go hands.

Statement of Purpose

"This is the season of the waxing dark. The seed of darkness that was born at the Summer Solstice now grows…the dark part of the days grows visibly longer. Earth's tilt is taking us back away from the Sun. This is the time when we celebrate dissolution; each unique self lets go, to the Darkness. It is the time of ending, when the grain, the fruit, is harvested. We meet to remember the Dark Sentience, the All-Nourishing Abyss, She from whom we arise, in whom we are immersed and to whom, we return.

This is the time of the Crone, the Wise Dark One, who accepts and receives our harvest, who grinds the grain, who dismantles what has gone before. She is Hecate, Lillith, Medusa, Kali, Erishkagel, Chamunda, Coatlique—Divine Compassionate One. We meet to accept Her transformative embrace, trusting Her knowing, which is beyond all knowledge."

"Let us slip between the worlds into Her dark space. Let us begin by remembering Her Recipe, the elements in Her Cauldron from whence we come."

Creating the Sacred Space

All turning to the East
"Hail the East: Water we are—
filled with the ocean tides—in Her Cauldron of Creativity!"
Drum for several beats—water person wait.
Each presented with cauldron (clay pot) of water, ladles it into their hand, holds it to the East and responds:
"Water I am!—in Her cauldron of Creativity! (—add whatever else)." (sip the water)

All turning to the North
"Hail the North: Fire we are—
sparks of ancient heat—in Her Cauldron of Creativity!"
Drum for several beats—fire person to wait.
Each presented with the firepot, lights a match from the firepot, holds it to the North and responds:
"Fire I am!—in Her cauldron of Creativity! (—add whatever else)." (dead match into a clay pot held by an assistant)

All turning to the West.
"Hail the West: Earth we are—
geoformations—in Her Cauldron of Creativity!"
Drum for several beats—earth person to wait.
Each presented with cauldron of earth, takes some, holds it to the West and responds: "Earth I am!—in Her cauldron of Creativity! (—add whatever else)."
(Put earth back, and touch 'dirty' hand to own forehead/throat/chest)

All turning to the South.
"Hail the South: Air we are—
particles of light and inspiration—in Her Cauldron of Creativity!"
Drum for several beats—air person to wait.
Each presented with the cauldron with lit smudge stick in it, lifts it out, holds it to the South and responds:
"Air I am!—in Her cauldron of Creativity!" (—add whatever else)." (put smudge stick back)

All turning to the Centre.
"This is Her recipe—Water, Fire, Earth and Air (PACING THE CIRCLE)—we are made from this, these are our Origins. We are at the Centre, in Her Cauldron of Creativity—in this Dark Realm of Manifesting. Her Centre is Here.
The circle is cast, we are between the worlds, beyond the bounds of space and time, where light and dark, birth and death, joy and sorrow meet as one."
(light centre candle)

Invocation

Bowl of ash and basket of wheat grains in one hand and arm.
Celebrant to each: "......*you* are the grain that is harvested—you are Her Harvest (put wheat in their hand); remember Her Dark Sentience within you (touch their forehead with ash), that you are She—the Transformation of the Ages."
Response: "I am She, Dark and Ancient Wise One." (add or express own words)

Sitting (with music[56])

"Contemplate Her now within you—this Dark and Ancient Wise One."

---

56. I use "Ignacio" by Vangelis Papathanassiou. Belaphon BLPS-19242, which Jean Houston has used in her Underworld experience (referred to in Chapter 6 fn29).

After a few moments or more:
"All stand—put your grains in the centre".

Dissolution—the Bread Figures[57]

Celebrant (with black veil over her face) picks up empty basket and invites each to place their bread figure in the basket:
"I am the Dark One come to claim you—what would you let go of? What do you fear? What do you have for-giving? What do you wish to surrender to my cloak of transformation?"
Each person speaks if they wish, placing their bread figure in Her basket, and summarizes with one or a few words that the group can repeat in a chant.
Celebrant and the group repeat the answer—chant style with DRUM.
Let energy build for each response. Those choosing not to speak still have the drum for their intention.
(Celebrant unveils while she answers the question)
When circle is complete, Dark One holds up the basket of bread figures, and says:
"I am the Old Compassionate One—the Creative One who receives all, transforms all." Dark One leads procession to the fire. Someone go ahead to light fire. Dark One tosses bread figures into fire—slowly, one at a time, repeating: "For transformation".

Silence

"Everything passes, all fades away.[58] May we open our Hearts."
A few moments of silence as we watch the bread figures burn.

"I am Love"

Celebrant (holding the basket of stars): "She says: I am Love, I am the All-Nourishing Abyss. All manifestation springs from me—you have given yourself back.

---

57. Based on the process in Starhawk, *The Spiral Dance*, p.191.
58. Starhawk, *The Spiral Dance*, p.191.

You will reap the harvest, you will proceed in joy and abundance…for this is the Mystery."

The Hoped for Harvest[59]

Celebrant takes the basket of star carrots/cookies around to each.
"What do you hope to harvest? What do you hope for?"
Each responds, then summarizes with one or a few words that the group can repeat in a chant.
Celebrant and the group repeat the answer—chant style (a few times).
After circle is complete: "Let us carry all our hopes back to the circle and gestate them."
Each chant again, their own hopes primarily, as the group processes back to the circle.
Celebrant holds up her star: "May all these hoped for harvests be so."
All respond: "May it be so!"
All eat the stars.

Music[60]

Communion

Celebrant hold up plate of dark rye bread and decanter of dark beer:
"May you be nourished by Her Harvest. Let Her Rich Creative Darkness soak through you."
Pass the bread to people either side (two plates, bread on each):
"May you be nourished by Her Harvest."
Each repeat the blessing around the circle, as they offer the bread.

(Assistant distribute glasses to each person)
Pass the dark beer to people either side (2 decanters):
"Let Her Rich Creative Darkness soak through you."
Each repeat the blessing around the circle, as they offer the beer/wine/juice.

---

59. based on the process in Starhawk, *The Spiral Dance*, p.191-192.
60. I use *Le Fleuve* from *Odes* by Irene Papas and Vangelis Papathanassiou. Polydor

Offer other dark foods—licorice, prunes, dark olives.

Story Space

"Perhaps there are stories of things you are letting go of, perhaps stories of loss, perhaps stories of harvests."

Dance—Harvest Dance[61]

"Let us dance in celebration of the Harvest—our harvests and the Harvest of these times. Can the grub imagine the butterfly she will become? Can we imagine what will emerge?"

Open the Circle

All turning to South
"We have remembered that we are Her recipe—
that we are Air, in Her Cauldron. May there be peace within us."
All: May there be peace within us.

All turning to the West
"We have remembered that we are Earth in her Cauldron. May there be peace within us."
All: May there be peace within us.

All turning to the North
"We have remembered that we are Fire, in Her Cauldron. May there be peace within us."
All: May there be peace within us.

---

61. I call this "The Harvest Dance"—the version we do is based on the Menousis dance that I learnt from Jean Houston. As we have been doing it: form a circle holding hands, take three steps to the right, pause, then three more steps to the right, pause and sway LRL. Take three more steps to the right, pause, take two steps into centre with right foot each step, two steps back out with left foot each step, the sway RL. Add gathering motions of joined hands with the steps into the centre. The music, named *Menousis*, is on *Odes* referred to in fn.60.

All turning to the East
"We have remembered that we are Water, in Her Cauldron. May there be peace within us."
All: May there be peace within us.

All turning to the Centre
"We have remembered that we are Divine—Sacred and Ancient Wise One, we have remembered the Dark Sentience, the All-Nourishing Abyss to whom we belong, in whom we are immersed. We have remembered our fears and our hopes. We have remembered that our harvest is Her Harvest.
May there be peace within us and between us." (all join hands)
All: May there be peace within us and between us.

"The circle is open but unbroken. May the Wisdom and Compassion of Goddess—the Mystery—go in our hearts."

All: It has been a merry meeting
It is a merry parting
May we merry meet again
Blessed Be!

(Pass the kiss in both directions)

Music[62]

Points for individual contemplation prior to the ritual:

—your own demise, the passing of your breath, the passing on of your "harvest".
—the Dark and ancient Wise One within you—how you are this, the Wisdom and Transformations of the Ages of Gaia within you.
—-your bread figure—what do you fear? What do you have for-giving? What do you wish to surrender to Her cloak of transformation?"
—What do you hope to "harvest"—what are your hopes?

---

62. I have used Leornard Cohen,"Dance me to the End of Love" available on *Leonard Cohen: More Best Of* 1997 Sony Music Entertainment, and "Lady Midnight" available on various compilations as referrred to at http://www.leornardcohenfiles.com/lp-compil.html

MABON

Wreath with wheat/grain heads and Autumn leaves, around centre candle. Three wheat stalks tied with red ribbon for each partticipant—all wrapped in cloth and tied ceremoniously with long thick red ribbon. Purple triangle overlaid on autumn coloured altar cloth.[63] Basket of bulbs. Each bring fruit or wine or juice or cake/cookies/fancy bread—next to themselves in circle. Glasses, plates, cutlery, bottle openers ready. Each bring a plant pot with soil—put outside (in "Underworld") near large pot full of soil, with small spades. Garden flame torches to light path to the pots. Lantern. Each bring a shawl—and stories of loss/grief. Tissues. Bells. Bowl of water and towel near "gate" of the "Underworld" for handwashing. Music ready. Bowl of pomegranate seeds in Underworld. Red threads available.

Call to Gather—energetic drumming

Statement of Purpose and Centering

"This is the time of Mabon, the Autumnal Equinox, the moment of balance of light and dark in the dark part of the cycle. The light and dark parts of the day in the South and in the North of our planet, are of equal length this day.

Feel the balance in this moment—Earth as She is poised in relationship with the Sun. Feel for your own balance of light and dark within. Breathe into it. Breathe in the light, swell with it, let your breath go into the dark, stay with it. Feel for your centre, shift on your feet, from left to right,..... breathe into it.

In our part of Earth, the balance is about to tip into the dark. Feel the shift within you, see in your mind's eye the descent ahead, the darkness growing, remember the coolness of it. This is the time when we give thanks for our harvests—the abundance we have reaped. Yet we remember too the losses. The story of Old tells us that Persephone is given the wheat—the Mystery, knowledge of life and death—for this she gives thanks. But she sets forth into the darkness—both Mother and Daughter grieve that it is so.

---

63. The triangle recalls that Demeter was the "Mother of the Great Triangle of Life, the Mystery of the Universe, complete in all Her parts: Creator, Preserver, Destroyer." Carolyn McVickar Edwards, *The Storyteller's Goddess*, p.178. The purple is a colour I associate with the grief of this season, as well as with the status of Sovereignty/royalty, which the Beloved One-Persephone is descending to.

Let us enter the sacred space, wherein we may speak the Mystery. Let us begin by remembering who we are and from whence we come."

Creating the Sacred Space

All turning to the East
"We are from the East, and we remember that we are Water.
She is alive in us and we in Her."
......carry water around and sprinkle it on participants. (AVANTI)
Each respond as they feel the water: "I remember that I am Water. She is alive in me and I in Her." (producing a cacophony effect)

All turning to the North
"We are from the North and we remember that we are Fire.
She is alive in us and we in Her."
......light and carry the fire around the circle. (AVANTI)
Each respond as they feel the fire: "I remember that I am Fire. She is alive in me and I in Her." (producing a cacophony effect)

All turning to the West
"We are from the West and we remember that we are Earth.
She is alive in us and we in Her."
......carry a rock or bowl of earth around for each to touch. (AVANTI)
Each responds as they feel the earth:"I remember that I am Earth. She is alive in me, and I in Her." (producing a cacophony effect)

All turning to the South
"We are from the South and we remember that we are Air.
She is alive in us and we in Her."
......light and carry smudge around. (AVANTI)
Each responds as they smell the smudge: "I remember that I am Air. She is alive in me, and I in Her." (producing a cacophony effect)

All turning to the Centre
"We remember that we have been present you and I, in the East, in the North, in the West, in the South, we have been present always in each stage of Gaia's story—She is alive in us and we in Her. We are at Centre, which is everywhere.

The circle is cast, we are between the worlds, beyond the bounds of space and time, where light and dark, birth and death, joy and sorrow meet as One."
(light centre candle)

Invocation

"Let us call Demeter."
Chant and drums—with a facilitator to co-ordinate and orchestrate.
All (as celebrant ties on mask of Demeter, adds to her costume and picks up bundles of wheat): "Demeter, Demeter—Mother we call you, Mother we call you."
LET ENERGY BUILD
When "Demeter" is ready and standing waiting, the group finishes with "Demeter!"
"Demeter" walks the circle twice ceremoniously untying the ribbon and unwrapping the cloth. She holds up the wheat bundles for all to see, stating:
"You are given the wheat in every moment."

"Demeter" goes to each one:
"(name), I give you the wheat—the Mystery—the knowledge of life and death. I let you go as Daughter(Child),[64] most loved of Mine…you become Queen(Sovereign).[65] You will return as Mother,[66] co-Creator with me. You are the Seed in the Fruit, that becomes the Fruit in the Seed. Inner Wisdom guides your path."

---

64. "Child" may be preferred for male participants particularly, though some may choose to identify with and respond with "Daughter" as the ancient initiates—female and male—possibly did in the Eleusinian Mysteries. See Rachel Pollack, *The Body of the Goddess*, p.220-221. The term "Son" is not really an appropriate alternative given that the Mysteries are specifically a Mother-Daughter story, and also given that the Christian heritage of some participants may affect the Earthly-egalitarian significance of this male term; that is, in the patriarchal heritage "Son" has been above "Daughter".

65. "Sovereign" may be a preferred term, although women may enjoy reclaiming "Queen". Male participants may prefer "Sovereign" given other cultural connotations of "Queen" for males and the desired solemnity of the moment! The alternative of "King" seems undesirable as it tends to designate dominance and highest status in the current cultural context.

66. All the ancients in the Eleusinian Mysteries—female and male—identified with Demeter. See Rachel Pollack, *The Body of the Goddess*, p.220-221. This is an identification with the Mother of all Life, the Universe.

Response: "It is so. I am Daughter(Child), becoming Mother—Seed becoming Fruit. The Mother knowledge grows within me." (each may vary and add words as desired to express self)

Celebrant takes off her mask and extra "Demeter" garments, and is given the wheat and invocation by another participant.

Thanksgiving for the Harvest

"Let us give thanks for our harvests—this harvest we are given in every moment, all that we have gained."

Each one picks up their "harvest" and puts it in the centre, stating:
"I give thanks for my harvest of…"
Response: "Your life, it is blessed." OR "Your harvest, it is wonderful. We hear your joy."

Celebrant; "We have harvested much, our lives are blessed. We are Daughters and Sons of the Mother."

Remembering the Losses and Sorrow[67]

"It is time now to take our Wisdom, and remember the sorrows—the losses involved. Let us put on our shawls and remember the grief of the Mother, of mothers and lovers[68] everywhere, our grief."

---

67. This process is based on a ritual done with Women-Church in Sydney in 1990. Its primary author was Christine Doyle. The ritual was partly relating with the grief of the mothers of the "disappeared" in Argentina, but also with the grief of mothers everywhere who lose their children, grown or small, through war, violence and ecological mismanagement. In this ritual, it is a process for grief of any kind.

68. This term "lovers" was chosen as the term to include men in the process, as I felt that the term "fathers" was inappropriate to the ritual story. Also, frequently much of the pain and loss experienced by both the women and men present is directly associated with the "father"—personal and/or collective. Certainly "fathers" in almost any global cultural context are simply different from "mothers". With the term "lovers" men may include themselves, and it remains appropriate to traditional Goddess story, as well as avoiding the possibility of patriarchal metaphoric imposition.

All put shawls on—may put shawls over head.

MUSIC[69] on.
"Persephone descends. The Beloved One is lost."
All process in a circle.

Participants may speak names and events etc for whom and what they grieve spontaneously as the music plays.[70] "I remember…"
Response: "For this we grieve."

Repeat for as long as necessary.

Celebrant: "Sit with a partner now and tell each other anything further in your heart, the losses you grieve…or just sit with each other in silence."

Celebrant ring bell after a few minutes as the cue to switch.

Ring bell to bring to silence.

Song (start softly)

"Ancient Mother we hear you calling, ancient Mother we hear your song.
Ancient Mother our grief and pain is yours, ancient Mother we taste your tears."[71]

Silence

The Hope of Persephone

The basket of bulbs is passed around. Each take one.

---

69. I have used "Gentle Sorrows" on the audio tape *Dreams* by Sky, 1988 copyright Ronny R. Bunke, Magic Music PO Box 1111, Mill Valley CA 94942. I copy it three times in sequence so that it runs for the time needed.
70. Each one used to pause the music to speak, but one year we found this was unnecessary, and that it flowed better when the music was left on and the procession could keep going.
71. An adapted version of an old chant.

"Persephone goes forth into the darkness to become Queen of that world. She tends the sorrows. These represent our Persephones, who tends the sorrows. Let us go out into the night with Her and plant our seeds."

All begin singing the chorus of "Changing Woman":[72]
"She changes everything She touches, everything She touches, changes."
Celebrant takes the lit lantern, and all follow her outside (to the "Underworld"). Each plants their bulb in their pot, as the singing continues. Co-celebrants may sing the verses of the song.

Story

When all are done planting, a co-celebrant reads an excerpt of the story of Persephone.[73]

"In the crook of Her arm Persephone held Her Mother's wheat close to Her breast, while Her other arm held the torch aloft. She was startled by the chill as She descended, but She was not afraid. Deeper and deeper into the darkness She continued, picking her way along the rocky path. For many hours She was surrounded only by silence. Gradually She became aware of a low moaning sound. It grew in intensity until She rounded a corner and entered an enormous cavern, where thousands of the dead milled about aimlessly, hugging themselves, shaking their heads, and moaning in despair.

Persephone moved through the forms to a large, flat rock and ascended. She produced a stand for her torch, a vase for Her Mother's grain, and a large shallow bowl piled with pomegranate seeds, the food of the dead. As She stood before them, Her aura increased in brightness and in warmth.

> *"I am Persephone and I have come to be your Queen. Each of you has left the body you knew, and resides in the realm of the manifesting—the realm of the dead. If you come to Me, I will initiate you into your new world."*

---

72. This has been sung by many, but the version I have is by The Gaia Choir on *WOM-ANSONG*. Byron Bay: BAHLOO MUSIC, 1992. Starhawk also refers to this chorus as "the Kore Chant", *The Spiral Dance*, p.188.
73. Charlene Spretnak, *Lost Goddesses of Early Greece*, p.114-116, with some of my own changes.

She beckoned those nearest to step up onto the rock close to Her. As each one came before Her Persephone embraced them and then stepped back and gazed into the eyes. She reached for a few pomegranate seeds, squeezing them between Her fingers. She painted the forehead with a broad swatch of the red juice and slowly pronounced:

> *"You have waxed into the fullness of life,*
> *And waned into darkness;*
> *May you be renewed in tranquility and wisdom."*

Pomegranate Seeds

Pass pomegranate seeds around. Each squeeze a few and mark another on the forehead, repeating the blessing if they like.
Moment of silence—then return to:
"She changes everything She touches, everything She touches, changes", as all move back inside, carrying the pots with them.

An attendant at the door helps with holding pots while each rinses their hands.

Communion

Celebrant holds the pot up:
"These represent our hope. The Seed of life never fades away. She is always present. Blessed be the Mother of all life. Blessed be the life that comes from Her and returns to Her."[74]

"Let us eat, drink and enjoy Her gifts and give thanks."
All join in cutting cake or whatever is there, opening wine, and serving each other.

---

74.   Partly from Starhawk, *The Spiral Dance*, p.193.

Storytelling

Red Threads (See p.304 for significance)
"Let us tie red threads on each other: we participate in the Vision of the Seed—of the continuity of Life. We are initiates into the Mysteries."

Open the Circle

All turning to the South
"We have remembered that we are Air, that She is alive in us and we in Her. May there be peace within us."
All: May there be peace within us.

All turning to the West
"We have remembered that we are Earth, that She is alive in us and we in Her. May there be peace within us."
All: May there be peace within us.

All turning to the North
"We have remembered that we are Fire, that She is alive in us and we in Her. May there be peace within us."
All: May there be peace within us.

All turning to the East
"We have remembered that we are Water, that She is alive in us and we in Her. May there be peace within us."
All: May there be peace within us.

All turning to the Centre
"Take up your sheaves of wheat, and your pots. We have remembered that we have been given the Mystery—Her knowledge is within us. We are the Seed in the Fruit, becoming the Fruit in the Seed. We have remembered our harvests, our sorrows and our hope—the blessed Harmony/Balance of the Cosmos—the Thread of Life, the Seed that never fades away.
May there be peace within us and between us." (all join hands)
All: May there be peace within us and between us.

Pass the kiss in both directions.

Song

"The circle is open but unbroken. May the peace of the Goddess be ever in our hearts. Merry meet, and merry part, and merry meet again.'

All: Blessed Be!

Points for individual contemplation prior to the ritual:

—your response to receiving the wheat from Demeter.
—your "harvest"—all that you have gained.
—the losses that you grieve—personal, cultural, Gaian.

8

Being in Place

The Place of Story as the Story of Place

In the Old Western Way,

> The receipt of story by eyes or ears was regarded as a vital pathway of blessing, if the reader or listener were in a state of proper attention and respect. Those who merely siphoned the words off the page like a vacuum cleaner, those who sat inattentively, mentally wool-gathering did not receive the blessing. Our own saturation with printed materials sometimes renders us insensible to the sacred blessing of story and its many gifts.…But when we memorize a story, its blessing works at a deeper level within us. It is then that we enter fully into its workings; it is then that we become the story. When we become garments of story, we are able to clothe others with blessing.[1]

The process of participating in "sacred space"—conscious ritual—is different from simply being lectured to or told something, or from having a discussion. In sacred space, the whole being is engaged; we are able to speak and hear the depths of our felt knowings. In sacred space, we are close to the blueprint of our lives, as close as each is able to be; and that ability within each is varied and complex and unknowable. The variation of ability to approach the "blueprint", from time to time within the same person, and then from person to person, affects what a participant will gain and possibly integrate. But the reaching for it, co-creates the very receptor that is required—as surely as the chlorophyll molecule was co-created by Earth and Sun, as Earth reached for nourishment; as surely as the ear was co-created by subject and sound, as the subject reached for an unknown signal.

Personally this practice has taken me from fragmentation and alienation to wholeness and belonging, as I reached for She Who Is, She Who Will Be, and

---

1.   Caitlin Matthews, *The Celtic Spirit*, p. 334.

She Who is the Transformation of the Ages. It has brought me through so much, sustained my personal evolution. It has been "geotherapy"—a term Brian Swimme uses to speak of how the vision of the whole story of Earth, of the Universe may enable the human to proceed from the present alienated pathological mode of being to wholeness—as we learn our Story.[2] I have personally responded to the re-storying of the Female Metaphor, associating Her with Cosmogenesis—the Unfolding of the Cosmos, and embodying Her in Seasonal ritual. My Search has been an intensely personal one, but it has been earthed and patterned in an ecological psychology that has been able to bless and "clothe" others as well. This blessing has been a completely reciprocal process, wherein they blessed me as they resonated with the story within me, and I resonated with their response—I unfolded, they unfolded, we were delighted…as something new came into being. We found and expressed a resonance with Gaia's Seasons and Her Creative Unfolding, we noticed Her more—around us and in us. It is deeply personal yet related, each one's unique poetry and life story finding a Place in other and all-that-is, and vice versa.

Some personal journal notes from different years:

WINTER SOLSTICE:
As I walk the spiral at the Winter Solstice with a candle in my hand, images flash to mind of walking the spiral in this same space at Summer Solstice, with a rose in my hand. The experience and the images—the candle, the rose, the spiral, in the same space—is a Sense, a Knowing of a pattern, that is forming in me. As I look at the tree in my backyard with her Winter nakedness, I remember her Summer dress, and how I have celebrated both—I have not let her beauty and her phases pass by without note. As I put the candle of Winter on the altar and express my wish for the world—"the flame in my heart"—images of past Winter rituals arise; I spontaneously recall the same moments of putting the candle down, or lighting the candle, and the intentions I expressed then…and I wonder at the magic I have witnessed in that time, how I feel the movement, the growing strength and capacity in me, and the keen delight of others. I spontaneously "see" and feel the movement we have celebrated into Light and into Dark, the Pattern we have danced many times. It is a rhythm I am coming to Know.

EOSTAR:
Walking—instead of driving—has become part of the practice, a way of coming to know. As the poem quoted by Fransisco Varela says "Wanderer, the road is your footsteps, nothing else; wanderer, there is no path; you lay down the path in walk-

---

2.   Brian Swimme, *Canticle to the Cosmos*, video 8.

ing…".[3] We step into power, leaving behind the binds of the past, co-create the present and future.

BELTANE:
As I do the breath meditation in preparation for the ritual, I know this as the Beltane Moment of the breath…images and memory flash in my mind of the Eostar breath meditation, the Imbolc breath meditation…I sense these other Moments in relation to this one in my breath.

SUMMER SOLSTICE:
Standing in the same location at Summer Solstice as at Winter Solstice, and stating the purpose for our gathering—to celebrate the time when the light part of the day is longest. There is a clear sense *of it, as I recall in the instant the darkness and cold of the Winter Solstice in this exact location and similar time of day.*

Often when we humans can describe gravity, the weather, our bodyminds and more, we think we know what they are—we can sum these things up. But it is simply a different kind of knowledge of Her; it is not Her sentience, which must be *felt*. This cosmology is about sensing an organic space and time, Being in Place—knowing that the dimensions of Self-place, Earth-place, and Universe-place are not separate; that this is all one's "country". Another word for this "country" may be the Welsh word "cynefin" (pronounced KUN-EV'IN). It has been literally translated into English as "habitat" or "place", but the sense of it is more: the word articulates a reciprocal relationship with one's particular place, and may be understood to consciously include the multivalent dimensions of this nested reality of Place. "Cynefin", like "country", includes the stories of one's multiple belongings—personal, cultural, geographic, cosmic…they are all *religious* in the sense of *connecting*, and more than we can know.[4] This "cynefin", this "country"—a PaGaian sense of habitat—includes knowing that one IS a Place, a place of the Sacred Interchange of Life—with all the complex web of stories, to which one belongs, and with which one acts. It is an intimate reality, but remains mysterious and unknowable in its infinite dimensions of belonging and action.

---

3.   A poem by Antonio Machado referred to by Sarah A. Conn, "The Self-World Connection", Woman of Power, Issue 20, p.74.

4.   At the website http://www.cynefin.net/, "cynefin" is described as "more properly understood as the place of our multiple belongings;"…wherein our interactions are frequently determined by the patterns of our multiple experiences—personal and collective—"expressed as stories". My understanding of the word as being similar to "country", comes from Taffy Seaborne's stories of his childhood experience in Wales and his later experience in central Australia.

The breath comes in—a gift of all that has gone before. You are the Place where it is received, changed and given forth again; your organism is the Dynamic Place of this exchange. You are then the gift as your breath is released.

This Place of Being is not static, it reaches in and reaches out—a place of reciprocal interchange. Perceptual psychologist, Laura Sewall advocates awakening our sensory systems, which are "exquisitely evolved channels for translating between 'in-here' and 'out-there'" and she describes this skillful ecological perception as a "devotional practice",[5] of coming to recognize Earth's call.[6] Sewall lists five "perceptual practices":

> (1) learning to attend, or to be mindful, within the visual domain; (2) learning to perceive relationships, context and interfaces; (3) developing perceptual flexibility across spatial and temporal scales; (4) learning to reperceive depth; and (5) the intentional use of imagination.[7]

The practice of celebrating the PaGaian Cosmology as it has been described in this book may meet all of these practices, (re-)developing ecological perception. It is a "devotional practice"—of becoming receptive to Gaia's speech, heard deep within and deep without. Her speech is like a ghetto-blaster really when we pay attention, find an art form to receive Her, a place to hold a Conversation or a Dance. We come to *feel* the infinite belonging and to act in accord. And there is no need to go to Eleusis to find this place, or rely on external authorities…this practice is Home-ly.[8]

Desire

Place of Being is a passionate place, where desire draws forth what is sought, co-creates what is needed; in a Con-text, a Story, where love of self, other and all-that-is are indistinguishable…they are nested within each other.

---

5.   Laura Sewall, "The Skill of Ecological Perception" in *Ecopsychology: Restoring the Earth, Healing the Mind.* p.203.

6.   Laura Sewall, "The Skill of Ecological Perception" in *Ecopsychology: Restoring the Earth, Healing the Mind.* p.224-215.

7.   Laura Sewall, "The Skill of Ecological Perception" in *Ecopsychology: Restoring the Earth, Healing the Mind.* p.204.

8.   as this term is described in chapter 2, p.66.

I begin to understand Desire afresh: this renewed understanding has been an emergent property of this religious practice. The Poem of Old says She is "that which is attained at the end of Desire." I begin to realize how Desire turns the Wheel. As the light part of the cycle waxes, form/life builds in Desire. At Beltane, Desire runs wild, at Summer Solstice, it peaks into Creative Fullness, Union…and breaks Open into the Dark part of the cycle—Dissolution. She becomes the Dark One, who receives us back—the end of Desire.

It has been a popular notion in the Christian West, that the beautiful virgin lures men (sic) to their destruction, and as I perceive the Wheel, it is indeed Virgin who moves in Her wild delight, towards entropy/dissolution; however in a cosmology that is in relationship with the Dark, this is not perceived as a negative thing. Also, in this cosmology, there is the balancing factor of the Crone's movement towards new life—a dynamic and story that has not been a popular notion in recent millennia.

Desire seems not so much a grasping, as a receiving, an ability or capacity to open and dissolve. I think of an image of an open bowl as a signifier of the Virgin's Gift. The increasing Light is Received, and causes the Opening, which will become a dispersal of form—entropy, if you like. This is Beltane—the Desire that is celebrated is a movement towards dis-solution…that is its direction. In contrast, and in balance, Samhain celebrates Re-solution which is a movement towards form—it is a materializing gathering into form, as the increasing Darkness is received. It seems it is Darkness that creates form, as it gathers into itself—as many ancient stories say, and it is Light that creates dispersal. And yet I see that the opposite is true also.

I think of how there is a desire for this work, for whatever one does—it is then already being received. Desire is receiving. What if I wrote this, and it was not received or welcomed in some way. But the Desire for it is already there, and perhaps the Desire made it manifest. Perhaps the Desire draws forth Manifestation, even at Winter Solstice, even at Imbolc, as we head towards Beltane—it is Desire that is drawing that forth, drawing that Process around. Desire is already receiving, it is Open. Its receptivity draws forth the Manifestation. And then the Manifestation climaxes at Summer and dissolves into the Manifesting, which is perhaps where the Desire is coming from—the Desire is in the Darkness, in the Dark's receptivity.[9] It becomes very active at the time of Beltane, it lures the differentiated beings back into Her. So the lure at Beltane is the luring of differentiated beings into a Holy Lust, into a froth and dance of Life, whereupon they dissolve ecstatically back into Her—She is "that which is attained at the end of Desire." And in the dissolution, we sink deeper into that, and begin again. All the time, it is Desire that is luring the manifest into the manifesting, and the manifesting into the manifest. Passion is the Glue, the underlying Dynamic that streams through it All—through the Light and the Dark, the Virgin-Mother-Crone, Differentiation-Communion-Autopoiesis.

If desire/allurement is the same cosmic dynamic as gravity as Swimme suggests,[10] then desire like gravity is the dynamic that links us to our Place, to "that which is", as philosopher Linda Holler describes the effect of gravity.[11] Held in relationship by desire/allurement we lose abstraction and artificial boundaries, and "become embodied and grow heavy with the weight of the earth."[12] We then know that "being is being-in relation-to".[13] Holler says that when we think with the weight of Earth, space becomes "thick" as this "relational presence...turns notes into melodies, words into phrases with meaning, and space into vital forms with color and content, (and) also holds the knower in the world."[14] Thus, *I* at last become a particular, a subject, a felt being in the world—a Place laden with content, sentient.

A Meta-religious Metaphor

Thomas Berry has said that we need to understand that the challenge of our time—that is, the apparent planetary siege by the human, is not just an outcome of the last few hundred years of Western scientific thinking. It is not just Cartesian, it is not just economics; this moment, he says, has required everything. He calls the challenge of this moment, "meta-religious".[15] He says that we, as a spe-

---

9. Perhaps the popular cultural association of the darkness/black lingerie etc. with erotica is an expression/"memory" of this deep Truth.

10. Brian Swimme, *The Universe is a Green Dragon*, p.43.

11. Linda Holler, "Thinking with the Weight of the Earth: Feminist Contributions to an Epistemology of Concreteness", Hypatia, Vol. 5 No. 1, p.2.

12. Linda Holler, "Thinking with the Weight of the Earth: Feminist Contributions to an Epistemology of Concreteness", Hypatia, Vol. 5 No. 1, p.2.

13. Linda Holler, "Thinking with the Weight of the Earth: Feminist Contributions to an Epistemology of Concreteness", Hypatia, Vol. 5 No. 1, p.2.

14. Linda Holler, "Thinking with the Weight of the Earth: Feminist Contributions to an Epistemology of Concreteness", Hypatia, Vol. 5 No. 1, p.2.

cies and as a planet, are in a "moment of transformation". It is my understanding that part of what that means for humans, is to realize that we are not in control—we never have been, and never will be. While it is true that we participate, that we are in it, that it is our Story, we are not *the* Story. It is Gaia's Story. We are participants through whom Creativity proceeds…whether consciously or not, whether as compost or new growth, we participate, and She proceeds with Her Creativity.

Berry lists three rights of all creatures: the right to Be, the right to Habitat, and the right to Fulfill its role in all existence.[16] In my mind these three rights correspond to the three faces of the evolutionary cosmic dynamics: it is an ethics based on the Creative impetus of Gaia, an ethics that may enable Life as we know it and as we don't yet know it, to proceed. Intrinsic to it is a balance and a recognition of, Love of Self, Love of Other, and Love of All-That-Is. It is based in a balance and recognition of, Urge to unfold, Place to be, and Subjective Space. Deep in the present moment, all the Creativity that is necessary, is present.

I notice in myself and others who continue to participate in the seasonal ritual celebrations, an opening to subtle perceptions and sensitivities that do enable and evoke a passion for adopting everyday changes to our domestic lives; that is, how we relate to the water we use, the food we eat, the methods of transport we choose, the social and cultural context. It seems that as each actually feels what Charlene Spretnak calls "the unitive dimension of existence"[17]—as one may in ritual over time, feels themselves to be "a node within a vast network of creative dynamics",[18] becomes more mindful of flux, wonder and awe[19]—as one may with artful practice of this Cosmology, that we do in fact begin to devise strategies for change in our lives. The strategies for change are ones whereby we may be more authentic in our relationship with this expressly sentient Earth and Cos-

---

15.   Thomas Berry, "The University: Its Response to the Ecological Crisis", a paper delivered before the Divinity School and the University Committee on Environment at Harvard University, p.8.

16.   Thomas Berry defines these in a talk he gave on June 4 2000, at the Center for Ecology and Spirituality, Port Burwell Ontario. It was a 5 day colloquim on "The Cosmology of Religion". He also suggests them in "The University: Its Response to the Ecological Crisis", p. 5.

17.   Charlene Spretnak, *States of Grace*, p.22.

18.   Charlene Spretnak, *States of Grace*, p.22.

19.   Charlene Spretnak, *States of Grace*, p.22.

mos. Some participants have given up their cars, found ways to reuse water, are learning how to garden organically, relate more consciously with the flora and fauna around them—care more, and feel that their small care does make a difference.

This translates on a broader scale to an increasing ability in the hearts and minds of participants to step outside the anthropocentric frame, as increasingly each one becomes more conscious of an "Earth Jurisprudence",[20] that is, that Earth Herself has innate wisdom and integrity. It is a wisdom that they can sense and come into relationship with, that is primordial, as they do constantly express and enact in the rituals. There is in participants more humility about the place of the human in the scale of things, more willingness to step back from the human impress on the planet and other beings, and to reframe more inclusively.

There is nothing comprehensive about this particular "re-inventing" as I have described it so far herein—it is a beginning, as other participants and I are aware. We are novices, most of us. Each year that I celebrate the Sabbats, I understand a little more. And it is new as well as old. In these times, any of us comes to it all with different minds than our forebears did—this is somewhat of a disadvantage, but the novice has a freshness too.

The Snake Bites Her Tail—the Circle Comes Around

In Chapter 1 I stated that "This book itself, as with any creative work, as it progresses, is ordered, structured and organized by these features"[21]—the three-fold creative principle. This work had so many disparate parts at the beginning (differentiation)…and where was its beginning (in the complex plenum—auto-poiesis/subjectivity)? It had many threads, and each of those threads had their own three features of creation. Each was complex, and the threads criss-crossed in no perceivable pattern. Part of the Search process was allowing the disparate parts to reveal their relationship, to show their resonances. This was largely conceptual at first, then another part of the Search was taking the courage to weave the threads (communion), and see how they responded. The weaving into a fabric was a work and a skill—a crafting—and then watching—"did it sit well?", and perhaps "did it take on an energy, a life of it's own—was there a communion into

---

20. Mike Bell, "Thomas Berry and an Earth Jurisprudence".
21. Chapter 1 p.48.

which they arrived, a deeper relationship that already existed there?" This was the production—done with receptivity. Then there was allowing and witnessing the synergy, the self of the work to come through—witnessing the conflagration, the transformation of the parts into one, a gestalt, becoming its unique self. This was active receiving of the work's autopoiesis, which flowed back into a new differentiated being.

Now as the Wheel continues to turn, and the work is given over again to something Larger—it disperses. It becomes many seeds in the minds and hearts of readers who may take it further. This is the Return of the "finished" work. It is consumed by the reader—the audience. It loses itself in a new context, many new contexts—it becomes many seeds—to come to life in a new way, within others. The cycle begins again in many new Places.

"ToGaianess"

Re-inventing language is something humans have always done—it is a most fluid medium, like the ocean we once swam in as early creatures. Language, Poetry, pattern and symbols are the seeds in our psyches, the transgenetic codings with which humans—personally and collectively—have expressed and shaped the world, our habitat; and we continue to.

"ToGaianess" is a term coined by my partner and beloved, for how in relationship we draw each other into Gaia, into Her True Being—real space and time, into the seamless Whole. We encourage each other in our practice, lure each other more deeply each day. Communities may do this for each other; I have come to know this experience particularly with my beloved. In Summer Solstice process one year, I noted how we lure each other into clear eyes, into seeing with clear sight. I felt "clear sight" to be knowing that we are "flashes", "events", passing through this place; and then being able to make it as creative and joyful as possible—why not?—it seems better for self and other certainly, and we can only assume the ripples go on indefinitely to all-that-is, from whence it comes. Thus it goes full circle.

An Australian Aboriginal expression that seems similar in meaning is "Ngapartji-ngapartji". It has generally been translated into English as "giving something in return"—taking turns at being given to;[22] but this is really a very poor sense of it. "Ngapartji-ngapartji" is more like being pleasure's source and pleasure's home at the same time[23]—not knowing when one is "giving" or "receiving": receiving is a giving, and giving is a receiving.[24] The closest translation of the Aboriginal term (and mode of being) may be "reciprocity": it is an exchange that happens simultaneously like it does in the peaking of the breath. It is not considered, it simply happens—is done. "ToGaianess" is like this; it is knowing self and other are one in the ground of our being (Gaia)—we are in the same breath—feeling it, and being able then to act accordingly.

"Careflow"

This is a term for going carefully with the flow.[25] The flow is the ongoing flow of Creativity. We may build care into our flow. We may slow down to care, to co-create what is important to us. We may decide to be care-full, to act because we care, and to not allow the distractions—the distractions from our true heart's desires. It is more easily done as we align ourselves with Her rhythms. Brian Swimme speaks of the "care in the curvature":[26] how the exquisite balance of the curvature of space-time that brings all forth, that allows the form-ation of being, may be described as "care"—that it has "care" built into it. This is not anthropomorphizing the Universe, this is articulating a power of the Universe that has been noticed as innate and unfolding: we may call it a dimension of "care" which we as some of its creatures have come to perceive.[27] "Careflow" is participating consciously—decidedly—in this power.

In a similar way one may come to use the word "organ-ised". If shifted in meaning, "organised" may be an alignment with one's organism or behaving organically; that is, a conscious participation in the self-organising creative cosmos. It

22.   As it is translated for example in *Pitjantjatjara/Yankunytjatjara to English Dictionary* 2nd edition compiled by Cliff Goddard, p.84.

23.   This is a state that Brian Swimme describes in *The Universe is a Green Dragon*, p.79, when he is speaking of "Allurement".

24.   Taffy Seaborne has this understanding of "Ngapartji—ngapartji" gathered from his own reflections and experience and conversations with Anangu elders of Uluru.

25.   A term coined by Taffy Seaborne.

26.   Brian Swimme, "The Care in Curvature", a talk given at the Journey into Wholeness conference, North Carolina, Spring 2003. Available on audio tape at http://www.JourneyintoWholeness.org/media/tapeset_brians.shtm

27.   Brian Swimme describes this "care" as a Power of the Universe that he names "Interrelatedness", in *The Powers of the Universe*, lecture 9.

may be understood as a kind of "careflow". "Organ-isation" can become an identification with the Organism-Universe even as we speak—a recognition of an wholistic state of being.

Language began with an "organ-ic" basis, and we may become more conscious of that again, as we now extend our sense of the "organic" to the Universe, as we extend our sense of "country".

A Prayer in Process

Sometimes it has been a useful exercise to re-write prayers or songs that I learnt perhaps too well as a child or later, to re-speak them and imbue them carefully with my new understandings. It is another way of spelling one's self, of changing one's mind—to articulate one's own prayers and with each word and phrase to honour what one now truly believes to be so. It is also the case that many of the prayers and praises that are found in the patriarchal religions of recent human history are quite often founded upon the expressions of some earlier Earth-based Goddess religion that is now unmentioned and buried. So any re-writing and listening to one's own interpretations of the pattern of the prayer may end up being closer to its original sense, as well as speaking a new moment.

One of the prayers I re-wrote for myself is one that is central to anyone of Christian heritage.[28] I continued to change it as my understandings shifted, so that over a period of years I could see an evolution, an unfolding of perception. Following is the latest rendition of that prayer. I named it a "Goddess Prayer" and dated it each time I re-wrote it.

Goddess Prayer 2005 C.E.

Mother—She who I am Who is deeply related
Virgin—She who I am Who is ever new
Crone—She who I am Who is creative return to All
     Holy is my Being.
This Mystery pervades all.
May I understand my Inner Guidance,
and graciously receive the infinite daily abundance.

---

28. It is known as "The Lord's Prayer".

May I forgive my insensitivities and lack of skill
     —and forgive others the same.
May I respond to my Divine Passion.
          I am in Awe…
and give thanks to the Light&Dark within.

There is also another version that cropped up recently, that was inspired by a re-scribing of the word "Kingdom" to form "Kin-dom".[29] So I wrote the following in collaboration with my partner, addressing the Universe as "Our Mother". Some may find it useful as it is, and may also renew it further.

Our Mother
  Who is with us,
Holy is Our Being.
Thy Kin-dom is present.
Thy Desire is received throughout the Cosmos.
We graciously receive your infinite daily abundance.
May we forgive each other our lack of skill and insensitivity.
May we understand our inner guidance,
  and perceive each other's needs.
For Thine is the Kin-dom, the Power and the Story,
          forever and ever.
Blessed Be.

The Three Candles Meditation—resonances with the three phases/dynamics of the "Great Creative One"

This meditation was mentioned in the Introduction, as being part of my daily practice. The three candles with associated objects remain a permanent arrangement on my altar, and I usually light the candles with some version of the following—sometimes shorter or longer—or sometimes non-verbally, simply allowing the sense of each one. It has continued to evolve and simplify, and is really at the heart of the three-lined prayer that concludes this chapter.

---

29.   Karen Davis, "A Peacable Kin-dom and the Ethics of Eating", EarthLight, Issue 51 Vol 14 No.2, p.54.

Light the 1st candle:
I remember She within me Who is deeply related—the Mother—the Matrix, the Intricate Web—She Who Is—everything within me that connects me to the past, upon which the present is built—the Depth of this moment. I remember the Sangha, the community around the globe that supports Life, those in particular that have and do support my life—all those who have been my teachers.

Light the 2nd candle:
I remember She within me Who is ever new—the Virgin—the Urge budding forth—She Who will Be—the future, the children, the descendants of body and mind—the much More in myself and all selves. I remember the Buddha, the Self, the Shining One within all, for whom I refine the gold—for whom this life is given, those whom I support.

Light the 3rd candle:
I remember She within me Who returns me to All-That-Is, to the Great Subject—the Old One—She within Who creates the Space to Be, Who dissolves the old in every moment, Who is the transformations of the Ages—Who knows the Truth of all things—Who is the Sentience within all. I remember the Dharma, She within whose Wisdom is beyond all knowledge.

This is the Creative Context in which we are held—in the Context of all that supports this present moment, in the Context of the future that is being conceived and nurtured right here, and in the Context of the Old all-Knowing Compassionate One who receives all—all three present within each unique being…right Here.

A PaGaian Breath Meditation

Going within for the moment and becoming aware of your breath, feeling this cycle within.

With your imagination, remember all the breathing happening right now on the planet—feel/sense it with each breath.
The entire planet is breathing.

Remember the constant dawning and setting of the Sun—happening right now,
as Earth turns…the constant dawn and dusk.

Remember the constant facing into the light of the Sun—our Star,
and the constant facing into the dark of the Cosmos, happening right now,
as She turns…
the constant moving fullness of light and dark on opposite sides of the planet.

Remember the constant coming into being and passing away happening right now,
as She turns.
The entire Wheel as we have celebrated it is happening right now—all at once.

We are at the Centre of the Wheel.
She waxes into fullness, and wanes into darkness—She grows into form, and
dissolves back into that great Plenum from which all emerges.
There is in every moment:
constant novelty—infinite particularity,
constant communion—infinite relationship,
constant dissolution—trans-formation…making way for the new.

Feel this breath, your breath. We participate in Her constant Creativity,
from this Centre.

A Creative Place of the Cosmological Unfolding

With the inbreath I remember that I am ever-new. I receive the Gift—the right
to Be. I am Virgin.

With the peaking of the breath I remember that I am in this Place—this dynamic
Place. I am the Place—the right to Habitat. I am Mother.

With the outbreath I remember that I am the ancient One ever-transformed. I
am the Gift—the right to fulfill my role in existence. I am Crone.

**Another version—because Virgin and Old One are particularly interchange-
able…the clarity of the beginning and the end is not always apparent:[30] and
the Three are always "fuzzy".**

With every breath in, I receive the Gift of All—the Transformations of the Ages, the Old One.

With every breath out, I am the Gift to All—again renewed, the Virgin.

I am the Sentient Place of Now, receiving All of the Ages, budding forth with it renewed, the Sacred Interchange, the Mother.

And very simply—and best done with expressive body movements, that perhaps call to bodymind, images (ancient or contemporary) of She Who is the Universe—as one feels them: remembering that you are Home.

I am the Ancient One,
ever-New,
in this Place.

---

30.   as referred to in the last section of Chapter 5.

Appendices

APPENDIX A

Thomas Berry's Twelve Principles of a Functional Cosmology

1. The universe, the solar system, and the planet Earth in themselves and in their evolutionary emergence constitute for the human community the primary revelation of that ultimate mystery whence all things emerge into being.

2. The universe is a unity, an interacting and genetically related community of beings bound together in an inseparable relationship in space and time. The unity of the planet Earth is especially clear; each being of the planet is profoundly implicated in the existence and functioning of every other being of the planet.

3. From its beginning the universe is a psychic as well as a physical reality.

4. The three basic laws of the universe at all levels of reality are differentiation, subjectivity, and communion. These laws identify the reality of the universe, the values of the universe, and the directions in which the universe is proceeding.

5. The universe has a violent as well as a harmonious aspect, but it is consistently creative in the larger arc of its development.

6. The Earth, within the solar system, is a self-emergent, self-propagating, self-nourishing, self-educating, self-governing, self-healing, self-fulfilling community. All particular life forms must integrate their functioning with this larger complex of mutually dependent Earth systems.

7. Genetic coding process is the process through which the world of the living articulates itself and its being and its activities. The great wonder is the creative interaction of the multiple codings among themselves.

8. The human is that being in whom the universe activates, reflects upon, and celebrates itself in conscious self-awareness.

9. At the human level genetic coding mandates a further trans-genetic coding by which specific human qualities find expression. Cultural coding is carried on by educational processes.

10. The emergent process of the universe is irreversible and non-repeatable in the existing world order. The movement from non-life to life on the planet Earth is a one-time event. So, too, the movement from life to the human form of consciousness. So also the transition from the earlier to the later forms of human culture.

11. The historical sequence of cultural periods can be identified as the tribal-shamanic period, the neolithic-village period, the classical civilizational period, and the emerging Ecozoic era.

12. The main task of the immediate future is to assist in activating the inter-communion of all the living and non-living components of the Earth community in what can be considered the emerging Ecozoic era of Earth development.

Appendix B

Song of Hecate

✦

(to be read uproariously)

let birds out of cages!
let bitches bitch!
and dogs be dogs
screech and moan to the moon
let crows de-feet the plastic surgeons
and cry "faarck" to the open sky
we will have age in all her beauty.

rivers of tears and mountains of groaning
The seas are thick with my blood

and yet i live with every baby's first cry

to cleanse the earth of the sins of adam

xxx

i am old—so old: and yet
methinks this is the dawn of time

from the deepest caverns of earth
the cry goes forth
"no! no! no more!
until the final "no" has been uttered.

– – – – – – – – – – – – –

......all is still under the fullest moon.
now the great "yes" arises
out of the sea......

Bridget McKern 1993

Appendix C

The Wheel of the Year—Southern Hemisphere

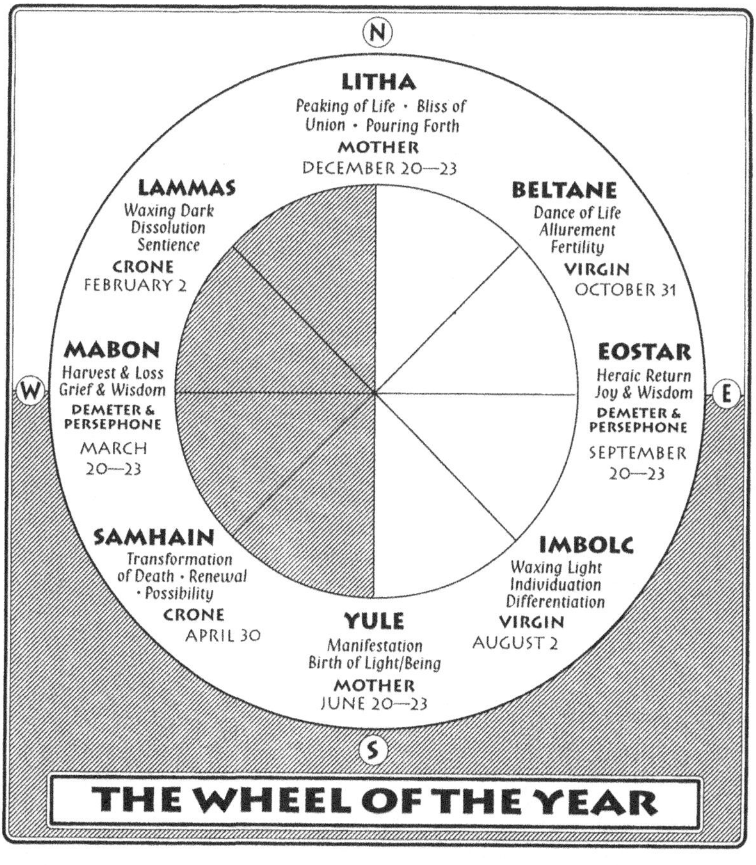
N
LITHA
Peaking of Life • Bliss of Union • Pouring Forth
MOTHER
DECEMBER 20—23
LAMMAS
Waxing Dark
Dissolution
Sentience
CRONE
FEBRUARY 2
BELTANE
Dance of Life
Allurement
Fertility
VIRGIN
OCTOBER 31
W
MABON
Harvest & Loss
Grief & Wisdom
DEMETER & PERSEPHONE
MARCH 20—23
EOSTAR
Heraic Return
Joy & Wisdom
DEMETER & PERSEPHONE
SEPTEMBER 20—23
E
SAMHAIN
Transformation of Death • Renewal • Possibility
CRONE
APRIL 30
IMBOLC
Waxing Light
Individuation
Differentiation
VIRGIN
AUGUST 2
YULE
Manifestation
Birth of Light/Being
MOTHER
JUNE 20—23
S
THE WHEEL OF THE YEAR

APPENDIX D

The Wheel of the Year as the Star of Aphrodite

✦

(as referred to in Chapter 5, page 153)

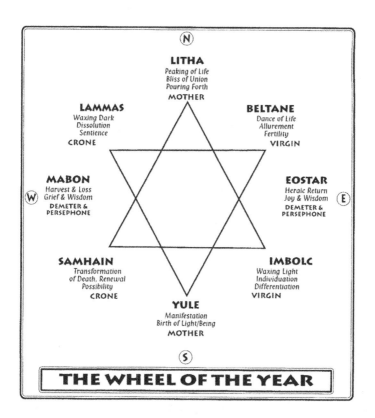

N

LITHA
Peaking of Life
Bliss of Union
Pouring Forth
MOTHER

LAMMAS
Waxing Dark
Dissolution
Sentience
CRONE

BELTANE
Dance of Life
Allurement
Fertility
VIRGIN

MABON
Harvest & Loss
Grief & Wisdom
DEMETER &
PERSEPHONE

W

EOSTAR
Heroic Return
Joy & Wisdom
DEMETER &
PERSEPHONE

E

SAMHAIN
Transformation
of Death, Renewal
Possibility
CRONE

IMBOLC
Waxing Light
Individuation
Differentiation
VIRGIN

YULE
Manifestation
Birth of Light/Being
MOTHER

S

THE WHEEL OF THE YEAR

APPENDIX E

Another Southern View of the Wheel of the Year

THE WHEEL OF THE YEAR

The Wheel of the Year celebrates the larger cycles of life's rites of passage as well as the seasonal cycles. In the southern hemisphere the wheel moves counter clockwise

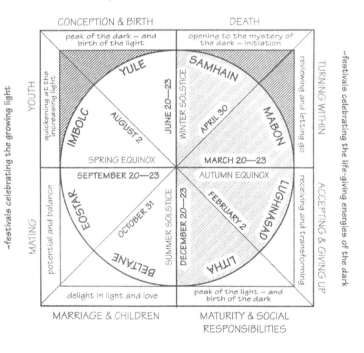

~at Spring Equinox the amount of light in a day starts to outweigh the dark
~at Autumn Equinox the balance tips and darkness gradually increases

REFERENCE: Annabelle Solomon, *The Wheel of the Year*, p.105.

273

APPENDIX F

Teachings for the Sabbat Rituals

The understanding of any of the Sabbats is always multivalent. The following "teachings" are a synthesis of my understandings and the work of many others, and form what I call a PaGaian perspective. They are presented here as they are currently—they are my notes for the teaching part of preparing the group for the ritual, as referred to in Ch. 7, p.180.

SAMHAIN

This is a celebration of deep Autumn. It has been known in Christian times as "Halloween"—since the church in the Northern Hemisphere adopted it as "All Hallow's eve" (31ˢᵗ October N.H.) or "all saint's day" (1ˢᵗ November N.H.). This "Deep Autumn" festival as it may be known in our times, was known in old Celtic times as Samhain, which is an Irish Gaelic word, with a likely meaning of "Summer's end", since it is the time of the ending of the Spring-Summer growth. The leaves are turning and falling. It was thus felt as the end of the year, and hence the New Year. It was and is noted as the beginning of Winter—the darkest phase of the year between the old and the new. It was the traditional time for bringing in the animals from the outdoor pastures, and when many of them were slaughtered.

Earth's tilt is continuing to move us away from the Sun at this time of year in our part of the world: our region is continuing into darkness, from where it seems all new things begin. As with any New Year, between the old and the new, in that moment, all is possible. We may choose in that moment what to pass to the future, and what to relegate to compost. Samhain may be understood as the Space between the breaths. It is a generative Space—the Source of all. There is particular magic in being with this Dark Space. This Dark Space which is ever present, may be named as the "All Nourishing Abyss" (Swimme 1996), the "Ever-Present Origin" (Gebser 1985). It is a generative Place, and we may feel it particularly at this time of year, and call it to consciousness in the celebration.

In this Earth based spiritual tradition, we say that at this Seasonal Moment, "the veil is thin that divides the worlds". The old story tells that on this night, we travel in the Womb of the Mother—the vast sunless sea within, and that we step ashore the Shining Isle, which is the egg—the ovum—of conception.[1] This is the Poetry that is used traditionally. There is death and there is conception. So in the celebration, we remember the dead—(i) our ancestors and those who have gone before (ii) we remember our old selves—who we have been (iii) the old cultural selves—collective—what we have done, what we are doing, some of the horrors…the ongoing wars, the inquisitions, the holocausts, the genocides, the geocide. We recall the ancestors, selves and cultural/historical events that have brought us to this moment. Now is the time for re-imagining the New—what we would become, personally and collectively.

The purpose of optional costume at this celebration is to emphasize possibilities—to entertain your imagination, your dreams and wild places. The Cosmos Herself, and as Earth, has come through so many wild, amazing changes in Her 13.7 billion year story…was it possible to imagine what was next? In the earliest of Earth's days could the first cells have been imagined? Could the advent of eyes, or the music we now experience have been imagined? So too, in our particular lives, could we have imagined our own advents? Can we imagine the More, the Not-Yet culturally? We can at least allow the Space for it.

In the ritual there is a place where you will be invited to name yourself "as you will": this is also a recognition that all is possible. We may identify with the mythic and grow ourselves into larger aspects of ourselves. It may be an opportunity for you to express something about yourself that gets little "airplay"; for example, I often do a modified version of my actual name, that expresses another realm or dimension of my being. You may choose to name yourself as you *are* named.

At Autumn Equinox—the previous Sabbat—Persephone (Beloved One) descended to became Queen of the Dead/the Underworld, the Dark Shining One within, Goddess of Transformation. Samhain is about celebration of the process that takes place in the dark chrysalis. If we have the eyes to see, this is what Death is…Transformation—thus all the gold decorative fabric. Persephone's dark aspect has also been known as Hecate. Another Death Goddess,

---

1.   Starhawk, *The Spiral Dance*, p.194.

Selket—known to the ancients as a Goddess of Transformation—is golden: the ancients seem to have known something that we have forgotten and are trying to remember. Other Dark Ones of this Season are Medusa, Lillith, Coatelique.

Samhain/Halloween is a celebration of the Old phase of the Goddess, the Crone who is primarily in relationship with All-That-Is (where the Virgin face is primarily in relationship with Self, and Mother is primarily in relationship with Other). The Crone/Old One is that movement back into the Great Sentience out of which All arises. Samhain particularly is a celebration of Her *process* of the end of things and transformation. The Crone aspect is the contraction if you like, that may be understood as a systole, a contraction of the heart by which the blood is forced onward and the circulation enabled. She is the systole that carries All away—She is about loss, but the contraction of the heart is obviously a creative one, it is the pulse of life. Perhaps it is only our short-sightedness that keeps us from seeing contraction/death that way: we insist on taking it all so personally, when it is not, in fact?

The falling apart, the disintegration can be, and usually is, felt as a scary or depressing thing. It is the loss of the known, perhaps the loss of a worldview, the loss of a world. Samhain is a time for such reflection—facing our deep fears and contemplating our demise. We usually confront fears or depression when we feel that our lives are changing—the world is falling apart. Samhain is about understanding that the Dark is a fertile place—in its decay and rot it seethes with many unseen complex Golden Threads connected to the wealth of Creativity of all that has gone before—like any compost. So it is in these dark times culturally, and so it may be—we may be some of the Golden Threads. We must retrain our perception to see the Beauty of new form possible in the old decaying fermenting compost. While our ancestors may have wondered whether they would make it through the coming Winter, we may wonder in our times whether we will make it through the global spasms and impending Gaian changes—and in what form.

Life will persist…such hope is represented by the Seed in the Fruit (show cut apple). There is a thread of life that has eternally endured. There is the Seed within us, the Dark Shining One, already present, simply awaiting its time of awakening. It may not be in the form we had in mind. To perform the magic, we accept all the old shapes of our lives, and ultimately of our culture, as compost for the new. We accept the unknowing. We put it all in the pot, consume it all…feed our imaginations good food so that the new may emerge. We may make "re-solutions". We transform the old into the new in our own bodyminds—we are the transformers. While it is true that we give ourselves over to the Great Transformer, the Old One's Process—we are She, and thus we play our part in the transforming, in the imagining, in the manifesting.

The format of this celebration is based on part of a poem by Robin Morgan,[2] slightly reworded. The metaphor of the snake is used because it is a symbol of renewal with its shedding skin.
Robin Morgan says:
> Drawn from the first by what you might become,
> you did not know how simple this secret could be....
> The shed skin lies upon the ground.
> Devour now all your old shapes, wasting no part...

In this process of transformation Gaia wastes nothing.
For the rebuilding then, the metaphor of the spider's thread is used because she weaves her home from her own bodymind with the strongest natural fibre known. The spider is a great example of Creator. Morgan says:
> Having devoured your old shapes, wasting no part...
> you are now free to radiate whatever you conceive,
> to exclaim the strongest natural fibre known—
> into such art, such architecture
> as can house a world made sacred by your building.

The strongest natural fibre known is perhaps our imaginations, our creative selves. We will represent it with golden thread. Samhain, this Seasonal Moment, is the time for conceiving and imagining the Not-Yet—for dreaming the new.

At Lammas—the beginning of the Dark cycle—we fell into Her Dark Sentience, Her "dis-solution". Now at Samhain—deep Autumn—we remember the Creativity of the Dark Process, it's fertile regenerative quality, its Power for "re-solution". We make New Year re-Solutions. We may "say what we will". We are performing the Act of co-Creator...the Power of Conception in the Dark available Space.

OTHER RITUAL NOTES:
We will be eating apples for communion tonight. The ancients understood the apple as the Goddess' sacred heart of immortality or "never-ending renewal". It

---

2.   Robin Morgan, "The Network of the Imaginary Mother", *Lady of the Beasts*, p.84.

contained the Mystery—the seed in the fruit, the fruit in the seed; the Daughter in the Mother, the Mother in the Daughter—the continuity of Life (show the cut apple). The pentacle was a sign of Kore (Core), another name for Persephone—in the heart of the Mother:[3] She, the Beloved Daughter—the Young One, is the World Soul and Self-Knowledge hidden in the Heart of the Mother. In eating the apples and drinking apple juice tonight, we will taste and enjoy the fruit of never-ending renewal, and deeper self-knowledge in the Heart of the Mother.

We will use scissors to cut free each other's conceptions—they are one of the tools of the Crone, for the finishing: at the same time the creating. This is one of her sacred processes, that all constantly participates in…and we may do so consciously.

WINTER SOLSTICE/YULE

Tonight we celebrate the longest night of the year. Traditionally it has been celebrated by the ancients—our Gaian ancestors in many regions—as the birth of Light, the birth of Form. The stories of many cultures tell of the Great Mother giving birth to the Divine Child at this time of year. It is this Sabbat for which the ancient pre-Celtic indigenous Europeans apparently built New Grange in 3200 B.C.E.. New Grange has been thought to be a temple-tomb, but it is possible that the great stone bowls there were not for remains of the dead, "but in fact contained water to act as reflective surfaces designed to interact with the sun-beam" that enters the chamber.[4] This is a very recent re-membering and conjecture about what was central to the spirituality of these ancient forebears.

The inner chamber wall of this mound is carved with the triple spiral, and at the Winter Solstice it is briefly illuminated by the rising sun. (SHOW the Triple Spiral image)[5] This was confirmed by modern academia only in 1969[6]—with minds that that at that time had little comprehension of what its significance may be. Some have said recently that the illumination immortalizes "earth's power to give

---

3.   Barbara Walker, *The Woman's Encyclopaedia of Myths and Secrets*, p.49.
4.   Paul Devereaux, *Earth Memory: The Holistic Earth Mysteries Approach to Decoding Ancient Sacred Sites*, p.124.
5.   Michael Dames, *Ireland: A Sacred Journey* p.192.
6.   Paul Devereaux, *Earth Memory: The Holistic Earth Mysteries Approach to Decoding Ancient Sacred Sites*, p.120.

new life to the sun",[7] some say it is the other way around.[8] Few accounts really understand the significance of the triple spiral at this stage, though Michael Dames in 2000 referred to the association of it with the Triple Goddess. Most mythographers at this point in time have not been prepared to allow the Goddess any cosmic function, as Claire French noted in 2001[9] or take seriously Her aspects. Another example of this is the lack of comprehension of the significance of Silbury Hill at Avebury, for so long, until Michael Dames came along with a goddess oriented mind with which to be able to take it in. He wrote "The Silbury Treasure" and published it in1976. It seems that New Grange—constructed to mark the Winter Solstice—celebrates the significance of Earth-Sun relationship in some way that we can only begin to guess at and re-member for ourselves. It apparently does celebrate the triple faced Cosmic Dynamic—as it is carved on the illuminated inner chamber wall.[10]

So we will participate with these ancient forebears in their celebration of the Triple Spiral tonight—deepening into our understanding of it. We will dance it—I am sure the old ones would be pleased…it's been a long time. The dance has three layers of equal significance—it may be perceived as the Triple Spiral Dynamic, or a breath. I have re-named the dance—the "Cosmogenesis Dance". Winter Solstice is a celebration of Cosmogenesis—the ongoing Birth of All, enabled and characterised by this Creative Triplicity. It seems the ancients understood that from their rock inscription—they left us a story, a code. The annual return of the Light at this Seasonal Moment, is a microcosm of the Birth of it All—and the Dynamic that births it all. Nothing is excluded from this triple-faced Dynamic—not Earth, nor Sun, nor you or me. It is the "triskele" of energy (that is the Celtic word), "the innate triplicity of the Cosmos…that runs through every part of the Universe".[11]

THE "COSMOGENESIS DANCE": The dance has three layers, representing the three aspects of the Goddess, the triple Spiral Dynamic that the ancients were aware of—the dynamic that they understood as unfolding the Cosmos. The three aspects celebrate Virgin—the ever new differentiated being, Mother—the deeply related interwoven web, and Crone—the eternal creative return to All-That-Is.

---

7.   Elinor Gadon, *The Once and Future Goddess* p.346.
8.   Anne Baring and Jules Cashford, *The Myth of the Goddess*, p.98.
9.   Claire French, *The Celtic Goddess*, p.22.
10.   See also http://gofree.indigo.ie/~thall/newgrange.html
11.   Caitlin Matthews, *The Celtic Spirit*, p.366.

The three layers of the dance may be understood to embody these. The Dance represents the flow and balance of these three—a balance and flow of Self, Other and All-That-Is. It may be experienced like a breath, that we breathe together—as we do co-create the Cosmos. That is part of our job this evening.

Winter Solstice is a Birthing Place, the Gateway from the dark part of the year to the light part. It particularly celebrates the Mother aspect of the Triple Goddess. At this Seasonal Moment, Darkness reaches its peak, its fertile fullness, and breaks into form. The face of the Goddess moves from Crone of the Dark part of the cycle through Mother at this Winter Gateway, to Virgin—the birth of Form, of Life. This is how it happens—out of her fertile Dark Matter. Winter Solstice is a time of receiving the Gift of the Dark, which is Birth, of Form—in its Depth and Breadth. To help you get a feel for this, the breath meditation tonight will be a contemplation of some of Gaia's birthings happening right now and throughout the eons.

And when we light the Fire Cauldron, we will recall Our Great Origin which has never ceased to pour forth and unfold. We receive it in every Moment and in all that we have inherited from the beings and ancestors of the past, and in the infinite Web we are part of in the present. It is the Ever Present Origin. We will recall the Grandmother Supernova that birthed our Solar system some 4.6 billion years ago—that is our lineage. We are celebrating this Cosmic lineage. Our birthing supernova has been named Tiamat by Thomas Berry, and I have adopted that. Tiamat was the ancient Babylonian name for the Great Mother of us all. We are Her star-stuff. Tiamat as the Babylonians storied her was a sea-serpent in form. We could just as well call our supernova "Rainbow Serpent"—in Australian indigenous tradition. The important thing is that we remember where we come from—our Gaian lineage, and receive Her Gift. Then we may choose to express Joy and Gratitude. There may be pain and joy in birthing—coming into Form. The dark is not necessarily felt as negative, the light not necessarily felt as positive: birthing may be felt as a separation, a leaving. But the new Being IS birthed.

Winter Solstice ritual is actually then, our Birth-day celebrations, a Birthday we all share. We celebrate that we are each 13.7 billion years old together with Earth and Sun. Winter Solstice is a special annual moment for expressing what new things are being born in you in the year ahead, rejoicing in all the new things being born in every moment, and the Unimaginable More that we, and Gaia will yet become.

IMBOLC

This is the celebration of the waxing Light—"Early Spring" as it may be named. The hours of light have been growing since the Winter Solstice, when we entered the Light part of the cycle of the year—out of the Fullness of the Dark. Earth's tilt has begun taking us back toward the Sun. Traditionally this Seasonal Point has been a time of nurturing the new life that is beginning to show itself—around us and within. It is a time of committing one's self to the new life and inspiration—in the garden, in the soul, and in the Cosmos. We may celebrate the new young Cosmos—that time in our Cosmic story when She was only a billion years old and galaxies were forming, as well as the New that is ever coming forth. This first Seasonal Point of the light part of the cycle has been named "Imbolc"—Imbolc is thought to mean "ewe's milk" from the word "Oimelc", as it is the time when lambs were/are born, and milk was in plentiful supply. It is also known as "the Feast of Brigid". The Great Goddess Brigid of the Celtic peoples, is classically associated with early Spring since the earliest of times, but her symbology has evolved with the changing eras—sea, grain, cow. All of these Sabbats have complex histories, because that is how the human story is. As you develop your own relationship with these points, they may take ever-new dimensions, and perhaps be re-named. We could associate this Sabbat with the Milky Way, our own galaxy that nurtures our life—Brigid's jurisdiction has been extended.

Some sources say that Imbolc means "in the belly of the Mother". In either case of its meaning, this celebration is in direct relation to, and an extension of, the Winter Solstice—when we celebrated the Birth of all. We are celebrating the Urge to Be, the Virgin dynamic of the Triple Goddess—the One/Energy deeply resolute about Being. She is willful in that way. In the ancient Celtic tradition Brigid has been strongly identified with this role of tending the Flame of Being, and with the Flame itself. Brigid has been described: "...Great Moon Mother, patroness of poetry and of all 'making' and of the arts of healing".[12] She is Poet,

---

12.   Lawrence Durdin-Robertson, *The Year of the Goddess*, p.36, quoting Denning M. et al, *The Magical Philosophy III*, p.166.

physician/healer, smith-artisan. When we invoke Her we invoke all these qualities in ourselves.

Brigid's priestesses tended a flame—like the one lit at Winter Solstice signifying
the Origin of All, and the small candles we lit signifying the new being birthing
in us. This flame within is to be protected and nurtured. In places of new growth
we are all young and vulnerable, perhaps uncertain—we need care and tending in
those places. The "new green shoots", the new Being, requires dedication. So
there is a "dedication" in the ritual, which is traditionally thought of as a "Bridal"
dedication—a "Brigid-ine" commitment. "Bride" is a derivative of the name
"Brigid". Her "virgin" integrity of being At-One-In-Herself is little understood in
our times: it has been trivialised to a level of debate about unbroken hymens. A
commitment to Brigid, to Her Virgin integrity, is a dedication to tending your-
Self, understanding that Self as an expression of the Whole.

Brigid is praised as of "the holy well and the sacred Flame".[13] The "Well" designates the Source of Life, to which the new tender being is intimately connected.
It may be understood as the Well of Creativity[14] of the Cosmos to which we are
seamlessly connected. A dedication to Brigid means a dedication to the Being and
Beauty of particular small self, and knowing deeply its Source—as the infant
knows deeply its dependence on the Mother, as the new shoot on the tree knows
intimately its dependence on the branch and whole tree, as the new star's being is
connected to the supernova. It is a dedication to the being of your particular
beautiful Self, rooted seamlessly in the whole of Gaia. The "Well" of Brigid then,
is not only the well into Earth-Gaia, but also Universe-Gaia's Well of Creativity.
Brigid has extended Her "country".

Imbolc ritual is a celebration of the sheer magic of this energy to Be. If one has
ever been deprived of it—in depression, illness, uncertainty, the mists of apa-
thy—one knows the Beauty of this Urge to Be and its preciousness. When it
arrives we may consciously nurture it, tend it, rejoice in it—Life/Creativity WILL
proceed!! It is a Blessed thing—it is an Annunciation—the knowledge that
Divine Life IS within: you are carrying it in your Being. Note that the words you
are blessed with at communion are echoes of the words traditionally attributed to
the angel's words to Mary—the "Annunciation"—but in this Cosmology we all

---

13.   Starhawk, *Truth or Dare*, p.289-295.
14.   Brian Swimme, *Canticle to the Cosmos*, video 10.

bear the Promised One. We *are* the Promised One. You have a particular Creativity to deliver that no-one else can, and this ritual is an opportunity to say "Yes" and commit yourself to the flourishing of your small part, which is a totally unique Beauty in the history of the Universe.

In the calling of the elements—creating the sacred space—I like to structure it for Imbolc so that we remain very conscious of the space within, and how we can sense/feel the elements in our manifest form, our bodies.

We will light candles again, contemplating the ever-new being in us, represented in the flame. We will affirm that we are this Young One—this shining ever-new Beauty or Promise of Life (however you'd like to express it). We will invoke Artemis who has traditionally been understood to midwife the new life, because of Her Passion for Being. The herbs given to ease the pain of childbirth were named *Artemisia*. We will taste them in the ritual—they are bitter, and we may remember this taste as part of the experience of expansion, of Creativity, of coming into Being, of *admitting* the New. Artemis is also the Archer, the one within whose arrow flies true and on centre—we will each hold Her arrow and remember the Power and Presence of this desire in us…to fly true and on Centre.

Coming into Being takes courage and daring. Thus the Virgin aspect is often understood as spiritual warrior. Esther Harding has described the Virgin thus:

> The one who is virgin, does what they do—not because of any desire to please, not to be liked, or to be approved, even by herself; not because of any desire to gain power over another…but because what they do is true.[15]

The Virgin's motivation for action is not guilt, fear, envy…but the truth of your being. This is Her purity and her freedom. This is what we affirm in ourselves tonight—this is the One we seek to nurture in ourselves.

Traditionally, Imbolc is a time of purification and strengthening[16]—that is what the nurturing of the new requires—care and vigilance and sometimes discipline. We will pass a bowl of salt water around and dip our hands in it, and each may express what it is that damages the New One, what weakens its life-force ("Nwyfre" is a Welsh word for this). We will pass it back in the other direction and each

---

15.   Esther M. Harding, *Woman's Mysteries: Ancient and Modern*, p.125.
16.   Starhawk, *Truth or Dare*, p.304.

may express what it is that strengthens this Urge to Be. This process of "purification and strengthening" may be understood as feeling for where it is in us that the Universe is acting now—where each one feels the excitement of Creativity calling to them in their lives.

There is risk and resistance to coming into Being. The Universe itself knew it when it encountered gravitational resistance to expansion, in our very beginnings, in the Primordial Flaring Forth. It was never without Creative Tension. The Universe knows it daily, in every moment. Imbolc can be a time of remembering some of your vulnerabilities, feeling them and accepting them, but remaining resolute in your birthing and tending of the new, your listening for the Urge of the Creative Universe within.

The lace on the altar and around the place is meant to signify the delicate web of Life that we are part of and that we nurture—the Promise of Life that we tend, in Ourselves and in each Other, and in All. The early Universe itself had a lacy pattern caused by quantum fluctuations that enabled the galaxies to form. Swimme and Berry describe the young billion year old universe:

> After the fireball ended, the Universe's primordial blaze extinguished itself, only to burn once more in the form of lacy veils of galaxies filling all one billion years of space-time existence.[17]

You may think of the lace as the web of the young Universe itself, and what Creativity it has taken to bring forth all that we witness.

NOTE the changes to Imbolc celebrations in the Christian era: it became "Candlemas", a time for purifying the "polluted" mother—40 days after Solstice Birthing, and invoking the asexual "virgin bride".[18] This is in contrast to how we are celebrating it.

At the beginning of the ritual, we will be invited to speak the Mother's word of Creation: "Om". This is how the Great Goddess Kali brought creation into being—with Her Word, *Om*, an invocation of her own 'pregnant belly'.[19] Kali was understood as Creator as well as Destroyer—that was what Her darkness was

---

17. Brian Swimme and Thomas Berry, *The Universe Story*, p.34.
18. Vivianne Crowley, *Celtic Wisdom: Seasonal Rituals and Festivals*, p.37.
19. Barbara Walker, *The Woman's Encyclopaedia of Myths and Secrets*, p.546.

for—Creativity. Kali's *Om* was the primordial Logos, 'the supreme syllable, the mother of all sound'.[20] It has derivatives in many cultures. In many cultural creation stories the world proceeds from sound. The letters of the Sanskrit alphabet were called "mothers", matrika. *Om* was the *mantramatrika*, Mother of Mantras.[21] The Celts called their Moon-mother *Omh*.

We will use the word then, but the essence of it is the *speaking*, the *spelling*—how we create the world with language, the words we choose: and we do/may choose so much of our expression. With your self-expression, your *Om*, you are spoken and collectively we speak. Imbolc is a time for being mindful of our creations—our spelling, how each unique self participates in creation. We will join and weave our *Om's* together.

The ringing of the bell, which is our call to gather this evening, is meant to signify the Beauty of the singular Being. Hear it as your Beauty ringing clearly and uniquely.

We have a red aisle for procession for your Brigid-ine dedication. This is a tradition that has its roots in the ancient Goddess integral understandings of the blood of the Mother being "wise blood". To walk on the red processional aisle was to be honored and recognized as participating in the Wisdom of the Mother—to be in Her Creative Flow and Timing—nurtured by Her Wisdom: that is how our Creativity happens.

EOSTAR

(Show a daffodil with bulb and roots exposed)—signifying the *full* story of Spring Equinox, which is, emergence from the dark: the joy of this blossoming is rooted in the journey through the dark. Both Equinoxes celebrate this sacred balance, and they are both celebrations of the Mystery of the Seed. The Seed is essentially the deep Creativity within—that manifests in the Spring as flower, or green emerged One.

---

20. Barbara Walker, *The Woman's Encyclopaedia of Myths and Secrets*, p.546 quoting Upanishads, p.53
21. Barbara Walker, *The Woman's Encyclopaedia of Myths and Secrets*, p.546.

As the new young light continues to grow, it comes into balance with the dark. Eostar, or Spring Equinox, is one of two points in the year when the Sun is equidistant between North and South, creating this light and dark balance. Yet the trend at this Equinox is toward increasing light—longer hours of light. It is about the Power of Being—Life is stepping into it. Earth in this region is tilting further toward the Sun. Traditionally it is storied as the joyful celebration of Persephone's return from the underworld—Her return and re-union with her Mother who has waited and longed for Her. Persephone, the Beloved Daughter—the Seed—has navigated the darkness successfully, has enriched it with Her presence and also gained its riches. Eostar is the magic of the unexpected, yet long awaited, green emergence from under the ground, and then the flower: especially profound as it is from a seed that has lain dormant for months or longer—much like the magic of desert blooms after long periods of drought.

This seasonal point is often named as "Eostar" which comes from the Saxon Goddess Eostre/Ostara—the northern form of the Sumerian Astarte.[22] The Christian festival was named "Easter" as of the Middle Ages. The date of Easter—set for Northern Hemispheric seasons—is still based on the lunar/menstrual calendar; that is, the 1st Sunday after the first full Moon after Spring Equinox. (In Australia "Easter" is celebrated in Autumn!) There are other names for "Eostar" in other places...the Welsh name for the Spring Equinox celebration is Eilir, meaning 'regeneration' or 'spring'—or 'earth'.[23]

The story that this celebration is based on is that of Demeter and Persephone—the traditional version that we understand as pre-patriarchal, from Old Europe. In Greece for millennia, Spring Equinox was celebrated as the return of Persephone from the Underworld. And other cultures celebrated it as the Return of the Beloved One—Dumuzi in Sumeria for instance. In the oldest stories we have, Persephone descended to the underworld voluntarily. She is a courageous seeker of Wisdom, a compassionate receiver of the dead. She represents—IS—the Seed of Life that never fades away. Spring Equinox is a celebration of Her return, Life's continual return, and also our own personal emergences/returns. We may contemplate the *collective* emergence/return also—especially in our times.

---

22.   Barbara Walker, *The Woman's Encyclopaedia of Myths and Secrets*, p.267.
23.   Emma Restall Orr, *Spirits of the Sacred Grove: The World of a Druid Priestess*, p.235.

I describe Persephone as a "hera", which of old was a term for a courageous One. "Hera" was a pre-Hellenic name for the Goddess in general.[24] "Hera" was the indigenous Queen Goddess of pre-Olympic Greece, before She was married off to Zeus. "Hero" was a term for the brave male Heracles who carried out tasks for his Goddess Hera: "The derivative form 'heroine' is therefore completely unnecessary."[25] "Hera" may be used as a term for any courageous individual. You may use it in the ritual to name yourself.

The pre-"Olympic" games of Greece were Hera's games, held at Her Heraion/temple.[26] The winners were "heras"—gaining the status of being like Her. The runners were female in the earliest of times selected from three age groups representing the three phases of the moon. This was so until about the seventh century B.C.E. when the boys' races were introduced.[27] In the earliest of times Hera was not the bickering, jealous wife of the Olympian pantheon. Hera, in the most ancient of stories was commonly identified with Gaia as "expressive of the creative, sustaining earth".[28] Marija Gimbutas tells us that Hera was called the 'origin of all things' by Greek writers as late as the sixth century B.C.E., that "Her name is cognate with Hora, season", that Hera created and restored life through the touch of a plant.[29] You may use the term in the ritual if you are able to shake off or reach through the patriarchal stories/images you may have in your mind about Hera. You may announce yourself at the invocation as a "Hera" today if you wish—to identify with Her as we once knew Her, and to express yourself as a courageous One, a "winner". You may also choose to use "hero", or simply "Courageous One", or "Beloved One", or "Persephone".

"Persephone" in each of us, courageous One, steps with new Wisdom, into Power—the Power that all Beings must have, Power from within—Gaian power, the Power of the Cosmos. We may identify ourselves with Her as Courageous Ones, rejoicing in how we have made it through, having faced our fears and our demise (in its various forms), had "close shaves"—perhaps physically as well as psychicly and emotionally. It is a time to welcome back that which was lost, and

---

24.   Charlene Spretnak, *The Politics of Women's Spirituality*, p.87.
25.   Charlene Spretnak, *The Politics of Women's Spirituality*, p.87.
26.   Charlene Spretnak, *Lost Goddesses of Early Greece*, p.87-88 referring to Jane Ellen Harrison, Myths of Greece and Rome, p.18.
27.   Charlene Spretnak, *Lost Goddesses of Early Greece*, p.88
28.   Pamela Berger, *The Goddess Obscured*. p.16.
29.   Marija Gimbutas, *The Language of the Goddess*, p.134.

step into the strength of Being. Eostar is the time for enjoying the fruits of the descent, of the journey taken into the darkness. Demeter, the Mother, receives Persephone—each of us—joyously. The young tender Selves we celebrated and committed to at Imbolc, are received into communal relationship and empowerment.

This may be understood as an individual experience, but also as a collective experience—as we emerge into a new Era as a species. Thomas Berry and Brian Swimme speak of the ending of the 65 million year geological Era—the Cenozoic Era—in our times, and our possible emergence into an Ecozoic Era. They describe the Ecozoic Era as a time when "the curvature of the universe, the curvature of the earth, and the curvature of the human are once more in their proper relation."[30] Joanna Macy speaks of the "Great Turning" of our times.[31] Collectively we have been away from the Mother for some time—and there is a lot of pain. As we each take the lantern and the seed, and wander into the house (the "Underworld") before coming to the "gate" of emergence, we may contemplate not only our own individual "lost" wanderings, but also that of the human species. We are part of a much Bigger Return that is happening. The Beloved One is returning on a collective level as well—we are part of making it happen. It is a return to the Mother in Self, Earth and Cosmos.

In the ritual tonight, as each one goes out of the circle and into the "Underworld", the rest of us will watch and wait—like Demeter. We each are Persephone, and we each are Demeter. We will all welcome the lost Ones, the Wise returned Ones.

Swimme and Berry say that: "With the beginning of each new era of the universe, activity and its multiform possibilities undergo a creative transformation."[32] This is true of ourselves as well. Something completely new is possible—new synergies can come into being with the stepping onto a new platform, into a new strength of being. Swimme speaks of this as "space-time binding", where all the transformations of the past are held within the present moment, making a completely new leap possible[33]—into "what", we can only guess at. But the creative track record is good.

---

30. Brian Swimme and Thomas Berry, *The Universe Story*, p.261.
31. Joanna Macy and Molly Young Brown, *Coming Back to Life*. p.77ff.
32. Brian Swimme and Thomas Berry, *The Universe Story*, p.63.
33. Brian Swimme, *Powers of the Universe*, lecture 9.

Spring Equinox is a balance point, a fertile balance of tensions. Light and dark parts of the day are of equal length for a moment. Equinox is a celebration of the Creative Curve between the compost and the lotus...the creative edge in which Life is born; it is the delicate balance that scientists know as "the curvature of space-time". This delicate balance makes possible the Creativity that we witness, that we are part of, that enables this celebration of Stepping into the Power of Growth and Being.

OTHER RITUAL NOTES:
• the rock/stone we will hold up at the invocation and announce ourselves: it is meant to represent the precious stone of Wisdom gained, from our journeys into darkness. It represents your courageous self returned and present with us. You may take it with you in your meditation, placing it back in the basket when you come to the circle.

• Communion poppyseed cake: the poppy is associated with Persephone because of its many seeds. The cake celebrates the rich fertility of the dark brought to light—manifest: the full story of the bulb and the flower. It is a holy cake. We will eat it in remembrance of She who gives Life—the Seed that never fades away.

• the eggs: they recall "the myths of Hathor-Astarte who laid the Golden Egg of the Sun."[34] The stories of the "Easter Bunny" came from the Moon-Hare sacred to the Goddess—the stories got linked over the millennia. A tradition of giving eggs at Eostar developed. Many primordial Goddesses laid Golden Eggs. You will be offered golden eggs tonight to remind you of the Ancient One who lays the Golden Egg—the Sun, the Gift of Life given everyday.

• the calling of the elements—as our true Powers of Life, and our *knowing* of them—our *certain* sensing of them as powers that manifest in various ways (whereas at Imbolc our sensing of them was more basic and tentative). Part of the describing of the elements as we do it tonight, is inspired by eco-psychologist Sarah A. Conn's aspects of global responsibility—which happen to correspond to the elemental characteristics. Emotional response or feeling or what Sarah Conn calls "direct experience", the ability to shape or integrate the information or what

---

34.   Barbara Walker, *The Woman's Encyclopaedia of Myths and Secrets*, p.267.

Conn calls "understanding", the willingness to take action, and awareness/the ability to perceive global problems.[35] (These are not in the order she has.)

• taking the Seed, as well as the lantern, for your Journey of lost wonderings: the Seed may remind you of the positive quality of the dark, how essential to your knowledge and strength and being—like the earth is to the seed.

BELTANE

Earth's tilt is continuing to move us closer to the Sun, in our part of Earth at this time: Light is dominating the day and will continue to do so increasingly until Summer Solstice. This is the time for virulent growth of the plants, and life. The energy of Spring has grown from the new and tender of Imbolc to the strong and virulent of Beltane. The story as we have been telling it is that the Virgin/Urge to Be of early Spring has stepped into Her Power (at Eostar) and is now coming into the Passion of Life and fertility; Her face is changing into the Mother of Summer—when She will be full. She is, at this time of Beltane, entering into relationship with the Other. The fruiting begins. It is time for celebrating the Dance of Life. Beltane is a celebration of this Passion—Holy Desire…that which unites the Cosmos and holds all things in form.

This Desire is multivalent—has many layers to it, and needs to be understood as a Cosmic Dynamic, a "Power of the Universe" as Brian Swimme expresses it—he calls it Allurement. It is preternatural, primordial—we didn't invent it. It has been present from the beginning and has many manifestations. As this Cosmic Allurement, one of its manifestations is Gravity. I like to think of it as Holy Lust—the dynamic at the core of manifest form. I regard Aphrodite as the embodiment of this dynamic; She was celebrated by the ancients as the One who united the Cosmos and brought forth all things—held all things in form. She willed the three-fold fates! In other words, these ancients understood that desire or Allurement *directs* the Dance—stronger than the three-fold fates, is at the Source of the Dance, turns the Wheel. Of old, Aphrodite, as Allurement, was understood as the pure essence of Creation—nothing existed without Her, without this Desire. As the Charge of the Goddess says: "I have been with you from the beginning, and I am that which is attained at the end of Desire."

---

35.   Sarah A. Conn. "The Self-World Connection" Woman of Power, Issue 20, p.73.

Beltane is traditionally a celebration of fertility—genetic fertility—and the mating of Goddess and God—that is the exoteric festival form of it: thus the "Maypole" or "Novapole" as I name it in our Southern Hemisphere, and the traditional red and white ribbons—the red signifies the Goddess, and the white the God, matching the body fluids that that mark the onset of fertility. Beltane is for some, a traditional time for Lovers to marry in this Earth tradition—it is called handfasting. It is also a time when new partners may be taken—a *trans*personal celebration of sexuality. In terms of the story of the Universe, Beltane is a celebration of the advent of meiotic sex—of the male or gender. This was a significant moment of Cosmogenesis—the Creative Unfolding of the Universe; it took a deeper leap into differentiation, communion and subjectivity—into deeper intimacy. That is a further dimension of the "Novapole" ritual—when we dance the Dance of Life, a celebration of the Cosmogenetic power of meiotic sexuality, as well as an affirmation of Allurement in general in all its forms.

Beltane is a celebration of Desire on all levels—microcosm and on the macrocosm, the exoteric and the esoteric. It brought you forth physically, and it brings forth all that you produce in your life, and it keeps the Cosmos spinning. It is felt in you as Desire, it urges you on. It is the deep awesome dynamic that pervades the Cosmos and brings forth all things—babies, meals, gardens, careers, books and solar systems. We have often been taught to pay it as little attention as possible, whereas it should be the cause of much more meditation/attention: tracing it to its deepest Place in us. What are our deepest desires beneath our surface desires. What if we enter more deeply into this feeling, this power? It may be a place where the Universe is a deep reciprocity—a receiving and giving that is One. Brian Swimme says: "Our most mature hope is to become pleasure's source and pleasure's home simultaneously. So it is with all the allurements of life: we become beauty to ignite the beauty of others."[36]

Beltane is a good time to contemplate this animal bodymind that you are: how it seeks *real* pleasure. What is your real pleasure? Be gracious with this bodymind and in awe of this form, this wonder.

Beltane is a good time to contemplate light—and its effects on our bodyminds as it enters into us—how our animal bodyminds respond directly to the Sun's light, which apparently may awaken physical desires. Light vibrates into us—different

---

36.   Brian Swimme, *The Universe is a Green Dragon*, p.79.

wavelengths different colours—and shifts to pulse. It is felt most fully in Spring-time ("spring fever")—light courses down a direct neural line from retina to pineal gland. When the pineal gland receives the light pulse it releases "a cascade of hormones, drenching the body in hunger, thirst, or great desire."[37] We respond directly to Sun as an organism.

OTHER RITUAL NOTES:
• We will "call" the elements by sensing our Desire for each of them:
Water—Desire manifests as thirst
Fire—Desire manifests in the gathering round
Earth—Desire manifests in the urge to make our mark, what we want to do That is, the work that we each do, the particular allurements that we feel and follow, *is/are* the mark we make that serves the Creative Cosmos—Gaia. It is the Creative Cosmos/Gaia in us—in our particular Passions—that makes the mark, with our own unique print. We will each make a print in mud with our hands, to signify this. It recalls some of the first marks humans ever made.
Air—Desire manifests in our reaching for breath.
And we remember primarily their presence, that is, our Desire is met...we are not left wanting. We didn't make up this Desire, it is the Universe desiring in us. It is our nature.
We are united in these Desires, that is, we all experience these Desires. And we are united in our Desire with all others who have gone before and all who will come after, in their Desires.

• In the breath meditation at the beginning, I note that we are present to all who have gone before us, in one deep breath each takes. I want you to be aware that this is not just poetry, it is empirical fact apparently.[38] We will breathe deeply and contemplate the Presence of all those who have gone before, and all those who come after us. Also, in the centering meditation at the beginning, there will be opportunity to make a simple physical gesture to embrace this Presence and the Present Moment. This is a suggestion.

• The invocation: you may identify with the beauty of the flower (the rose is Aphrodite's flower of choice), tree, bird, ocean—something that you may find particularly beautiful—it may be a Place, something that reveals to you the Beauty at

---

37.   Laura Sewall, "Earth Eros, Sky", EarthLight, p.22.
38.   Brian Swimme, *Canticle to the Cosmos.*

the Heart of the Universe. You are encouraged to identify with this Beauty—if you can recognize it, it must be in you. And you may speak of being Desirable, and the Desire that you feel—the sacredness or holiness of it.

• We will dance the Dance, "weaving in what we will."

• We will leap the flames, leaving behind what we will. Traditionally in pastoral cultures of old, at this time of year, the cattle were let out of their Winter housing and driven between fires to rid them of their Winter bugs and ticks. The people too decided to purify themselves this way, by leaping the flames. The flame of Allurement—of Love—is understood to be purifying and creative.

• Communion: we will consume pink ring cake with rose honey on it, in honour of Aphrodite; and be encouraged to consume our desire, to consummate it. We will drink sweet wine, and be encouraged to enjoy the sweetness of life: don't miss the Moment.

SUMMER SOLSTICE/LITHA

Summer Solstice is the celebration of the peaking of the Light in the annual cycle—many of the fruits of Earth come to their fullness in Summer, many grains ripen, deciduous trees peak in their greenery, lots of bugs and creatures are bursting with business and creativity. We may celebrate our own ripening, maturing of creativity, the bliss of our full expression—in every moment, as well as in special achievements, and ultimately. Some of us celebrated the Child of Promise in us early in the Spring—at Imbolc, when we remembered the tenderness and vulnerability of our Being. At this season of Summer Solstice we may celebrate the Promise growing to fullness in us—expressed as the Sacred Fullness of the Mother.

The Beauty that we dedicated ourselves to at Imbolc (the differentiated self), that we identified with at Beltane (I am the Beauty)—is now Given Back, Given Away, ripe for Consuming. This is its purpose, its sacred Destiny. We do desire to be received—to be consumed—it is our Joy and our Grief.

Summer Solstice is the peaking of potential, and also then the point of the return to the Dark part of the cycle of the year—it is the "Great Omega"…as Winter Solstice is the "Om", the beginning of form. The little spark of Winter Solstice has grown to fullness. Now, in this season, it is the Dark that is born, and that will grow. (The Solstices are points of Exchange between Light and Dark—Gateways.) This Dark that is born at the peak of Summer, is the fulfillment of Bliss—that is, the Bliss of fulfilling your creative purpose—and it is the dissolution of the fulfilled self, given over. It is the beginning of the Return to the "Manifesting", from whence all comes. We celebrate Light's fullness, our fullness—a peaking of potential in us, and acknowledge that it is not ours to hold—like a breath; it is given over to the Bigger Picture…passed on to the next Urge. The fullness of our bliss, our Passion, our Creativity is what moves the world—we give it daily, and ultimately, as Earth does and all Creation does. The breathing, including the releasing, sustains the world. We celebrate our realized Creativity, and acknowledge its Source. Summer then is like the Rose, as it says in this tradition—blossom and thorn…beautiful, fragrant, full—yet it comes with thorns that open the skin. All is given over.

In one traditional version, the story is that the Goddess and God, Beloved and Lover, reach the full expression of Their Love at this time—the Allurement of Beltane/High Spring, finds its Maturation. Beloved and Lover embrace, in a Love so complete, that all dissolves, into a single Song of Ecstasy that moves the worlds. It is the Big Orgasm—the "little death" as it is known in some cultures—the realization of Union with the Beloved. This is the Sabbat for which they postulate that Stonehenge was built—the Summer Solstice. The Old story tells us then that this Ecstasy of union is at the core of the Mystery of Existence—it is the Fullness and End of Desire. In Their Union—Beloved and Lover—the boundaries of the self are broken, they merge, All is Given Away—All is poured forth, the deep rich dark Stream of Life flows out. We affirm in the Summer ritual that each of us is "Gift"—that means that we are both Given and Received—all at the same time. The breath is given and life is received. We receive the Gift—with each breath in, and we are the Gift—with each breath out.

Summer is a time when Earth pours forth Her abundance, so we celebrate the infinite daily abundance that is always given, and ours to receive. We live amongst pure gift—we daily build our lives on the work/creativity of the ancestors and ancient creatures that went before us. And what we do/create each day builds it further for those to come; we too give it away & add to the abundance. As Brian Swimme says: "Every moment of our lives disappears into the ongoing story of the Universe. Our creativity is energising the whole."[39] That is what is meant today when we affirm that we are the Bread of Life. Being the Bread of Life—Food—means being consumed, but it also means being received and enjoyed. We are Creators everyday—our small efforts sustain the world—daily and ultimately. We are constantly consuming the work and creativity of others and we are constantly being consumed. Who are you feeding?

Summer Solstice is a good time to contemplate how the Sun is in all we are and do, all that we eat and think—that it is the Sun in us, that has ripened, that is in our every thought and action. We are the Sun, coming to Fullness in its creative engagement with Earth. We affirm this in this ritual, with: "It is the Sun that is in you, see how you shine".

Summer Solstice particularly is a celebration of the Fullness of the Mother—in ourselves, in Earth, in the Cosmos; as is the Winter Solstice in a different way—at Winter Solstice, it is a Fullness of Darkness—a pregnancy that bursts into Form. At Summer Solstice the Fullness of Form bursts back into the Dark.

Throughout the Spring we have been celebrating the Virgin aspect, with Her face gradually changing to the Mother—coming into Power at Eostar, into Fertility at Beltane, and now birthing the fruits and fullness of being; and through the Autumn we will be celebrating the Crone, whose face will gradually change also, back to the Mother.

OTHER RITUAL NOTES
• Giving the full rose/flower to the fire as we will, may be seen in many ways—you will have your own subtle understandings. Essentially it is to signify the giving away of the fullness of our creative selves (counter to the "birth" of this creative self at Winter Solstice—when we light candles to signify that). Throwing the rose/flower on the fire may be seen as a commitment to follow your Passion, and to release it, express it—to feed the world with your Fullness—the Fullness of your particular Self, wherein the Universe speaks. This tradition is about fulfillment of the self—giving *that* to the Universe, not self-abnegation. (This is not about burning away negatives in yourself, it is about giving your full potential and becoming that—in every moment, and ultimately.)
• the Spiral Dance: at Winter Solstice we did this spiral with lit candles in our hands, representing the small flames being born in us. Now at Summer Solstice,

---

39.   Brian Swimme, *Canticle to the Cosmos*, video 5.

we do the spiral with the full rose signifying the full radiance of what we may/
have become—that is given back to Source.

• the wreath will be upheld for each of us:
—for you to look through it to the fire, being admonished and encouraged to see
with clear sight. This will be invoked for you—clarity of vision—of Life and
Death, the "Om" and the "Omega".
—Held aloft for you to see the circle of full roses—to affirm the unbroken circle.
She goes on, in Her creative spin. Nothing is wasted—all comes full circle and
goes on. You will have your own understandings of that.

• the invocation: we will pronounce each other "Queen of Summer" or "Summer
King". To the ancients of this tradition, "Summer" was a Place (similar to
"heaven" of the Christian mind), but it was a Place here on Earth, a Place of
abundance, ripeness and eternal fulfillment—it was "Avalon". There was nothing
"pie in the sky" about it. "Summer" is a Place where we may dwell now—even in
the midst of discomfort or the awesomeness of Life—where we know within that
we are in the flow, immersed in the richness of the Universe. So to be "Queen of
Summer" or "Summer King' is to be blessed with a sense of abundance, Creativity and Union.

• the toning that we will do as a culmination of the invocation: it may be felt as
an exercise in relationship with self, other and all-that-is…the three layers of Cosmogenesis. Each is feeling for their own true expressive voice, listening for the
others, and it is all coming out of and going into a Larger Self: the toning that
arises is co-created and yet it is coming from the Well of Creativity itself.

LAMMAS

This is the seasonal moment of celebration of the waxing dark, as Earth's tilt
takes us back away from the Sun, after the Summer Solstice peaking of light. This
Sabbat has traditionally been a joyous event, celebrated as the first harvest festival—and there are remnants of it in places still. "Lammas" is an old name for it:
this is a Saxon word for the feast of Bread, the festival of the Great Goddess of the
grain, of sustenance.[40] "Lughnasad" is a later Celtic name for it. In the Celtic
story, this festival is the wake of Lugh, the Grain God, who is sacrificed/har-

---

40. Barbara Walker, *The Woman's Encyclopaedia of Myths and Secrets*, p.527.

vested. There is rejoicing in this harvest—of food, of life. In the pre-Celtic stories of the Goddess tradition, *She* embodied all the transformations—She was the Reaper and the Reaped. She went through all the changes Herself. "The community reflected on the reality that the Mother aspect of the Goddess, having come to fruition, from Lammas on would enter the Earth and slowly become transformed into the Old Woman-Hecate-Cailleach aspect…"[41] And so, might we understand ourselves—as embodying all the transformations, because we do actually. *We* are the harvest—it is our "wake" also. We are the transformations of the Ages, we each hold the memory of all Gaia's transitions; and we are each the Grain that is harvested, we—our lives—are the sacred Grain. We are the Reaper—we each reap our small harvests, and we are the Reaped—our small harvests are reaped by the Universe—by Her. This is a continuation of the Summer Solstice theme, where we affirmed that we are the Bread of Life. Just as the Food harvested nourishes us, so our lives may nourish the world.

In its depth significance Lammas celebrates the Harvest of Life, the cutting of the ripe food, the releasing of Gaia's breath which peaked at Summer Solstice. Her outbreath enables Life to go on—just as ours does. It is the time to celebrate dissolution, the return to Source. Like Imbolc, it is a time of dedication—this time, dedication to the Larger Self. It is the time for "making sacred", which is the meaning of the term "sacrifice". It is not a self-abnegation, it is a fulfillment of purpose, a fulfillment of the Passion that is in you—like the fruit fulfills its purpose in the eating. Your passion, your work, is fulfilled in the consumption. Whereas Imbolc is a Bridal commitment to Being and form, where we are the Promise of Life; Lammas is a kind of commitment marriage to the Dark within—we accept the *Harvest* of that Promise, the cutting of it. We remember that the Promise is returned to Source. "The forces which began to rise out of the Earth at the festival of Bride now return at Lammas."[42]

As it is said, She is "that which is attained at the end of Desire": the same Desire we celebrated at Beltane, has peaked at Summer and is now dissolving form, Returning to Source to nourish the Plenum, the manifesting—as all form does. This Seasonal Moment of Lammas celebrates the beginning of dismantling, destructuring. Gaia-Universe has done a lot of this de-structuring—it is in Her nature to return all to the "Sentient Soup"…nothing is wasted. We recall the

---

41.   Adam McLean, *The Four Fire Festivals*, p.21.
42.   Adam McLean, *The Four Fire Festivals*, p.22.

Dark Sentience, the "All-Nourishing Abyss" at the base of Being, as we enter this
Dark part of the cycle of the year.

It is the season of the Crone, the Old Wise One—who returns us to the Dark or
the Deep from which we all arise. This Dark/Deep at the base of being, to whom
we are returned, may be understood as the Sentience within all—within the
entire sentient Universe. The dictionary definition of sentience is: "intelligence",
"feeling", "the readiness to receive sensation, idea or image; unstructured available consciousness", "a state of elementary or undifferentiated consciousness". [43]

The Old Wise One is the aspect that returns us to this Sentience, the Great Subject out of whom we arise. We are subjects within the Great Subject—the sentient Universe; we are not a collection of objects, as Thomas Berry says. This
Sentience within, this Readiness-To-Receive, is a dark Space, as all places of ending and beginning are. Mystics of all religious traditions have understood the
quintessential Darkness of the Divinity, known often as the Abyss. Goddesses
such as Nammu and Tiamat and Kali are the anthropomorphic forms of this
Abyss/Sea of Darkness that existed before creation. She is really, the Matrix of the
Universe. This Sentience is ever present and dynamic. It could be understood as
the Dark Matter that is now recognized to form most of the Universe. We will
recognize it as Her "Cauldron of Creativity" in the ritual. Her Cauldron of Creativity is the constant flux of all form in the Universe—all matter is constantly
transforming. *We* are constantly transforming on every level.

These times that we find ourselves in have been storied as the Age of Kali, the Age
of Caillaech—the Age of the Crone. There is much that is being turned over,
much that will be dismantled. We are in the midst of the revealing of compost,
and transformation—social, cultural, and geophysical. Kali is not a pretty
one—but we trust She is transformer, and creative in the long term. She has a
good track record. Our main problem is that we tend to take it personally.

The Crone—the Old Phase of the cycle, *creates the Space to Be*—(whereas the
Virgin, whom we celebrated at Imbolc, after the Winter Solstice, is the *Urge* to
Be; the Mother is the *Place* to Be). Lammas is the particular celebration of the
Beauty of this Awesome One. She is symbolized and expressed in the image of
the waning moon, filling with darkness. She is the Nurturant Darkness that may

---

43. *Webster's Third International Dictionary of the English Language.*

fill your being, comfort the Sentience in you, that will eventually allow new constellations to gestate in you, renew you. So in this celebration we will contemplate opening to Her—our fears and our hopes involved in that. She is the Great Receiver—receives all, and as such She is the Great Compassionate One. Her Darkness may be understood as a Depth of Love. And She is Compassionate because of Her dismantling...where we may not have the will. We do want to be ever fresh, ever new—it is not possible without the Wise Old One, who will mercifully shake us loose from our tracks.

Often we have only feared Her. But the harvest of our lives—everyday and ultimately—may also be a deeply joyful thing, as it is received and made into food to nourish the world. Sometimes the changes that need to be made are awesome...we would not have chosen them, but they serve us deeply. The Zen Buddhist tradition speaks of the "tiger's kindness", that is, we *want* to change, but may not have the will. (The tiger fears the human heart, the human fears the tiger's kindness).[44]

This Sabbat is about trusting and rejoicing in the kindness and Creativity of the Dark—knowing it is centrally part of us and we are part of it. Loren Eiseley describes his pulse as "a minute pulse like the eternal pulse that lifts Himalayas and which, in the following systole, will carry them away."[45] Our organisms are constantly a microcosm of the cataclysmic transformations of Gaia—transformations that allow the life of the organism to go on, be that our small self or that of the Large Self of Earth or the Universe. This Sabbat is like a funeral, and we may understand the event as a "wake"—a celebration of life.

OTHER RITUAL NOTES:
• breath Meditation: reference is made to the breath as yours but not yours. It is borrowed by you, by each of us, for a while—like a relay, you will let it go, pass it on. The Air remains, altered by your (our) presence and actions, for those who come next.

• Invocation: At Imbolc we affirmed that we are the shining and New One—ever the Urge to Be—the Beauty of the particular and emerging Self. Now at Lammas we will affirm that we are the Dark and Ancient Wise One—ever in the process

---

44. Susan Murphy, *upside-down zen*, p.89-93.
45. Loren Eiseley, *The Immense Journey*, p.20.

of dissolving and recycling, creating the Space to Be. We are as ancient as Gaia Herself—ever She who has transformed over and over. Ten percent of our bodies are hydrogen—direct from the primordial fireball, the rest made in Tiamat—grandmother supernova—recycled over and over. We hold all of the evolutionary wisdom within our cells—Her ancient story is your story. The invocation affirms that. You may vary the words—make it meaningful for you.

And the Darkness that you may identify with may be imagined as shining or velvety if you like. The Dark can have many beautiful textures—which you might like to imagine. This dark One has Her own kind of Beauty. This Darkness is a Native Place for us—a part of us does recognize it, and love it—as we love to close our eyes and sleep.

• your bread figures will be given to the fire: She is the Compassionate One…She receives all, and She transforms all. So much of our being yearns for this compassion and "forgiveness" (which is a "receiving"), for transformation. We have to be able to trust that there is a MUCH BIGGER PICTURE that we don't usually see. So we trust Her knowing, which is beyond all knowledge. She knows how to dismantle the old, sweep it clean, create a Space for the new and hoped for. We will each contemplate what holds us back? What holds you back from letting go to passion and transformation? What are your fears?

• we will chant or repeat each one's expressed fears: this is to help reflect them back to you. Then when repeating them yourself in a kind of chant, you are saying them out loud more or less to yourself—hearing them and pondering them as you take them for transformation. In this process you may discover other dimensions to these fears.

MABON

The dark part of the day has continued to grow since Summer Solstice, and at this time of year has now reached the point of balance with the light. It will continue to wax from this point of balance, until it reaches its fullness. Mabon/ Autumn Equinox is the point of balance of light and dark in the dark part of the cycle. Sun is equidistant between North and South, as it was at Spring Equinox, but in this phase of the cycle, the trend is toward increasing dark. Autumn Equinox is a time of thanksgiving for the harvest—for its empowerment and nourishment, and it is also a time of leavetaking and sorrow, as Life declines.[46] For millennia, in Greece, this Sabbat has been the holy celebration of Persephone's descent to the Underworld, and in the earliest Goddess tradition, She descends of Her own volition—She is the Seed planted in the Earth, that will sprout again.

Like the Spring Equinox which is a "stepping into power" of form and light, Autumn Equinox is also a "stepping into power", but it is not necessarily perceived as such; it is usually felt as loss. It is a "stepping into power" of the dark, through which we may grow in Wisdom—yet there is pain in it. Autumn Equinox is a time for grieving our many losses, as individuals, as a culture, as Earth-Gaia. At this time we may join Demeter—and any other Mother Goddess from around the globe—in Her weeping for all that has been lost. The Mother weeps and rages, the Daughter leaves courageously, the Old One beckons with Her Wisdom and Promise of Transformation.

In the Celtic tradition, Autumn Equinox celebration is commonly named "Mabon". Mabon is the name of the Son of Modron—the Matrona or Mother of earliest times. His name is not a name, but is a title "Mab ap Modron" meaning "Son of the Great Mother". In later tales and songs the divine Mabon is transformed in the role model for the Western knight.[47] Mabon is taken from His Mother when only three nights old as the story goes in the Mabignogion. "He is the primal child…"[48] He represents an innocence. In the still strong mysteries of Mabon and Modron the Mother, he is lost and imprisoned, but his primal innocence is held to turn away harm. Though he is lost he has the power of the protecting Life. It has similarities to the multivalence of the Demeter-Persphone story.

Our celebration tonight is based on the mysteries of Demeter and Persephone—the Eleusinian Mysteries, but as with any great story, it includes the echoes of many. The Mysteries of Eleusis was a nine day ritual celebration of Mother and Daughter that took place annually for 2000 years, at Eleusis in Greece. These Mysteries were thought to hold the entire human race together—partly because people came from every corner of the Earth to be initiated.[49] (We will recall that in the way we create the sacred space tonight—that we too, do indeed come from every corner of the Earth).

46.   Starhawk, *The Spiral Dance*, p.192.
47.   Claire French, *The Celtic Goddess*, p.58.
48.   Caitlin and John Matthews, *The Western Way*, p.83.
49.   Lawrence Durdin-Robertson, *The Year of the Goddess*, p.158.

I base the celebration on Charlene Spretnak's version of Persephone's descent[50]—wherein Persephone descends of Her own volition, She is not forced. She descends to "tend the dead". In this pre-patriarchal story Persephone is a Hera (the original word for "hero").[51] Persephone descends for the tending of sorrows in the Underworld—because as the Seed She represents hope for rejuvenation. This is the integrity with which it was initially celebrated. In Carolyn McVikar-Edwards' version, Persephone descends for the gaining of Wisdom.[52] In pre and post-patriarchal understandings, Persephone is the Wisdom Redeemer figure within all Being. She, like the Seed, is the Mother Knowledge who grows within. This is also represented in the apple—She is the Seed in the Fruit becoming the Fruit in the Seed…and so we will affirm of ourselves tonight. SHOW AN APPLE CUT ACROSS.

Although we use the story of Demeter and Persphone, for this celebration, I want to mention the oldest story of descent and return, that humanity knows—that of Inanna. Inanna was the "primary one" of Sumeria for 3500 years, and made the heraic journey into the Underworld to become Queen of that Realm. There is also the story of the descent of Dumuzi, Her Beloved—for whom She grieves.

SHOW ICON OF DEMETER HANDING PERSEPHONE THE WHEAT (FROM 500 B.C.E.)[53] This image is central to tonight's celebration, and the understanding of Demeter and Persephone—so just receive it as best you can. I suggest having this image of Wisdom present to you all year round. Demeter is passing on the Knowledge—of Life and Death—the Mystery, which is represented by the wheat. For Persephone, it is an acknowledgement and an initiation…acknowledgement of Her maturity and readiness for Power, as well as an initiation into that. (Whereas in our cultural context, one usually "ascends" to Power). We will enact this tonight—how you have grown in Wisdom, and are also an initiate.

The icon is about a complex reality:
• It is Demeter's gift of agriculture to the world—humans becoming aware of the planting of the seed—and the awesome power of the seed, moving out of simply

---

50.   Charlene Spretnak, *Lost Goddesses of Early Greece*, p.112-116.
51.   Charlene Spretnak, *The Politics of Women's Spirituality*, p.87.
52.   Carolyn McVikar-Edwards, *The Storyteller's Goddess*, p.178-183.
53.   See Figure 2, Chapter 6.

hunting and gathering. This domestication of seed occurred about 10,000 years ago, wheat and barley being the earliest.

• And the handing of the wheat, is at the same time, Demeter's gift of the Mysteries—moving into death with awareness, eyes open, in that sense, coming into Power. Persephone "becomes Queen of that realm"—her name means "She who shines in the Dark". The Mysteries then identify each Initiate with the seed that falls from the dying plant to lie underground, hidden from life, and yet sprouts again—in some form, shape or other. We will all be lost—we have been lost. Everything lost is found again, in a new form, in a new way. We are the Beloved Ones who are lost, along with everything else.

• the Wheat represents a harvest of Life that we are given—we are Given all that went before us—it is handed to us. We may rejoice in it and give thanks. But like the Seed that goes into the Earth, every moment of Life is Lost—it dissolves, and is never repeated. Also it has had a cost. This moment and all that we enjoy, has had a cost. Every moment in our lives and in the entire history of Gaia-Universe is never repeated—it is lost. That means it is also ever-new. That is the Mystery—it is lost, but it is ever-new. There is a place on that Edge—of the grief and the joy, where the Universe hums in balance—a creative tension (some may call it the "curvature of space-time"). It is what enables Creativity to go on...in our lives and in the Cosmos. This may be represented by the Seed (SHOW IT), the "Persephone" that goes down into the Dark Earth, and will sprout yet again. It is also represented in the red thread I use on the wheat—initiates sometimes wore a red thread. I offer you red threads to wear tonight if you like. It represents the sacred Thread of Life that has never faded away (if it had we would not be here). Demeter gives the sheaf of wheat to Her Daughter Persephone—representing the Knowledge, and also the continuity, the unbroken thread of life.[54]

The ancients were awestruck when the wheat was upheld towards the end of the ritual in Eleusis. They appreciated the Magic of the seed, of the grain. The wheat was understood to reveal the Mystery of Being. Demeter is Mother of the grain, of wheat ("corn" as it was known). It was a 'Vision into the Abyss of the Seed', it was a vision of the Vulva/Yoni—Mother of all Life.[55] The grain of wheat is both the beginning and the end of the cycle—representing the Alpha and the Omega, it is seed and also food. It is our daily sustenance/bread. Thereby it may represent what we are given in every moment. In a different culture it could be corn or rice.

---

54.   Erich Neumann, *The Great Mother*, p.142.
55.   Lawrence Durdin-Robertson, *The Year of the Goddess*, p.166.

To be aware of this Gift, the Gift of the present moment—its depth—is sacred knowledge—Divine Wisdom.

When you are handed the wheat tonight, you may feel it in many ways. You may acknowledge new Power, a new coherence—you have received something, but you are also an initiate. The handing of the wheat, and the Seed itself that we will plant tonight, represents the continuous thread that enables life to go on—despite all the loss, and usually because of it.

In that sense the Seed is our Hope. She—Persephone—tends the sorrows, soothes the losses. She is an energy present in the bulbs, in each person, creature, all of existence—at the heart of matter, of Life, of the Mother—that never fades away. So we each will take a bulb, which represents something lost yet also something extremely powerful—filled with the essence of life. It is Wisdom to understand this, and its revelation is Awesome.

There are lots of layers to this celebration—multivalent—and there are infinite ways to receive it.

OTHER RITUAL NOTES:
• the Invocation words: At Eleusis, all the celebrants identified themselves with Demeter. "Men who took part were given names with feminine endings. All the mystae wore the same clothes, simple robes…"[56] Men too acted out the myth of loss and recovery. "All people became the Mother in the Mysteries. They may also have identified powerfully with Persephone…."[57] So the Mother will be invoked in all—women and men. She whom we become is the Mother of all Life. And we are all Persephones—the Sacred Receiver and Carrier of the Thread. But anyone may choose to use the word "Child" instead of "Daughter", or you may use both.

---

56. Rachel Pollack, *The Body of the Goddess*, p.220.
57. Rachel Pollack, *The Body of the Goddess*, p.221.

NOTE RE THE DAWN ON EQUINOX MORNING:
It may have been a traditional part of the Eleusinian Mysteries for initiates to witness the dawn.[58] Let the light permeate your being as it enters you through your eyes—the Promise of Inner Wisdom, She who shines in the Dark.

---

58. Mara Lynn Keller, "The Eleusinian Mysteries: Ancient Nature Religion of Demeter and Persephone" in *Reweaving the World: the Emergence of Ecofeminism.* Irene Diamond & Gloria Feman Orenstein (eds.), p.50.

Appendix G

PaGaian Joy to the World

✦

(for Winter Solstice ritual referred to in Chapter 7)

Joy to the World
The light returns
Let All receive Her Love

CHORUS:
Let every Heart
Let every tongue
Repeat the sounding Joy
Repeat the sounding Joy
Let Creatures, and all of Nature sing

She moves the stars
With Her Desire
Let All receive Her Power

She grows the seed
With all Her Love
Let All receive Her Wisdom

She lights our Hearts
She grows our food
Let All receive Her Joy

Joy to the World
The Light returns
Let All receive Her Love

These words may be sung to the tune of "Joy to the World".

APPENDIX H

SHINE

✦

by Wendy Rule
(for Eostar ritual referred to in Chapter 7)

You were bound, You were lost, You were captured...
With Your infinite soul counting hours,
In a web where each thread held a future,
And the future holds infinite powers.
You are braver than mythical heros.
You have rescued the Child of the Dreamland.
You have conquered the beast of the Shadow.
Well...the Universe is Centred on where You stand.

Feel the world at Your feet,
Freedom calls You from time...
And all because You shine.
You...You...You
Are drinking a Nectar Divine.

You have broken the rings that hold Saturn.
You are shedding the clothes of Your sorrow.
And the Summer is singing its Passion.
And the Universe calls You to follow.

Feel the world at Your feet,
Freedom calls You from time...
And all because You shine.
You...You...You
Are drinking a Nectar Divine.

REFERENCE: *Deity* by Wendy Rule. Shock Records, 1998. WENDY007.

APPENDIX I

Instructions for the "Cosmogenesis Dance"

—to the music "Adoramus Te Domine" (as referred to in Chapter 6 fn 20)

Start with a partner, decide who are #1's and #2's.

#1's form the inner circle with their arms raised, holding hands.
(This has been known as the Stillpoint of the dance, and as such it has been regarded as more significant than the other two layers. I like to weight its significance as the same as the other layers, as is the case for the three aspects of Cosmogenesis. This layer then may be identified with autopoiesis, the centre of creativity that each being is.)

#2's are eight steps behind their partner, and take one step to Right before dance, not holding hands, standing still.

On the second measure, the inner circle takes four steps backward, slowly lowering arms, and at the SAME time, the outer circle takes four steps forward and reaches in front of the inner circle people to grasp the hands of others in the outer circle.
(This forms an interwoven basket weave. This layer may be identified with the communion of being.)

On Adoramus Te, when the circles are interwoven, everyone sways to the left first, then to the right. Then #1's drop hands—#2's continue to hold hands. #1's take four steps backwards, #2's take four steps forward holding hands and raising their arms slowly. On the second Adoramus Te, the 2's (inner circle) are standing still holding the Stillpoint. The outer circle people are swaying (to the left first), not holding hands.
(This layer is the form of unique individuals. It may be identified with differentiation.)

ACKNOWLEDGEMENTS

It takes the whole Story of the Universe to get to any moment, and so, I am thankful for it all. I have been blessed to learn some of the infinite events and beings that form Now and what*ever* anyone is able to do or be. My understanding of this is largely the gift of Brian Swimme and Thomas Berry.

Amongst my particular genetic forebears, whom I thank, is my Nana, Winifred Smith Seng, whose life of hard work in country Australia, laid down a foundation for me. She had little schooling, did not see the ocean until she was in her forties, and worked to sustain the world with very few requests for herself; and I know that she dreamed. She did not feel hard done by, yet she did hope for something she could not quite express. I felt this hope, this desire from her, and also learned something from her organic, older world. She named her first married home "Avalon", though I never knew why.

In terms of the particular transgenetic codings essential to the conceiving and unfolding of this book, it is the work and inspiration of Starhawk and Charlene Spretnak, at the base initially decades ago and throughout the years since. And the research of Marija Gimbutas has formed a core. There were also many other "mothers" and "spin-sters" there in the conception, awakening me with their swords of insight and nurturing me with their poetry: Mary Daly, Adrienne Rich, Hélène Cixous, Robin Morgan, and Batya Podos being of significant note. Dr. Jean Houston has been this work's midwife: her experiential teaching enabled the capacity in me to carry forth the poetic rituals essential to the whole process.

My partner and beloved, Taffy Robert Seaborne has collaborated in the manifestation of this book. The term "PaGaian" itself is one that he coined in the midst of a synergistic discussion we had. Taffy's magical presence and our discussions have been crucial in recent years. His Earth-Wisdom, present from a childhood in his country of Wales, and developed in relationship with the Anangu traditional elders of Uluru, has supported and lured me into further insight and articulation of this work's celebration of Being.

For providing nurturant places, spaces and developmental networks, I am thankful to these past Sydney groups: the Women's Academy, the Australian Transpersonal Association, and Women-Church (which still exists in new form). In particular I thank Marie Tulip, Erin White, and Graham Bird for their friendship and ovarian support. I thank the women of an early Moon Circle group, particularly Annabelle Solomon and Annie Byron. I thank thea Gaia for her friendship and support through early and hard times of daring the new pathway. I thank the University of Western Sydney for a scholarship, which afforded me time for the real growth of the rituals and reflective process in recent years. The magnificent people who staff the Social Ecology School of the University of Western Sydney gave a context of integral vision and applicable guidance for the research phase; particularly I thank Dr. Susan Murphy for her wise counsel, presence and generosity. I thank my doctoral thesis examiners who gave encouraging and clarifying assessment. I am deeply grateful to all the participants in the ritual celebrations and classes over the years, and particularly Debbie Dunn, Loret Runagall, Lyn Ward, Kaye Tanttu, Helen Martin, Carrick Martin, Louise Stammers and Sheila Quonoey.

I am thankful for the powerful Gaian philosophy and storytelling, and personal encouragement of Dr. Elisabet Sahtouris, and for the enthusiasm and encouragement of Connie Barlow.

I am thankful for the support of my Mum, Beryl Hosking, through years of uncertainty, and for the teachings of my children—all three, and the generosity of spirit of Joachim and Jesslyn.

Helen Martin gave the manuscript very valuable and detailed attention, and Carrick Martin assisted. Judith Kohlhagen enjoyed reading it! Julie Cunningham did the artwork for the front cover, and made helpful suggestions. Donald MacLean gave generous technical help. I thank these friends, and many more.

BIBLIOGRAPHY

Abram, David. *The Spell of the Sensuous.* NY: Vintage Books, 1997.

_____ "The Mechanical and the Organic: Epistemological Conse-quences of the Gaia Hypothesis", in *Gaia in Action.* Peter Bunyard (ed). Edinburgh: Floris Books, 1996, pp. 234–247.

Adler, Rachel. "A Mother in Israel", in *Beyond Androcentrism: Essays on Women and Religion*. Rita Gross (ed). Montana: Scholar's Press, 1977, pp. 237–255.

Allen, Paula Gunn. *The Sacred Hoop: Recovering the Feminine in American Indian Traditions*. Boston: Beacon, 1992.

Anderson, William. *Green Man: The Archetype of our Oneness with the Earth*. Helhoughton FAKENHAM:COMPASSbooks, 1998.

Ardinger, Barbara. *A Woman's Book of Rituals and Celebrations*. Novato CA: New World Library, 1995.

Ashe, Geoffrey. *The Virgin*. NY: Arkana, 1988.

Badinter, Elisabeth. *Mother Love: Myth and Reality*. NY: Macmillan, 1981.

Baring, Anne, and Cashford, Jules. *The Myth of the Goddess: Evolution of an Image.* Penguin Group, 1993.

Barfield. Owen. *History, Guilt and Habitat.* Middletown, Conn.: Wesleyan University Press, 1979.

Barlow, Connie. *Green Space, Green Time*. NY: Springer-Verlag, 1997.

Barlow, Connie (ed). *From Gaia to Selfish Genes: selected writings in the Life Sciences*. Massachusetts: MIT Press, 1994.

Berger, Pamela. *The Goddess Obscured*. Boston: Beacon Press, 1985.

Bernard, Jessie. *The Future of Motherhood*. NY: Penguin Books, 1975.

Bell, Mike. "Thomas Berry and an Earth Jurisprudence". Unpublished manuscript. Yellowknife Canada, June 2001.

Berry, Thomas. *The Great Work*. NY: Bell Tower, 1999.

_____ "The University: Its Response to the Ecological Crisis". A paper delivered before the Divinity School and the University Committee on Environment at Harvard University, April 11 1996. htpp://www.ecoethics.net/ops/univers.htm

_____ "The Universe Story". Keynote address to International Transpersonal Association Conference. Killarney Ireland, 1994.

_____ *The Dream of the Earth*. SF: Sierra Club Books, 1990.

Bohm, David. *Wholeness and the Implicate Order*. NY: Routledge, 1995.

Braud, W. and Anderson, R. *Transpersonal Research Methods for the Social Sciences*. London: Sage, 1998.

Bridle, Susan. "Comprehensive Compassion: An Interview with Brian Swimme". **What Is Enlightenment?** No. 19, Spring/Summer 2001, pp. 35–42, 133–135.

Brock, Rita. "Can These Bones Live? Feminist Critiques of the Atonement" in *What's God Got to Do With It? Challenges facing feminism, theology, and conceptions of women and the divine in the new millennium. CONFERENCE PROCEEDINGS*, Kathleen McPhillips (ed). University of Western Sydney Hawkesbury Publications, December 2000, pp. 17-30.

_____ *Journeys by Heart: A Christology of Erotic Power*. NY: Crossroad, 1988.

Bullough, Vern L. *The Subordinate Sex*. Chicago: University of Illinois Press, 1973.

Campbell, Joseph. *The Inner Reaches of Outer Space: Metaphor as Myth and as Religion*. NY: HarperPerrenial, 1995.

_____ *The Power of Myth with Bill Moyers.* NY: Doubleday, 1988.

_____ *Myths To Live By.* NY: Bantam Books, 1973.

Capra, Fritjof. *The Tao of Physics.* NY: Bantam Books, 1975.

Caputi, Jane. "On Psychic Activism: Feminist Mythmaking" in *The Feminist Companion to Mythology.* Carolyne Larrington (ed). London: Pandora, 1992, pp. 425–440.

Chicago, Judy. *The Dinner Party.* Hammondsworth: Penguin, 1996.

Chittick, William C. and Wilson, Peter Lamborn (trans). *Fakhruddin 'Iraqi: Divine Flashes.* London: SPCK, 1982.

Christ, Carol. *Rebirth of the Goddess.* US: Addison-Wesley, 1997.

_____ *Diving Deep and Surfacing.* Boston: Beacon Press, 1980.

Cirlot, Juan Eduardo. (trans. Jack Sage). *A Dictionary of Symbols.* London and Henley: Routledge & Kegan Paul, 1978.

Cixous, Hélène. "The Laugh of the Medusa" (trans. Keith Cohen and Paula Cohen). **Signs** 1 no. 22, Summer 1976, p.875-893.

Coates, Irene. *The Seed Bearers—the Role of the Female in Biology and Genetics.* Durham: Pentland Press, 1993.

Colgrave, S. *The Spirit of the Valley: Androgyny and Chinese Thought.* London: Virago, 1979.

Conn, Sarah A.. "When Earth Hurts, Who Responds?" in *Ecopsychology: Restoring the Earth, Healing the Mind.* Roszak, T, Gomes, M E, & Kanner, A D. (eds). San Fransisco: Sierra Books, 1995, pp. 156–171.

_____ "The Self-World Connection" **Woman of Power** Issue 20, Spring 1991, pp. 71-77.

Costigan, Phillip. "An Australian Man in Search of an Embodied Spirituality", Ph.D. thesis, Griffith University, 2005.

Cousins, Ewert H. (ed). *Process Theology.* NY: Newman Press, 1971.

Crowley, Vivianne. *Celtic Wisdom: Seasonal Rituals and Festivals*. NY: Sterling, 1998.

Dames, Michael. *Ireland: A Sacred Journey*. ELEMENT BOOKS, 2000.

_____. *The Silbury Treasure: The Great Goddess Rediscovered*. London: Thames and Hudson,1976.

Daly, Mary. *Pure Lust: Elemental Feminist Philosophy*. Boston: Beacon Press, 1984.

_____ *Gyn/Ecology: The Metaethics of Radical Feminism*. London: The Women's Press, 1979.

Davis, Karen. "A Peacable Kin-dom and the Ethics of Eating", **EarthLight**, Issue 51 Vol 14 No.2., Autumn 2004. p.54-57.

Dawson, L.L. and Prus, R.C. "Interactionist Ethnography and Postmodern Discourse: Affinities and Disjunctures in Approaching Human Lived Experience". **Studies in Symbolic Interaction**. 15, 1993, pp. 147–77.

de Beauvoir, Simone. *The Second Sex*. (trans. H.M. Parshley). NY: Knopf, 1953.

Delacott, Philip (trans.). Aeschylus, *The Oresteian Trilogy*. Penguin Classics, 1966.

Denning, M. et al. *The Magical Philosophy III*. Minnesota: St.Paul, 1974.

Devereux, Paul. *Earth Memory: The Holistic Earth Mysteries Approach to Decoding Ancient Sacred Sites*. London: Quantum, 1991.

Denzin, Norman K. & Lincoln, Yvonna S. (eds). *Handbook of Qualitative Research*. London: Sage, 1994.

Dimitrov, Vladimir. "Fuzzy Logic in Service to a Better World: the Social Dimensions of Fuzzy Sets", IMACS/IEEE CSCC Conference, Athens, Greece July 4-8, 1999; published in *Complexity, Organisations, Fuzziness*, University of Western Sydney Reader 2000.

Diner, Helen. *Mothers and Amazons*. NY: Anchor Press, 1973.

Downing, Christine. *The Goddess: Mythological Images of the Feminine.* NY: Crossroad, 1984.

Durdin-Robertson, Lawrence. *The Year of the Goddess.* Wellingborough: Aquarian Press, 1990.

Edwards, Carolyn McVickar. *The Storyteller's Goddess.* NY: HarperCollins, 1991.

Eisler, Riane. *The Chalice and the Blade.* San Fransisco: Harper and Row, 1987.

Eiseley, Loren. *The Immense Journey.* NY: Vintage Books, 1957.

Eliade, Mircea. *Myths, Dreams and Mysteries.* NY: Harper Colophon, 1975.

Feuerstein, Georg. "Towards a New Consciousness: A Review Essay on Jean Gebser". **Noetic Sciences Review**, No. 7, Summer 1988, pp. 23–26.

Flamiano, Dominic. "A Conversation with Brian Swimme". **Original Blessing**, Nov/Dec 1997, pp. 8–11.

Forman, K.C. (ed.). *The Problem of Pure Consciousness.* NY: Oxford University Press, 1990.

Frank, Irene M. and Brownstone, David M. *Women's World: A Timeline of Women in History.* NY: HarperCollins, 1995.

French, Claire. *The Celtic Goddess.* Edinburgh: Floris Books, 2001.

Gadon, Elinor W. *The Once and Future Goddess.* Northamptonshire: Aquarian, 1990.

Gebser, Jean. *The Ever-Present Origin* (translation by Noel Barstad with Algis Mickunas). Athens Ohio: Ohio University Press, 1985.

George, Demetra. "Mysteries of the Dark Moon". **Woman of Power**, issue 8, Winter 1988, pp. 30–34.

_____ *Mysteries of the Dark Moon.* SF: HarperCollins, 1992.

Gimbutas, Marija. *The Language of the Goddess.* NY: HarperCollins, 1991.

_____ *The Goddesses and Gods of Old Europe*. Berkeley and Los Angeles: University of California Press, 1982.

Goddard, Cliff. *Pitjantjatjara/Yankunytjatjara to English Dictionary*, 2nd edition. Institute for Aboriginal Development, Alice Springs, 1992.

Goodenough, Ursula. *The Sacred Depths of Nature.* New York and Oxford: Oxford University Press, 1998.

Göttner-Abendroth, Heide and Marler, Joan. "Cultures of the Goddess: A Discussion". **ReVision**, Vol. 20,No.3, Winter 1998, pp. 44–48.

_____ *The Goddess and Her Heros.* (trans. Lilian Friedberg), Massachusetts: Anthony Publishing Company, 1995.

Gould, Stephen Jay. *Ontology and Phylogeny.* Cambridge Mass.: Belknap Press of Harvard Univerrsity Press, 1977.

Grahn, Judy. *Blood, Bread and Roses: How Menstruation Created the World*. Boston: Beacon Press 1993.

Graves, Robert. *The White Goddess*. Grevel Lindop (ed). Manchester: Faber & Faber, 1999.

Gray, Susan. *The Woman's Book of Runes.* NY: Barnes and Noble, 1999.

Greene, Brian. *The Elegant Universe*. London: Vintage, 2000.

Griffin, Susan. *Woman and Nature: The Roaring Inside Her*. NY: Harper Colophon, 1980.

Gross, Rita. "The Feminine Principle in Tibetan Vajrayana Buddhism." **The Journal of Transpersonal Psychology**. Vol.16 No.2,1984, pp.179–182.

Guthrie, W. K. C. *The Greek Philosophers*. NY: Harper Torch Books, 1960.

Halifax, Joan. *Being With Dying*. (Audio cassettes) Colorado: Sounds True, 1997.

Harding, M. Esther. *Women's Mysteries, Ancient and Modern*. London: Rider & Company, 1955.

Harman, W. & Sahtouris, E. *Biology Revisioned.* Berkeley: North Atlantic Books, 1998.

Harrison, Jane Ellen. *Prolegomena to the Study of Greek Religion.* NY: Meridian Books, 1957.

_____ *Myths of Greece and Rome.* London: Ernest Benn Ltd., 1927.

_____ *Themis: A Study of the Origins of Greek Religion.* Cambridge: Cambridge University Press, 1912.

Heron, John. *Sacred Science: Person-Centred Inquiry into the Spiritual and the Subtle.* Ross-on-Way Herfordshire: PCCS Books, 1998.

Hillman, James. "A Psyche the Size of Earth" in *Ecopsychology: Restoring the Earth, Healing the Mind.* Roszak, T, Gomes, M E, & Kanner, A D. (eds). San Fransisco: Sierra Books, 1995, pp. xvii—xxiii.

_____ (ed). *Facing the Gods.* Irving Texas: Spring Publications, 1980.

Ho, Mae-Wan. "Natural Being and Coherent Society" in *Gaia in Action.* Peter Bunyard (ed). Edinburgh: Floris Books, 1996, pp. 286–307.

Holler, Linda. "Thinking with the Weight of the Earth: Feminist Contributions to an Epistemology of Concreteness". **Hypatia** Vol. 5 No. 1, Spring 1990, pp. 1–22.

Houston, Jean. *A Mythic Life.* NY: Harper Collins, 1996.

_____ *The Hero and the Goddess.* NY: Aquarian Press, 1993.

_____ *The Search for the Beloved.* Los Angeles: Jeremy P. Tarcher, 1987.

Howell, Nancy R. *A Feminist Cosmology: Ecology, Solidarity, and Metaphysics.* New Jersey: Humanities Press, 2000.

Iglehart Austen, Hallie. *The Heart of the Goddess.* Berkeley: Wingbow Press, 1990.

Irigaray, Luce. *An Ethics of Sexual Difference*. (trans. Carolyn Burke and Gillian C. Gill) NY: Cornell University Press, 1993.

Johnson, Elizabeth. *She Who Is: The Mystery of God in Feminist Theological Discourse.* NY: Crossroad Publishing Co, 1994.

Johnson, Robert A. *She: Understanding Feminine Psychology.* NY: Harper and Row, 1977.

Keller, Catherine. *From a Broken Web: Separation, Sexism and Self.* Boston: Beacon Press, 1986.

Keller, Mara Lynn. "The Eleusinian Mysteries: Ancient Nature Religion of Demeter and Persephone" in *Reweaving the World: the Emergence of Ecofeminism.* Irene Diamond & Gloria Feman Orenstein (eds). SF: Sierra Club Books, 1990, pp. 41–51.

Kremer, Jürgen W. "The Dark Night of the Scholar: Reflections on Culture and Ways of Knowing". **ReVision**, Vol.14, No.4, Spring 1992, pp.169-178.

_____ 1992b. "Post-modern Shamanism and the Evolution of Consciousness", paper delivered at the International Transpersonal Association Conference, Prague, June 20-25. Audio tape available from http://www.conferencerecording.com/conflists/itc92.htm.

Lao Tzu. *The Way of Life.* (trans by Witter Bynner). NY: Capricorn Books, 1962.

Lakoff, George and Johnson, Mark.. *Philosophy in the Flesh: The Embodied Mind and its Challenge to Western Thought.* NY: Basic Books, 1999.

_____ *Metaphors We Live By.* Chicago: University of Chicago Press, 1980.

Larousse Encyclopedia of Mythology, London: Hamlyn Publishing Group Ltd., 1968.

Larrington, Carolyne (ed). *The Feminist Companion to Mythology.* London: Pandora, 1992.

Le Guin, Ursula. *Dancing at the Edge of the World.* NY: Harper & Row, 1989.

Lerner, Gerda. *The Creation of Feminist Consciousness*. NY: Oxford University Press, 1993.

Liebes, Sidney, Sahtouris, Elisabet and Swimme, Brian. *A Walk Through Time: From Stardust to Us.* NY: John Wiley & Sons Inc., 1998.

Ling, Coralie. "Sophialogy and Croning Rituals" in *What's God Got to Do With It? Challenges facing feminism, theology, and conceptions of women and the divine in the new millennium. CONFERENCE PROCEEDINGS*, Kathleen McPhillips (ed). University of Western Sydney Hawkesbury Publications, December 2000, pp. 83–90.

Livingstone, Glenys. *The Female Metaphor—Virgin, Mother, Crone—of the Dynamic Cosmological Unfolding: Her Embodiment in Seasonal Ritual as catalyst for Personal and Cultural Change.* Ph.D. thesis, University of Western Sydney, 2002.

Lorde, Audre. "Uses of the Erotic" in *Weaving the Visions: New Patterns in Feminist Spirituality.* Judith Plaskow & Carol Christ (eds). NY: HarperCollins, 1989, pp. 208–213.

Macy, Joanna. "Working Through Environmental Despair" in *Ecopsychology: Restoring the Earth, Healing the Mind.* Roszak, T, Gomes, M E, & Kanner, A D. (eds). San Francisco: Sierra Books, 1995, pp. 240–262.

Macy, Joanna and Brown, Molly Young. *Coming Back to Life*. Gabriola Island, Canada: New Society Publishers, 1998.

Madison, Gary Brent. *The Phenomenology of Merleau—Ponty*. Ohio University Press, 1981.

Marshack, Alexander. *The Roots of Civilization*. London: Weidenfeld & Nicolson, 1972.

Matousek, Mark. "Reinventing the Human". **Common Boundary,** Vol. 8, No. 3, May/June 1990, pp. 31–34.

Matthews, Caitlin. *The Celtic Spirit*. London: Hodder and Stoughton, 2000.

Matthews, Caitlin and John. *The Western Way*. London: Penguin, 1994.

Mayr, Ernst. *The Growth of Biological Thought: Diversity Evolution and Inheritance.* Cambridge Mass.: Belknap Press, 1982.

McDonald, Heather. *Blood, Bones and Spirit: Aboriginal Christianity in an East Kimberley Town.* Melbourne: Melbourne University Press, 2001.

McLean, Adam. *The Triple Goddess*. Grand Rapids MI: Phanes Press, 1989.

_____ *The Four Fire Festivals*. Edinburgh: Megalithic Research Publications, 1979.

Merleau-Ponty, Maurice. *The Invisible and the Invisible*. (trans. Alphonso Lingis). Evanston, Illinois: Northwestern University Press, 1968.

Meis, M. & Shiva, V. *Ecofeminism*. London: Zed Books, 1993.

Monaghan, Patricia. *O Mother Sun! A New View of the Cosmic Feminine*. Freedom CA: Crossing Press, 1994.

Morgan, Robin. *Lady of the Beasts*. NY: Random House, 1976.

Morton, Nelle. *The Journey is Home*. Boston: Beacon Press,1985.

Mumford, Lewis. *The City in History*. NY: Harcourt, Brace and World, 1961.

_____ *The Transformations of Man*. London: Allen and Unwin, 1957.

Murphy, Susan. *upside-down zen: a direct path into reality.* Melbourne: Lothian, 2004.

Neumann, Erich. *The Great Mother*. Princeton: Princeton University Press, 1974.

Nichols, Mike. "The First Harvest", Pagan Alliance Newsletter NSW Australia, Lughnasad 2000, Vol. 4, No. 7, p.1.

_____ "Yule", Pagan Alliance Newsletter NSW Australia, Yule 1999, Vol. 4, No. 2, p.1.

Noble, Vicki. "Female Blood Roots of Shamanism". **Shaman's Drum**, No. 4, Spring 1986.

Orr, David W. *The Last Refuge: Patriotism, Politics and the Environment in an Age of Terror.* Island Press, 2004.

Orr, Emma Restall. *Spirits of the Sacred Grove.* London: Thorsons, 1998.

Osborne, Ken (ed). *Stonehenge and Neighbouring Monuments.* London: English Heritage, 1999.

Perera, Sylvia Brinton. *Descent to the Goddess: A Way of Initiation for Women.* Toronto: Inner City Books, 1981.

Plumwood, Val. *Feminism and the Mastery of Nature.* NY: Routledge, 1993.

_____ "Gaia, Good for Women?" **Refactory Girl.** No.41, Summer 1991.

Podos, Batya. *The Triple Aspect of the Goddess.* Unpublished paper, SF, 1978.

Pollack, Rachel. *The Body of the Goddess.* Brisbane:Element Books, 1997.

Qualls-Corbett, Nancy. *The Sacred Prostitute.* Toronto: Inner City Books, 1988.

Raphael, Melissa. *Thealogy and Embodiment: the Post-Patriarchal Reconstruction of Female Sexuality.* Sheffield: Sheffield Press, 1996.

Reader's Digest Association. *The Last Two Million Years.* London, 1974.

Reason, Peter. *Participation in Human Inquiry.* London: Sage,1994.

Reason, Peter & Rowan, John (eds). *Human Inquiry: A Sourcebook of New Paradigm Research.* NY: John Wiley, 1981.

Reis, Patricia. "The Dark Goddess". **Woman of Power** Issue 8, Winter 1988, pp. 24–27, 82.

_____ "A Woman Artist's Journey". **Common Boundary** Vol. 5 Issue 4, July/August 1987, p. 7.

Restall-Orr, Emma. *Spirits of the Sacred Grove: The World of a Druid Priestess.* London:Thorsons, 1998.

Reuther, Rosemary. "Women's Body and Blood: the Sacred and the Impure" in *Through the Devil's Gateway: Women, Religion and Taboo.* Alison Joseph (ed). London: SPCK, 1990.

Rich, Adrienne. *Of Woman Born.* NY: Bantam, 1977.

Ricoeur, Paul. *The Symbolism of Evil.* (trans. E Buchanan). Boston: Beacon Press, 1969.

Rilke, Rainer Maria. *Letters To a Young Poet.* (trans. M.D. Herter Norton). NY: W.W. Norton & Company, 1954.

Robbins Dexter, Miriam. *Whence the Goddesses: A Source Book.* NY: Teacher's College Press, 1990.

Ross, Nancy Wilson. *Three Ways of Asian Wisdom.* NY:Simon & Schuster, 1966.

Rothery, Andrew. "The Science of the Green Man", **Gatherings: journal of the international community for ecopsychology**, June 28 2004. Available at **http://www.ecopsychology.org/ezine/gatherings.html**

Sahtouris, Elisabet. *Earthdance: Living Systems in Evolution.* Lincoln NE: iUniverse Press, 2000.

Shuttle, Penelope and Redgrove, Peter. *The Wise Wound: Menstruation and Everywoman.* London: Paladin Books, 1986.

Simpson, G.G. *The Major Features of Evolution.* NY: Columbia University Press, 1953.

Sewall, Laura. "The Skill of Ecological Perception" in *Ecopsychology: Restoring the Earth, Healing the Mind.* Roszak, T, Gomes, M E, & Kanner, A D. (eds). San Francisco: Sierra Books, 1995, pp. 201–215.

_____ "Earth Eros, Sky" in **EarthLight**, Winter 2000, p.22-25.

Smart, Ninian. *The World's Religions.* Cambridge University Press, 1998.

Smith, Joanmarie. "Hen, Homemaker and Goddess". PACE 14 Issues-D. Winona Minnesota: St. Mary's Press, 1983-84.

Solomon, Annabelle. *The Wheel of the Year.* Winmalee: Pentacle Press, 1999.

Spretnak, Charlene. *The Resurgence of the Real: Body, Nature and Place in a Hypermodern World.* NY: Routledge, 1999.

_____ *States of Grace: The Recovery of Meaning in the Postmodern Age.* SF: HarperCollins, 1993.

_____ *Lost Goddesses of Early Greece.* Boston: Beacon Press, 1992.

_____ "Gaian Spirituality". **Woman of Power** Issue 20, Spring 1991, pp. 10–17.

_____ (ed). *The Politics of Women's Spirituality.* NY: Doubleday, 1982.

Stanley, Julia P. and Robbins, Susan W."Going Through the Changes: The Pronoun *She* in Middle English" *Papers in Linguistics*, Vol. 9, Nos. 3-4 (Fall 1977).

Starhawk. *Truth or Dare.* SF: Harper and Row, 1990.

_____ *The Spiral Dance: A Rebirth of the Ancient Religion of the Great Goddess.* NY: Harper and Row, 1989.

Stockton, Eugene (ed). *Blue Mountains Dreaming.* Winmalee: Three Sisters Productions, 1996.

Stone, Merlin. *Ancient Mirrors of Womanhood.* Boston: Beacon Press, 1984.

_____ *When God was a Woman.* London: Harvest/HBJ, 1978.

Swimme, Brian. *The Powers of the Universe.* (DVD series). 2004.

_____ *The Hidden Heart of the Cosmos.* NY: Orbis, 1996.

_____ *Canticle to the Cosmos.* (Video series). CA: Tides Foundation, 1990.

_____ *The Universe is a Green Dragon.* Santa Fe: Bear & Co., 1984.

Swimme, Brian and Berry, Thomas. *The Universe Story*. NY: HarperCollins, 1992.

Tacey, David. "Spirit and Place", **EarthSong journal**, issue 1, Spring 2004, pp.7-10 and pp.32-35.

Taylor, Dena. *Red Flower: Rethinking Menstruation*. Freedom CA: Crossing Press, 1988.

Tedlock, Dennis, and Barbara Tedlock, (eds). *Teachings from the American Earth*. NY: Liveright, 1975.

Theatana, Kathryn. "Priestesses of Hecate". **Woman of Power**, issue 8, Winter 1988, pp. 35–37.

Thompson, William Irwin. *Coming into Being*. NY: St. Martin's Press, 1998.

_____ *Gaia: A Way of Knowing*. NY: Lindisfarne Press, 1987.

Toulson, Shirley. *The Celtic Year.* Dorset: Element Books Ltd., 1993.

Vare, Ethlie Ann, & Ptacek, Greg. *Mothers of Invention.* NY: Quill, 1987.

Vernadsky, Vladimir. *The Biosphere.* London: Synergetic Press, 1986.

Volk, Tyler. *Gaia's Body*. NY: Springer-Verlag, 1998.

Walker, Barbara G. *Restoring the Goddess*. NY: Prometheus Books, 2000.

_____ *The Woman's Encyclopaedia of Myths and Secrets*. San Francisco: Harper and Row, 1983.

Warner, Marina. *Alone of All Her Sex*. NY: Alfred Knopf, 1976.

Webster's Third International Dictionary of the English Language Unabridged. Encyclopaedia Britannica, 1986.

Wertheim, Margaret. *Pythagoras' Trousers*. NY: Times Books, 1995.

Whitehead, Alfred North. *Process and Reality*. NY: Macmillan, 1929.

Whitmont, Edward C. *The Return of the Goddess*. London: Routledge and Kegan Paul, 1983.

Wicken, Jeffrey S. *Evolution, Thermodynamics and Information: Extending the Darwinian Program*. NY/Oxford: Oxford University Press, 1987.

Wilber, Ken. *A Brief History of Everything*. Massachusetts: Shambhala, 1996.

Wilson, Colin. *The Outsider*. Boston: Houghton Mifflin, 1956.

Wilson, E.O. *The Diversity of Life.* Cambridge Mass.: Belknap Press of Harvard University Press, 1992.

_____ *On Human Nature.* Cambridge Mass.: Harvard University Press, 1978.

Wittig, Monique. *Les Guerilleres*. NY: Avon Books, 1973.

Woodman, Marion. *The Pregnant Virgin*. Toronto: Inner City Books, 1985.

Woodroffe, Sir John (trans). *Mahanirvanatra*. NY: Dover Publications, 1972.

Wright, Pam. "Living With Death as a Teacher". **Woman of Power**, issue 8, Winter 1988, pp. 12–13, 90.

Index

About the Author

Glenys Livingstone lives in the Blue Mountains, West of Sydney Australia, where she and her partner Taffy Seaborne hold sacred space for the celebration of Earth's holy-days with a small open community, according to their place on the planet. She also teaches and writes about this ecospiritual practice. Glenys' websites are http://pagaian.org and www.divinexpressions.com.au

978-0-595-34990-6
0-595-34990-0